PERENNIALS
FOR THE
PACIFIC NORTHWEST

PERENNIALS FOR THE PACIFIC NORTHWEST

A Comprehensive Guide

RUTH ROGERS CLAUSEN & THOMAS CHRISTOPHER

TIMBER PRESS
PORTLAND, OREGON

Photo and illustration credits appear on page 390.

Timber Press
Workman Publishing
Hachette Book Group, Inc.
1290 Avenue of the Americas
New York, New York 10104
timberpress.com

Timber Press is an imprint of Workman Publishing, a division of Hachette Book Group, Inc. The Timber Press name and logo are registered trademarks of Hachette Book Group, Inc.

Printed in Dongguan, China, (TLF) on responsibly sourced paper

Series design by Will Brown

The publisher is not responsible for websites (or their content) that are not owned by the publisher.

ISBN 978-1-64326-452-3

A catalog record for this book is available from the Library of Congress.

CONTENTS

Introduction 8

Perennial Basics 16

PERENNIALS A–Z 27

Appendix—Planting Ideas

- Shade Lovers 381
- Drought Resistant 382
- Deer Resistant 383
- Continual Bloomers 384
- Native Plants 385
- Pollinator Paradise 386
- Rabbit Resistant 387
- Best for Slopes 388
- Best for Wet Areas 389

Photo Credits 390

Index 394

INTRODUCTION

ANY EXPERIENCED GARDENER knows that perennials—herbaceous or more-or-less non-woody plants that go dormant in fall and return in the spring—are the main fabric of an ornamental garden. Trees and shrubs provide architecture, and annuals may embroider the design, but it's the perennials that supply the enduring keynotes of texture, and the calculated sequences and rhythms of colors and forms. Perennials dominate through persistence. Choose your plants carefully and lay down a theme in perennials; it will return year after year, becoming the framework around which other plants and furnishings are arranged.

This is why selecting your perennials wisely is such an important process—your decisions can and should have long-lasting repercussions. The process of selection is demanding. Indeed, because of our good fortune, it's more challenging, or at least more complicated, than ever before. In the last few decades, American gardeners have moved from a situation of perennial famine to one of feast. Hundreds of new plant species and countless cultivars (plant types or varieties selected for desirable traits) have been added to our garden flora. Online shopping has made virtually all of them readily available in any region of the country. The choices are stunning, even overwhelming. Currently, for example, the registry of the American Hosta Society records the names and descriptions of some 7200 distinct hosta cultivars. A central purpose of this guide is to help you connect with the plants that you will find most rewarding.

Addressing New Challenges

As plant offerings have burgeoned, gardeners have gained a growing awareness of environmental issues, resulting in the addition of new criteria to the selection process beyond traditional aesthetics. The implications of these new standards are practical in nature, but also have an impact on what we see as the potential roles that our gardens can play in addition to delighting our senses.

Climate change, for example, is bringing drought, intermittent and seasonal, to regions of North America that in the past haven't had to worry as much about the water supply. In such areas, responsible gardeners are searching for plants adapted to withstanding dry conditions. The adoption of such plants reduces the need to irrigate as frequently, which in turn reduces the demand on the local water supply system. Other regions, including most of the Northeast where we authors reside, are experiencing an increase in precipitation, but rain or snow may be delivered in less frequent but more violent storms. In those regions, perennial plants must be able to cope with periodic soakings while also being able to cope with the dry spells between storms.

Many gardeners also wish to reduce their contributions of greenhouse gases to the atmosphere and help in the effort to control climate change. In fact, traditional gardening practices can be a substantial liability in this respect. Synthetic fertilizers, a longtime horticultural mainstay, are produced with enormous consumption of fossil fuels. To produce one ton of ammonia, for example—the principal source of nitrate and the first number in the three number ratio on the fertilizer bag—requires the consumption of 33 million British thermal units (BTUs) of natural gas. Organic fertilizers may also be significant contributors of greenhouse gases. Some formulations release nitrous oxide (N_2O), a greenhouse gas 265 times as potent as the more familiar carbon dioxide (CO_2), as they decompose. By selecting perennials whose fertility needs match the natural character of your soil, you can greatly reduce your dependence on fertilizers while also saving yourself money and work. Sending a sample of your soil to your state soil testing laboratory will provide you with precise knowledge of your soil's texture, organic content, and levels of principal nutrients, allowing you to make informed decisions about plant choices and garden maintenance.

Biodiversity, or the degree of genetic diversity in your landscape, has also become a concern in recent years as natural wildlife and plant populations have both declined nationally. These two, plant diversity and wildlife diversity, are inextricably linked, for plants are the basis of the natural food chain, and many insects and birds are highly dependent on particular plant species for their diet and reproduction. Insects such as butterflies, for instance, not only need nectar on which to feed but also specific plants on which to lay their eggs and raise caterpillars. In turn, songbirds commonly rely on caterpillars as a food for their chicks; a pair of chickadees must gather 6000 to 9000 caterpillars to nourish a single nestful of babies. Not surprisingly, biodiversity and including a broad selection of perennials in their plantings has become a concern of thoughtful gardeners.

Finally, gardeners also need to know what is safe to plant in their region. The alarming spread of invasive nonnative plants introduced to North America as garden plants has prompted increasing numbers of gardeners to demand assurance that perennials they introduce into their gardens will not jump the fence and crowd the native flora out of adjacent natural areas. Readers may rest assured that every effort has been made not to include known invasives among the perennials featured in this guide.

Using This Book

This book is focused on taking readers step-by-step through the process of successful perennial selection. It begins, as any gardener should, with a broader survey designed to identify groups of plants that are both adapted to the conditions in your garden and suited to your design goals. Accordingly, the individual perennials here are grouped together by genus. Note, too, that each genus is listed with its botanical family, a more inclusive category that indicates other genera to which a genus is related. If you find the plants of some genus particularly appealing or successful in your garden, you'll surely want to explore their relatives.

Under each genus heading in this book, you'll find a succinct description of its attractions and benefits. Also included here are notes about any serious liabilities associated with that particular genus—even the most essential plant genus may suffer from susceptibility to insect pests and diseases, for example. Browsing these notes and scanning the photographs will allow you to identify quickly those that appeal to you. Occasionally this preamble may include a warning as well. Some genera, for example, may have proved too hardy and vigorous, becoming invasive in certain areas. If so, this fact is prominently noted. Historically, gardeners have been responsible for introducing many foreign (exotic) plants into their own countries. Japanese barberry (*Berberis japonica*) and purple loosestrife (*Lythrum salicaria*), for instance, have escaped from cultivation and proliferated freely, displacing natives and becoming threats to regional ecosystems. One of the missions of this book is to help gardeners ensure that this sort of mistake is not repeated. If in doubt about a particular perennial, contact your local Cooperative Extension Office.

Plant Attributes

A number of characteristics play a central role in determining whether a particular perennial is likely to perform well in your garden; to simplify your selection process, this book addresses these key characteristics at the beginning of each species description.

- Flower color and season of bloom. If a flower won't please your eye or provide color when you want it to, then you will not want to grow it. The season of bloom is expressed as a range, from the season when you can expect flowering to begin to the season when you can expect it to end.
- Height and width are expressed as ranges of inches or feet, such as 1.5–2 ft. × 18–30 in., which describes a plant that grows to a height of 1.5 to 2 feet and a width or spread of 18 to 30 inches. If the perennial won't fit in the space you can give it, you don't want to plant it.
- The amount of light a perennial requires for healthy growth. **Sun** means that this particular plant requires exposure to at least six hours of direct sunlight a day, preferably from midmorning to midafternoon, when sunlight is most intense. **Part shade** means it will flourish with exposure to less than six hours of sun daily, but that it requires some direct sunlight or, alternatively, day-long dappled sunlight filtered through an

intermittent canopy of high tree branches. **Shade** means that this species can subsist without any direct sunlight, just light reflected off trees, pavement, or buildings. By observing the conditions found in different parts of your garden, you can use these notes on light to determine if a particular plant is suited to the available location.

- Winter hardiness is expressed as a range of zones, such as Z4–9; the zones correspond to geographical areas outlined on the USDA Plant Hardiness Zone Map. This map uses the average coldest winter temperature experienced in each region to divide the United States into 13 zones. If a perennial is listed as hardy from zones 4 through 9, that means that if given an adequate site and care, typically it will persist from year to year within the area from the northern border of zone 4 to the southern border of zone 9. The USDA Plant Hardiness Zone Map is the standard reference of the nursery industry and as such is indispensable when making decisions about plant selection. However, winter temperatures vary locally in response to altitude, proximity of large bodies of water, and garden microclimates. Also, snow cover acts as insulating mulch; plants growing in areas where snowfall is infrequent are more vulnerable to extreme cold and bitter winds. Treat hardiness ratings only as a guide.

In some instances you will find the letters HS (heat sensitive) following the zone description. This indicates that the perennial in question is sensitive to a combination of summer heat and humidity. Alternatively, a plant may be exceptionally well adapted to heat and humidity, in which case, the hardiness description will be followed with the letters HT (heat tolerant).

Other Information

Following each species name, you will also find listed any obsolete or alternative botanical names (e.g., syn. *Acanthus balcanicus*, *A. longifolius*). Botanists are constantly revising and correcting the nomenclature—a plant known as one thing today may overnight become something else. Sometimes this is a mere updating or a consolidation of species names; in other cases, plants may be assigned to new genera. For example, the huge *Chrysanthemum* genus has been split several times, so that many former members are now classified in *Dendranthema*, *Argyranthemum*, *Tanacetum*, and *Leucanthemum*. We have used the most up-to-date botanical nomenclature, but we include also the former names, as some nurseries still sell the plants under those labels. In a few cases where the nursery industry as a whole has continued to use the obsolete name, this book lists the species under that name while noting the update. At the start of each species description, you will also find the most widely used common names for that plant.

Native Ranges

A good way to determine whether a perennial is likely to thrive for you is to check its native climate and habitat. Clearly, if you are planning a garden in a groomed woodland area, where you have cleared the brush and weed trees to let in more light, it would be wise to select plants native to open woodlands in climates similar to your own. Perennials for a meadow garden should be grassland or prairie plants; dryland perennials are the obvious choice for arid or semi-arid gardens. That's why we have included (following the common names) information in each plant entry about the habitat and geographical area in which that species is found in the wild. Many gardeners choose to focus their attention only on plants native to their region. This greatly reduces the chance of introducing invasive species into the local ecosystem, and can be a means of restoring natural biodiversity.

Plant Descriptions and Cultural Tips

After common names and native ranges, foliage is generally addressed next in each plant description because it has the most persistent influence on a plant's visual impact—the flowers may be spectacular, but their season is limited, whereas the foliage is mostly a garden presence throughout the growing season; that of evergreen perennials shines through the winter, too.

Cultural information is critical and includes the type of soil the plant prefers, and its need (if any) for irrigation. Although the soil type recommended may vary from sandy to organic-enriched, and from dry to moist, in most instances the cultural tips call for one that is "well drained." Soil drainage denotes the ease with which water passes through the soil, and that depends on how porous the soil is. Clay soil, composed of very fine particles, is naturally dense with small pores; any water deposited on it will pass through only very slowly—a soil of this kind is "poorly drained." Soil with coarser particles, such as loam or a sandy soil, has larger pore spaces that allow water to pass through more quickly. The novice may wonder how a soil that is moist can also drain well. Particles of decomposed organic material (compost or rotted leaves, for example) in the soil act like sponges absorbing and retaining moisture. The addition of organic matter creates a soil that is both well drained and consistently moist. Such a soil will satisfy the needs of peonies and other perennials and also remain sufficiently moist to satisfy moisture-loving Japanese iris and hostas.

Additional information in the genus descriptions includes usual propagation methods, tips about where to site the plants, and which plants are compatible companions. Notes on drought resistance, and deer and critter resistance are also included, along with any problems or pests. Below the species description, outstanding cultivars or hybrids are included. These are by no means comprehensive, but rather focus on noting the very best, a pool of selections that will provide the gardener with the most outstanding options.

Some plants included in this book, including colocasias (elephant ears), dahlias, and impatiens, have been regarded traditionally as annuals in chillier zones due to their sensitivity to cold. However, in mild zones where not subjected to significant winter cold, these plants perform as perennials. As American gardening has become less parochial over the last generation, these plants have reclaimed their true identity. Gardeners in cold-winter regions have come to value the perennial character of these tender plants as the fashion has arisen for using them as dramatic additions to summertime container displays (some refer to them as temperennials).

One further note: most of the plants included in this book are commonly seen in garden centers and catalogs, but in an effort to collect the very best and most useful perennials, this book also describes many lesser-known species and cultivars. All those described, however, are commercially available.

Regional Focus

North America is a place of many climates and soils and vastly different topographies. In the past, American gardeners have tended to ignore that, following a similar pattern of European-derived garden design across the continent. Too often, we have used unsustainable inputs of resources, such as irrigation and soil amendments, to enable us to grow a similar selection of traditional gardening favorites wherever we gardened.

More recently, though, gardeners have begun to celebrate the unique beauties of their local landscapes. Garden design has become more regional in its character, with Midwesterners incorporating the sweep of prairies into their landscapes, and gardeners in the Deep South often adopting a subtropical lushness. This regional focus has led to a transformative rethinking of the process of plant selection. Bringing the garden more into harmony with the surrounding regional character has encouraged gardeners to select plants that are better adapted to their local conditions.

Gardeners in the Southwest, for example, are less prone now to opt for a lawn of water-thirsty imported turf grasses, and more likely to create displays of plants that appreciate the intense sunlight, arid or semi-arid climate, and organic matter–poor soils of their regions. In addition, they are more likely to consult the way that plants grow naturally in their region. Those gardeners are learning to avoid the use of groundcovers, and instead space their plants more widely so that each has access to a broader reservoir of soil moisture. Moister, cooler, and cloudier regions, in contrast, call for a different plant palette and a denser, more verdant style of cultivation.

The Pacific Northwest

The Pacific Northwest is in many respects the most permissive place to garden in North America. In coastal areas, the proximity of the Pacific Ocean helps to moderate temperatures throughout the year so that winters tend to be mild and summers not too hot. Winters in coastal areas are typically wet, and summers sunny and drier but still marked by several rains every month. Farther inland, east of the mountain ranges that parallel the coast, summer and winter temperatures tend to be more extreme and precipitation much lower, creating true desert conditions in some areas and dry grassland conditions in others. The bulk of the population, however, lives and gardens in communities near the coast, where an extraordinary diversity of plants flourish and the growing season may last through seven months of the year.

It's important to note, though, that climate change is making extreme weather events more common in the Pacific Northwest. "Atmospheric rivers" have been bringing record rainstorms and, conversely, a decline in summer precipitation in many areas that has brought drought. Average temperatures in the region have risen by only 2°F since 1900, but heat waves have become less of a rarity. Gardeners need to keep the threat of such anomalies in mind when selecting plants, and understand that the collection of climate-challenged plant rarities, a popular activity in the past, is likely to lead to severe losses in this new era.

Clay and sandy soils are both common in the Pacific Northwest and present challenges for gardeners. Clay soils are slow to absorb water and slow to drain once wet. Sandy soils drain rapidly, do not hold moisture during dry spells, and are low in plant nutrients. Fortunately, there is a relatively easy fix for both conditions.

A generous application of compost will improve the drainage of a clay soil and increase the absorption and fertility of a sandy one. Typically, digging in 3 to 4 inches of compost when creating a new bed, and spreading another half inch over the planted bed every fall when the garden is dormant, will be beneficial to both clay and sandy soils. Before adding anything to your soil, however, it is wise to submit a soil sample to your state's soil testing laboratory to get exact recommendations.

A Note About Nomenclature

The most basic step in selecting and obtaining a particular perennial is getting the name correct. That involves becoming comfortable with botanical nomenclature. It's true that many of us use common (or English) names to identify individual plants when we discuss gardens among ourselves, but in communicating with nurseries and garden centers—and especially online—we are better advised to use the botanical (or Latin) nomenclature. Often the common name for a plant varies regionally or even within the same region: your beebalm may be someone else's bergamot. These differences in common names lead to misunderstandings, so that what you receive in a shipment from a nursery is not always what you had anticipated. For each plant species, however, there is only a single botanical name, composed of the genus and the species. Thus, mahogany trout lily, a beautiful native of coastal regions from northern California to British Columbia, is also sometimes known by the common names "coast fawn lily" and "pink fawn lily." Its one and only botanical name, however, is *Erythronium revolutum,* which signifies that it belongs to the species *revolutum* of the related group of perennials in the genus *Erythronium.*

Botanical names not only offer precision, they also provide an insight into plant relationships. *Erythronium revolutum,* for instance, identifies that West Coast perennial as a close relative of the East Coast native, *Erythronium americanum,* the yellow trout lily. This information can be useful to the gardener in that both relatives are adapted to part shade and moist woodlands, and so will flourish in similar settings.

PERENNIAL BASICS

IN MANY RESPECTS, garden plants constitute what an investment adviser would describe as "fungible assets"—that is, they are interchangeable, at least in the sense that if you can grow one successfully, you can apply those same techniques to others. You can, for example, use the skills you perfected in growing tomatoes to grow other annuals such as petunias (which are, in fact, close relatives of tomatoes). But when you move on to more dissimilar plants, you do have to make adjustments. Cultivating orchids with exactly the same techniques you perfected with cacti will result in disappointment.

That may seem obvious, but many gardeners who have developed their skills on annuals and food crops don't bother to inform themselves about the special needs of perennials before they begin to invest in them, and the results can be painful. What follows is a rundown of special points that gardeners new to perennials—or even those with more experience—should keep in mind when embarking on perennial gardening.

From the Ground Up

When cultivating annuals or vegetables, you have the opportunity to refresh and redig the soil (if necessary) every growing season. With perennials, however, this is not possible, so extra care must be taken to prepare the soil well and thoroughly before planting.

The details of soil preparation will depend partly on what sorts of perennials you plan to grow. A soil test is the first step in designing any perennial planting (this can be done at nominal cost from your state's Cooperative Extension Service or from the agricultural division of your state's land-grant university). It will tell you your soil's pH (its relative acidity) and type (loam, clay, silt, or sand, or any combination of these)—both will determine which types of perennials will grow there successfully. Some gardeners insist on trying to modify their soil to suit their favorite plants, but typically this involves a great deal of work and expense, and rarely produces results as good as selecting plants that are adapted to the kind of soil you already have.

One requirement that is common for the vast majority of perennials is the need for a well-drained soil. There are exceptions, and these have been noted in this book's plant descriptions, but they are few. You'll know that the soil in your garden or prospective border doesn't qualify if it puddles up or remains waterlogged overnight or even longer after at least an inch of rain has fallen.

If necessary, there are several ways to improve the drainage of your soil:

- Apply a layer of decomposed organic material, such as compost or leaf mold, to a depth of several inches. Dig this in about 8 in. or more deep; it will help to increase the porosity of the soil. By increasing the soil's bulk, it helps to raise the surface of the treated area above its surroundings, allowing gravity to pull the water out of the soil more efficiently.
- If you are planting species that prefer a sandy or gritty soil—those recommended for rock gardens generally require such conditions—improve the existing drainage by digging in a fifty-fifty mixture of organic matter and coarse, sharp sand or grit. Coarse sand is sold by masonry supply companies, and turkey grit is available from feed stores. Avoid the sand sold in bags at the big-box home and garden stores, as it is too fine to be effective and, if the existing soil is clayey, will turn it into something like concrete.
- The classic location for a rock garden is on a sunny slope. A sloping site enhances the drainage of the soil naturally by allowing excess water to run off.
- To improve the drainage of soils in a flat or low-lying area, installing raised beds is the most effective technique. To make a raised bed, heap up the soil so that it sits above the level of the surrounding ground, thus enabling excess water to drain away. In a formal design, raised beds may be edged and contained with timber, bricks, or stones; an informal effect can be achieved by grading the edges of the raised area into a stable slope. To be effective, soil in a raised bed should stand at least 6 in. higher than its surroundings; in really damp locations, 8 in. is better.

An additional advantage of a raised bed is that the soil warms up more quickly in spring. Thus the growing season is lengthened in chilly northern or high-altitude climates, which can be a significant advantage for perennials planted there. However, due to their enhanced drainage, raised beds are also more susceptible to drought, and require more frequent irrigation during dry spells.

Shopping for Perennials

The prime key to success with perennials is to start out with healthy, pest- and disease-free stock. This is critical with perennials, since you expect to grow them in the garden for several years; an underperforming weakling may dog you for a long time. Taking full advantage of the perennials described in this book means coming to terms with bare-root (no soil on the roots) nursery stock. This is a traditional but somewhat outdated method of raising perennials in which plants are field grown, dug when dormant, and kept in cold storage over the winter. In late winter or early spring, the still-dormant plants have the soil washed from their roots, and are packed and shipped to customers. These are not the most inspiring sight when you first remove them from their shipping containers. In fact, with their brown roots and withered remains of last year's leaves, new arrivals may appear lifeless to a novice. However, if the nursery has handled and packed the plants carefully, and if you plant them promptly upon receipt, the survival rate of bare-root plants is excellent. After recovery, they'll start into growth fast. Such plants do, however, require special treatment during transplanting into your garden:

1 | When a shipment arrives from the grower, open the box immediately and inspect the contents. If the plants inside seem dry, moisten them. Set the box in a cool place, such as a basement or garage, until you can find time to plant the contents. If the plants are moldy or decaying at the time of arrival, call the retailer and demand replacements.

2 | Don't procrastinate. Ideally, bare-root plants should be planted within a day of their arrival on your doorstep. Kept moist and cool, bare-root plants will generally survive a few days without planting, but every day of delay decreases the odds of success. If the plants arrive when the garden soil is unsuitable (frozen or just thawed, or too cold and wet to be worked), pot them, water them, and hold them in a sheltered sunny spot until you can plant them. They will be fine for several weeks if kept moist.

3 | Stand bare-root plants in a bucket of water for a couple of hours before planting to rehydrate the roots. They are likely to have become somewhat desiccated during storage and shipping.

4 | To plant, dig a hole in a well-prepared bed, deep enough and wide enough to accommodate the roots of the plant. Mound soil into a cone in the center of the hole, and set the plant on top, draping the roots over the sides. Position the plant so that its crown—the point where the stem and roots connect—is at or just below the level of the surrounding bed. Refill the hole with soil, gently working it in, over, and among the roots with your fingertips. Firm all around gently with your foot.

5 | Water well. If the soil settles as it absorbs the water, top up with more soil as necessary, and water again. In a sunny location, drape floating row cover material over the plant to protect it from sunburn and dehydration for the first week or so.

Today, however, most perennials are container grown—raised in pots rather than in the ground—which does offer some advantages. If properly cared for, they can sit for weeks in a nursery's yard without harm, which extends the shopping and planting season, and makes impulse purchases possible. Container-grown plants are sold while in active growth, so it is easier for an inexperienced shopper to tell whether they are healthy. Here are some easily observed clues that reveal the status of a plant's health:

- When shopping at the local garden center or retail nursery, fight the temptation to select the largest specimens. Extra-large plants, out of scale and too large for their containers, have been sitting in their pots too long; this neglect stunts the plant's growth and has long-term effects on their health and vigor. Roots emerging from the drainage holes in the bottom of a container are another sign that the plant has been in the container too long.

- Always inspect the roots of any plant you contemplate buying. With the nursery's permission, slip the plant out of its nursery pot—the roots should be crisp and white, reaching out over the exterior of the soil ball but not overly long so that they've wrapped themselves around it. That condition, known as being "pot bound," also indicates that the plant has been left too long in its container.

- Check the leaves—tops and bottoms—and along the stems for insects or insect eggs; flecks of discoloration on the leaves can also be a sign of insect infestation. Bringing home infested plants releases pests into your garden that may prove difficult to eradicate.

- Unless you are inspecting a cultivar that is supposed to feature variegated foliage, yellowing leaves or ones blotched with pale patches are signs of trouble. Such off-colored leaves may be a sign of disease or mistreatment by the retailer; in either case, you don't want that plant in your garden.

In addition, container-grown plants forgive procrastination; if you leave them in the shade on the porch for a few days and keep them watered until you have time to get them in the ground, container-grown plants seldom suffer any significant harm—that said, make the time delay as short as possible.

Relying on container-grown perennials to stock your garden, however, entails a couple of serious disadvantages. They tend to be more expensive than their bare-root equivalents, and some nurseries prefer to ship plants bare-root because it is much more economical to do so. Consequently, customers of container-grown plants are forced to rely mainly on local retail nurseries and garden centers that may stock only a small selection of top sellers. If you want not just a phlox, but a phlox that is mildew resistant and has flowers of a particular shade of lavender or pink, you'll probably have to have the plants shipped to you. Similarly, if you want not just the most popular perennials, but those best adapted to your conditions and needs, you may have to shop online or by catalog.

Keep in mind, however, that the retail nursery business is subject to constant change, with a large number of small specialist firms. Be adventurous in your online and catalog shopping, but keep track of the performance of the nurseries you patronize. Some do a better job of storing, packing, and shipping bare-root plants, which is reflected in the higher survival rate (and sometimes price) of their plants. Gardening forums on the internet, such as Dave's Garden, are helpful with this kind of shopping; many include nursery reviews detailing other gardeners' experiences.

Maintenance

Because of their distinctive, cyclical pattern of growth, perennials require a somewhat different kind of care from annuals or woody plants.

Winter vs. Summer Hardiness

Because our gardening tradition came to us mostly from northern Europe, Americans have focused on tolerance for winter cold as the criterion of a plant's hardiness. This attitude is reflected in the USDA Plant Hardiness Zone Map, which defines its geographical zones by the average lowest winter temperatures experienced in each region. Similar maps have been developed for Canada and Britain and may be found at www.plantmaps.com, and the Australian National Botanic Gardens have created a plant hardiness map for their continent. It defines zones by somewhat different criteria from those used by the USDA, but includes a tool for correlating the two systems.

This continues to be a useful guide to the likelihood of any perennial's survival in a given region. But as southern parts of our country have come to play a larger role in American gardening, and as climate change continues to make summers everywhere hotter, drier, and longer, summer hardiness has become an issue too. An inch-deep layer of some organic mulch, including pine needles or shredded bark, helps keep the soil moist and cool, protecting perennials against high summer temperatures; siting plants so they receive some afternoon shade from deciduous trees when sunlight is particularly intense is also beneficial—deciduous shade is preferable, as it allows the plants to enjoy winter sun during short days.

The combination of heat and humidity is particularly challenging to many perennials. It's best to select plants that are adapted to this sort of climate. In addition, provide protective afternoon shade; grow plants in raised beds to improve free-air circulation, thus reducing the effects of humidity; and top-dress humidity-sensitive plants with sand, gravel, or grit to enable surface moisture to drain quickly—this looks particularly appropriate in rock gardens.

Irrigation

Gardeners whose experience has been principally with annuals and vegetables will find that the styles of watering they used successfully with those plants are less beneficial when applied to perennials. Annuals and most vegetables complete their life cycle in a single growing season and so respond best to generous watering and fertilization. Perennials, on the other hand, aside from those recommended for xeriscapes and dry soils, need adequate and consistent moisture for satisfactory growth and flowering; too generous irrigation results in soft growth. This leaves plants susceptible to pests and diseases, and also prone to sprawl.

Fundamental to supplying your perennials the level of moisture they prefer is thorough preparation of the soil before planting. Dig and amend the soil to a depth of at least 10 in.—ideally twice the length of your spade—through double digging. In situations where shallow soil makes that impractical, deepen the layer of fertile, porous soil by spreading layers of amendments over the beds and forking them in—or create raised beds.

The amendments you add will depend on the preferences of the plants you intend to grow. For most rock-garden plants and those that prefer a gritty or sandy soil, the principal amendment should be coarse, sharp sand combined with a modest amount of poultry grit. For perennials that prefer a woodland-type soil (organically enriched and evenly moist), a fitting amendment is decomposed organic matter, such as compost or leaf mold. In either case, the goal is to create soil that naturally retains the level of moisture preferred by the plants grown in it.

With a properly prepared soil, irrigation should be deep and infrequent. An inch of water administered once a week during periods of hot, dry weather is sufficient for perennials that require a moist soil; similarly, deep watering once every two weeks or even less during droughts should satisfy a xeriscape. An easy way to test if the irrigation has penetrated through the root zone is to poke a metal rod into the soil—it will slip with relatively little resistance through wet soils and stop penetrating when its tip encounters dry soil.

Remember that it's not only how much water you apply, but how you apply it that's important. Soaker hoses or drip irrigation systems apply water directly to the soil surface. They not only minimize water lost to evaporation during irrigation but also avoid wetting plant foliage, reducing the danger of infection and spread of fungal diseases. When irrigating really dry soils, as in xeric conditions, it is most effective to apply water in two stages. Allow the first application to soak through the soil before applying the second. This deepens penetration and reduces water loss to surface runoff.

Pinching and Deadheading

The tasks of pinching and deadheading both involve narrowly targeted, low-impact pruning that requires very little labor. However, if completed in a timely fashion, these tactics greatly enhance the form and bloom of many perennials.

Pinching consists of removing the growing tip from a plant stem with your thumb and fingertip or with a pair of clippers. The result is to awaken dormant buds farther back along the stem and encourage branching, leading to more compact, bushier growth. This makes the plant stouter, reducing or even eliminating the need for staking, and often increases flowering.

Late-blooming perennials such as chrysanthemums, asters, and sedums are commonly treated this way. Otherwise they are likely to produce long, floppy stems rather than the more attractive cushion-like growth for which such plants are known. These examples are pinched at 6 in. tall, and again as the stems add each new 6-in. increment, until early July when flower buds should be allowed to develop. Summer-blooming perennials that tend to flop, such as summer phlox and beebalms, benefit from a curtailed version of this treatment: shear stems back by half in mid-spring (known as the Chelsea chop) to encourage sturdier growth.

Perennial species that bear their leaves in basal rosettes and their flowers on long, upright spikes do not respond positively to pinching. Among these unpinchables are columbines, astilbes, delphiniums, daylilies, coral bells, hostas, irises, foxgloves, and dianthus.

Deadheading is more of an ad hoc process that is applicable to virtually all perennials—it just involves snipping or pinching off spent or aging flowers as they fade. Most plants stop producing flowers as they begin to set seed; by preventing them from reaching this point, deadheading helps extend bloom time. Spike-forming perennials—delphiniums, monkshood, and the like—are best deadheaded to the base of the spike to encourage later bloom on laterals; those that have solitary flowerheads on long stems, such as coreopsis and other daisies, are deadheaded to the base of the leafless stem—don't just pop off the heads, which leaves an ugly "porcupine" effect. On other perennials, look for shoots emerging lower down the stem, and cut the spent one just above it. In many cases (as noted in the species entries), the more drastic treatment of shearing a plant back by a third or a half after bloom time will provoke a burst of new growth and often a second round of flowering.

Staking and Support

Taller perennials, especially the more spectacular, spike-flowering types such as delphiniums, monkshood, and foxgloves, may require support to keep flower stems from toppling, especially on windy sites. Staking is also an effective way to keep heavy-headed flowers such as peonies from sprawling.

Staking is an art form. The secret of providing effective and unobtrusive support for your plants is to do your installations early in the season. Plants will then grow up, through, and around the stakes or other support, camouflaging them so that they provide an internal structural skeleton or corset while the plants preserve a natural appearance. Waiting until the plants are already sprawling or on the verge of collapse, and then cinching them with stakes and twine, yields a constricted, unnatural look.

The traditional means of supporting perennials is called brushing up. Find some brushy twigs—short and branching wild cherry and birch are favorites, but virtually any twiggy branches will work. Clip them to a length so that the tops stand a few inches below the expected height of the plant, adding perhaps an extra 10 in. to allow enough length to anchor them in the ground. Insert the branches around and among the stems of each perennial that needs support, pushing the bases firmly into the ground. This process, also known as pea-sticking, is effective for clump-forming and mounded perennials, including chrysanthemums, coreopsis, asters, and summer phlox. A less laborious, but more expensive, alternative is to encircle the plants with circular metal supports sold as peony rings. These wire rings with wire legs vary in diameter. Position the ring over the newly sprouted perennial in spring and push the legs into the soil so that the ring is about 6 in. or so above the soil surface. As the stems grow, the legs of the ring can be slipped up a bit with them. There are many other staking products on the market, as well; choose what works best for you.

Support spike-forming perennials, such as delphiniums, individually with bamboo or metal stakes pushed into the ground near the base of the plant in spring. As the flowering spikes emerge, tie them loosely to the stakes in a figure eight with soft twine; as the spikes grow, retie every foot or so. Avoid tying too tightly and bruising—or worse, breaking the stems.

Winter and Summer Mulches

The benefits of organic mulch to perennials in summertime have already been mentioned. It's worth noting that by insulating the soil and reducing evaporation of soil moisture into the atmosphere, an organic mulch can reduce the need for summertime irrigation by as much as half. As the mulch decomposes, it slowly adds humus to the surface soil. In a garden where chemicals are used with restraint, earthworms flourish and carry decomposing organic matter down to their burrows, thus adding to the organic content of the soil and improving soil drainage.

A winter mulch, applied in very late fall, is a lifesaver for perennials in cold-winter regions. Dormant perennials cope better with consistent cold than with rapid temperature fluctuations and the resulting cycle of freeze, thaw, and refreeze. Wait until the ground is frozen, then apply an insulating blanket of evergreen boughs or several inches of a loose, fast-draining mulch (straw, shredded leaves, etc.) and your borders will overwinter well with little damage. Remove the mulch in early spring as new growth begins.

Unsold Christmas trees, mostly available free and often in bulk the day after Christmas, are excellent and economical sources of winter mulch material. Watch for neighbors putting out their discarded trees for collection.

Coping with Pests and Diseases

The best defense against the twin threats of pests and diseases is to plant healthy specimens of resistant plants, and then provide good care. Insects can sense when a plant's natural defense system has been compromised by stressors such as drought or inadequate light, and predators will deliberately target these vulnerable victims. Weak plants are also more susceptible to diseases and less able to cope with them once infected. Weeds serve as hosts for insect pests, and compete for resources, starving adjacent desirable plants. Avoid overly generous fertilization and irrigation that encourages soft, lush growth that makes the garden a target for insect pests, deer, and other browsing animals.

Even the best-cultivated gardens, however, sometimes fall prey to such invaders. It is important that you deal promptly with any infestations before they become too general or entrenched. A good policy is to inspect the garden for pests and diseases daily. Information about possible pests and diseases is included in the species descriptions in this book to help you identify incipient problems promptly.

Methods for controlling pests and diseases continue to evolve, often rapidly, as older pesticides lose their effectiveness or are taken off the market, and biological controls are developed and introduced. To secure the most up-to-date information about pest and disease control, contact your state's Cooperative Extension Service—most local offices keep a horticulturist on staff or can refer gardeners to an appropriate specialist with the state university system or a Master Gardener. Help with the diagnosis of what is troubling your plant and advice on recommended responses is usually free and, above all, reliable.

Propagation

Having bought a plant that turns out to be a favorite, you will probably want to have more of the same. Of course you can always buy more, but it is more economical and fun to increase your own. This is known as propagation, and may be vegetative or asexual by several methods, or sexual by seed.

Dividing Perennials

Division is a simple procedure that allows gardeners to increase their stock of perennials; it also reinvigorates some plants, returning aging specimens to a younger, healthier type of growth. Division produces offspring that are genetically identical to the parent plant. This method is ideal to propagate cultivars or hybrids that do not reproduce true to type by seed, but isn't applicable to all perennials. Taprooted plants such as poppies, sea hollies, and hollyhocks typically resent any disturbance to their roots. When division is inappropriate, this fact has been noted in the individual entries in this book. (One caveat: Propagating patented cultivars is prohibited.)

Divide fibrous-rooted perennials such as summer phlox by inserting a pair of garden forks, back-to-back, into the excavated root mass and prying it apart into two pieces; with a large clump, this process may be repeated one or more times to subdivide the root mass into a number of pieces. Save the healthiest divisions.

Some perennials, including campions and some irises, prove short-lived unless reinvigorated by division every three or four years. The plants die out in the center of the clump after a couple of years; remedy this by digging and separating the strongest outside pieces from the clump and discarding the dead center.

Timing is crucial to the success of this operation. In cold-winter regions, early spring, just as new growth is emerging, is usually the best time to divide perennials, as the leaves and stems are still small and less easily damaged, and the root systems are full of stored energy that helps the divisions recover and make new growth. Spring divisions have an entire growing season to reestablish, before facing the challenge of winter. In hot and dry climates, with mild winters and torrid, droughty summers, early fall can be a better season to divide perennials. Some perennials, such as bearded and Siberian irises, Asiatic lilies, daylilies, summer phlox, Jacob's ladders, Oriental poppies, and herbaceous peonies, prefer fall division, regardless of climate.

Propagation by Cuttings

Another method of increasing stock is by taking cuttings. These may be made from soft, young growth, from semi-ripe growth that is slightly hardened at the base, or from hardwood cuttings, which are reserved for woody plants. For a few perennials, Oriental poppies for example, root cuttings can be taken from fat roots, usually in winter.

Softwood or stem cuttings and basal cuttings are pieces of stem or young shoots that are cut off the mother plant. Trim cuttings to about 3–6 in. long, depending upon the species, cutting preferably just below a node where leaves emerge. Remove the bottom leaves, dip the base in rooting compound (to stimulate root production) and tap off excess, then insert the cuttings into a container of seed mix, sand, or peat or perlite mix (this is called sticking). Gently firm the cuttings and water from below or lightly from on top. Place the containers in plastic bags, blow up, and seal. Place them in a shaded spot until rooting occurs. Most species take at least two to four weeks or more to root, although chrysanthemums, for instance, root from 2- to 3-in. cuttings in a week if conditions are ideal.

Semi-ripe cuttings are taken much the same way, although the cuttings are probably longer. These are often taken with a heel—that is, with a piece of the mother stem attached. Strip the side branch from the mother, pulling downward to take a short spur of tissue with the cutting. Trim it up before sticking.

Root cuttings are taken from species such as bleeding heart and some peonies that have thick, fleshy roots. Look for roots that are about as thick as a pencil, sever a few pieces, and trim them up. Make a slanted cut at the end of the root that was closest to the plant and a horizontal cut at the other end. The roots can then be laid horizontally on top of a rooting soil mix and covered to about the depth of their thickness. Water carefully.

Layering is a method used to increase some perennials, especially dianthus. Bend the stem down if necessary, then nick no more than a third of the way through the underside of it with a sharp knife or razor blade. Open the wound and sprinkle a little rooting hormone on the cut, then peg it down to the soil (a hairpin or opened paperclip works well). Cover the wounded section with a mound of mixed soil, peat, and sand, and keep evenly moist until rooting occurs.

Starting from Seeds

Starting plants from seed is an economical and easy—albeit slow—way to furnish your perennial beds. The caveat is that sexual reproduction (seed production) results in some reshuffling of genetic material. Offspring will be variable and not always exact copies of their parents. Plant breeders, however, have created many desirable hybrid strains, which can be relied upon to come true and which are sold as seed. Propagation by seed is arguably the best way to secure a quantity of plants for a wild or meadow garden; by introducing genetic variability into your planting, it increases its resilience to pests, diseases, and extreme weather. No matter what the challenge, a less homogenous, seed-propagated population is likely to contain some individuals with natural resistance; conversely, a garden planted with a handful of spectacular cloned (genetically uniform), named cultivars may be more susceptible.

As a rule, the instructions printed on the seed packet offer a good guide to the proper treatment of that particular perennial. The following tricks, however, may be helpful to ensure your success. Start the seeds indoors, in shallow containers (with drainage holes in the bottom, of course) filled with your favorite soilless seed-starting mix. Starting indoors produces the best results because you can protect the germinating seeds from fluctuations in temperature and moisture, as well as from insects and birds. These mixes are naturally sterile and greatly reduce the danger of fungi that might attack newly sprouted seedlings. A dressing of coarse grit also reduces the threat of damping off, a fungal disease. (Milled sphagnum, once popular for this use, has fallen out of favor because sphagnum production is so environmentally destructive and contributes to climate change.) Fluorescent fixtures, outfitted with a combination of "warm-white" and "cool-white" tubes provides a nearly ideal light source.

The following are some ideas for pre-treatments that will help you get the most from your seeds:

- Some seeds, including baptisia, thermopsis, and hardy geraniums, have thick, hard seed coats that prevent water from penetrating, causing delayed germination. Scarify the seed coats by rubbing the seeds lightly over coarse sandpaper; then soak them in water overnight prior to sowing to increase both the speed and rate of germination.

- To delay germination until spring arrives, the seeds of perennials that evolved in very harsh climates often remain dormant and require a winter-like period of moisture and chilling (stratification) to break dormancy. To satisfy this requirement, after sowing the seeds, enclose the containers in sealed plastic bags and store them in the refrigerator or outdoors for winter chill for a minimum of eight weeks. If germination doesn't occur when the containers are brought back into warmer temperatures, don't throw them out—they may simply need another chilling cycle.

- Gentle, even warmth enhances the germination rate of many perennial seeds. The best way to provide this is to set your seed-starting containers on a waterproof, thermostatically controlled heating mat—these devices are available from many nurseries and horticultural supply companies, as well as some online seed catalogs. Failing that, you can put them on top of the refrigerator, but make sure to monitor them closely.

PERENNIALS A–Z

ASTER | MICHAELMAS DAISY

Aster, Symphyotrichum | ASTERACEAE

ONCE A SPRAWLING GENUS of some 600 species, recently asters have been reorganized by botanists so that all except one of the North American members have been assigned to other genera (*Eurybia, Doellingeria*, etc.). However you name them, this invaluable, colorful group of plants includes many tough and persistent species. Some, like the attractive Siberian *Aster tataricus*, can be too successful, even invasive; others are well-behaved stalwarts of summer and fall displays in gardens of all kinds. Asters bear composite daisy-like flowers, typically in great abundance, with petals (ray flowers) in shades of blue, purple, white, and pink. The centers (disks) of each blossom (actually a head of flowers composed of countless individual flowers) are usually yellow.

The *Symphyotrichum* genus includes several species formerly listed as asters, but based on genetic studies, they are now classified separately. This move, of course, has not changed these plants' cultural needs or aesthetic potential.

While some species may be invasive, several others serve as staples in summer and fall displays in meadow and prairie plantings, and as sources of cut flowers. The taller, fall-blooming types, New England (*Symphyotrichum novae-angliae*) and New York asters (*S. novi-belgii*), partner well with ornamental grasses; purple-flowered cultivars provide an especially effective complement to switch grass cultivars such as 'Shenandoah', whose foliage becomes reddish in autumn. Symphyotrichums offer especially fine blues—dropping one of these into the middle of a sea of yellow flowers, or swamp sunflowers, for example, really energizes such a display.

Similar to asters, symphyotrichums bear composite, daisy-like flowerheads, typically in great abundance, in shades of blue, purple, white, and pink. The centers of each flowerhead are usually yellow. As the common name Michaelmas daisy (which correctly refers to New York asters but is often applied more broadly) indicates, symphyotrichums tend to bloom late in the growing season—the feast of St. Michaels falls on September 29, when asters are in bloom in many regions, often persisting until the arrival of a killing frost.

As a rule, asters and their kin prefer a well-drained, organic-rich soil, and struggle if planted in dense clays; they do well in coastal, sandy soils. Full sun is best for most species, though some tolerate part shade. Taller species benefit from being cut back by half before midsummer to promote branching and more compact growth that can forgo staking. Asters are prone to foliar diseases including powdery mildew and rust, as well as some insect pests including aphids, leafhoppers, and spider mites. Though such infestations rarely kill the plants, they disfigure them and may affect garden neighbors. Search out disease- and pest-resistant cultivars. Deer seldom browse asters; butterflies flock to their flowers.

Divide mature clumps of any of these in spring or fall, or take softwood stem cuttings in late spring. Start seed indoors in late winter.

Aster ×frikartii

🖌	lavender
📅	early summer to fall
✥	2–3 ft. × 1.5 ft.
☼	sun, part shade
📍	Z5–10, HS

FRICKART'S ASTER This *A. amellus* × *A. thompsonii* hybrid isn't as pest and disease resistant as some of the species, but it blooms early and long from late spring to midfall if deadheaded conscientiously. Vivid, fragrant flowers, 2.5 in. wide, top loose mounds of dark green, oval leaves. Protect dormant plants with mulch of evergreen boughs through winter in cold zones; well-drained soil is essential. Superb for containers.

'Flora's Delight', an introduction by Alan Bloom, is more compact (1.5–2 ft.) with 2-in., lilac-colored flowers. Somewhat less cold hardy than other members of this group. **'Monch'** bears 2-in., lavender flowers with yellow centers. 2 ft. tall. **'Wonder of Staffa'** has slightly paler lavender flowers but is hard to distinguish from 'Monch'. 2 ft.

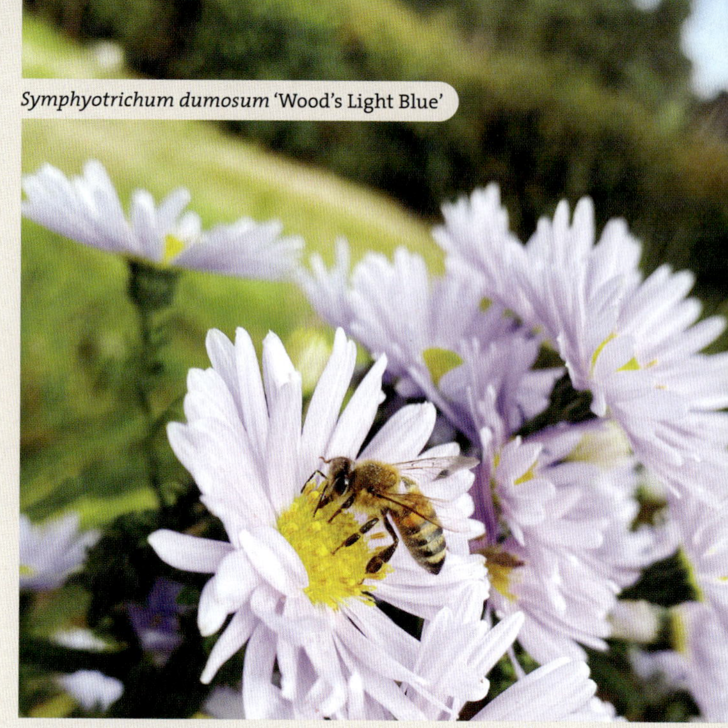

Symphyotrichum dumosum 'Wood's Light Blue'

Aster tongolensis

Color	blue, purple
Bloom time	early summer
Size	1–1.5 ft. × 1 ft.
Light	sun
Zones	Z3–9

EAST INDIES ASTER Western China. Stoloniferous and mat forming, with oval leaves in a slowly spreading cushion; in early summer, erect, thick, and hairy, almost leafless stems branch at the top and bear solitary, 6-in.-wide, violet-blue flowers centered with orange-yellow. Ideal for rock gardens, troughs, and the front of borders.

'Berggarten' blooms prolifically with 2- to 3-in.-wide, orange-eyed, bright violet-blue flowers. 24 in. tall. **'Napsbury'** has light violet-blue flowers with slender rays. 18 in. **'Wartburg Star'** is 1.5–2 ft. high and wide, with long-blooming, 2-in., violet-blue flowers.

Symphyotrichum dumosum

syn. *Aster dumosus*

Color	pale violet
Bloom time	late summer to early fall
Size	3–4 ft. × 1–3 ft.
Light	sun, part shade
Zones	Z3–8

RICE BUTTON ASTER Native throughout the eastern United States. Naturally bushy with 3-in., lanceolate leaves; unlike many asters, remains clothed with foliage to the ground throughout the growing season. Large clusters of small flowerheads congregate at the branch tips; pinch young shoots in spring to encourage more prolific flowering. Disease and pest resistant.

'Wood's Light Blue' is compact with light blue flowers. Superior rust and mildew resistance. 12–14 in. **'Wood's Pink'** is similar with clear pink flowers. 12–16 in. **'Wood's Purple'** has blue-violet to purple flowers. 12–18 in.

Symphyotrichum ericoides

syn. ***Aster ericoides***

Color	white
Bloom time	late summer to fall
Size	1–3 ft. × 1–1.5 ft.
Light	sun
Zone	Z3–10

HEATH ASTER Native to open, dryish sites throughout eastern and central North America. Needle-like foliage; yellow-centered, 0.5-in., white flowers are borne in profuse sprays that persist well into autumn. Disease and pest resistant; tolerates dry soils and drought; performs well in ordinary garden conditions.

'Blue Star' produces a multitude of dark blue, starry flowers. 3 ft. **'Esther'** has pink-tinged, white flowers. 18–24 in. **'Snow Flurry'** is prostrate, 6–8 in. tall and to 2 ft. wide. Valued as a dense groundcover with abundant white bloom. Excellent for containers.

Symphyotrichum laeve

syn. ***Aster laevis***

Color	purple
Bloom time	fall
Size	2–4 ft. × 1–2 ft.
Light	sun
Zone	Z3–8

SMOOTH ASTER A native of the northeastern United States that offers disease and pest resistance, and tolerance for droughty, poor soils. Smooth green, mostly toothed, 5-in. leaves clothe unbranched stems topped with loose, 6-in.-wide clusters of yellow-centered, 0.75- to 1.25-in., violet-blue or purple flowerheads. Striking with goldenrods.

'Bluebird' has violet-blue flowers

Symphyotrichum lateriflorum

syn. *Aster lateriflorus, A. diffusus*

Color	white
Season	fall
Size	2–3 ft. × 1 ft.
Exposure	sun, part shade
Zones	Z3–9

CALICO ASTER Another disease- and pest-resistant species native to eastern North America. Clumps of branching stems clothed with lance-shaped leaves to 5 in. long, toothed or entire along the edges; 0.3-in., white flowers, with yellow centers that age to maroon.

'Horizontalis' (var. *horizontalis*) has horizontal branched stems, and carries tiny but abundant pinkish brown–eyed white flowers. Very bushy, with dark foliage. Full sun. 2 ft. tall. **'Lady in Black'** makes mounds of deep purplish leaves that become blanketed with red-centered, white flowers. Foliage color is best in sites with full sun.

Symphyotrichum novae-angliae 'Alma Potschke'

Symphyotrichum novae-angliae

syn. *Aster novae-angliae*

🖌	purple
📅	late summer to fall
✥	3–6 ft. × 2–3 ft.
☼	sun
📍	Z4–8

NEW ENGLAND ASTER Eastern United States. Robust and easily grown in average, well-drained but moist soils. Hairy, lance-shaped leaves to 4 in. long clasp the hairy stems. Generous crops of 1.5-in., yellow-centered, purple flowers. Good air circulation and full sun restrain susceptibility to mildew. Pinch back stem tips several times before midsummer to encourage compact growth and limit the need for staking. Excellent cut flowers; wear gloves to protect from the hairy stems. Cultivars abound; this is a sampling:

'Alma Potschke' ('Andenkan an Alma Potschke') has 1- to 2-in., bright magenta-pink flowerheads; disease-resistant foliage. Early. 4 ft. **'Harrington's Pink'** bears 1.5-in., clear pink heads. Mildew- and rust-resistant foliage. 3–5 ft. **'Hella Lacy'**. Plants are smothered with 2-in.-wide, blue-violet daisies. 3–4 ft. Named for garden writer Allen Lacy's wife, Hella. **'Purple Dome'** has vibrant deep purple flowers with yellow centers. Foliage resists mildew and rust. Compact at 18–24 in. **'Wedding Lace'** has pure white flowers; outstanding resistance to rust. 3–4 ft.

Symphyotrichum novi-belgii 'Raspberry Swirl'

Symphyotrichum novi-belgii

syn. *Aster novi-belgii*

Color	blue, purple
Bloom	late summer to early fall
Size	2–4 ft. × 3 ft.
Light	sun
Zone	Z4–8

NEW YORK ASTER Native to northeastern North America. Similar in habit and bloom to the New England asters but less leggy; stem-clasping leaves are smooth. Not as full flowered as the preceding species, and not as good for cutting. Provide good air circulation and consistent soil moisture to reduce vulnerability to diseases. Tall (4 ft. or more), medium (under 4 ft.), and dwarf (up to 15 in.) cultivars are available. Medium and dwarf plants are most useful, unless space is unlimited. British breeders have developed a host of cultivars offering diverse colors, as well as compact plants that need no staking. Tall cultivars are not suitable for most gardens unless they are pinched when young and are well supported.

'Professor Anton Kippenburg' has semi-double, lavender-blue flowerheads; mildew-resistant foliage. Compact. 12–18 in. tall. **'Raspberry Swirl'** has a rounded form; abundant raspberry-pink flowers; mildew resistant. Compact. 18–24 in. **'Royal Opal'** sports light blue flowerheads; mildew and insect resistant. 16 in. high and wide. **'Tiny Tot'** is a dwarf with bright purple flowers; mildew resistant. 4–8 in. **'Winston Churchill'** has bright red daisies, good for cutting. Tolerates heat and humidity. 2–3 ft. tall.

Symphyotrichum oblongifolium 'October Skies'

Symphyotrichum oblongifolium

syn. *Aster oblongifolius*

Color	blue, purple
Bloom time	late summer to fall
Size	1–3 ft. high and wide
Light	sun
Zones	Z3–8

AROMATIC ASTER Native from the eastern seaboard of North America into the Rocky Mountains. This adaptable, compact, bushy plant tolerates numerous challenges including clay, rocky soils, and drought. Blue-green, 4-in., oblong leaves are aromatic; yellow-centered, violet-blue, 1-in. flowerheads. An outstanding cut flower. Plant where passersby will brush against foliage and release the minty fragrance.

'October Skies' has deep sky-blue flowers. Introduced by Primrose Path Nursery. 1.5–2 ft. high and wide. **'Raydon's Favorite'** bears abundant 1.25-in., lavender flowerheads on stiff, hairy stems. Late blooming. 3 ft. × 4 ft.

ASTILBE | PLUME FLOWER

Astilbe | SAXIFRAGACEAE

A MOIST, SHADED GARDEN without astilbes is like a cock without its crow! Their beautiful fluffy plumes of pink, red, purple, or white flowers and attractive fern-like leaves would earn them a place even without their tolerance of shade and easy-care ways. And as a bonus, deer don't seem to find them tasty.

Astilbes are indigenous to damp woodlands and streamsides in China and Japan, as well as the United States (for example, *Astilbe biternata*). The bulk of the named selections on the market are the result of extensive hybridization between species. Clumps of astilbe grow from a mass of rhizomes that becomes woody with age. Young foliage, two- or three-times divided into toothed leaflets, erupts in spring. Leaf color is variable, mostly dark or mid-green; red-flowered selections often display young, deep red foliage. Fluffy plumes of tiny flowers are borne mostly above the foliage mass in summer on leafless stems of varying heights. Bloom time runs from late spring (early) through to mid- to late summer (late). Catalogs may list selections as early, midseason, or late. Seedheads and leaves become an attractive rusty brown and can provide interest through the winter months. Allowed to remain intact, these provide unusual contrast to early-blooming stinking hellebores or Italian arum, for example, and are interesting in dried flower arrangements.

Provide rich, acid soil that remains moist but does not become waterlogged; be sure plants remain well watered in hot weather, as drying out results in crisping of the leaf margins. Amend the soil with plenty of organic matter, as astilbes are greedy feeders; an annual dressing of rotted manure or compost is beneficial. Divide the woody rootstocks every three to four years in spring or fall to maintain vigor or to propagate.

Astilbes are often major players in moist, shaded beds and borders, and beside streams or ponds, where they may be massed to provide large drifts of color or grouped with other shade lovers. Among their most popular companions are bold-leaved hostas, hellebores, lungworts, hardy begonias, and ferns. The tall types look well among flowering shrubs, especially early- or late-blooming ones to extend the season of interest. Both compact and tall astilbes grace any container solo or mixed with other plants that like damp feet.

Pests and diseases are few, although leaf spots and mildew may damage the foliage. Ignored by deer and rabbits.

Increase by dividing the clumps in spring; pot up or replant at once.

Astilbe ×*arendsii* 'Deutschland'

Astilbe ×arendsii

Color	red, pink, white, purple
Bloom time	late spring to midsummer
Size	2–4 ft. × 2 ft.
Light	part shade
Zones	Z3–8

HYBRID ASTILBE This hybrid group displays amazing variety in all aspects, and includes the bulk of available cultivars. Flowering time varies from early to late, enabling gardeners to have color over many weeks.

'Amethyst' has robust lavender plumes. Early to late. 18–24 in. **'Bridal Veil'** ('Brautschleier'). Thick plumes of white flowers. Midseason. 18–24 in. **'Deutschland'** may be the whitest of whites, not turning ivory. A strong grower. Early. **'Fanal'**. Dark red flowers bloom above bronzy foliage. Early. 24 in. **'Montgomery'** has bright red plumes with green foliage. Midseason. 20–24 in. **Music Series** blooms mid- to late season: 'Jump and Jive', bright pink with dark foliage, 12–16 in. 'Rhythm and Beat', fuchsia pink with medium green leaves, 14–18 in., reblooms. 'Rhythm and Blues', hot pink over dark leaves, 20–24 in. 'Rock and Roll', black-stemmed, white plumes above bronzy leaves; 18–24 in.; reblooms. **'Peach Blossom'**. Light salmon-pink flowers. Reliable old variety, often listed under *Astilbe ×japonica* or *A. ×rosea*. 24 in. Z4–9. **'Prof. van der Wielen'** has open plumes of white flowers. Late. 30–48 in. Z4–9. **'Straussenfeder'** ('Ostrich Plume') has elegant branched, pendulous inflorescences of hot-pink flowers. Tolerates heat and humidity. Has *A. thunbergii* blood. 3 ft.

Astilbe chinensis syn. *A. rubra*

flower color	white, pink
bloom time	mid- to late summer
size	10–36 in. × 24 in.
light	sun, part shade
zones	Z3–8

CHINESE ASTILBE Siberia, China. Vigorous, with bronzy, softly hairy leaves divided into three rounded leaflets rimmed with double teeth. The species is seldom cultivated, but there are plenty of superior selections.

'Diamonds and Pearls' has dense plumes of pure white flowers above dark green foliage. Heat and humidity tolerant. 2 ft. tall. **'Finale'**. Leaves are bronzy green and lacy. Lavender-pink flowers. Appropriately named, blooming into early fall. 15–18 in. **'Maggie Daley'**. Bright fuchsia-pink plumes over green foliage. A strong grower. Midseason. 28 in. **'Pumila'** has lilac-pink plumes on 10-in. stems. Good groundcover if kept damp, but often displays unattractive half-spent plumes. May be a hybrid. Fast spreader. Late. **'Visions'** is compact with upright bright raspberry flower plumes. Bronze green foliage. Mid- to late season. 15 in. Others in the excellent **Visions Series** include pale 'Visions in Pink' (18 in., mid- to late season) with bluish green leaves, 'Visions in Red' (15 in., midseason), with bronze foliage, and 'Visions in White' (20–30 in., early) with soft white plumes.

Astilbe chinensis 'Visions'

Astilbe ×crispa 'Lilliput'

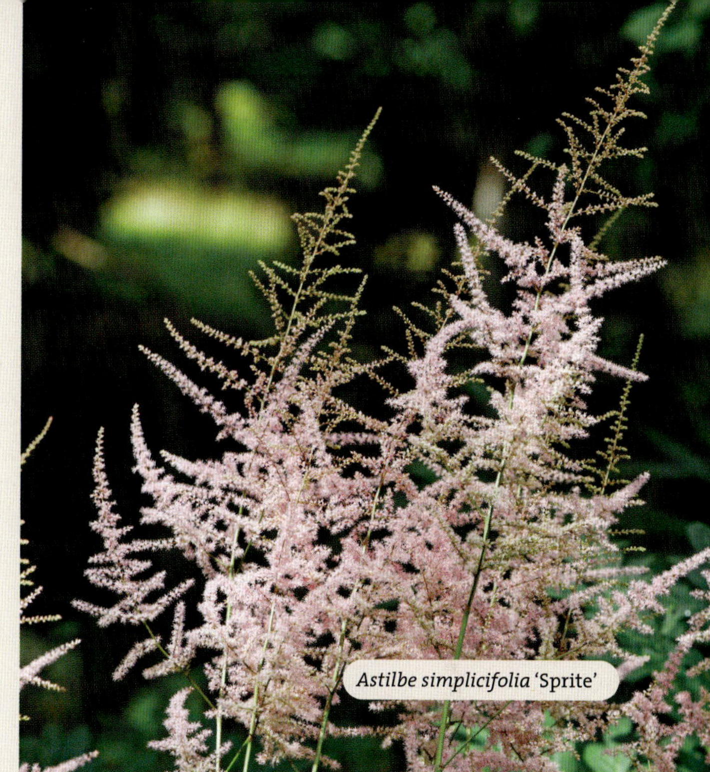
Astilbe simplicifolia 'Sprite'

Astilbe ×crispa

syn. *A. crispa*

Flower color	pink
Bloom time	early to midsummer
Size	6–10 in. × 10 in.
Light	part shade, shade
Zone	Z4–8

CRISP-LEAVED HYBRID ASTILBE This diminutive hybrid has crimped, deep green leaves below a full complement of fluffy flower plumes. Excellent for rock gardens, containers, or as edging along shaded pathways

'Lilliput' has light salmon flowers. 6–8 in. **'Perkeo'** ('Peter Pan') has deep rose-salmon plumes. 8–10 in.

Astilbe simplicifolia

Flower color	pink, white, magenta
Bloom time	early to midsummer
Size	12–18 in. × 24 in.
Light	sun, part shade
Zone	Z3–8

STAR ASTILBE Japan. This short species is best known for its contribution as a parent to many superior hybrid selections:

'Key West' has mounds of dark burgundy leaves, with feathery plumes of carmine red. Excellent for cutting and in containers. Midseason. 16–20 in. **'Pink Lightning'**. Open, pale pink plumes over dark lustrous leaves. Early. 16–20 in. **'Sprite'** is a favorite, with airy shell-pink flower plumes and bronzy leaves. Late. 12 in. An Alan Bloom selection. Perennial Plant of the Year 1994. **'White Sensation'** is particularly compact with 10-in. mounds of glossy green foliage. Dainty white flowers. Mid- to late season. 18 in.

BABY'S BREATH

Gypsophila | CARYOPHYLLACEAE

COMMONLY USED AS FILLER by the floral industry in arrangements focused on more dramatic flowers such as roses and lilies, gypsophilas can serve a similar purpose in the perennial garden. The airy clouds of small, white flowers that they display through most of the summer furnish a delicate counterpoint to the stronger colors and forms of more assertive blossoms and foliage. Gypsophilas are also useful for filling the gaps left in the garden by early spring bulbs, wildflowers, and summer-dormant perennials, including Oriental poppies, when they retreat back into dormancy in late spring. And, of course, gypsophilas are a handy source of cut flowers.

Gypsophila means "gypsum-" or "chalk loving," and most members of this genus prefer an alkaline soil. Add lime to acid soils, and top-dress with limestone chips in rock gardens. Gypsophilas do best in sunny spots and are generally pest and disease free, although poor drainage may cause root rot. Seldom browsed by deer.

Start seed indoors in winter or outdoors in a cold frame in spring. Root cuttings may be taken from the species in late winter.

Gypsophila cerastioides

Color	white
Bloom time	late spring to midsummer
Size	4–8 in. × 8–12 in.
Light	sun
Zones	Z3–7, HS

BABY'S BREATH Himalayas. Forms a compact mound of small, rounded, fresh green foliage, from which emerge taller, branching stems that carry the small, pink-veined, white, starry flowers. Drought tolerant; attracts butterflies. Evergreen in mild winters. Valuable for rock gardens, sunny banks, edging along pathways, and at the front of sunny borders, or in containers. Intolerant of heat combined with humidity.

Gypsophila repens

(color)	white
(bloom time)	early to late summer
(size)	4–12 in. × 18 in.
(light)	sun
(zone)	Z3–8, HS

CREEPING BABY'S BREATH Low-growing European species, commonly 6 in. tall, forms spreading cushions of gray-green, lanceolate foliage. Smothered in early summer with tiny, white, five-petaled flowers. Beautiful groundcover for sunny, well-drained spots, also works well as edging for a path or border, or spilling over the edge of a retaining wall or container. A gem for rock gardens and containers, and for planting into crevices of a south- or west-facing retaining wall, or between flagstones on a sunny terrace. Drought tolerant, but regular irrigation during dry spells in spring and early summer is critical to the flower quality. Difficult in hot and humid gardens.

'Alba' is white flowered. 4 in. tall **'Dorothy Teacher'** has a low, neat habit with soft pink flowers that darken with age. Bluish green foliage. 2 in. **'Filou Rose'** has a long season of bloom from late spring to late summer. It bears large, bright pink flowers. **'Fratensis'** (syn. *Gypsophila franzii* 'Nana Compacta') makes a low cushion of blue-green foliage, 2–3 in. high and 6 in. wide, from which emerge wiry stems bearing a wealth of tiny, pale pink flowers. Z4–7.

BANEBERRY | BUGBANE

Actaea | RANUNCULACEAE

IN RECENT YEARS BOTANISTS have expanded the genus *Actaea* to include all the plants formerly classified as species of *Cimicifuga* (*C. japonica, C. matsumurae, C. racemosa*, and *C. simplex*). Many nurseries still sell these plants under their old names, so these have been included here as synonyms.

Natives of temperate Northern Hemisphere woodlands, baneberries flourish in moist, well-drained, humus-rich soils in situations of partial shade, dappled sunlight, or even full shade. Their combination of attractive foliage, small but elegant flowerheads, and ornamental fruits make them good choices for a woodland or wild garden. Those formerly classified as *Cimicifuga* are stately, elegant perennials, with lacy foliage and fluffy spires of sweetly scented, small, starlike flowers borne atop soaring, erect, or arching stems. All are intolerant of dry conditions but otherwise easy to grow, with few serious pests or other problems. Deer appear to ignore them. Typically long-lived if their basic needs are met, actaeas often naturalize in hospitable locations.

Be warned that many members of this genus are poisonous in some or all their parts, especially the fruits (which are, however, attractive fare for many birds).

To propagate, sow seed in containers in fall and overwinter outdoors in a cold, but protected spot, or divide mature plants in early spring.

Actaea japonica

syn. *Cimicifuga japonica*

flower color	white
bloom time	late summer
size	36–48 in. × 22 in.
light	part shade, shade
zones	Z3–9

JAPANESE BUGBANE Japan. Blooming later than most baneberries, this Japanese native has just three large leaflets per leaf and flowers borne in branching panicles. The best Actaea for the hot, humid southeastern United States.

'Cheju Island Form' is compact, making a mound of foliage just 12–14 in. high. Flower stems might reach 4–5 ft.; floriferous—a single mature plant may bear 12–15 flower spikes.

Actaea matsumurae

syn. *Cimicifuga matsumurae*, *C. simplex* var. *matsumurae*

flower color	white
bloom time	late summer to early fall
size	3–4 ft. × 2–3 ft.
light	part shade, shade
zones	Z4–9, HS

BUGBANE Central and eastern Asia. Chiefly available as the cultivar **'White Pearl'** (syn. *Cimicifuga simplex* 'White Pearl'). Arching, bottlebrush-like racemes to 24 in. long with small, white flowers borne on slender stems; these rise well above the mound of dissected, fern-like, medium green leaves that emerge late in spring.

Actaea pachypoda

syn. ***Cimicifuga pachypoda***

Color	white
Bloom time	mid- to late spring
Size	1.5–2.5 ft. × 2–3 ft.
Exposure	part shade, shade
Zones	Z3–8

WHITE BANEBERRY, WHITE COHOSH, DOLL'S EYES Eastern North America. This low-key but charming woodland wildflower thrives under tree canopies and in clearings. Astilbe-like, compound leaves of three-toothed leaflets remain attractive all season. Sweetly scented, tiny, white flowers in oblong clusters are held aloft on long stems that turn red as the pea-sized white berries, each with a single purple spot, develop. The berries do indeed resemble doll's eyes but are extremely poisonous, making white baneberry a poor choice for households with children. The toxicity deters wildlife, so the fruit display lasts typically until a killing autumn frost. Ideal in woodland or shade gardens, as well as in shady borders. Long-lived, it often naturalizes and forms colonies. Ferns, blue sedge, bugbanes, and goldenseal are good companions.

'Misty Blue' has delicate blue-green foliage together with white springtime flowers. Poisonous white berries follow. 2–3 ft.

Actaea racemosa

syn. ***Cimicifuga racemosa***

Color	white
Bloom time	late spring to early summer
Size	4–6 ft. × 2–4 ft.
Exposure	part shade, shade
Zones	Z3–8, HS

BLACK BUGBANE, BLACK SNAKEROOT, BLACK COHOSH Rocky woods throughout most of the United States east of the Mississippi. Produces white-flowered spikes that may soar to 8 ft. in ideal conditions—humus-rich, evenly moist soil, and a sheltered, semi-shaded site. Astilbe-like foliage, three times divided, is an attractive deep green. Provide support for flower spikes, especially in windy spots.

Actaea rubra

(flower)	white
(bloom time)	mid- to late spring
(size)	1–3 ft. × 6–12 in.
(light)	part shade, shade
(zones)	Z4–8, HS

RED BANEBERRY Cool, moist, nutrient-rich sites throughout the northeastern and midwestern United States, the Rocky Mountains, and Pacific Coast regions. Stems bear few coarsely toothed, deeply lobed leaves that emerge in a bushy clump. Clusters of lightly rose-scented, small, delicate, white flowers open above the foliage; conspicuous glossy red or occasionally white berries follow in late summer and fall. The fruits are favorites of many birds, including grouse, gray catbirds, and robins. Best in woodland gardens where meadow rues, gaultheria, and false Solomon's seal are appropriate native companions.

Actaea simplex Atropurpurea Group

Actaea simplex

syn. *Cimicifuga simplex, C. ramosa*

(flower color)	white
(bloom time)	late summer to early fall
(size)	3–4 ft. × 2–3 ft.
(exposure)	part shade, shade
(hardiness)	Z4–8, HS

BUGBANE, KAMCHATKA BUGBANE Mongolia, eastern Russia, and Japan. Late in the season numerous small, creamy-white, strongly scented flowers bloom in fluffy spires atop tall, upright, wiry stems. Attractive dark green, astilbe-like foliage, compound with deeply cut leaflets. Often self-seeds and naturalizes. Provide support for flowering stems; best where sheltered from strong winds. Bugbane is an asset in woodland gardens, among shrubs, in cottage gardens, and naturalized areas. Most attractive when planted in multiples; white spires show up well against dark backgrounds.

Atropurpurea Group (black bugbane) includes a number of dark-leaved cultivars that are still listed in many catalogs under *Cimicifuga ramosa*: 'Atropurpurea', 6 ft.; look for clones with darker-hued foliage. **'Black Negligee'** is vigorous, with deeply cut, black-purple foliage on dark stems and bottlebrushes of purple-tinged, white flowers; to 5 ft. **'Brunette'** has bronze-hued foliage to set off the white, sometimes pink-tinged wands of flowers, each about 8 in. in length. Fragrant **'Hillside Black Beauty'** has black stems up to 7 ft. that bear white flowers; dark, coppery-purple foliage. **'James Compton'** is compact with deep bronze foliage and white, sometimes pink-tinged flowers; its clumps are 2–3 ft. × 1.5–2 ft.

BASKET-OF-GOLD

Aurinia | BRASSICACEAE

LIKE ITS CLOSE RELATIVES *Aubrieta* and *Arabis*, this genus provides a host of spring-blooming prizes for rock gardens, for spilling over walls, and for tucking into crevices. Woody at the base, basket-of-gold's upper growth forms loose clumps of evergreen, grayish, spoon-shaped leaves to 5 in. long. This superstructure bears masses of brilliant school bus–yellow flowers that bloom over several weeks from spring into early summer. Best in full sun, basket-of-gold thrives in well-drained, poor to average soil but is not fussy as long as the roots do not remain wet; rich soil promotes soft, leggy growth, susceptible to insects. Established plants are drought tolerant. Shear after bloom for neatness and to ensure vigor.

Sow seed in late fall outdoors or with protection in very early spring. Named cultivars must be propagated vegetatively: summer cuttings usually root easily, but attempting division in fall is not reliable.

Aurinia saxatilis 'Compactum'

Aurinia saxatilis

syn. *Alyssum saxatile*

flower color	yellow
bloom time	spring to early summer
size	8–12 in. × 12–18 in.
light	sun
zones	Z3–8, HS

BASKET-OF-GOLD, GOLDENTUFT, MADWORT Southeastern and central Europe. This cheerful plant is easy to grow and provides dramatic spring color. Rather floppy foliage is mostly grayish, felted with hairs, and a perfect foil for the flowers. Replace old woody plants with young stock; plants may self-seed freely unless cut back before seed set.

'Citrinum' ('Luteum', 'Sulphureum') has pale lemon-yellow flowers. **'Compactum'** is a 4- to 8-in. miniature form. **'Compactum Flore-Pleno'** ('Plena') has double flowers. **'Dudley Neville Variegated'** has cream-edged foliage and is beautiful throughout the season, especially with yellow corydalis. Apricot buff flowers. In hot climates, provide midday shade, or treat as an annual. **'Golden Flourish'** was bred for container cultivation. Masses of mustard-yellow flowers above green foliage. Eye-catching spilling over the edges of planters with tulips, pansies, daffodils, and other early bloomers. **'Sunny Border Apricot'** has soft orange-yellow flowers. A Sunny Border Nursery introduction. Z6–9.

BEARDTONGUE | PENSTEMON

Penstemon | PLANTAGINACEAE

A TREASURE TROVE FOR GARDENERS who favor North American natives, the genus *Penstemon* includes over 300 species, only one of which originated outside this continent. Ranging from coast to coast, and from the Arctic tundra to the mountains of Guatemala, penstemons have achieved their greatest diversity and splendor in the western United States. Yet we owe the domestication and hybridization of these plants to the late nineteenth- and twentieth-century European plant breeders. The recent quest for water-conserving gardens, however, has brought increased attention to drought-tolerant Western penstemons; many are available now, especially from regionally focused nurseries.

Not surprisingly, such a large group of plants offers great variety. Penstemons range in height from 1–2 in. to 7-ft. giants. Leaves are alternate; funnel-shaped or tubular flowers are borne typically in spikes. Flower color ranges from white to blue, violet, purple, pink, magenta, red, and occasionally yellow. Individual blooms are two lipped like a gaping mouth, from which protrudes a long, frequently hairy staminode—the source of the common name, beardtongue. Attracts a variety of pollinators including butterflies and hummingbirds; deer resistant.

Most penstemons are "pioneer" plants, adapted to colonizing disturbed soils. They tolerate and favor nutrient-poor, very well-drained, even gritty soils; consistently moist conditions with poor drainage commonly cause root rot. Mulch with gravel or leave soil bare; avoid moisture-retaining, organic mulch, such as ground bark. Seldom browsed by deer or rabbits. Some species of penstemons are somewhat demanding outside their native habitats; the following are among the easiest to grow.

Propagate by seed, division, stem cuttings, or layer species with prostrate stems.

Penstemon barbatus

color	red
bloom time	late spring to early summer
size	1.5–3 ft. × 1–2 ft.
exposure	sun
zones	Z4–9

BEARDTONGUE Rocky slopes and open woodlands from Utah to Arizona, east into Colorado. Clump forming with evergreen, oblong to ovate basal foliage, and clasping, willow-like stem leaves, 2–6 in. long. Terminal racemes of tubular, 2-in., orange-red flowers; deadhead to extend flowering. Tolerates shallow, rocky soils. Good for sunny, dry borders and rock gardens, naturalized in cottage gardens and meadows, open woods.

'Jingle Bells' (var. *coccineus* 'Jingle Bells') has scarlet flowers. Grow from seed. **'Rubycunda'** has slightly fragrant, scarlet flowers with contrasting white throats.

Penstemon cardinalis

color	red
bloom time	midsummer
size	24–30 in. × 24 in.
exposure	sun
zones	Z5–9

CARDINAL BEARDTONGUE Southern New Mexico, west Texas. Rosettes of large, evergreen, deep green leaves; ruby-red, tubular flowers dangle from upright stems. Withstands intense sun, but tolerates very light shade. Exceptionally drought tolerant once established; will succeed in very well-drained soil in moister climates. Best for rock gardens or dry borders; a premier hummingbird plant.

Penstemon davidsonii

Color	blue, purple
Bloom	midsummer
Size	2–5 in. × 12 in.
Light	sun, part shade
Zone	Z6–8

DAVIDSON'S PENSTEMON Mountains of the West Coast from California through British Columbia. Dense mats of creeping, woody stems with small, leathery, evergreen, oval leaves. Broad, tubular flowers, 0.75–1.5 in. long and blue-lavender to purple, rise on very short stems. Sensitive to summer drought; best where snow cover is reliable, or protect with evergreen boughs in winter (extends hardiness through zone 5). Unusual, handsome groundcover for rock gardens, sunny, sandy, or gravelly banks, or dry borders.

Var. *menziesii* 'Microphyllus' is compact (2 in. × 10–12 in.) and hardier with small, more finely textured, evergreen leaves that turn burgundy color in winter. Z4.

Penstemon digitalis

Color	white
Bloom	midspring to early summer
Size	3–5 ft. × 1.5–2 ft.
Light	sun
Zone	Z3–8

BEARDTONGUE Native to prairies, fields, woodland edges in eastern and southeastern United States. Recommended as easy and reliable for Pacific Northwest gardens by the American Penstemon Society. Clump forming with elliptical basal leaves, becoming lanceolate to oblong higher up the stems. Panicles of white, tubular, 1- to 1.25-in. flowers. Provide average, dry to moderately moist, well-drained soil; resents wet, poorly drained ones. Striking massed in sunny borders, wild gardens, prairie plantings, or well-drained rain gardens. Generally trouble free if drainage is adequate.

'Husker Red' has non-fading, deep burgundy foliage, and white or blush-pink flowers. Compact at 2–3 ft. × 1–2 ft. 1996 Perennial Plant Association Plant of the Year. **'Mystica'** foliage emerges green, becoming dark maroon-red during the summer, and blazing red in the fall. Clusters of lavender-pink flowers. 30 in. × 20 in.

Penstemon heterophyllus

color	blue
bloom time	late spring to early summer
size	12–18 in. × 12–18 in.
light	sun
zones	Z6–10

FOOTHILL PENSTEMON Grasslands, chaparral, and open woodlands of California's mountain foothills. Clump forming, with narrow, lanceolate to linear stem leaves, 2–4 in. long, and 1.5-in. tubular, gentian-blue flowers in terminal racemes on erect, spreading stems. Remove spent flowering racemes to prolong bloom time. Sunny, dry borders, rock gardens, and dry, rocky banks and slopes.

'Electric Blue' has flowers of more intense, uniform blue than the species.

Penstemon pinifolius

color	red
bloom time	late spring to early summer
size	10–12 in. × 12–18 in.
light	sun
zones	Z4–9

PINELEAF BEARDTONGUE Arizona, New Mexico, northern Mexico. Forms low, bushy mound of needle-like foliage, evergreen where winters are mild. Constricted, tubular, orange-red flowers with fringed mouths borne over two-month season. Cut back hard as growth resumes in early spring to remove old woody growth. Glorious in rock gardens, walls, or troughs; very drought tolerant, a natural for xeriscapes.

'Magdalena Sunshine' has yellow flowers. Z5–9.

Other Notable Cultivars

Hybrids commonly offer a greatly prolonged season of bloom and a wider color range; superior in the border.

'Blackbird' bears raspberry-purple flowers; deep green leaves. 18–24 in. × 12–18 in. **'Blue Midnight'** has large, deep blue-purple flowers with white, burgundy-streaked throats. 30 in. × 36 in. Z6–9. **'Dark Towers'** has abundant pale pink flowers, above non-fading, deep burgundy foliage. 18–36 in. Z3–8. **'Elfin Pink'**. Broad mats of glossy foliage; 12- to 18-in. spikes of salmon-pink flowers. Sun, partial shade. Z4–9. **'Prairie Dusk'**. Tubular, rose-purple flowers on 20-in. stems. Deadhead for long bloom. **'Red Riding Hood'** bears vivid, coral-red flowers from late spring through summer. 24–30 in. × 18–24 in. Z5–8.

BEAR'S BREECH

Acanthus | ACANTHACEAE

ONE OF THE MOST architectural of perennials, bear's breech's bold leaves—variously lobed, cut, and divided, some tipped with spines—inspired the decorative foliage on Corinthian column capitals. The bracted, tubular flowers, borne in dramatic spikes above the foliage, are mostly white, often almost concealed by a purple or mauve hood, and are excellent for cut flowers, fresh or dried.

These are not plants for tight conditions or for the faint of heart. Bear's breech can take over a small space and is considered by some to be invasive, especially on favorable sites—its tenacious roots are almost impossible to eradicate. Established plants tolerate drought well, though good drainage is critical. In cold-winter areas, apply a protective winter mulch.

A fine subject for large containers for a deck or patio, bear's breech also stands out massed beside lightly shaded driveways or on the edge of woodlands, where it can spread freely. In flower borders, protect from intense sun. Garden phlox, upright milky campanula, and meadow rue are good back-of-the-border companions. Underplant with geranium 'Rozanne' or sweet woodruff. Seldom browsed by deer.

Propagate by division or by detaching young plants from the base in spring or fall. Sow seed in spring, or take root cuttings when the plants are dormant.

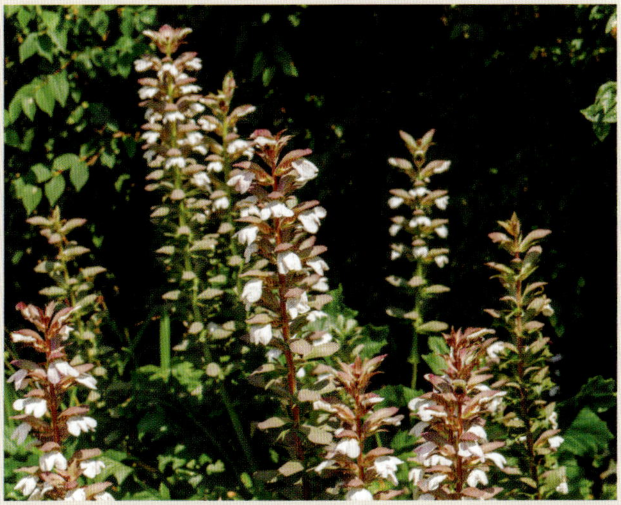

Acanthus hungaricus

syn. *A. balcanicus, A. longifolius*

flower color	white, purple
bloom time	late spring to summer
size	3–4 ft. × 3 ft.
exposure	sun, part shade
zones	Z6–10

BALKAN BEAR'S BREECH Southeastern Europe. Clumps of deeply divided, dull green leaves are thistle-like but lack spines. White flowers are hooded with plum bracts equipped with spines.

Acanthus mollis

(flower color)	white, purple
(bloom time)	late spring to summer
(size)	4 ft. × 3 ft.
(exposure)	sun, part shade
(zones)	Z7–10, HS

BEAR'S BREECH Southeastern Europe, northwestern Africa. Deeply lobed, glossy leaves to 2 ft. long. Slow to establish, especially when grown from seed. Intolerant of heat coupled with humidity.

'Hollard's Gold' emerges with bright gold foliage in spring, which unfortunately matures to green. Can be used as a startling focal point to contrast with ostrich fern (*Matteuccia struthiopteris*, syn. *Onoclea struthiopteris*) in light shade, or as a specimen or container plant. Spikes of white and wine-colored flowers rise to 5 ft. tall all summer long. **'Rue Ledan'** thrives in hot, humid conditions. Clumps of handsome, shiny leaves may reach 3 ft. across. Spikes of pure white flowers rise to 3 ft. Not as heat tolerant. Z6–8. **'Whitewater'** bears eye-catching, deeply cut leaves generously splashed and tipped with white, and white-and-pink snapdragon-like flowers in summer. Tough, excellent in difficult areas.

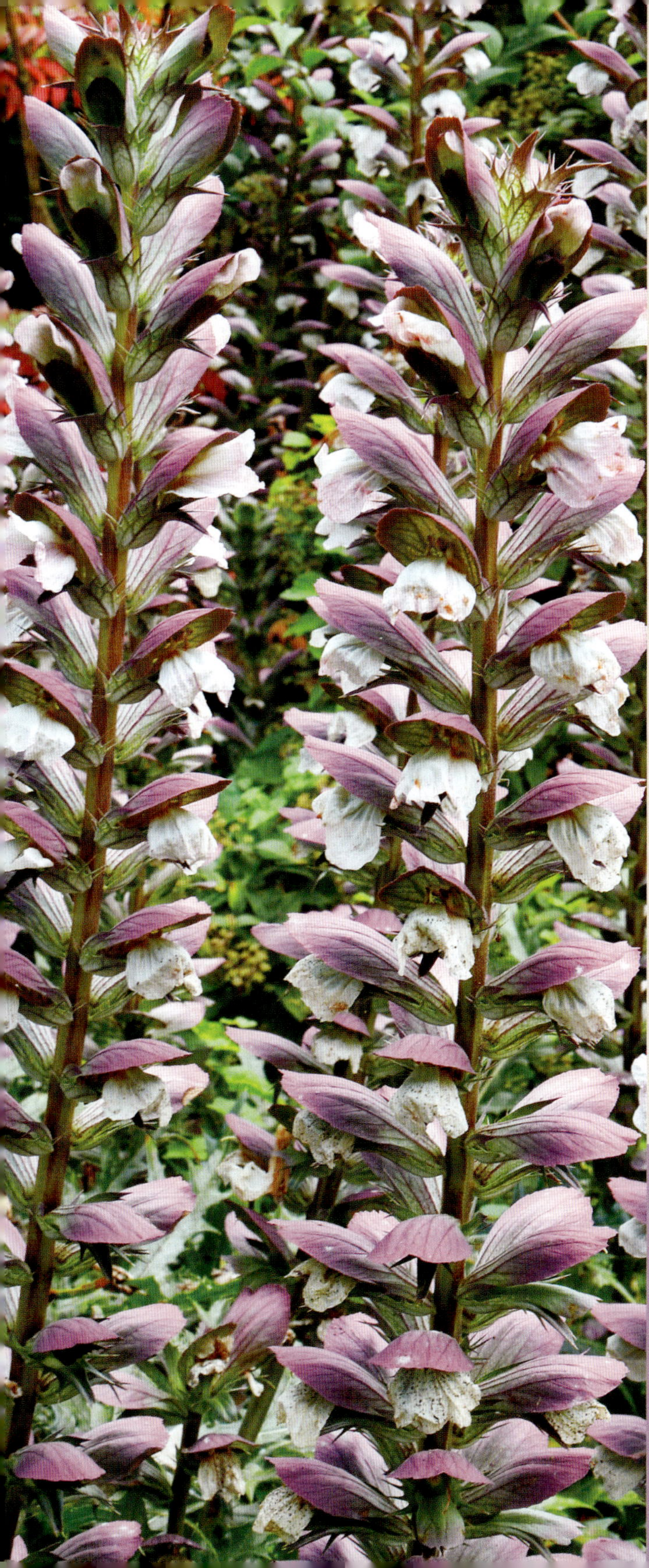

Acanthus spinosus

syn. ***A. spinossissimus***

Color	white, purple
Bloom time	summer
Size	3–4 ft. × 2–3 ft.
Light	sun, part shade
Zone	Z6–9

BEAR'S BREECH Eastern Mediterranean. This species does not establish quickly but is worth the wait. The thistle-like, dark green leaves are glossy and variably spiny.

Other Notable Cultivars

'Holland Days', often listed under *Acanthus spinosus*, has deeply cut, sharply pointed (but not spiny) leaves, and purple-bracted, white flowers. Ideal for smaller gardens, but beware of its aggressive tendencies. 1 ft. × 3 ft. Z6–10. **'Summer Beauty'** sports huge, deeply cut, shiny, dark leaves; 4- to 6-foot flower stems with mauve-bracted, white flowers. Tolerates heat and humidity. Z6–10.

BEEBALM | BERGAMOT

Monarda

LAMIACEAE

USED BY INDIGENOUS PEOPLES as a treatment for a wide variety of ailments, this genus of North American wildflowers continues to supply the antiseptic, thymol, employed in many modern mouthwashes. Gardeners value these hardy mint relatives for their aromatic foliage and long-lasting bloom. Like the mints, beebalms have square stems and small, tubular flowers borne in dense, mop-headed clusters.

Flourishing on a wide range of soils, beebalms prefer a moderately moist, well-drained site, but tolerate some drought once established. As their common name suggests, their nectar-rich flowers attract bees as well as butterflies and hummingbirds. The more refined hybrid selections hold their own in mixed borders; as a group, however, beebalms appear more at home in less formal meadows, native plant gardens, and open woods, or alongside ponds and streams. They have the rare ability to grow under black walnut trees. Good companions include black-eyed Susans, coneflowers, Shasta daisies, and gayfeathers. Little troubled by insect pests, deer, or rabbits, beebalms are, however, susceptible to powdery mildew. Search out mildew-resistant selections.

Propagate by seed; take stem cuttings or divide named cultivars in late spring.

Monarda didyma

	red
	early to late summer
	2–4 ft. × 2–3 ft.
	sun, part shade
	Z4–9

OSWEGO TEA, BEEBALM Eastern United States and Canada. Clumps of stems clothed with aromatic, alternate, lanceolate, 3- to 5-in. leaves rimmed with teeth. Dense terminal heads of red flowers top whorls of showy red-tinged, leafy bracts. Shade from intense sun. Unlike other beebalms, this species must not dry out; a good choice for rain gardens.

'Adam' has red flowers. More drought tolerant than the species. **'Croftway Pink'** is a lovely rosy pink. Susceptible to mildew. **'Grand Parade'** offers lavender-purple flowers. 13–16 in. × 16–20 in. Z3–8. **'Jacob Cline'** has outstandingly large, brilliant red flowers. Largely mildew resistant. **'Purple Rooster'** displays large, rich purple flowers. Mildew resistant. 36 in. × 26 in.

Monarda fistulosa

	pink, lavender
	early to late summer
	2–4 ft. × 2–3 ft.
	sun, part shade
	Z3–9

WILD BERGAMOT Native to prairies; dry, rocky woods and woodland margins; and in unplanted fields and along roadsides in United States, Canada, and Mexico. Clump forming with oblong, grayish green leaves to 4 in. long. Two-lipped, lavender flowers cluster in terminal, globular heads above whorls of showy, pinkish bracts. Prefers dry to moderately moist, well-drained soil, but tolerates clay; shallow, rocky soils; and some drought. Reseeds; best for naturalized informal plantings. Prone to powdery mildew.

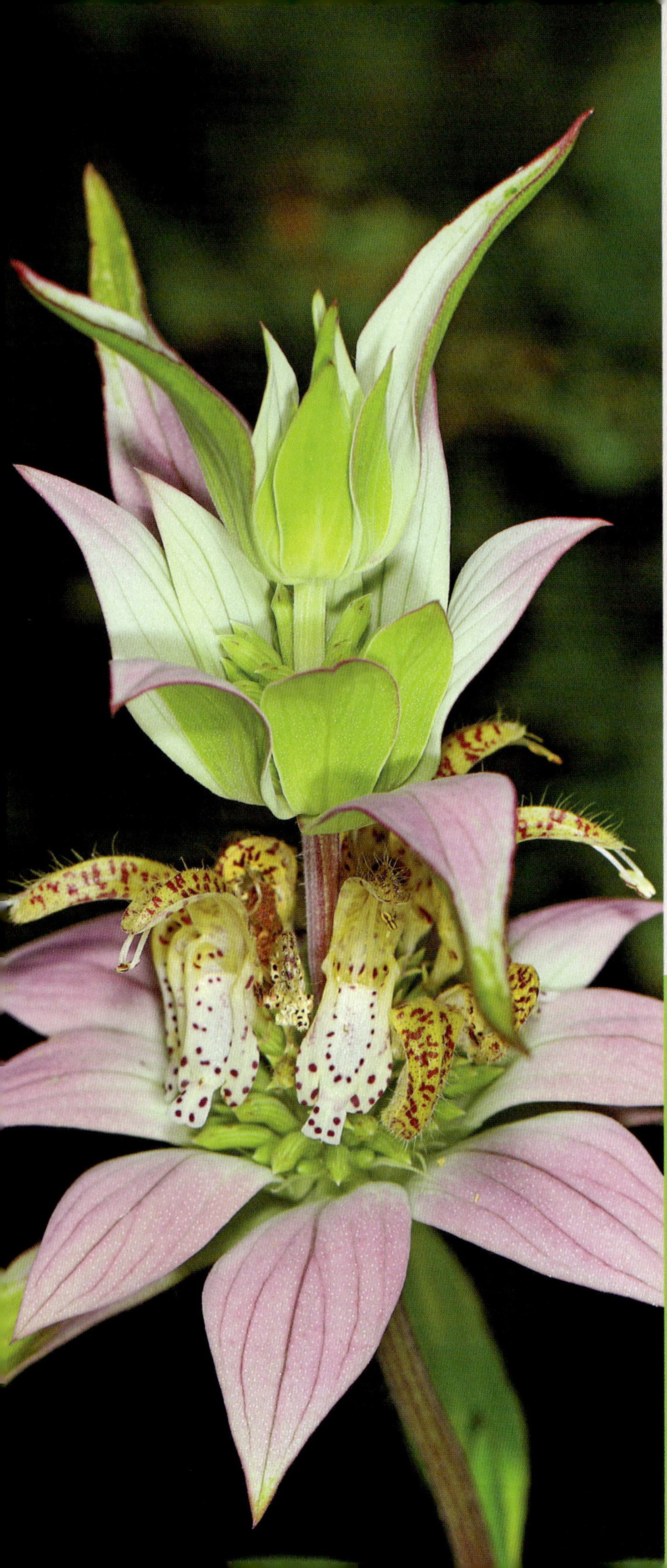

Monarda punctata

Flower color	yellow, purple
Bloom time	early summer
Size	18–24 in. × 9–12 in.
Exposure	sun, part shade
Zones	Z3–8

DOTTED BEEBALM, SPOTTED HORSEMINT Eastern United States. Clump forming with toothed, aromatic, oblong leaves to 3 in. long. Two-lipped, tubular flowers are yellow, spotted with purple. They are borne in upper leaf axils and at stem ends in tiered, stem-encircling clusters supported on whorls of showy, pinkish bracts. Prefers dry to moderately moist, well-drained soil; tolerates poor soils and some drought. Self-seeds.

'Fantasy' is an exceptionally robust cultivar. 2–2.5 ft. × 2–3 ft.

Other Notable Cultivars

'Blue Stocking' ('Blaustrumpf') has deep lilac flowers. Quite heat and drought tolerant. 36–60 in. × 24 in. Z4–10. **'Colrain Red'** has deep red flowers. Mildew resistant. 3–4 ft. Z4–9. **'Gardenview Scarlet'** has bright rose-red flowers; mildew resistant. Introduced by Henry Ross, Gardenview Park, Ohio. Has largely replaced mildew-prone **'Cambridge Scarlet'**. 36 in. × 24 in. Z4–10. **'Marshall's Delight'**. A mildew-resistant Canadian introduction with densely packed heads of showy pink flowers. 36–48 in. × 24–36 in. Z4–9. **'Pardon My Purple'** is dwarf with 2.5- to 3-in., fuchsia-purple flowers. 12 in. tall. **'Petite Delight'** is dwarf with lavender-pink flowers. Mildew resistant. 12–15 in. × 18–24 in. Z2–8.

BELLFLOWER

Campanula | CAMPANULACEAE

THIS LARGE AND DIVERSE GENUS of about 420 species includes plants of many different habits—from upright to creeping—whose diversity enables them to fill niches in plantings ranging from perennial borders to rock gardens. A large number of species is native to North America, with its western mountains being an especially rich source. Campanulas supply some of the finest, clearest blues in the garden, though the palette of floral colors found in this genus extends to a range of whites and pinks as well. It should be noted that the species *Campanula armena* was formerly sold under the name of *Symphyandra*, but since being reclassified, most nurseries are now advertising them under the new name.

As the common name indicates, campanula flowers are often bell shaped, although there are species with tubular, star-, or cup-and-saucer-shaped blossoms as well. Conscientious deadheading prolongs the season of bloom.

Note that several bellflower species tend to be invasive. Creeping or roving bellflower (*C. rapunculoides*—not described here) is one to avoid. Once introduced it is almost impossible to eradicate. Another hardy, though less aggressive species worth investigating is *C. rotundifolia*, native to most of North America and northern Europe.

Though usually easy to grow, bellflowers are susceptible to snails, slugs, spider mites, and aphids. Powdery mildew and rust may also be problems. As a group, campanulas attract hummingbirds, but resist deer browsing. The longer-stemmed species are decorative as cut flowers; sear the base of the stems to avoid the milky sap fouling the vase water.

Sow seed in containers in spring or early fall (overwinter with protection), by division in spring or autumn, or by basal stem cuttings from new spring growth.

Campanula carpatica 'Blue Clips'

Campanula armena

syn. *Symphyandra armena*

Color	blue, white
Bloom time	late spring to early summer
Size	15 in. × 12 in.
Light	sun, part shade
Zone	Z7–8

RING BELLFLOWER Caucasus, Turkey, Iran. Deeply toothed, heart-shaped, hairy leaves on domed networks of branching stems. Nodding, bell-shaped, lavender-blue or white flowers are borne prolifically. At home in any light, well-drained garden soil. Long-lived treasure for rock gardens or border foregrounds.

Campanula carpatica

Color	blue, purple, white
Bloom time	early to late summer
Size	6–12 in. × 1–3 ft.
Light	sun, part shade
Zone	Z4–7

CARPATHIAN HAREBELL Mountains of eastern Europe. A species of modest vigor and stature best suited to the front of a border, rock, or cottage garden, or for display in a container. Heart-shaped, dark green leaves form neat tussocks that in summer are covered with bell-shaped flowers with a diameter of 2–3 in. Well-drained soil—regularly moistened but allowed to dry between waterings—promotes good growth.

'Blue Clips' is low growing and spreading with violet-blue flowers. **'Pearl Deep Blue'** blooms heavily with large, bright blue flowers. **'White Clips'** is compact, 6–8 in., with pure white flowers.

Campanula cochlearifolia

(color)	blue, purple
(bloom time)	early to late summer
(size)	2–4 in. × 6–8 in.
(light)	sun, part shade
(zone)	Z3–8

FAIRY'S THIMBLE European mountains. This fast-growing, even aggressive, species has a low and spreading habit that makes it valuable for edgings or as an underplanting for taller perennials. The dense mat of diminutive leaves provides a pretty backdrop for the showy 0.5-in. bells.

'Bavaria Blue' has sky-blue flowers. **'Bavaria White'** bears heavy crops of pure white flowers. **'Elizabeth Oliver'** bears intricate double, pale lavender flowers.

Campanula glomerata

(color)	blue, purple
(bloom time)	summer
(size)	12–24 in. × 15–24 in.
(light)	sun, part shade
(zone)	Z3–8

CLUSTERED BELLFLOWER Europe, Asia. Free blooming; forms clumps of upright stems above basal rosettes of long-stemmed oval, toothed leaves 4–5 in. long. Lacking petioles, the stem leaves are sometimes clasping and smaller. Dense but rather ungainly clusters of funnel-shaped, 0.75- to 1-in., bright purple flowers clump at the stem tips and in leaf axils. Long lasting as cut flowers. Provide part shade in hot areas; full sun is preferable in cooler climates. Group with daylilies, tickseeds, Helen's flower, and summer phlox.

'Crown of Snow' ('Schneeckrone') has pure white flowers. 18–24 in. **'Freya'**, named for the Norse goddess of love and fertility, produces starry, lilac-purple flowers on the top two-thirds of the stems. Late spring to summer. Non-invasive. 10–15 in. tall. **'Joan Elliot'** blooms early with upward-facing, light purple-blue flowers. Good for cutting. Tolerates wet soils. 18 in. **'Superba'** is a strong grower with bright purple-violet flowers. 24 in.

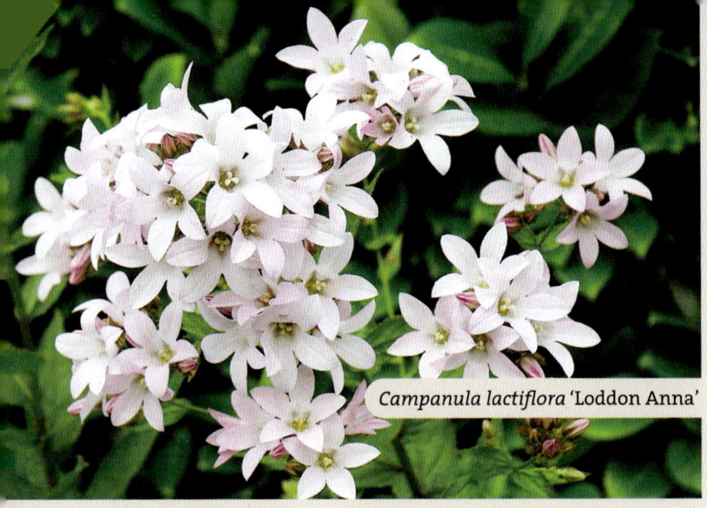

Campanula lactiflora 'Loddon Anna'

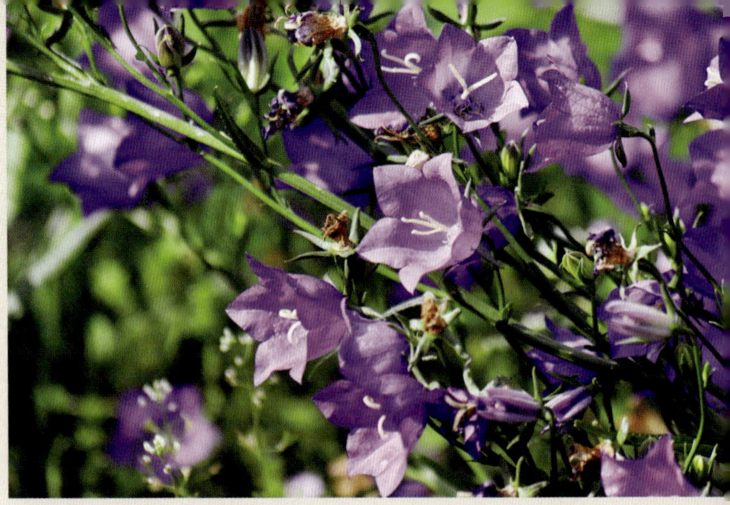

Campanula lactiflora

(color)	blue, purple, white
(bloom time)	midsummer to early fall
(size)	3–5 ft. × 1–3 ft.
(light)	sun, part shade
(zones)	Z4–10, HS

MILKY BELLFLOWER Caucasus. Long-lived and imposing, milky bellflower forms a group of tall stems clothed with rounded leaves and topped with conical spires of sweet-scented, 1.5-in., bell-shaped flowers. Cut back to 1 ft. in midspring to encourage denser, sturdy growth that doesn't require staking. Performs best on rich, moist but well-drained soils. Self-seeds. Combine at the back of the border with hollyhocks.

'Alba' has white flowers, but is otherwise similar to the species. **'Dwarf Pink'** is compact but floriferous, bearing an abundance of pink flowers. Late spring to early summer. 18–24 in. **'Loddon Anna'** bears pale pink flowers. **'Pfouffe'** is dwarf, with an abundance of pale blue flowers. 1–2 ft. tall. **'Pritchard's Variety'** bears violet-blue flowers over an extended season. 3 ft.

Campanula persicifolia

(color)	blue, purple, white
(bloom time)	late spring to early fall
(size)	1–3 ft. × 1–1.5 ft.
(light)	sun, part shade
(zones)	Z3–8, HS

PEACH-LEAVED BELLFLOWER Mountainous areas of Europe, northern Africa, and northern and western Asia. Forms a rosette of narrow, glossy, bright green leaves. Cup-shaped flowers in shades of blue, lilac, or white borne along the full length of tall, slender stems. Prefers an evenly moist soil that drains well, and some afternoon shade in places where sun is intense. Does not tolerate summer heat and humidity well. Self-seeds readily and also spreads by rhizomes. Appropriate in cottage gardens, borders, and open woodlands, and as a cut flower. Good companions include catmint, daylilies, hardy geraniums, and lilies.

'Alba' is white flowered. **'Chettle Charm'** has flowers that are creamy white, edged with lavender-blue. **'Kelly's Gold'** has bright golden foliage and white flowers tinged blue around the edges. **'La Belle'** is compact, with small, double flowers, deep blue with a silver gloss, borne all summer. To 24 in. **'Telham Beauty'** is extra vigorous (to 4 ft. tall) with porcelain-blue flowers.

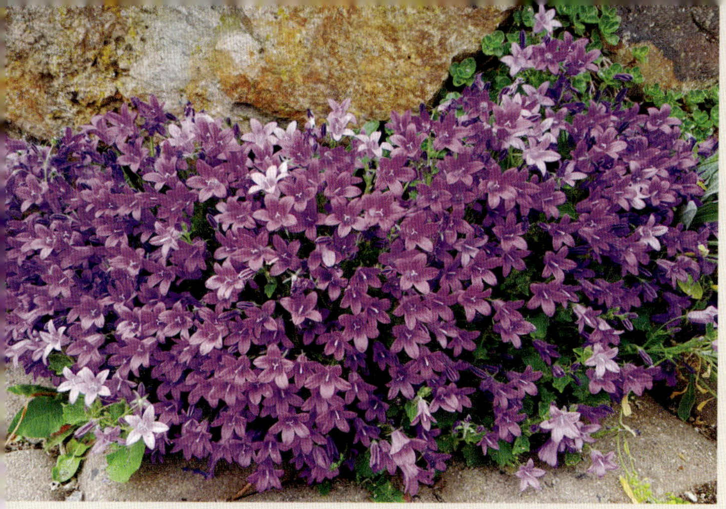

Campanula portenschlagiana

syn. ***C. muralis***

	blue, purple
	late spring to midsummer
	3–6 in. × 1–3 ft.
	sun, part shade
	Z4–8

DALMATIAN BELLFLOWER Rocky uplands of Dalmatia, Croatia. In favorable locations, this low, mat-forming plant spreads rapidly by rhizomes. Heart-shaped, dark-green leaves with toothed edges; abundant 1-in., funnel-shaped, blue to purple flowers. Protect from the early afternoon sun in hot climates. Suitable for rock gardens, edgings, and containers.

Var. *alba* is white flowered. **'Aurea'** has golden foliage. **'Birch Hybrid'** makes a neat cushion, 4–6 in. tall and 20 in. across, covered with cupped, blue-purple flowers from early summer into fall. **'Resholt Variety'** bears intensely violet-blue flowers.

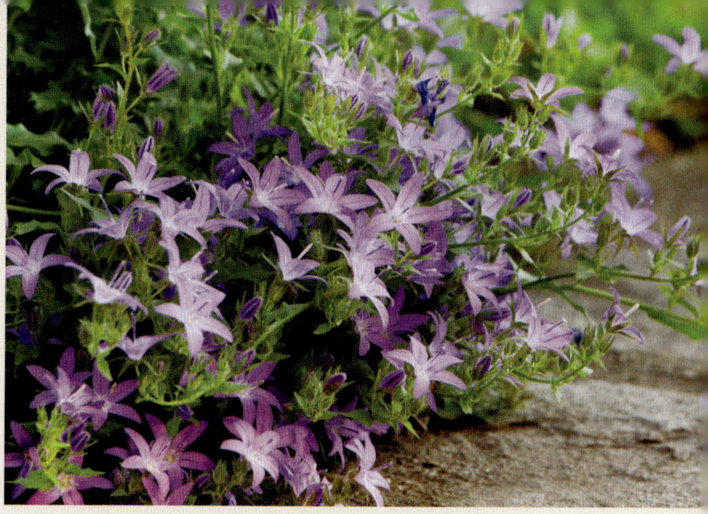

Campanula poscharskyana

	blue
	midspring to early summer
	4–12 in. × 1–1.5 ft.
	sun, part shade
	Z3–8

SERBIAN BELLFLOWER, DALMATIAN BELLFLOWER Northern Balkans. A sprawling, prostrate species that forms a low, mounded groundcover of oval to cordate, medium green leaves to 1.5 in. long. Evergreen where winters are mild. Lilac-colored, star-shaped, 1-in. flowers borne in loose panicles along the stems. Excellent as edgings along a path or around a patio, in containers, or spilling over the top of a retaining wall or down a bank.

'Blue Waterfall' bears an abundance of lavender-blue flowers. 8–10 in. **'Blue Rivulet'** is a similar but more compact form of 'Blue Waterfall'. Perfect for containers and small gardens. 6–7 in. **'E. H. Frost'** has white flowers. Excellent tumbling over walls and rocks. 8 in. **'Stella'** has violet-blue flowers. 6–12 in.

Campanula punctata

Color	pink, white
Bloom time	early to midsummer
Size	1–2 ft. × 1–1.5 ft.
Light	sun, part shade
Zone	Z5–7

SPOTTED BELLFLOWER Siberia and Japan. Long blooming and easily grown; forms basal rosettes of rounded, toothed, green leaves to 5 in. long, from which rise arching stems. These sport racemes of nodding, tubular, white to pale pink flowers as much as 2 in. long, spotted purple inside to guide foraging bees. Spreads freely by rhizomes or self-sown seeds and can become thuggish; suitable for informal borders, cottage gardens, and lightly shaded woodland settings. Keep under control.

'Bowl of Cherries' has pink to dark purple-red bells on 15-in. plants. Remove spent flowers for later rebloom. Vigorous. Z5–9. **'Cherry Bells'** has rose-red flowers. Tolerates heat and humidity well. 24 in. **'Hot Lips'** is dwarf, with large, bell-shaped, pale pink flowers, speckled burgundy inside, above rich dark green foliage. 10–12 in. **'Kent Belle'** has glossy violet-blue flowers on upright stems. Tolerates heat and humidity. Sterile. Striking with silver-leaved companions. 24 in. Z5–9. **'Pink Chimes'** has nodding, pink flowers. 9–18 in. tall.

Campanula takesimana

Color	pink
Bloom time	mid- to late summer
Size	18–24 in. × 24 in.
Light	sun, part shade
Zone	Z5–8

KOREAN BELLFLOWER Korea. Rhizomatous roots produce basal rosettes of heart-shaped leaves, 3–4 in. long, above which rise winged flower stems. Branching sprays of nodding, tubular, pink-flushed, white flowers, 2–3 in. long, decorated inside with maroon spots and speckles. Deadhead routinely to keep neat. Spreads vigorously, valuable only in informal or very lightly shaded woodland, shrub, or wild gardens and for cutting.

'Elizabeth' blooms freely with plenty of purplish pink, speckled blooms. Vigorous.

Other Notable Cultivars

'Bumblebee' bears masses of small, upright, blue bellflowers in summer. Excellent in containers and crevices. 4 in. × 12 in. Z4–8. **'Sarastro'** is upright and compact. Abundant large, purple flowers from early summer, repeating until fall. 18 in. × 24 in. Z3–8. **'Viking'** displays tubular, light lavender flowers. Compact, excellent for the middle and front of borders, and cottage and cutting gardens. Spreads in a quiet, civilized way; sterile. Attracts hummingbirds and butterflies. 18 in. tall.

BERGENIA | PIGSQUEAK

Bergenia | SAXIFRAGACEAE

A WELL-GROWN GROUND COVER of bergenias is handsome indeed, though it can become shabby if neglected. These clumping perennials from rocky moors and meadows of Asia have large leaves like ping-pong paddles, often heart shaped at the base. Some are evergreen, and many turn red, purple, or bronze in cold weather. Clusters of pink, red, or white flowers, bell or funnel shaped, are borne atop thick succulent stems, sometimes pink tinged, branched or not.

Deadhead regularly to extend bloom time, and remove shabby foliage to the base as necessary. Foliage and flower buds of some are frost tender; flower buds brown and do not open, and leaves become black-brown and unsightly. This is not as prevalent where snow cover is reliable; elsewhere protect from searing winds and frost with a winter mulch applied in late fall.

In spite of the common recommendation to grow bergenias in shade, in temperate climes they do better in full sun. Part shade is also fine, but avoid deep shade. In general, bergenias are not well adapted to hot regions, and if attempted there, they must be protected from midday sun. Soil should be average, deep, moist, and enriched with well-rotted compost or manure. Heavy clay that waterlogs easily is not satisfactory; amend with organic matter to improve drainage. Resistant to deer and rabbits, but protect from slugs, which otherwise promote that shabby appearance.

Mass bergenias as a groundcover along with meadowsweets, foxgloves, and Siberian iris to create contrasts in height and foliage texture. Planted as a skirt beneath white-barked birches or red-stemmed dogwoods, they can create a memorable winter-garden tableau. Use as edging plants along pathways or to delimit flowerbeds. British garden designer Gertrude Jekyll edged many a small bed with bergenias, often accompanied by our delicate native white wood asters (*Eurybia divaricata*) that tumbled over the cabbage-like leaves. Other appropriate companions include columbines, lungworts, and ferns.

Propagate by division in spring or fall. Otherwise, at the end of the growing season, take 3-in. cuttings of the rhizomatous stems, making sure to include a bud. Propagate species by seed.

Bergenia ciliata

syn. *B. ligulata*

Flower color	white, pink
Bloom time	early spring
Size	6–12 in. × 12–24 in.
Light	part shade
Zones	Z5–8

WINTER BEGONIA, FRILLY BERGENIA, WINTER BERGENIA
Nepal. Grown mainly for its hairy, deciduous, rounded, wavy-edged, bright green leaves that may reach 12 in. across. Clumping, spreads slowly by rhizomes. Clusters of rose-flushed white or pink flowers.

Bergenia cordifolia 'Rotblum'

Bergenia cordifolia

syn. *B. crassifolia*

flower color	pink
bloom time	early spring
size	12–24 in. × 24–30 in.
light	sun, part shade
zones	Z3–8

HEART-LEAVED BERGENIA, PIGSQUEAK, WINTER BEGONIA
Central Asia. Creeping rhizomes give rise to shiny, thick, cabbagey leaves, heart shaped at the base, about 12 in. long. These may turn purple and bronze as temperatures fall; some cultivars display better winter color than others. Evergreen or nearly so, in all but the coldest places. Tight clusters of deep pink flowers with rosy centers and calyces top branched pink stems.

'Purpurea' (syn. *Bergenia purpurea*) has bright purple-red flowers on red, 20-in. stems. Purple winter foliage. **'Rotblum'** has red flowers and deep red winter foliage. 18 in.

Other Notable Cultivars

'Baby Doll' has maroon winter foliage color that contrasts well with the early spring clusters of pale pink flowers; these mature to hot pink over several weeks. Protect from intense sun. A heavy protective mulch in winter is beneficial. 8–10 in. Z6–8. **'Bressingham Ruby'**, a hybrid, is valued for its tolerance of dry shade. Large, cabbagey, dark green leaves become polished burgundy in cold weather. Clusters of rosy flowers above the leaves in spring. A great groundcover. 12–16 in. Z4–10. **'Cabernet'**. Large, deep green leaves emerge early, closely followed by the bud clusters carried on pink stems, which open to deep pink bells. Bloom continues through late spring. Fall foliage turns deep red when temperatures drop. Semi-evergreen in zone 6 and warmer. 10–12 in. tall. **'Eroica'**. A superior long-blooming selection, displays clusters of bright purple flowers held well above wine-flushed leaves. Requires moist soil. Considered by some to be an improvement on better-known **'Abendglocken'**. 12–14 in. Z4–8. **'Herbstblute'** (fall pigsqueak) tolerates heat and humidity well. Low basal rosettes of 6-in., rounded, dark green leaves. Light pink flowers in spring, and occasionally through the season. 6 in. Z2–7. **'Overture'** makes tight mounds of lustrous dark foliage, purple in fall. Clusters of dramatic fuchsia flowers open in midspring on fleshy stems above the leaves. Stunning when planted in drifts or massed in semi-shade. Z4-8. **'Winterglow'** ('Winterglut') has leathery, heart-shaped foliage with good substance. Fall color is ruby red. Clusters of deep pink flowers in spring, often with repeat bloom in fall. 12–15 in. Z3–8.

BISHOP'S HAT | BARRENWORT

Epimedium | BERBERIDACEAE

A LARGE GENUS OF HARDY, shade-tolerant perennials, epimediums have long been a go-to groundcover for woodland gardens; although they prefer a moist, humus-rich soil, they are among the select group of plants that succeeds in the dry shade found under shallow-rooted trees. The introduction of new species from China in recent years and new hybrids has broadened the color palette of both flowers and foliage, and many of the new types also display their blossoms more visibly, holding them higher above the foliage than older garden epimediums did.

The leaves, evergreen, semi-evergreen, or deciduous, are divided into heart-shaped, rounded, or even triangular leaflets that range in size from 0.5–6 in. long. The cup-shaped flowers are four-parted, often with petals that extend into long spurs that can lend the blossoms the look of an inverted crown (hence the common name bishop's hat).

Although persistent once established, bishop's hats are not aggressive; they form dense clumps that spread slowly by means of underground rhizomes. They make elegant edging plants and provide an effective counterpoint to other shade-tolerant foliage plants: lungworts (*Pulmonaria*), hardy gingers (*Asarum*), ferns, and sedges. Resistant to deer and rabbits, they are generally pest and disease free, though sloppy propagation in the nursery sometimes results in viral infections; plants whose leaves exhibit mosaic patterns of yellow should be discarded.

Propagate by division, in early spring or early fall for deciduous types, and in fall for evergreen ones, or by seed sown in late summer.

Epimedium alpinum

Color	red-and-yellow
Bloom	early spring to midspring
Size	6–9 in. × 9–12 in.
Light	part shade, shade
Zone	Z4–8

BISHOP'S HAT Southern Europe. This species spreads more rapidly than others. Foliage is deciduous to semi-evergreen (in mild climates); the heart-shaped leaflets have a pink tinge when they emerge in spring, maturing to a medium green and turning deep reddish bronze in fall. Flowers with yellow petals shrouded by red sepals are borne in racemes of 12 to 20.

Epimedium epsteinii

Color	white-and-purple
Bloom time	midspring to early summer
Size	12 in. × 18 in.
Light	part shade, shade
Zones	Z5–8

FAIRY WINGS This discovery from China is an excellent evergreen groundcover that spreads 6–8 in. annually. Glossy dark-green leaflets; 10 to 30 flowers per stem, with white inner sepals and plum-purple spurs. Named for the late Harold Epstein.

Epimedium grandiflorum

syn. *E. macranthum*

Color	pink, purple, white, yellow
Bloom time	midspring to late spring
Size	12–18 in. × 9–18 in.
Light	part shade, shade
Zones	Z5–8

LONGSPUR BARRENWORT, HORNY GOATWEED Native to China, Korea, and Japan. The dramatic long spurs formed by the petals of this flower are the inspiration for one common name; the other refers to a belief in Asian countries of this species' potency as an aphrodisiac. The deciduous, angel-wing leaflets are toothed along the margins, and are a red-tinged beige when young, maturing to light green and turning red in fall. There are numerous cultivars.

'Cranberry Sparkle' has young chocolate leaves and cranberry-red flowers. **'Lilafee'** ('Lilac Fairy') has bronze-mottled foliage and lavender-purple flowers. **'Pierre's Purple'** ('Pierre's Purple Fairy Wings') bears wine-purple flowers. **'Red Queen'** has carmine-red flowers. **'Tama-no-gempei'** has white petals inset into purple outer sepals.

Epimedium pinnatum

Color	red, white, pink, yellow
Bloom time	mid- to late spring
Size	8–10 in. × 15 in.
Light	part shade, shade
Zones	Z5–8

PERSIAN EPIMEDIUM, BARRENWORT Japan. Spiny-edged evergreen or deciduous leaves are excellent as a slow-growing groundcover in woodlands and beneath shrubs. Bronzy pink when young, the leaves mature to green, then turn bronze by fall. Airy spikes of long-lasting flowers dance above the foliage. Drought tolerant. Cut back in very early spring.

Subsp. *colchicum* 'Thunderbolt' bears foliage that slowly darkens in mid-autumn from deep green to blackish purple beneath a pattern of green veins. Z5–8.

Other Notable Cultivars

×*cantabrigiense* is evergreen and clump forming. Long-stalked leaves of up to 17 in number have lovely fall color. Spurless, two-toned, coppery pink-and-yellow flowers held above the leaves. **×*perralchicum* 'Frohnleiten'** is evergreen, 6–10 in., and spreads 6–8 in. annually. Elongated, spiny spring foliage, mottled rose-red, with bright green veins. Large, showy flowers: yellow inner sepals surround tiny, gold-and-red petals. Z5–8. **×*versicolor* 'Versicolor'** is deciduous; emerging foliage is deep rose-red with green veins; matures green, then dark brownish purple in fall. Flowers are rich salmon-pink with red-flushed spurs. Z4–8. 'Cupreum' has coppery flowers; 'Sulfureum' has deep yellow flowers. **×*youngianum*** is a deciduous clump former. Each stem has two to nine wavy-edged leaflets. White or pink, 0.5-in. flowers. 'Niveum' is white flowered; 'Roseum' ('Lilacinum') has grayish pink flowers.

BLACK-EYED SUSAN

Rudbeckia | ASTERACEAE

WITH THEIR BRIGHT FLOWERS, tolerance for drought, and prolonged bloom, these North American natives are a mainstay of midsummer and fall gardens. What they lack in subtlety, rudbeckias make up with their reliability and vigor. When massed in borders or meadows, their prolific daisy-like blooms in shades of yellow, chestnut, mahogany, or bronze are like bursts of distilled sunshine. Ranging in height from 1–7 ft., they fit many niches, and provide a generous source of showy cut flowers. Their warm floral tones make them excellent complements for the purples, mauves, and pinks of purple coneflowers and New England asters.

Rudbeckias grow from clumps of simple or branched stems, clothed with spirally arranged, somewhat coarse, hairy, entire to deeply lobed leaves, 2–10 in. long. The daisy-like flowerheads consist of gently drooping, petal-like ray florets arranged around a central cone of dark purplish brown to orange, yellow, or green disk florets. Flowerheads may be single, semi-double, or fully double.

Provide any average, dry to medium, well-drained soil; avoid overly rich ones and too generous fertilization, both of which promote soft, floppy growth. Best in full sun; tolerates hot and humid summers. Deadhead to encourage prolific bloom, leaving some seedheads to remain as winter food for seed-eating birds. Disease resistant; attracts butterflies. Deer resistant, but important rabbit food.

Other garden-worthy species not described here include cut-leaf coneflower (*Rudbeckia lacinata*).

Propagate by seed or division.

Rudbeckia fulgida var. *sullivantii* 'Goldsturm'

Rudbeckia hirta 'Cappuccino'

Rudbeckia fulgida

color	orange, yellow
bloom time	early summer to midfall
size	2–3 ft. × 2–2.5 ft.
exposure	sun
zones	Z3–9, HT

BLACK-EYED SUSAN Southeastern United States. Upright, rhizomatous, and clump forming, with oblong to lanceolate leaves. Prolific bearer of 2.5-in.-wide, yellow-rayed, daisy-like flowerheads with brownish purple central cones. Adapts to wide range of soils, including clays, dry soils, and shallow or rocky ones. Naturalizes readily. Tolerates air pollution. Mostly available in the form of cultivars.

Var. *deamii* (Deam's black-eyed Susan) grows to36 in., with slender, orange-yellow rays surrounding dark brown centers; late summer to midfall. Z4–9. **Var. *sullivantii* 'City Gardens'** displays golden, daisy-like flowerheads, in mid- to late summer. Suitable where space is limited. Compact at 12 in. **Var. *sullivantii* 'Goldsturm'** is uniform and bushy, 30–36 in., with blackish brown-centered, golden-yellow inflorescences. 1999 Perennial Plant Association Plant of the Year. Seed-produced Goldsturm Strain is not uniform. **'Viette's Little Suzy'** is similar but in a tidy, compact plant. 12–18 in. × 9–12 in.

Rudbeckia hirta

color	yellow
bloom time	early to late summer
size	2–3 ft. × 1–2 ft.
exposure	sun
zones	Z3–7

GLORIOSA DAISY, BLACK-EYED SUSAN Central United States. Biennial or short-lived perennial in mild regions, often grown as an annual where winters are cold. Hairy, lanceolate leaves, 3–7 in. long; 3-in.-wide inflorescences with yellow-orange rays and chocolate-brown central disks on stiff, erect stems. Prefers moist, organic-rich soils, but adapts to most well-drained ones. Tolerates heat and drought. Short-lived, but self-seeds freely, supplying its own replacements.

'Cappuccino' blooms heavily from late spring to fall; 4-in. flowerheads are orange at the margin, red toward the center. 18–20 in. × 12 in. Z5–8. **'Indian Summer'** bears huge, 6- to 9-in., single and semi-double, golden yellow flowerheads with brown centers. Z3–7. **'Maya'** has fully double, chrysanthemum-like, yellow flowerheads with brown centers on 18 in. × 12 in. plants. Z5–8. **'Prairie Sun'** displays 4- to 5-in., single flowerheads, with yellow-tipped, orange rays surrounding a green cone.

Rudbeckia maxima

color	yellow
bloom	early summer
size	5–7 ft. × 3–4 ft.
light	sun
zone	Z4–9

LARGE CONEFLOWER Central and southern United States. Basal clumps of dramatic waxy, blue-green, cabbage-like leaves to 24 in. long and 10 in. wide; evergreen in mild winters. Sturdy, sparsely leaved stalks bear 3-in.-wide inflorescences with drooping yellow rays and 2- to 6-in.-tall, dark brown central cones. Somewhat coarse but striking; good for wildflower meadows, prairies, and larger borders. Adapts to a wide range of soils. Be alert for snails and slugs on young foliage; susceptible to powdery mildew. Self-seeds in hospitable conditions, if seeds not eaten by goldfinches.

'Golda Emanis' has bright gold young foliage that matures to chartreuse; orange-yellow flowerheads.

Rudbeckia nitida

color	yellow
bloom	late summer to early fall
size	5–6 ft. × 3 ft.
light	sun, part shade
zone	Z4–9

SHINING CONEFLOWER Native in Georgia and Florida, west to Texas. Tall, hairy stems support 3- to 4-in. flowerheads with drooping, yellow ray flowers surrounding a greenish disk. Oval, toothed leaves are mostly basal. Rhizomes spread freely. Deadhead for further bloom.

'Herbstonne' ('Autumn Sun') is perhaps the showiest of the rudbeckias. Yellow-rayed heads centered with green disks may reach 4 in. across. Sometimes listed as a cultivar of *Rudbeckia laciniata*, or as a hybrid. 7 ft. tall.

Rudbeckia subtomentosa

flower color	yellow
bloom time	early summer to midfall
size	3–4 ft. × 1–2 ft.
exposure	sun, part shade
zones	Z4–8, HS

SWEET CONEFLOWER Central United States. Toothed, gray-green leaves, downy beneath and three lobed at base of plant. Anise-scented, 3-in. flowerheads with yellow rays and dark brownish purple cones are borne on branching stems. Thrives on average to clay soils, but intolerant of drought. Stake if necessary. Watch for snails and slugs, and powdery mildew. Appropriate in borders, meadow and prairie plantings, and cottage gardens.

'Henry Eilers' bears bright yellow flowers with narrow, quilled rays, and reddish brown cones.

Rudbeckia triloba

flower color	yellow
bloom time	early summer to midfall
size	2–3 ft. × 1–1.5 ft.
exposure	sun
zones	Z4–8

BROWN-EYED SUSAN Eastern and central United States. Biennial or short-lived perennial that self-seeds freely and often naturalizes. Clumps of densely branched stems bear three- or sometimes five- or seven-lobed, rough, coarse leaves. Yellow-rayed, 1- to 1.5-in. flowerheads with purple-brown disks bloom profusely through summer and fall. Prefers moist, humus-rich soil but adapts to any well-drained soil. Tolerates light shade, heat, moderate drought. Perfect for meadow and prairie plantings, good for cottage gardens. Deadhead to control self-seeding.

'Prairie Glow' has chocolate-centered heads with bicolored rays of burgundy, bronze, or reddish orange shades, always tipped with gold. 5 ft. × 3 ft.

BLANKET FLOWER | INDIAN BLANKET

Gaillardia

ASTERACEAE

BLANKET FLOWERS ARE AMONG North America's most showy native wildflowers, growing in huge sweeps across grasslands, mountain hillsides, high prairies, and meadows. Their floral hues are bold, bright, and earthy, recalling those of Native American weavings, as the common name indicates. Not surprisingly, gaillardias have in recent years attracted the attention of plant breeders, who have introduced a host of fine hybrids.

As members of the aster family, gaillardias bear their flowers in daisy-like heads consisting of deeply two- or three-lobed ray flowers (what appear to be petals) and a central button of disk flowers. The most common colors are shades of red and yellow.

Plant gaillardias in sunny spots with an average, well-drained soil; this latter quality is essential, and it is critically important, especially for the hybrids, that the plants do not go into cold weather with wet feet. Deadhead for neatness and to maintain vigor, but leave a few heads if you are collecting seed, or more if you want to feed seed-eating birds. Butterflies, bees, and birds can often be seen collecting nectar and pollen from blanket flowers, adding another dimension to the garden. Lovely in native and wild gardens, in wildlife meadows, and in cottage gardens, these plants also fit in more formal applications as edgings for flowerbeds or to brighten the midsections of beds or borders. The taller sorts furnish fine, long-lasting cut flowers.

Gaillardias sometimes prove susceptible to mildews, rust, and rots. The tender young leaves are a treat for slugs and snails; however, deer and rabbits seldom browse them.

Many of the hybrids are short-lived; divide established clumps in spring to maintain vigor. Propagate species by seed or division; cuttings may be difficult to root.

Gaillardia aestivalis

color	yellow
bloom	late spring to late fall
size	12–18 in. × 9–12 in.
light	sun
zones	Z5–9

FIREWHEEL, LANCE-LEAF BLANKET FLOWER Southeastern United States. Yellow-rayed, 3-in. flowerheads with purplish brown, rounded centers. Some rays occasionally appear to be missing, either partly or completely; the central disk persists like an attractive purple globe after "petal" drop. Provides food for goldfinches, and butterflies are frequent visitors during the long bloom period. Lanceolate, grayish green leaves. Short-lived, but self-seeds unless deadheaded.

Var. *winkleri* 'Grape Sensation' has 2-in., solid, deep lilac rays and black-currant disks. Clumps to 2 ft. × 3 ft. Long-lived with excellent drainage.

Gaillardia aristata

color	purple-red, yellow
bloom	summer
size	24–36 in. × 18 in.
light	sun
zones	Z3–9

BLANKET FLOWER North Dakota south to Colorado, west to California and British Columbia. Appropriate for dry, wild, and meadow gardens. Lobed and lance-shaped, basal leaves to 10 in.; stem leaves are sessile and not lobed. Flowerheads, 3–4 in. across, are yellow rayed, purple at the base with purple disks. This rather sprawling species is seldom cultivated except as a breeding parent. Seed takes two years to reach bloom size.

'Amber Wheels' has vibrant, frilled, gold rays with an amber-red disk. 30 in. Z3–9. **Bijou Strain.** Orange-red ray flowers tipped with yellow. Self-seeds. 10–12 in. Z4–7. **'Fanfare'** has 3-in. flowerheads with fluted, yellow rays with red tubes surrounding a deep red central disk. May be listed under *Gaillardia ×grandiflora*. Introduced by Plant Haven. Soil must be free draining. 15 in. Z3–9.

Gaillardia ×grandiflora

syn. *G. grandiflora*

(color)	red-and-yellow
(bloom time)	early summer to fall
(size)	24–36 in. × 18 in.
(light)	sun
(zones)	Z5–9

BLANKET FLOWER Of garden origin. This easy-to-grow cross (between the perennial *G. aristata* and annual *G. pulchella*) displays hybrid vigor in its offspring, many of which have been introduced to the marketplace. Mostly erect and somewhat spreading, with hairy, soft, dark basal foliage, lanceolate and lobed along the edges; stem leaves are sessile and entire. Showy heads of flowers may reach 4 in. across. Plants tend to be short-lived, often as a result of poor drainage; most resent winter wet. A few of the species shown here seed true, but uniformity is assured by propagating the named cultivars vegetatively, by division, or from cuttings.

Other Notable Cultivars

Most of the cultivars are hardy to Z3. Deadhead to extend bloom time.

'Arizona Red' has red flowerheads. **'Arizona Sun'** has red, 3- to 4-in. flowers with yellow margins. Both are Fleuroselect Gold Medal winners. 12 in. **'Baby Cole'** is maroon centered, with yellow-tipped, red rays. 6–8 in. **'Dazzler'** is similar but 24–30 in. tall. 'Burgundy' (syn. *Gaillardia aristata* **'Burgundy'**) has wine-red, 3-in. daisy flowers with red-and-yellow disks. 18–24 in. **Commotion Series**. These mounding selections have great vigor. Heads are fully semi-double, with fluted rays: Commotion 'Frenzy' has red petals tipped with yellow; Commotion 'Tizzy' has rosy red ray flowers. 18–24 in. Z5. **'Goblin'** ('Kobold') has large, deep red rays, irregularly bordered with yellow. 'Golden Goblin' is all yellow. Z3. **Monarch Strain** is a seed mix of yellow and orange to dark red flowers. 2–5 ft. tall. **'Oranges and Lemons'**. Bright cantaloupe rays tipped with lemon yellow; golden disk.

BLAZING STAR | GAYFEATHER

Liatris

ASTERACEAE

EXPECT FIREWORKS WHEN YOU include blazing stars in your planting: the spikes of vivid flowers that shoot up from the clumps of whorled, narrow foliage are like slow-motion rockets. Natives of New World grasslands, liatris have evolved to raise their heads above their neighbors, making them wonderful accent plants for sunny borders, as well as ideal vertical punctuation in meadow or prairie plantings. The striking look and form of the flower spikes makes blazing stars a good source of cut flowers that open gradually; their display, whether in a vase or in the garden, is long lasting.

Flower spikes are composed of multiple, closely set, button-like buds that open to produce a fluffy effect. Unusually, these open from the top down; in floral displays the spent tops can be snapped off, allowing for a longer vase life.

Like so many prairie and grassland plants, liatris have the ability to cope with adverse conditions: their cormous roots withstand prolonged drought, as well as summer heat and humidity, and winter cold. They thrive on moderate to nutrient-poor soils, as long as drainage is good; not tolerant of poorly drained, wet soil, especially in wintertime. Liatris blooms attract butterflies and hummingbirds, and later the seeds provide fall food for a variety of birds. Taller species and cultivars may require staking. They resist deer, and suffer from no serious pests and diseases.

Propagate by seed sown in fall as soon as it ripens; overwinter outdoors. Dig and divide corm clumps in late winter before they break dormancy. Softwood cuttings root readily in spring.

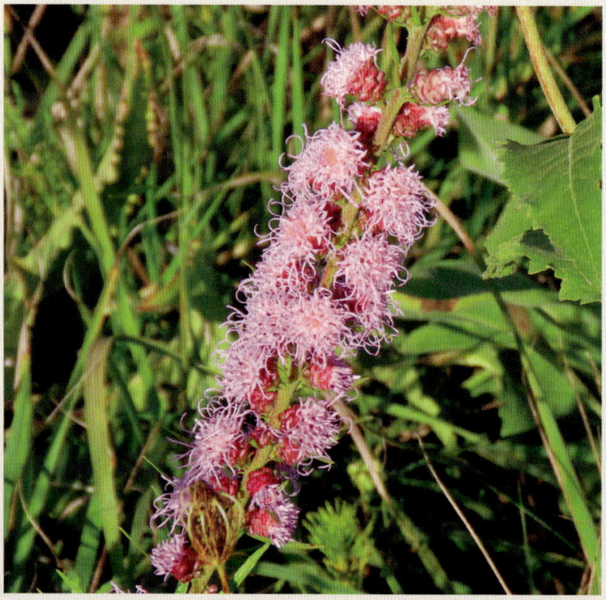

Liatris aspera

Color	purple
Bloom time	late summer to early fall
Size	2–5 ft. × 1–1.5 ft.
Light	sun
Zones	Z3–8

ROUGH GAYFEATHER Native to dryish soils in prairies, open woods, meadows, and along roads and railroad tracks throughout Eastern and Midwestern North America. This species produces basal tufts of rough, narrow, lanceolate leaves sometimes 12 in. long. Erect, leafy stalks rise from the base, topped with long spikes of rounded, fluffy, rose-purple flowerheads, each up to 0.75 in. across. Tolerates shallow, rocky soils.

Liatris microcephala

color	purple
bloom time	mid- to late summer
size	18–24 in. × 12–18 in.
exposure	sun, part shade
zones	Z4–7

DWARF BLAZING STAR Native to southern Appalachians. Basal rosettes of grassy leaves from which emerge several 12- to 24-in. spikes of rosy-purple flowerheads. A good species for planting among boulders in rock gardens or in the foreground of sunny borders.

Liatris pycnostachya

color	purple
bloom time	early to late summer
size	2–5 ft. × 1–2 ft.
exposure	sun
zones	Z3–9

PRAIRIE BLAZING STAR Native to central and southeastern United States. This robust, grassland perennial produces clumps of narrow, lanceolate leaves, to 12 in. long; fluffy flowerheads are deep rose-purple, to 0.75 in. across; they are borne in dense terminal spikes to 20 in. long. Tolerates well-drained clay or poor soils, and summer heat and humidity. Prairie blazing star may be too large and vigorous for most borders, but it is an asset in wild and native plant gardens, naturalized areas, prairie plantings, and meadows.

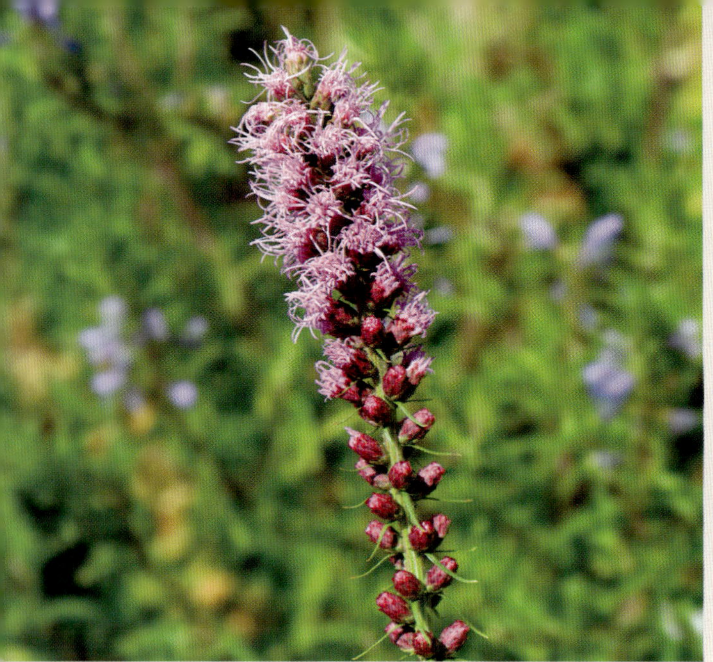

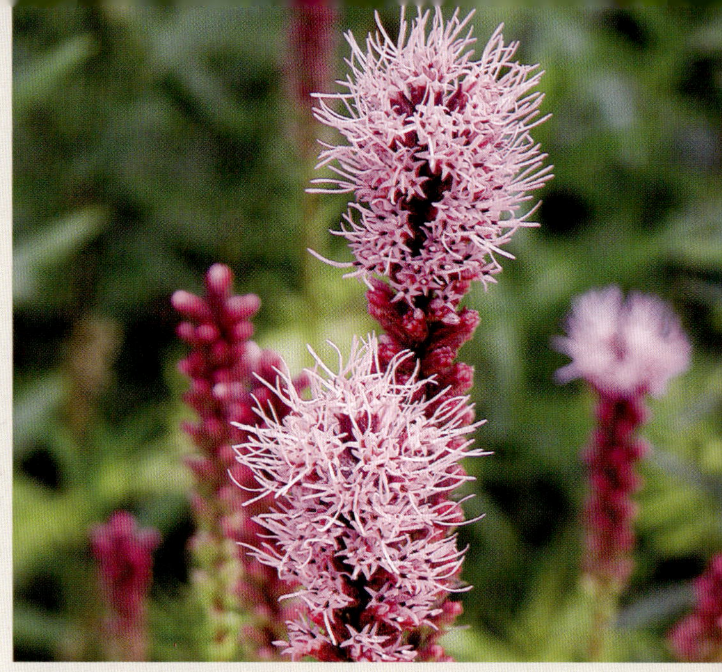

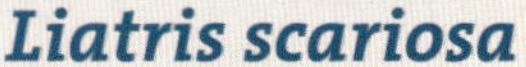

Liatris scariosa

	purple
	late summer to midfall
	2–4 ft. × 1–2 ft.
	sun
	Z3–8, HT

BLAZING STAR Native to rocky woods and slopes, grasslands, and gravelly streambanks from Maine, west to Wisconsin, and south to Mississippi and Georgia. Produces basal tufts of rough, narrow, ovate to lanceolate leaves, to 10 in. long; leaves become smaller as they ascend the stem. Fluffy, reddish purple flowerheads to 1 in. across top erect stems in columnar spikes, to 18 in. long. Prefers dry, sandy, or rocky soils; staking may be necessary if grown on more fertile soils. Intolerant of wet feet, especially in winter. May self-seed on favorable sites. Blazing stars are an excellent choice for borders, cottage gardens, meadow and prairie plantings, and naturalized landscapes.

Liatris spicata syn. *L. callilepis*

	purple
	midsummer to early fall
	3–5 ft. × 2 ft.
	sun, part shade
	Z3–9, HT

SPIKE GAYFEATHER, BUTTON SNAKEROOT, DENSE BLAZING STAR Native to low, moist sites throughout the eastern and southern United States. Grass-like leaves to 12 in. long are arranged in basal tufts; tall stems are topped with 6- to 12-in., terminal spikes of fluffy, mauve to deep purple flowerheads, to 0.75 in. in diameter. Spike gayfeather prefers moist, organic-rich soil, but ordinary garden soil suffices. It handles more moisture than other members of the genus; also tolerant of poor soil, heat, humidity, and drought. A favorite of the floral industry, a natural for cutting gardens, and as vertical accents in borders or damp meadows.

'Blue Bird' has blue-purple flowerheads. **'Kobold'** is compact, 2–2.5 ft., with deep purple flowerheads. **'Snow Queen'** has white flowerheads.

BLEEDING HEART

Dicentra; Lamprocapnos

FUMARIACEAE; PAPAVERACEAE

BLEEDING HEARTS ARE ONE OF the cottage garden plants that many of us remember from the gardens of our youth, and the virtues that made them popular then are just as relevant today. Indeed, the breeders have been busy with this genus, so there are many more cultivars from which to choose.

Several species of bleeding heart are native to North America; in the wild, they are usually found growing in partly shaded, damp spots among trees. The leaves are deeply divided and they often have a bluish cast that contrasts appealingly with the colorful flowers. The heart-shaped, mostly pink or white flowers are charmingly dainty, with inner petals protruding from the outer ones. Both flowers and leaves are carried on brittle, succulent stems.

Lamprocapnos is a genus of one species that was, until recently, classified with *Dicentra*; it is still listed mostly under its former name in nursery catalogs.

Provide bleeding hearts with humus-rich, well-drained, moisture-retentive soil. Some selections tolerate sun well, especially in cool summers, although only a few are happy in heat and humidity. As a group, they are best in light or partial shade, always with damp but not waterlogged soil.

Compatible companions for bleeding hearts include woodland natives such as bloodroot, columbines, Christmas fern, and wide blue sedge. Appropriate non-natives include spring bulbs, hellebores, lungworts, and hostas; lily-of-the-valley also mixes well. Bleeding hearts are excellent for brightening up beds and borders in spring, as a skirt around flowering shrubs, and for the edges of woodlands and paths. Compact selections are in scale in rock gardens and raised beds. Butterflies and hummingbirds often forage the flowers and foliage of bleeding hearts, making them appropriate for planting in wildlife gardens.

Bleeding hearts are deer and rabbit resistant and mostly pest and disease free, except for aphids. For the species, propagate by root cuttings in winter or by seed sown in containers as it becomes ripe or in spring. Divide named cultivars in early spring.

Dicentra cucullaria

(flower color)	white
(bloom time)	early spring
(size)	6–9 in. × 9 in.
(exposure)	part shade
(zones)	Z3–7

DUTCHMAN'S BREECHES, STAGGER WEED Native to open clearings in the woods from Nova Scotia south to North Carolina, and west to Kansas. Small, white tubers give rise to blue-green, finely dissected leaves that disappear quickly after bloom time. Spurred, white, 0.5-in. flowers, shaped like baggy, upside-down Dutchman's trousers, are arranged on short stems along arching, pinkish stems. Needs humus-rich soil. Toxic to livestock, but formerly used as a remedy for syphilis. Squirrel corn, *Dicentra canadensis*, is similar, but has less ferny foliage and heart-shaped, white flowers. Avoid planting too deeply. Becomes dormant shortly after blooming.

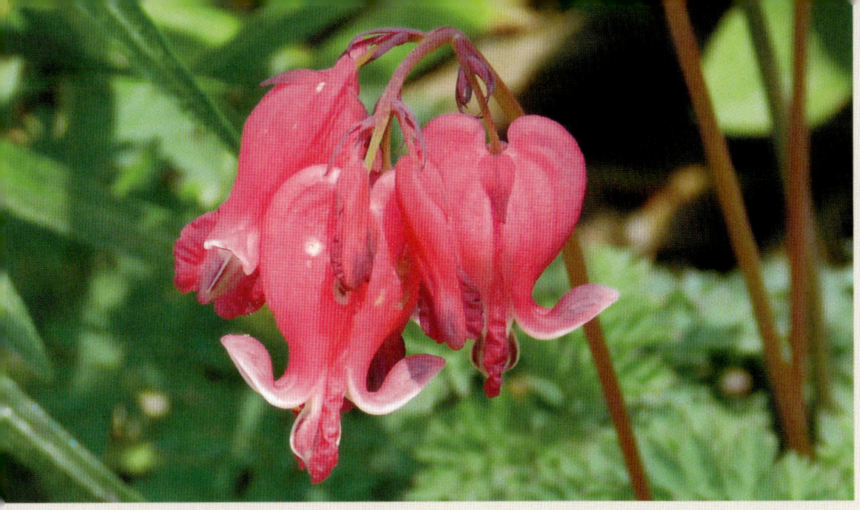

Dicentra eximia

(color)	pink
(bloom time)	late spring to fall
(size)	12–24 in. × 18 in.
(light)	part shade
(zones)	Z4–9

FRINGED BLEEDING HEART, TURKEY CORN Native to rich woodlands of the eastern United States, especially in the Appalachian region. Mounds of finely dissected, 6- to 18-in.-long, gray-green leaves rise from scaly, fleshy rootstocks and persist through the season if kept moist. Each arching, pink-tinged stem bears several nodding, rosy-pink, heart-shaped flowers on short pedicels (flower stems). The 1-in.-long flowers are produced for several weeks and then sporadically till fall. Seeds about. In the garden, plant with columbines, wild gingers, lungworts, woodland phlox, and other spring shade lovers. There has been a great deal of hybridization between this species and the western or Pacific bleeding heart, *Dicentra formosa*; many selections may be hybrids, although attributed to one species or the other. Other species are also involved.

'Alba' produces mounds of bright green, cut leaves and white flowers tipped with yellow. 12–30 in. Z3–9. **'Bacchanal'** has dusky red flowers in mid- to late spring. Gray-green leaves. 18 in. Z3–9. **'Dolly Sods'**, an introduction from Plant Delights Nursery in North Carolina, has pale pink flowers and is reputed to be the most heat tolerant of the bleeding hearts. Suitable for hot, humid summers. Z3–8. **Heart Series**, bred in Japan, has produced the following superior compact selections, all with lacy, bright blue-gray leaves. 'Burning Hearts' has deep rosy-red, heart-shaped flowers rimmed with white. 10 in. 'Ivory Hearts' has clean white flowers. 12 in. 'Candy Hearts' blooms with deep rose flowers. 6–12 in. All must remain damp in summer, and they bloom longer with routine deadheading to the base. Z5–9. **'King of Hearts'** has carmine flowers above compact, 6-in. foliage mounds in late spring. This older selection has similar genetics to the Heart Series. 9–18 in. Z3–8. **'Langtrees'** is possibly the best white. Charming delicate clusters of white hearts contrast with finely dissected, gray leaves. 12 in. Z4–8. **'Luxuriant'** is a popular selection for its late spring, cherry red flowers and bluish leaves. Very long blooming; sterile. Tolerates summer heat only if kept moist. 12–18 in. Z3–9. **'Stuart Boothman'** ('Boothman's Variety') has wonderful dissected, 4- to 8-in.-long, strong blue-green leaves that contrast beautifully with 0.5- to 1-in., deep rose flowers. 12 in. Z3–9. **'Zestful'**. Deep rose flowers above ferny, blue-green foliage. Almost nonstop blooming, even through warm weather if kept moist. 12–18 in. Z3–9.

Dicentra formosa

Color	pink, red
Bloom time	early spring to early summer
Size	15 in. × 18 in.
Light	sun, part shade
Zones	Z3–8

WESTERN BLEEDING HEART, PACIFIC BLEEDING HEART, LYREFLOWER Native to moist woodlands, along streambanks, and in meadows from northern California to British Columbia; the specific epithet means "beautiful." Similar to *Dicentra eximia*, spreading by underground rhizomes, this species colonizes quickly but not invasively. Rosy mauve-pink flowers hang from brittle, succulent stems; the basal foliage is finely dissected and bluish green. A nectar plant for hummingbirds and adult Clodius Parnassian (*Parnassius clodius*) butterflies and a larval plant for the caterpillars; ants spread the seeds. Valued in folk medicine in spite of all parts of the plant being toxic. Divide when dormant.

'Aurora' is more compact and possibly superior to 'Alba', with longer-blooming white flowers above mounds of ferny, blue-green leaves. Spring to summer. 12–15 in. **'Sweetheart'** has white flowers. 15 in.

Lamprocapnos spectabilis

syn. *Dicentra spectabilis*

Color	pink, white
Bloom time	mid- to late spring
Size	24–48 in. × 18 in.
Light	part shade, shade
Zones	Z3–8

OLD-FASHIONED BLEEDING HEART Japan, Korea, Siberia. Clump forming. Similar to the dicentras but soft green, lobed foliage is less deeply and intricately cut. Tall, arching stems laden on one side with pendent, broadly heart-shaped, 1-in. flowers with reflexed outer rose-pink petals, and exserted inner white petals. Spectacular foliage and floral display in midspring; unfortunately, usually becomes summer dormant, after an untidy interlude with scruffy yellow foliage. Excellent for cut flowers, often forced commercially for Valentine's Day; perfect for weddings. Plan to have companion plants to fill the gap after the bleeding hearts become dormant; hostas, toad lilies, astilbes, and balloon flowers are good choices.

'Alba' has pure white hearts dangling from its arching stems. **'Gold Heart'**. Pink hearts above deeply lobed golden leaves. **'Valentine'** has white-tipped, cherry-red flowers on arching, deep burgundy stems. Foliage matures to dark gray-green.

BLUESTAR

Amsonia

APOCYNACEAE

THE UNDERUSED BLUESTARS are mostly native North American perennials that create floral displays in spring, often followed by amazing autumn foliage color.

The durable clumps are tough and easy to grow in ordinary garden soils that drain well; established plants tolerate short periods of drought. Clusters of starry flowers in various shades of pale blue top foliage-clad stems and provide nectar for early scavenging butterflies, especially mourning cloaks. After bloom time, slender seedpods remain on the plants.

Little maintenance is required: bluestars seldom need division and require staking only if grown in too much shade. If the plants begin to flop, encircle with wire rings or "pea sticks" (bushy, woody stems saved from shrub pruning); cut back by 6 in. after bloom time. Mostly disease free although susceptible to rust, bluestars are generally free of pests too, including deer and rabbits.

If used as cut flowers, sear the base of the stems with a flame to prevent the milky sap from bleeding and fouling the water. Some people report skin irritation from contact with the sap.

Propagate by division or softwood cuttings in spring. Species seeds germinate readily in spring or fall.

Amsonia ciliata syn. *A. angustifolia*

ice blue
late spring
2–3 ft. high and wide
sun, part shade
Z5–9

DOWNY AMSONIA, FRINGED BLUESTAR Southeastern United States. Although it flourishes in the wild over a broad range, downy amsonia is not as popular for gardens as other species. However, it is an excellent plant, especially on sandy soils with pH above 7, amended with organic matter. Young growth is downy and silky soft. Showy clusters of flowers perch on erect but not very strong stems clothed with lanceolate, 1.5-in.-wide leaves. In sunny spots, fall foliage is brilliant yellow. If plants sprawl, prune gently into a rounded bush and support stems with pea sticks. Mass in native plant or wildlife gardens to attract butterflies and other insects. Astilbes and hardy geraniums are good border companions for spring; try goldenrods and blue leadwort for fall. Slow to establish.

'Spring Sky' has larger, longer-blooming flowers than the species. Fall color is yellow or bronze.

Amsonia hubrichtii

steel blue
late spring to early summer
3–4 ft. × 3 ft.
sun, part shade
Z5–9

ARKANSAS BLUESTAR, HUBRICHT'S AMSONIA, NARROW-LEAVED BLUESTAR Arkansas, Oklahoma. Not as stiffly upright as other species, this easy-care Arkansan native has smooth, thread-like leaves that present unusual textural beauty. Provide acid soil and a sunny site; in too much shade, plants will open up and sprawl. The showy powder-blue, 0.5-in., starry flowers cluster at the tops of the stems, where they attract butterflies; needle-like fruits follow. Cut back by 6–10 in. after bloom time to groom the plants into a neat mound of feathery foliage; the fruits will be lost in this process, but fall color will be more dramatic. Plants grown in full sun produce the best fall color, an arresting banana yellow and orange. Arkansas bluestar is perfect for native, wild, and wildlife gardens; in flower borders, combine with peonies, Oriental poppies, and late-blooming perennials, or provide a dark-leaved shrub, such as ninebark (*Physocarpus*) or *Weigela* 'Wine and Roses' ('Alexandra'), as a background. The brilliant fall foliage is eye-popping against tall sedums 'Matrona' and 'Autumn Joy'. Slow to establish. Named the Perennial Plant of the Year for 2011 by the Perennial Plant Association.

Amsonia montana

syn. *A. tabernaemontana* 'Montana', *A. tabernaemontana* var. *montana*

light blue

spring

12–24 in. × 9–12 in.

sun, part shade

Z3–9

DWARF BLUESTAR Massachusetts to Missouri. Now considered by some authorities to be a species in its own right, dwarf bluestar differs from *Amsonia tabernaemontana* in producing dense clusters of somewhat deeper blue flowers earlier in spring on more compact plants. Drought tolerant once established. In sun, the willowy leaves turn gold in fall.

'Short Stack' is a 12-in.-tall dwarf selection. Z5–9.

Amsonia orientalis

syn. *Rhazya orientalis*

lavender-blue

spring

18 in. high and wide

sun, part shade

Z6–9

BLUESTAR Greece, Turkey. A change in taxonomy has brought this European native into the *Amsonia* genus. Popular in the UK and Europe, this plant is quite similar to *A. tabernaemontana*, but with a more refined look. The flowers are larger and a stronger blue, best seen when plants are grown in part shade. Keep soil moist, especially in sunny places.

Amsonia tabernaemontana

syn. *Tabernaemontana amsonia*

(color)	pale blue
(bloom time)	mid- to late spring
(size)	2–3 ft. high and wide
(exposure)	sun, part shade
(zone)	Z3–9

BLUE STARFLOWER, BLUE DOGBANE, EASTERN BLUESTAR Eastern and central United States. Upright with somewhat stiff stems, blue starflower is clothed with smooth, willow-like leaves. In sun, these turn brilliant yellow come fall, though its color is not as spectacular as that of Arkansas bluestar. Pale blue, starry flowers cluster at the ends of the stems; spindle-like fruiting pods follow. This tough plant tolerates less than ideal conditions, but prefers a moist, well-drained soil. Spectacular massed in rough meadows or native plant gardens as well as in butterfly gardens where it provides food for coral hairstreak caterpillars. In beds and borders or among shrubs, group several plants together. An excellent cut flower, sear the base of the stems before conditioning them to prevent sap bleed. Lovely in front of shrubby yellow potentillas or dark-leaved ninebark.

Var. *salicifolia* (syn. *Amsonia salicifolia*), woodland or willow-leaved bluestar, has very slender leaves. 2–2.5 ft.

Other Notable Cultivars

'Blue Ice' is a hybrid selection from *Amsonia tabernaemontana*, possibly with *A. montana* or *A. orientalis*. Extremely long-blooming, with terminal clusters of intense deep lavender flowers, good for cutting. Tolerates part shade, but in sun foliage turns vivid yellow and orange in fall. Provide consistently moist, humus-rich soil; drought tolerant and adapts to hot, humid summers. Compact, ideal for small gardens. 15 in. × 24 in. Z5–9. **'Seaford Skies'** (*A. hubrichtii* × *A. tabernaemontana*) displays hybrid vigor. Pyramidal clusters of star-like, sky-blue flowers from mid- to late spring. Vibrant yellow fall color. Bred by noted garden writer Pam Harper. 3 ft. × 5 ft. Z5–9.

CALAMINT

Calamintha

LAMIACEAE

CALAMINTHA IS LITERALLY TRANSLATED as "beautiful mint," which accurately summarizes the virtues of this genus. The calamints are close relatives of the mints and have strongly aromatic foliage—plant one beside a path and every time you brush against it, the garden will be filled with a pleasant fruity, minty scent. The flowers are mint-like too, small but abundant, clustering in the leaf axils, tubular with a pair of lips framing the mouth. Calamints typically bloom for six weeks or more, attracting hosts of birds, butterflies, and hummingbirds. Calamints have the adaptability and persistence of mints, thriving in virtually any well-watered, well-drained soil, and in sun or part shade, but they lack mint's aggressive nature, and are not invasive or prone to weediness.

Though deer and insect resistant, calamints may be susceptible to powdery mildew; grow them in an open, airy location, especially where humidity is high. Propagate by seed or division in spring.

Calamintha nepeta

syn. *Clinopodium nepeta, C. nepeta* subsp. *nepeta*

Flower color	white, light blue
Bloom time	summer
Size	12–18 in. high and wide
Light	sun
Zone	Z5–7

LESSER CALAMINT Central and southern Europe. Bushy, dense, and sometimes sprawling with ovate, gray-green leaves to 0.75 in. long, and tiny but abundant flowers. It is perfect for edging walks, patios, or herb gardens, or at the front of a border. Allow to spill over retaining walls or showcase in a container. Drought tolerance makes this species suitable for rock gardens too. 2021's Perennial Plant Association Perennial Plant of the Year.

'Blue Cloud' is compact with light blue flowers and fine, gray-green foliage. To 15 in. high and wide. **'White Cloud'** has white blooms. **Subsp. *glandulosa*** is more vigorous than the species, with 1.25-in. leaves and slightly larger flowers that bloom all up and down the stems.

CAMPION | CATCHFLY

Lychnis — CARYOPHYLLACEAE

THIS GENUS OF ABOUT 20 species is closely related to *Silene* and *Agrostemma*, but over the years there has been considerable nomenclatural confusion. Nonetheless these usually short-lived perennials provide plenty of color, and are easy to grow.

Campions grow best in sun or partly sunny spots where soil is average to moderately fertile. Drainage must be excellent for gray-leaved species, but otherwise a dressing of moisture-retaining compost is appreciated. Deadhead to extend bloom time and to prevent self-seeding. Erect and sticky, branched stems bear pairs of clammy leaves at swollen nodes. The funnel- or star-shaped flowers have five brightly colored petals, centered with five styles, and followed by five-toothed seed capsules. These are major points of difference from *Silene*. Cut stems halfway back after blooming to encourage a further crop of flowers.

Lychnis has an interesting history. The name comes from *lychnos*, the Greek word for "lamp" derived from the usage of furry, felted rose campion (*L. coronaria*) leaves for lamp wicks. The popular Maltese cross (*L. chalcedonica*) was grown by Thomas Jefferson at Monticello and was popular among gardeners of the day.

Campions are susceptible to few pests and diseases, except slugs and snails, and resist rabbits and deer. They are larval food and nectar plants for several species of butterflies.

Plant small species to adorn rock gardens and crevice gardens; larger ones are suitable for wild and wildlife gardens, cutting gardens, beds and borders, and between low shrubs.

Start from seed in spring, barely covering them; early seeding may result in bloom the same year. Divide clumps in spring or fall.

Lychnis alpina

syn. *Silene suecica*

	pink
	spring
	4–6 in. × 6 in.
	sun, part shade
	Z4–7

ALPINE CAMPION, ALPINE CATCHFLY Sub-arctic and mountainous areas of the Northern Hemisphere. Low tufts of dark green, lanceolate, 1.5-in. leaves, from which rise short stems topped with clusters of bright pink, 0.75-in. flowers, with frilled, bi-lobed petals. Deadhead to extend bloom time. Appropriate for troughs, rock gardens, and crevices between pavers or flagstones.

Lychnis ×*arkwrightii*

	orange
	late spring to summer
	15–18 in. × 12 in.
	sun
	Z5–8

ARKWRIGHT'S CATCHFLY This short-lived hybrid (*L. chalcedonica* × *L. haageana)* has dark, hairy stems clothed with pairs of maroon-flushed green leaves. The 1.5-in., star-shaped flowers have notched petals, and are arranged in flat-topped clusters.

'Orange Dwarf' ('Orange Zwerg') has bronzy foliage that contrasts well with the brilliant orange-red flowers. 8–12 in. Z5–8. **'Vesuvius'** has screaming orange flowers. 18–24 in. Z3–10.

Lychnis chalcedonica 'Flore Pleno'

Lychnis chalcedonica

syn. *Silene chalcedonica*

color	scarlet
bloom time	summer
size	2–3.5 ft. × 1.5 ft.
light	sun
zones	Z3–10, HS

MALTESE CROSS, JERUSALEM CROSS, SCARLET LIGHTNING Native to European regions of Russia, Mongolia, and northwestern China. This old-fashioned cottage garden favorite makes clumps of upright, sticky, unbranched stems that carry pairs of clasping, ovate leaves, toothed along the edges, 2–4 in. long. Dense, terminal, umbel-like heads of flowers composed of numerous star-shaped, orange-red, 0.5- to 1-in. blooms, each with deeply notched petals. Plants are long-lived and very hardy, but not in high heat and humidity. Attracts butterflies and hummingbirds. If soil is rich, staking may be necessary; insert twiggy stems (pea sticks) early when shoots are about 6–8 in. Deadhead to discourage self-seeding. Silvery ornamental grasses make good companions. Mass among shrubs or in deep borders, or group in beds. Good cut flower.

'Alba' has pure white flowers. **'Alba Plena'** has double, white flowers.

'Dusky Salmon' has light salmon-pink blooms. Possibly a synonym for 'Carnea' and 'Morgenrot'. **'Flore Pleno'** has double, scarlet flowers. May be brighter than the species, and the double flowers pack more punch.

Lychnis coronaria

syn. *Agrostemma coronaria*, *Silene coronaria*

Color	cerise
Bloom time	late spring to early summer
Size	1.5–2.5 ft. × 1.5 ft.
Exposure	sun, part shade
Hardiness	Z3–9

ROSE CAMPION, MULLEIN PINK, DUSTY MILLER

Native to southeastern Europe, this easy and showy perennial makes spreading mats of woolly, silvery leaves. These are about 4 in. long, ovate, on short petioles; opposite stem leaves are smaller. Branched stems are topped with solitary, wheel-shaped, cerise flowers, about 1 in. across. Short-lived but self-seeds freely; deadhead routinely. Demands very good drainage; root rot may result from poor drainage. Drought tolerant, and suitable for dry gardens, as well as beds, borders, and wildlife gardens. Sometimes used for edging.

'Abbotswood Rose' has 2-in.-wide, electric pink flowers over woolly, silver-gray foliage. **'Alba'** is white flowered. **'Atrosanguinea'** ('Bloody William') has gaudy purplish scarlet flowers above silver foliage mats. More-or-less sterile, resulting in lack of seeds. **'Gardener's World'** ('Blych', syn. *Coronaria tomentosa*) has fully double, 1.5-in., deep red flowers. Sterile, thus does not seed about. Long blooming. 2 ft. tall. **'Oculata'** has white flowers centered with a spreading fuchsia eye. Z4–9.

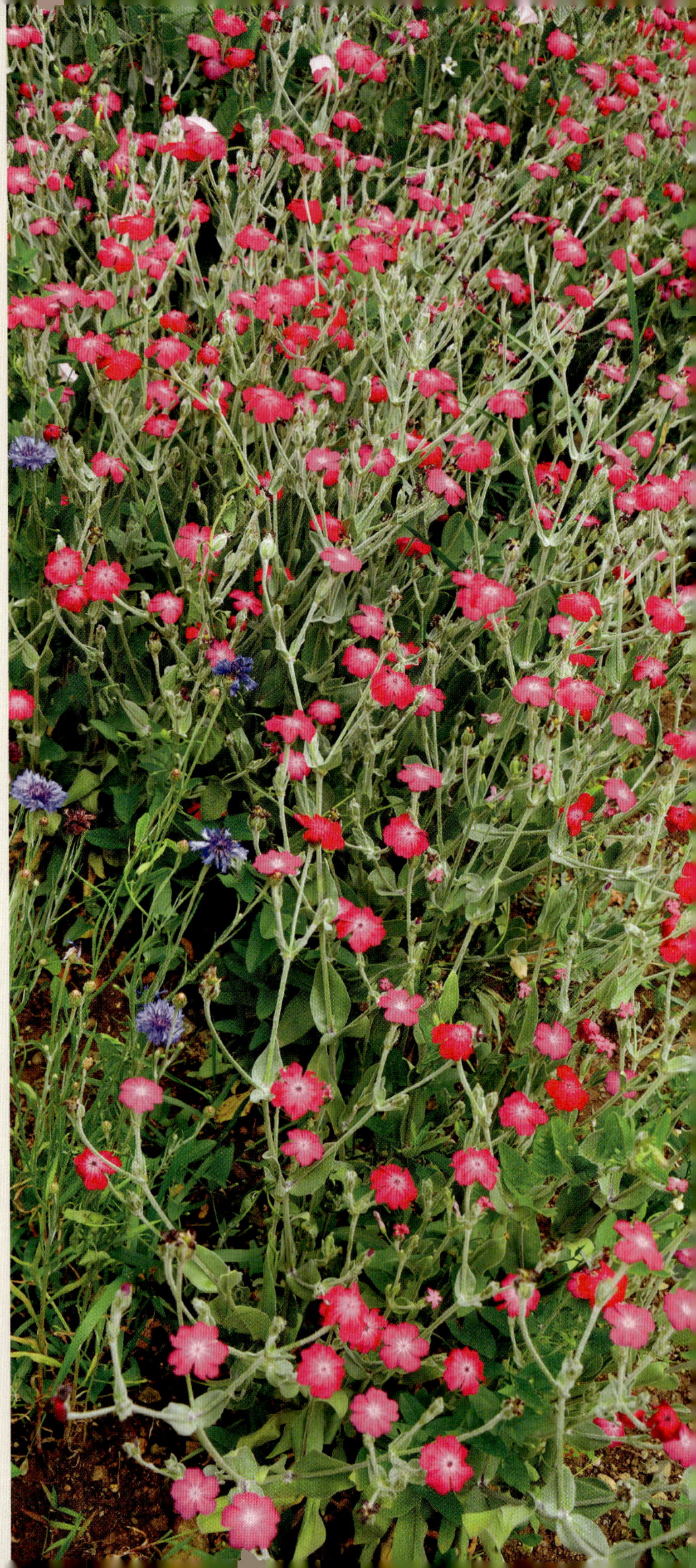

Lychnis flos-cuculi

Color	pink, white
Bloom time	late spring to early summer
Size	12–24 in. × 12 in.
Light	sun, part shade
Zone	Z3–7

RAGGED ROBIN Damp meadows of Europe, Caucasus, Russia. Low mats of grassy, bluish green, basal foliage. Loose, branched, umbel-like clusters of star-shaped magenta or sometimes white flowers. These are 1.5 in. across and shaggy looking, with double, deeply notched petals. Attracts pollinating butterflies and bees. Drought tolerant. Deadhead to curtail self-seeding.

'Alba' produces white flowers in early summer. 12–15 in. **'Jenny'** ('Nana') is double flowered with shaggy, pale lavender-pink blooms. Good for rock gardens, front of the border, for cutting, and in containers. 8–12 in. tall.

Lychnis viscaria syn. *Viscaria vulgaris*

Color	magenta
Bloom time	early to midsummer
Size	12–18 in. × 14–16 in.
Light	sun, part shade
Zone	Z3–7

GERMAN CATCHFLY, STICKY CATCHFLY Sandy meadows and dry clearings and roadsides from Europe to western Asia. Evergreen tufts of broadly oblong basal leaves, 3 in. long and without hairs. Stems, sticky with glandular hairs that rise above the foliage, bear slender spike-like clusters of three to five bright magenta flowers with notched petals, about 0.75 in. across. Drought tolerant. Long blooming; attracts butterflies and hummingbirds. Self-seeds. Suitable for lining paths, for rock gardens, or as a groundcover; also good for cutting.

'Alba' ('White Cockle') has white flowers. **'Fire'** ('Feuer') has orange-pink flowers, some double. Protect from intense sun. 18 in. Z3–8. **'Passion'** ('Splendens Plena', 'Flore-Plena') has double, hot-pink flowers.

CANDYTUFT

Iberis | BRASSICACEAE

CANDYTUFTS WERE FIXTURES in cottage and rock gardens of yesteryear, and endow even the most modern garden with a touch of nostalgic charm. The genus includes about 39 annual and perennial species; several of the latter are subshrubby. The name *Iberis* commemorates the fact that many candytufts hail from the Iberian Peninsula.

As the common name suggests, these plants grow in the form of tufts of dark green, alternate, linear, and entire leaves. Numerous flowers cluster into flattened corymbs or racemes above the foliage mass, sometimes hiding the leaves entirely. Each small flower is four petaled, with one pair of petals larger than the others. Seedpods are not decorative.

Plant in full sun or light shade in well-drained soil. Tolerates occasional drought. Shear plants after bloom by a third for neatness, and to prevent legginess. Every couple of years cut back the plants severely into old wood to rejuvenate them. Plants may be short-lived in less-than-ideal conditions. Protect in with evergreen boughs to mitigate winter burn from icy winds and sun.

Excellent in rock gardens, tumbling over rocks and walls, or between pavers and along pathways. *Iberis* can even be grown as an attractive low hedge, clipped to shape after bloom time. Choose compact selections for containers, window boxes, and planter boxes. Good companions include rock cress, pinks, basket-of-gold, and London Pride saxifrage along with small, spring-blooming bulbs. Attracts butterflies; resists deer.

Propagate cultivars from cuttings; start species from seed.

Iberis saxatilis

	white
	spring
	3–6 in. × 6 in.
	sun, part shade
	Z3–9

ROCK CANDYTUFT Native to rocky areas of southern Europe. Tight, low, almost prostrate cushions of evergreen, needle-like, 0.75-in.-long leaves become covered with flattened, 1.5-in. clusters of fragrant, white flowers that fade to lilac, held at the stem tips.

'Pygmaea' is very compact. 4 in.

Iberis sempervirens

	white, purple
	early spring to late spring
	9–12 in. × 18 in.
	sun
	Z3–8

PERENNIAL CANDYTUFT Southern Europe. Mounds of evergreen, needle-like, 1.5-in. leaves; flat, 2-in.-wide clusters of flowers borne in the leaf axils.

'Alexander's White' has dense clusters of chalk-white flowers. 8 in. Z4. **'Autumn Snow'** produces white flowers in spring; repeats in fall. Keep moist during hot weather. Possibly a better repeat-bloomer than **'October Glory'**. 8–10 in. **'Little Gem'** has pure white flowers. Very compact. 6–12 in. **'Masterpiece'** is a recent introduction with heads of white flowers, lilac-tinged buds. Mounding. 10 in. Z6. **'Snowball'** makes mounds of white flowers; early. 10 in.

CATMINT

Nepeta LAMIACEAE

A VERSATILE GROUP OF PLANTS that offer subtle but elegant colors and textures, together with aromatic foliage and a remarkably trouble-free experience for the gardener. For cats, of course, catmint, especially *Nepeta cataria*, provides a truly intoxicating experience.

Close cousins to mints, catmints have aromatic, opposite leaves, square stems, and tubular, two-lipped flowers. However, their roots are seldom as invasive. Commonly catmint foliage is gray-green; the flowers blue spotted with purple. Some species have pink, white, and lilac, even pale yellow blossoms.

Though flowers are individually small, they are borne in verticillasters that produce a more substantial effect. Valuable in several garden niches, catmints range in height from 1–4 ft. for beds and borders, rock gardens, or lining a path or bed. Traditionally, rosarians planted catmint to hide the "knees" or stick-like canes of rose bushes. The soft colors and textures of catmints are an attractive counterpoint to the bolder colors and foliage of roses.

Tolerant of dry soils, heat, and full sun, catmints are excellent for xeriscapes, though ordinary garden conditions suffice. They struggle and may melt in hot, humid summers; provide early afternoon shade. Cut back plants hard after their initial flush to promote rebloom. Outstanding for attracting butterflies and bees to the garden; deer resistant, and rarely troubled by insects and diseases.

Divide in spring or fall, or take spring or summer cuttings.

Nepeta govaniana

syn. *Dracocephalum govanianum*

yellow
mid- to late summer
1.5–3 ft. × 1.5–2 ft.
sun, part sun
Z5–9, HS

YELLOW CATMINT Himalayas, Pakistan, northern India. Branching stems with velvety, aromatic, gray-green leaves; open racemes of pale yellow, tubular, lipped flowers bloom over a long period. Available in United States primarily as seed; should be more readily available.

Nepeta grandiflora

blue
midsummer to midfall
24–36 in. × 9–12 in.
sun
Z4–9

CAUCASUS CATMINT Caucasus Mountains, eastern and central Europe. Velvety, aromatic, silver-gray leaves and tall, showy spikes of lavender to violet flowers. The following are commonly available as cultivars:

'Border Ballet' displays deep violet-blue, almost purple flowers. Start from seed. 18–24 in. **'Dawn to Dusk'** has soft pink flowers. 24–36 in. × 18–24 in. **'Pool Bank'** has rich blue flowers, with purple-blue bracts. 30–36 in. × 24 in. **'Wild Cat'** sports blue-violet flowers with purplish red calyxes. 3 ft. × 2 ft. Z5.

Nepeta racemosa syn. *N. mussinii*

color	purple, lavender
bloom time	midspring to early fall
size	9–12 in. × 12–18 in.
light	sun, part shade
zone	Z4–8, HS

CATMINT Caucasus, northern Iran. This low-growing species forms spreading clumps of decumbent stems with hairy, ovate leaves, with heart-shaped bases and crenate margins. Pale to dark violet flowers, 0.5 in. long. Shear spent blooms to encourage later rebloom. Exceptionally drought tolerant; outstanding for xeriscapes. Non-sterile varieties self-seed and become invasive. Useful for rock gardens, border fronts, herb gardens, for lining paths or beds, and as a groundcover.

'Walker's Low' produces abundant crops of lavender-blue flowers; deadhead spent flower spikes routinely for continuous bloom from spring to fall. Sterile. Named for a place, and not its habit. 2007 Perennial Plant Association Plant of the Year. 2.5 ft. × 3 ft.

Nepeta sibirica

syn. *Dracocephalum sibiricum*

color	purple
bloom time	early to late summer
size	30–48 in. × 12–24 in.
light	sun, part shade
zone	Z3–8, HS

SIBERIAN CATMINT Siberia. Upright with handsome, aromatic, soft gray-green foliage, and whorled clusters of rich blue flowers. Cold-hardiest catmint, but struggles with summer mugginess. Well-drained soil is essential. Fast growing, good as a low hedge, in coastal gardens, and on sunny banks. Adapts well to containers.

'Souvenir d'André Chaudron' has violet-blue flowers. Sometimes sold as 'Blue Beauty'. 12–18 in. high and wide.

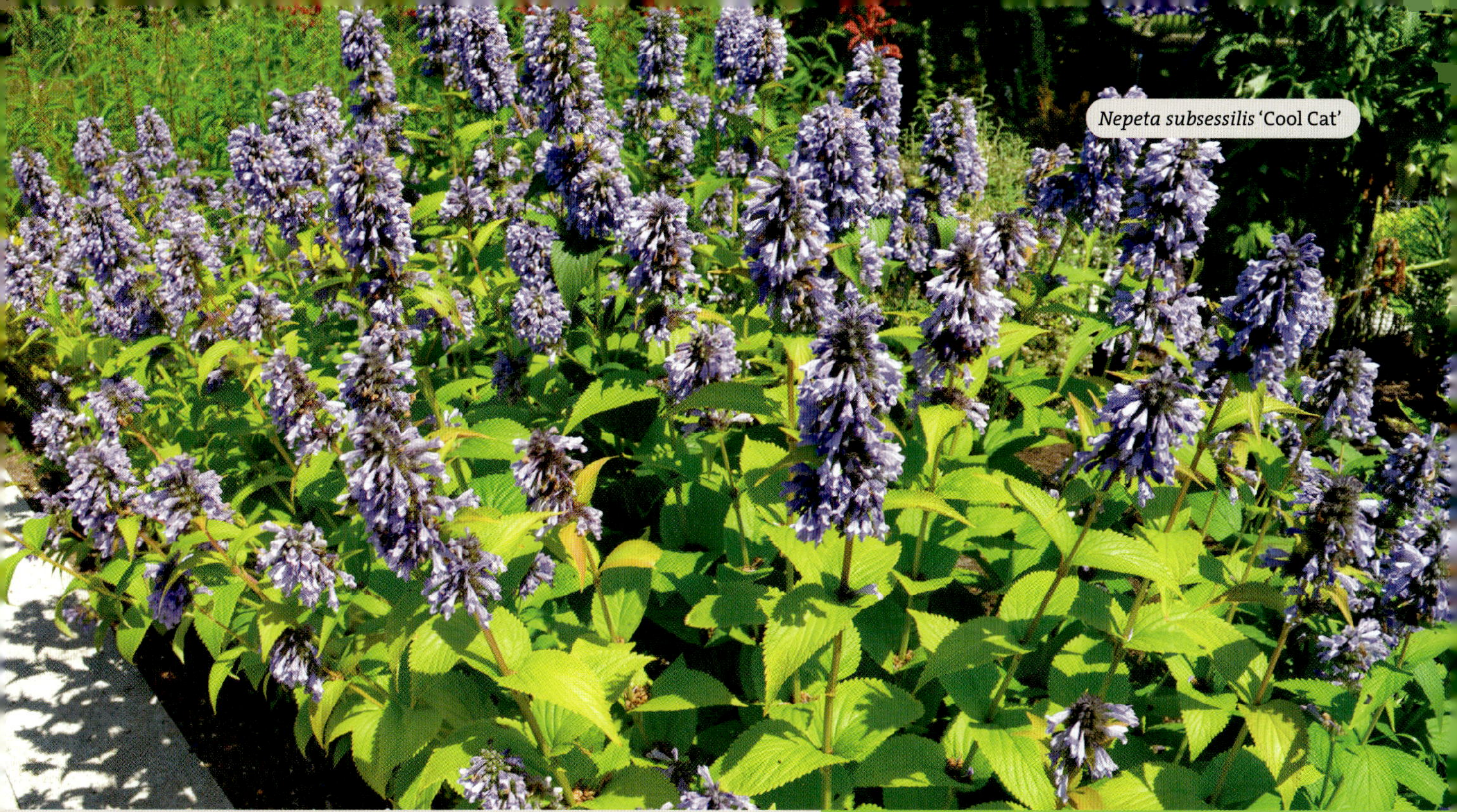

Nepeta subsessilis 'Cool Cat'

Nepeta subsessilis

Color	blue
Bloom time	midspring to early fall
Size	1.5–2 ft. × 1–1.5 ft.
Light	sun, part shade
Zone	Z4–8

JAPANESE CATMINT Moist Japanese mountainsides. Mounds of aromatic, toothed, green leaves, and showy spikes of 2-in., bell-shaped, maroon-spotted, deep violet-blue flowers. Not as drought tolerant. Plant in borders, herb gardens, or naturalized plantings; outstanding for rain gardens.

'Candy Cat'. Dense clusters of pale lavender-pink flowers. 2 ft. **'Cool Cat'** has white-specked, lavender-blue flowers. 2–2.5 ft. **'Sweet Dreams'** bears pink flowers with burgundy bracts. 18 in. **'Washfield'** carries erect branching spikes of vibrant blue-violet flowers. 1.5 ft.

Other Notable Cultivars

×*faassenii* Strain, typically sterile and non-invasive, includes: 'Blue Wonder', with dark blue flowers. 1–2 ft. 'Select Blue'. Long, tapered, gray-green leaves in neat mounds; long blooming. Vigorous and drought tolerant. 15 in. × 18 in. 'Six Hills Giant' displays 9- to 12-in.-long spikes of deep purple flowers. 3–4 ft. **'Joanna Read'** (*Nepeta sibirica* × *N.* × *faassenii*) has darker violet flowers than other nepetas, to 3 ft. Named for Pennsylvania plantswoman Joanna Read. Z3–8.

CHRYSANTHEMUM | MUM

Chrysanthemum | ASTERACEAE

CULTIVATED CHRYSANTHEMUMS DERIVE from an Asian tradition that focused on the development of spectacular blossoms, often at the expense of the vigor and hardiness of the plant. This trend has been perpetuated by many Western breeders who have created a wide variety of hybrids (often listed in catalogs as *Chrysanthemum* ×*morifolium*) whose magnificent blossoms make them the ultimate florist's flowers, but which generally will not flourish outside a greenhouse. As a rule, the plants sold in bloom by retailers in the fall belong to this category and should be regarded as annuals. However, a handful of perceptive horticulturists have focused on developing garden-hardy types that integrate readily into beds and borders, and overwinter reliably outdoors throughout much of North America and elsewhere. Typically, plants of this category are available only by special order.

Hardy chrysanthemums have the virtue of timeliness, bearing their flowers of golds, russets, oranges, reds, pinks, and white in late summer and fall when most other perennials are winding down. The foliage—typically rich green and deeply lobed—is attractive and, when well grown, chrysanthemums have a bushy form that makes them desirable garden elements even when not in flower. Although not long-lived, hardy mums are easily propagated.

For best results, give garden chrysanthemums a spot with at least six hours of direct sun daily and a well-drained, organic-enriched soil. Because they are shallow rooted, chrysanthemums need regular irrigation during dry spells to keep the soil consistently moist—these plants will survive some drought but their bloom will be severely diminished. Avoid setting chrysanthemums near a strong night-time light source, including street lamps, as this can prevent them from setting flower buds.

An early to midspring planting is best, although container-grown hardy chrysanthemums can be planted successfully in early summer. To keep plants compact and maximize bloom, pinch off the tip of each shoot every two to three weeks from the time when new growth reaches 4–6 in. until early June. Deadhead for neatness in warm areas, where the foliage will remain green into winter. In colder climates, leave the fading flowers and withering stems intact to provide winter protection. Cover dormant plants with a protective winter mulch, such as evergreen boughs, where winters are cold.

Hardy chrysanthemums combine well with other fall bloomers such as sedums, goldenrods, and Russian sage, and provide an attractive counterpoint to the russet fall foliage of ornamental grasses. Little troubled by pests aside from occasional visits from slugs and infestations of aphids and mites. Susceptible to a variety of diseases, but usually only when plants are stressed by an overly shady spot or poorly drained soil.

Divide established plants every third year in spring to renew their vigor. Propagate by stem cuttings taken from new growth in mid- to late spring.

Chrysanthemum arcticum

syn. *Arctanthemum arcticum*

flower color	white, pink
bloom time	late summer
size	10–16 in. × 12–24 in.
light	sun
zone	Z4–9

ARCTIC DAISY Native throughout the northern parts of the Northern Hemisphere, including most of Canada and Alaska. Forms cushions of medium green leaves, wedge shaped, semi-pinnatifid with three to five lobes or teeth; daisy-like flowerheads, up to a diameter of 2 in. and with yellow disk centers, are solitary but often borne in great profusion. Suitable for the border, rock garden, edging paths, or in mixed containers.

'Red Chimo' bears lavish crops of bright pink flowers. Continues to bloom even after light frost. Canadian bred.

Chrysanthemum ×koreana

flower color	yellow, orange, pink, red, white
bloom time	late summer to late fall
size	30–36 in. × 36 in.
light	sun, part shade
zone	Z4–9

KOREAN HYBRIDS Originals bred by Alex Cumming of Bristol Nurseries in Connecticut, from a plant collected in Korea, *Chrysanthemum zawadskii* var. *sibiricum*, which is also the principal parent of the *rubellum* hybrids. Korean hybrids were originally shorter and bushier than their ×*rubellum* relatives, with double, semi-double, or single, daisy-like flowers, although interbreeding has blurred the distinction.

NYBG Series. Bred at the New York Botanical Garden; large, single flowerheads in a range of colors. Excellent cut flowers. Selections include 'Painted Lady', 'Cambodian Queen', and 'Arizona Sunset'.

Chrysanthemum ×*rubellum*

color	yellow, pink, red
bloom	late summer to fall
size	24–36 in. high and wide
light	sun, part shade
zone	Z5–9

KOREAN MUM, RUBELLUM HYBRIDS This is the other major group of hardy garden hybrids, bred in Britain during the late nineteenth and early twentieth centuries. Several excellent examples are still commercially available.

'Clara Curtis' has pink, single, daisy-like flowers, with a diameter of 3 in. More shade tolerant than most chrysanthemums. 18–24 in. × 18 in. **'Emperor of China'** has double, rose-pink flowers in midfall; foliage turns mahogany-red as weather cools. 3–4 ft. × 1.5 ft. Z4–9. **'Mary Stoker'** has single, apricot-yellow flowers in early fall. 24–30 in. × 16 in.

Chrysanthemum weyrichii

syn. *Dendranthema zawadskii*

color	white, pink
bloom	late summer to late fall
size	6–12 in. × 18–24 in.
light	sun, part shade
zone	Z4–8

MIYABE Native from northern Japan to Alaska. Mat forming with toothed leaves and single flowers with yellow centers to 2 in. across, borne on short stems. Equally at home in rock gardens or the front of borders.

'Pink Bomb' has pale pink flowers. **'White Bomb'** has white flowers, dark green leaves, and purplish stems.

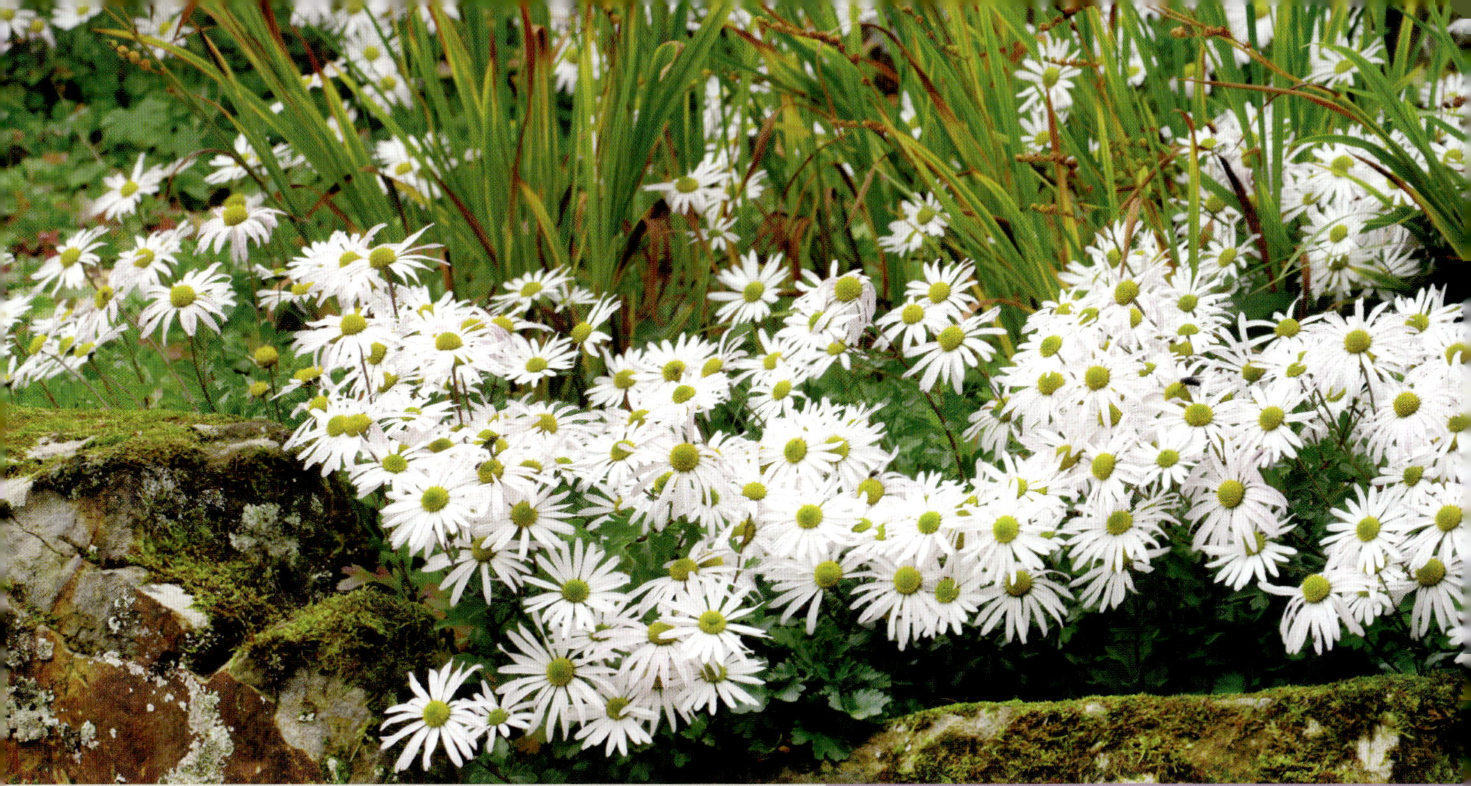

Chrysanthemum yezoense

syn. *Dendranthema arcticum* subsp. *maekawanum*

Flower color	white, purple
Bloom time	early fall to late fall
Size	3–8 in. × 2 ft.
Light	sun, part shade
Zones	Z5–9

GROUNDCOVER CHRYSANTHEMUM Ground-hugging Japanese coastal native, spreads slowly by rhizomes to an indefinite width. Long-stalked, evergreen, lobed and toothed leaves. Abundant display of 2-in., white or purplish flowers. Drought tolerant; handsome additions to rock gardens or cascading down a bank.

Other Notable Cultivars

'Autumn Moon'. Abundant 2.75-in., single flowers of pale yellow touched with pink. Late fall. 18–24 in. Z4–9. **'Glowing Ember'** bears prolific crops of 2.5-in., semi-double, red flowers edged with gold. Late fall. 22–24 in. Z4–9. **'Mei Kyo'** has small, double, lavender blooms in late fall; doesn't require the regular division needed to reinvigorate many other chrysanthemums. 36 in. high and wide. Z4–9. **'Ruby Mound'** has burgundy-centered, double, deep red flowers. 16–24 in. × 16 in. Z5–9. **'Sheffield Pink'**. Loose sprays of large, yellow-eyed, pale, single, salmon-pink flowers. Early to midfall. 24–36 in. high and wide. Z5–9. **'Single Apricot Korean'** bears 2.5-in., pale apricot-pink flowers. Midfall. 2–3 ft. × 2 ft. Z4–9.

CLEMATIS

Clematis | RANUNCULACEAE

MENTION CLEMATIS AND MOST gardeners think of tall vines sporting large open flowers in bright jewel tones, or clouds of small, white blossoms enveloping arbors. But there are also several non-climbing, upright weavers or sprawling species that deserve a place among herbaceous perennials. The weavers bring a sense of random informality in otherwise orderly beds; the sprawlers, supported by small shrubs, pea sticks, or rustic tepees, provide height in midborder.

Clematis have opposite leaves that are generally compound and composed of several leaflets. Instead of petals, flowers have four or five petaloid (petal-like) sepals that surround a central cluster or boss of yellow or white stamens. Some produce interesting plumed fruits. In chilly climates clematis do best in sun, but where sun is more intense they prefer lightly shaded spots. Averse to drought, they require evenly moist, average to rich soil, ideally amended with compost, and should never dry out. Stake as necessary. Blooms are borne on new growth; prune hard in spring. Slugs may damage young foliage; deer are seldom a problem. Clematis wilt is not as widespread on the herbaceous species as on the vining types, but gardeners should watch for the symptoms.

Propagate by cuttings taken from new shoots emerging from the base of the plant in spring, or by seed sown outdoors in fall, or stratified and sown indoors in containers in spring. Dividing non-climbing clematis is possible but risky, and best accomplished in late winter or early spring while the plant is still dormant.

Clematis heracleifolia 'Mrs. Robert Brydon'

Clematis heracleifolia

Color	blue
Bloom time	late summer
Size	2–3 ft. × 4 ft.
Exposure	sun, part shade
Zones	Z3–7

TUBE CLEMATIS, SHRUBBY CLEMATIS, BUSH CLEMATIS China. Tubular, variably fragrant, light blue flowers about 0.5 in. long are borne in dense clusters at the stem tips and leaf axils and are quite showy. Tips of the sepals reflex backward as with hyacinths. Bloom is more abundant in full sun, but the roots need cool, evenly moist conditions; mulch in spring. Large, three-parted leaves, with a larger middle leaflet. Mostly upright and bushy; plants can be staked if preferred. Attracts bees and butterflies. Tolerates deer and the toxic roots of black walnut trees. Rabbits dine on the young growth. Plants are reportedly poisonous. Most named selections are actually hybrids with other species.

'Blue Mood' is best planted among low shrubs such as fothergilla, bush cinquefoil, and Russian sage for support. True blue flowers. Z5–9. **'China Purple'** has clusters of small, violet-blue flowers. Prefers full sun. 2 ft. Z5–9. **'Mrs. Robert Brydon'** (*Clematis tubulosa* × *C. virginiana*) is a hybrid with bold dark leaves and a multitude of hyacinth-like, pale blue flowers. Excellent as a groundcover to suppress weeds. **'Rosea'** has fragrant, pink flowers similar to the species.

Clematis integrifolia

Color	blue
Bloom time	summer
Size	1.5–3 ft. × 4 ft.
Exposure	sun, part shade, shade
Zones	Z3–8

SOLITARY CLEMATIS Southern Europe. Solitary, 2-in., nodding, blue-lavender flowers, each with four twisted sepals borne at the tips of wiry stems; attractive heads of silvery seeds follow. Pairs of dark green, lance-shaped leaves sparsely clothe the stems. This sprawling species is excellent in beds and borders where it benefits from being staked with twiggy branches or pea sticks. In cottage and meadow gardens, allow it to ramble through other plants. Stems are less robust in shaded sites. Hardy geraniums, meadow sages, ornamental onions, and coreopsis are good companions.

'Hendersonii', often listed as a cultivar of solitary clematis but in fact a hybrid (*Clematis integrifolia* × *C. viticella*), is larger-flowered and indigo-blue. Long blooming. **'Rooguchi'** is a lax climber with non-woody stems. Fleshy plum-colored bell flowers.

Clematis recta

	white
	late spring to summer
	2–4 ft. × 2.5 ft.
	sun, part shade, shade
	Z3–9

GROUND CLEMATIS Native to southern Europe. Scrambling or more erect, with up to nine pointed, oval leaflets per leaf. Silvery seedheads follow frothy clouds of fragrant, 1-in., starry, white flowers borne in large clusters. Provide obelisks, tepees, or other structures for support, or plant alongside low shrubs through which the plants can ramble. Ground clematis may be confused with similar but vining sweet autumn clematis (*Clematis terniflora*).

'Purpurea' displays bronzy purple foliage. Variable; select a well-colored form. **'Purpurea Select'** has more intensely purple foliage; best in full sun.

Clematis tubulosa

syn. *C. tubulosa* var. *davidiana*, *C. heracleifolia* var. *davidiana*

	blue
	midsummer
	4 ft. high and wide
	sun, part shade
	Z3–7

TUBE CLEMATIS Central and northern China. Dense clusters of very fragrant, open, violet flowers that bloom a little earlier than most clematis. Leaves are also fragrant.

'Wyevale' is clump forming with fragrant, reflexed, mid-blue flowers. Attractive fluffy seedheads follow. Some authorities consider this to be a hybrid; others, a selection of *Clematis heracleifolia*.

COLUMBINE

Aquilegia | RANUNCULACEAE

BOTH THE SCIENTIFIC AND common names celebrate this plant's intriguing flower structure. *Aquilegia* derives from the Latin for "eagle," and refers to the five long, hollow spurs sweeping back from the flower's face, supposedly resembling the talons of a bird of prey; columbine (Latin for "dove") offers a gentler vision—turn the flower over and look for the resemblance to five doves perched around a fountain. In addition to the flowers, aquilegias offer daintily divided or lobed, rich green or blue-green foliage.

Easy to grow, columbines thrive in most soils as long as they drain well. To promote the best growth and bloom, water regularly but avoid soaking; overwatering is generally fatal. Full sun is fine in cooler, northern regions; morning sun with afternoon shade is preferable in warmer ones.

The most common pest is leaf miner, which disfigures the foliage by burrowing beneath the leaf surface, marking it with pale, winding tracks; cut back to the ground and destroy foliage of infested plants immediately after bloom time. This promotes healthy new growth. The seeds and roots of columbines are toxic, and should not be ingested. Resistant to deer and rabbits, but attractive to hummingbirds and butterflies.

Plant larger-flowered species and hybrids in borders with spring bulbs and perennials: perennial flax, dame's rocket, and spurges, for example. Less showy types adapt well to rock gardens and at woodland edges. Well suited to cottage gardens and excellent in containers and as cut flowers.

Easily started from seed; propagate named cultivars by dividing mature clumps carefully; columbines resent root disturbance and are slow to recover from such treatment.

Aquilegia alpina syn. *A. montana*

Color	blue
Bloom time	late spring
Size	1–2 ft. × 6–12 in.
Light	sun, part shade
Zone	Z4–8

ALPINE COLUMBINE European Alps. Flowers are cobalt blue, 2–3 in. across. Well-drained soil is essential; prefers partial shade in warmer, sunnier areas. Reseeds freely in hospitable locations.

Var. *alba* bears white flowers on slightly shorter plants.

Aquilegia caerulea

Color	blue, white
Bloom time	spring to early summer
Size	8–24 in. × 18–24 in.
Light	sun, part shade
Zone	Z3–8, HS

ROCKY MOUNTAIN COLUMBINE Rocky Mountain states. Large flowers to 3 in. across, white and pale to cerulean blue. Provide protection from afternoon sun in the warmer part of its range. Self-seeds in hospitable locations.

'Florida' has bicolored flowers of pale and golden yellow. **'Georgia'** has extra-large, red flowers with white corollas. **'Kristall'** is pure white. **'Red Hobbit'** is dwarf with carmine flowers with white corollas. 12–15 in.

Aquilegia canadensis

- pink, red-yellow
- mid- to late spring
- 2–3 ft. × 1–1.5 ft.
- sun, part shade
- Z3–8

CANADIAN COLUMBINE Rocky woods, slopes, and open areas throughout North America, east of the Rockies. Bright red flowers with yellow corollas dance in the slightest breeze. Adapts to a wide range of soils, including dry ones. Attractive to hummingbirds, well suited to wildlife gardens as well as native plant collections. Tolerates drought, deer, and rabbits. Self-seeds and naturalizes in hospitable locations. Reportedly resistant to leaf miners.

'Corbett' has pale yellow flowers on 8- to 10-in.-tall plants. May lack vigor. **'Little Lanterns'** is a dwarf that bears brilliant red flowers with yellow corollas. 8–10 in.

Aquilegia chrysantha

- yellow
- late spring to early summer
- 1–3 ft. × 1–3 ft.
- part shade, shade
- Z3–8

GOLDEN COLUMBINE Southwestern North America. Delicate flowers have gently curving spurs to 3 in. long. Fast growing and successful on a wide range of well-drained soils; keep well watered in full sun in cool climates; prefers partial shade elsewhere. Self-seeds in hospitable locations. Rust and powdery mildew may attack in dry summers; be alert for fungal leaf spots and the occasional blight.

'Yellow Queen' bears especially bright yellow-and-gold flowers.

Aquilegia ecalcarata

syn. *Semiaquilegia ecalcarata*

Color	red, purple
Season	spring
Size	15–18 in. × 12 in.
Light	sun, part shade
Zones	Z4–7

SPURLESS COLUMBINE Japan, China, Korea. This short-lived perennial has ternate, 10- to 12-in. basal leaves on long petioles. The leaflets are sometimes further divided. Starry burgundy to purple flowers nod in loose clusters atop branched stems; in this species, the floral spurs of other aquilegias are replaced by small pouches at the base of the flowers. *Semiaquilegia adoxoides* is similar but has pale pink flowers.

Aquilegia flabellata

syn. *A. atkinensis*

Color	purple, white
Season	1–3 ft. × 0.5–1 ft.
Size	sun, part shade
Light	Z4–8
Zones	

FAN COLUMBINE Japan and Korea. Flowers are bicolored, bluish purple with white tips and centers. Self-seeds in hospitable locations.

'Blackcurrant Ice' has a dark purple corolla with yellow sepals and spurs. **'Cameo Blue-and-White'** is extra compact with blue and white flowers. 6 in. **Var. *pumila*** is very dwarf, just 3–5 in., with blue-and-white flowers.

Aquilegia vulgaris

Color	blue, pink, white
Bloom time	early to late spring
Size	12–36 in. × 6–12 in.
Light	sun, part shade
Zones	Z3–8

EUROPEAN COLUMBINE, GRANNY'S BONNET Europe. The wild species has blue or purple-and-white flowers, but cultivars offer many other hues. Nodding flowers appear congested, with short, hooked spurs. Prefers humus-rich, moist but well-drained soils.

'Leprechaun Gold' has gold-marbled, bright green foliage and large, deep violet flowers borne on reddish pink stems. **'Nora Barlow'** has tightly double flowers of red and white with very short spurs. Named for Charles Darwin's granddaughter. **'Ruby Port'** has wine-red flowers; **'Variegated Ruby Port'** bears similar flowers with yellow-specked foliage. **'William Guiness'** ('Magpie') bears double flowers of black-purple, with white corollas, blooming from late spring through early summer.

Other Notable Cultivars

Biedermeier Mix has single and double, upward-facing blooms in violet, cream, lilac, pink, and deep red. 12–18 in. Z3–9. **Dragonfly Hybrids** strain is dwarf with blue, pink, red, salmon, white, or yellow flowers. 12–18 in. Z3–9. **McKana Hybrids** grow up to 24 in. tall and bear large, long-spurred flowers in a wide range of pastel colors. **Origami Series** (or Butterfly Series) is a hybrid mix with bicolored flowers with slender spurs. Often listed as *Aquilegia caerulea*, which is a prime parent. Superior named cultivars include 'Origami Red-and-White' and 'Origami Yellow-and-White'.

CONEFLOWER | PURPLE CONEFLOWER

Echinacea | ASTERACEAE

ITS EASY-CARE WAYS and long season of bloom has put *Echinacea* at the very top of the "essential perennials" list for many gardeners. And purple coneflowers are getting better all the time: during the past decade, plant breeders, most notably those at ItSaul Plants, the Chicago Botanic Garden, and Terra Nova Nurseries, have been releasing all sorts of exciting new cultivars and hybrids. Now, in addition to the familiar single, purple (and sometimes white), daisy-type blossoms, a host of echinaceas with flowers in exotic colors and forms, and often fragrant, are appearing in catalogs and garden centers. Yellows and oranges have been added to the color palette, as well as outrageous double-flowered forms and some with top knots.

Purple coneflowers are vigorous plants, clothed with mostly coarse, dark green, bristly, hairy foliage on strong, branching stems. Basal leaves usually have long petioles and may be toothed along their edges; stem leaves are narrower, often without petioles. The stems terminate in solitary, daisy-like flowers, good for cutting. The ray flowers (petals) surround a raised, prickly central disk that persists after flowers fade.

Purple coneflowers do best in sunny spots but tolerate light shade. They thrive in most well-drained soils, and even endure periods of drought once established; wet feet, however, especially in winter, is usually fatal. Plant in late spring or early summer so the roots have time to become established before cold weather arrives. Pollen and nectar-collecting songbirds, bees, and butterflies are frequent visitors through summer and fall. Regular deadheading results in an extended season of bloom. Allow late-season flowers to go to seed, to provide food for birds—seedeaters feast on the oil-rich seeds inside the central fruiting cone.

Purple coneflowers are versatile garden plants from the designer's perspective. Use tall selections among shrubs or at the back of the border, or mass them in informal meadows, wildlife gardens, or native plant gardens. Dwarf selections are ideal for containers, especially when combined with foliage plants such as coleus, gauras, or fountain grass. Seldom browsed by deer or rabbits, but mildew and Japanese beetles may be a problem.

Propagate species by seed sown outdoors in fall or in containers in spring and chilled for four weeks to break dormancy. Divide named cultivars and hybrids in spring.

Echinacea pallida

(color)	purple
(bloom time)	summer
(size)	2–3 ft. × 1–1.5 ft.
(exposure)	sun, part shade
(zones)	Z3-10, HT

PALE PURPLE CONEFLOWER Open areas along roadsides, fields, and grasslands of the eastern United States. Thrives in most soils, even poor ones, as long as they are well drained. Tolerates heat, humidity, and drought well. The mound of narrow, dark green leaves contrasts well with the light purplish, sweet-scented flowerheads above. These have extremely reflexed rays, giving the heads the appearance of a shuttlecock. Ideal in meadows, native plant gardens, and wildlife gardens, or massed in open spaces where they naturalize over time. Can also be used as a temporary summer hedge, perhaps interplanted with tall ornamental grasses.

Echinacea paradoxa

color	yellow
bloom time	summer
size	1–3 ft. × 1–1.5 ft.
light	sun
zone	Z5–8

YELLOW CONEFLOWER, OZARK CONEFLOWER, BUSH'S PURPLE CONEFLOWER Open areas of the Ozark region of Missouri and Arkansas in fertile, free-draining sites. Erect stems are topped with fragrant, showy, bright yellow, 3-in. flowerheads with swept-back rays surrounding a raised, chocolate-colored disk. Provide full sun and well-drained, even somewhat dry soil—very drought tolerant when established. Not as vigorous as *Echinacea purpurea*; may need support. If planting in fall, it is important to plant sufficiently early to give roots time to grow in well before very cold weather. New plants may not bloom the first summer. Group or mass to provide impact in meadows, or native plant and wildlife gardens. Striking at the back of the border, among shrubs such as chaste tree and butterfly bush, or *Miscanthus* and other bold ornamental grasses.

'Hula Skirts Yellow' is a particularly fine selection with larger flowers.

Echinacea purpurea

syn. ***Rudbeckia purpurea***

color	purple, white
bloom time	summer
size	2–4 ft. × 1.5–2 ft.
light	sun, part shade
zone	Z4–9

PURPLE CONEFLOWER, EASTERN PURPLE CONEFLOWER Florida and Texas north into Ontario. These plants were a dominant species of the prairies, and in gardens are especially handsome when massed in meadows or with other natives in wild gardens. They have strong root systems and must be planted before midsummer to establish and grow deep. The flowerheads of these traditionally purple or whitish daisies may reach 6 in. or so across, with slightly drooping ray flowers. The deep brown central disk becomes cone-like as it matures. Stiff orange bracts protrude from the cone.

Other Notable Cultivars

Countless selections and cultivars of purple coneflower are in the marketplace, with more almost daily. Hybrids are mostly the results of crossing *Echinacea paradoxa*, *E. purpurea*, and *E. angustifolia*. The following are just a small sampling of what is available.

'Art's Pride' ('Orange Meadowbrite') was the first orange coneflower—a color breakthrough—to appear on the market. Striking 5-in., coppery-orange flowerheads; slender, reflexed rays encircle raised, dark brown cones. 2–3 ft. Z3–8. **'Coconut Lime'** was the first white, double-flowered, purple coneflower; the flowers start out light green, maturing to greenish white. The full topknot of flowers, orange in the center, is long lasting above a fringe of drooping, white rays. 2–2.5 ft. Z4–9. **'Fragrant Angel'** has very large, fragrant, white flowers with gold cones. Partner with tall gayfeathers and daylilies. Prefers humus-rich soil. 3 ft. Z4–9. **'Green Envy'** is an unusual large-flowered novelty. The black, green-centered cones are surrounded by long ray flowers, pale green at the tips and pink toward the cone. A Mark Veeder selection. 3 ft. Z4–9. **'Green Jewel'** is perfect as a cut flower for St. Patrick's Day. The fragrant, bright green, 4-in. flowerheads have jade-green rays and deep green cones. Sturdy and compact, but demands good drainage. Ideal for containers. 1.5–2 ft. Z3–8. **'Harvest Moon'** ('Matthew Saul') belongs to the Big Sky Series from ItSaul Plants. Single, sorbet-yellow daisies with raised, orange cones on strong, branched stems. Broad ray flowers, gently reflexed, overlap slightly. 2–2.5 ft. Z4–9. **'Hot Papaya'**, a double Dutch selection, has fully double, fiery red pompon heads above a skirt of paprika-colored rays. Strong, maroon-marked stems. 2.5–3 ft. Z5–9. **'Kim's Knee High'**, a perennial dwarf purple coneflower, has strongly reflexed, purple-pink ray flowers and prominently raised, orange cones. Ideal in limited spaces. Drought tolerant. 1–2 ft. Z3–9. **'Magnus'** was the 1998 Perennial Plant Association Plant of the Year. Its hot-pink flowerheads accented with a copper-brown cone may reach 3–4 in. across on very strong stems. The broad rays are carried horizontally. Dramatic with 'Pomegranate' yarrow. 2.5–3 ft. Z3–9. **'Milkshake'** is a selection from the Dutch double-flowered Cone-fections Series. It has strongly reflexed, vanilla cream ray flowers above which the usual central cone is smothered with double, vanilla-cream flowers. 3 ft. Z5–9. **'Pink Double Delight'** offers "in-your-face" bright pink, double flowers. 1.5–2 ft. Z4–8. **'Razzmatazz'** was the first fully double (anemone type) purple coneflower on the market. It has an eye-popping rounded topknot of bright pink, double flowers and a fringe of drooping, dark purplish pink ray flowers. Long blooming; deadhead routinely. Suitable for containers, at the front of the border, and as cut flowers. 2.5–3 ft. Z4–8. **'Rubinsturn'** has carmine ray flowers that are held horizontally. Considered by some to be superior to the older 'Magnus'. Grown from seed stock. 40 in. Z4–9. **'Sunrise'** ('Big Sky Sunrise'). Fragrant, light greenish yellow daisies accented with a green-maturing-to-orange cone make a cool color combination. 2.5–3 ft. Z4–9. **'Tiki Torch'** is eye-catching with 3-in.-wide daisies; drooping, brilliant pumpkin to orange rays surround rounded, reddish cones. 2.5–3 ft. Z4–9. **'Tomato Soup'** has flowers that truly are the color of real red, ripe tomatoes. Large flowerheads, 5 in. or more across, bear slightly drooping rays around brown cones. 32 in. Z4–9. **'White Swan'**. Possibly the best white cultivar. Heat, drought, and humidity tolerant, even in poor soil. Vigorous, bears plenty of flowers with slightly drooping rays on strong erect stems. 2–3 ft. Z3–8.

CORAL BELLS | ALUMROOT

Heuchera | SAXIFRAGACEAE

FOR PERENNIAL GARDENERS who want to plant natives but prefer a bit of flamboyance in their gardens, this genus is invaluable. *Heuchera*'s 35 or more species inhabit a wide range of habitats—woodlands, prairies, and mountain peaks—from the Gulf Coast west to California and north into southern Canada; this diversity enables heucheras to fit into a wide range of garden niches.

Heucheras form rounded mounds of leaves with woody basal rootstocks; roots are shallow and prone to winter heaving. The hairy leaves vary in shape from rounded to palmately lobed and maple-like; over the last generation, a flood of new hybrids with vibrantly colored, even gaudy foliage have appeared on the market. The flowers, which may lack petals, are borne on tall stalks well above the foliage, mostly in late spring and early summer. Although not always as showy as the foliage, the blossoms attract hummingbirds; some make fine cut flowers.

These plants prefer partial shade; they'll survive full sun where light intensity is low, but nothing other than morning sun where it is intense. They prefer a rich, neutral to slightly acid soil; good drainage is a must, especially in shade. Deadhead to prolong bloom.

Heucheras integrate easily into woodland and rock gardens, semi-shaded borders, and container displays. Their evergreen foliage provides an attractive groundcover, especially when intermingled with contrasting, lacy-leaved plants such as ferns or astilbes. Juxtapose colorful-leaved cultivars with contrasting flowers or foliage—a purple-leaved heuchera, for example, alongside a yellow coreopsis or green-and-white-leaved *Carex* 'Ice Dance'.

Usually trouble-free, heucheras are prone to fungal diseases if grown in damp shade. Also susceptible to black vine weevil and deer, although dark-foliaged selections appear to be browsed less often.

In winter, cover with evergreen boughs after the ground is frozen. Start species from seed; propagate hybrids by division. Divide established plants every three to four years to prevent the centers from dying out and to reinvigorate.

Heuchera americana

Color	green, white
Bloom	late spring to early summer
Size	12–24 in. × 12–18 in.
Light	sun, part shade
Zones	Z4–9, HS

CORAL BELLS Rocky, open woodlands and rocky crevices throughout the eastern United States and southeastern Canada. Grown primarily for its 12- to 15-in. mounds of 3- to 5-in. leaves, heart shaped with five to seven lobes, marbled and veined with purplish brown at first, maturing to green. Airy panicles of tiny, bell-shaped flowers, greenish white tinged with red, rise atop tall, wiry stems.

'Dale's Strain' ('Dale's Variety') has silver-blue, marbled foliage accented with white flowers. 30 in. Nancy Goodwin, of the late, lamented Montrose Nursery in North Carolina, crossed 'Dale's Strain' with 'Palace Purple' to produce 'Montrose Ruby'. **'Garnet'** has bright garnet-colored new foliage that matures to green, veined with bronze. Fall and winter leaves bright garnet, with green margins. 18 in. **'Pewter Veil'** has copper-pink young leaves that mature to metallic pewter. 22 in.

Heuchera cylindrica

Color	white
Bloom	midspring
Size	0.5–3 ft. × 0.5–2 ft.
Light	sun, part shade
Zones	Z4–8, HS

ROUNDLEAF HEUCHERA East of the Cascade Mountains to western Montana. Mottled, dark green, slightly hairy leaves range from oval to round, with toothed and scalloped margins. Inflorescence is a tall, dense spike of 0.25-in., bell-shaped flowers, white with pink margins, that bees and butterflies enjoy.

'Greenfinch' has short, stiff panicles of green flowers. 30–36 in.

Heuchera micrantha

flower color	white
bloom time	midspring to midsummer
size	0.5–2 ft. × 1–2 ft.
exposure	sun, part shade
zones	Z4–8, HS

CREVICE ALUMROOT, SMALL-FLOWERED ALUMROOT Rocky slopes and cliffs from British Columbia to California. Evergreen, reddish green, 4-in.-wide, heart-shaped leaves with three to seven shallow lobes and toothed margins. Flowering is profuse on well-grown plants, with up to 100 reddish spikes of tiny, creamy-white blossoms. This species is more tolerant of wet soils than others. A parent of many superior selections.

Var. ***diversifolia*** **'Palace Purple'**, the first purple-leaved selection, was once widely popular but now largely replaced by superior purple-leaved hybrids. 18 in.

Heuchera sanguinea

flower color	pink, red, white
bloom time	mid- to late spring
size	12–18 in. × 9–12 in.
exposure	sun, part shade
zones	Z3–9

CORAL BELLS New Mexico and Arizona. A parent of so many fine selections, especially those bred for floral characteristics. This species is grown for its many 6-in.-long panicles of larger flowers. Blooms profusely and holds its abundant red blossoms well, even in hot weather; bloom time is long, especially when deadheaded. Evergreen leaves are kidney shaped to round, up to 2 in. wide with scalloped edges.

'Firefly' has dark red flowers. 30 in. **'Frosty'** has dark red flowers that tower over the white- to frosty-green leaves. 20 in. Dark red flowers tower over the white- to frosty-green leaves. 20 in. **'Ruby Bells'** has blood-red flowers. 18 in. **'Splendens'** has bright scarlet flowers. 28 in.

Heuchera villosa 'Tiramisu'

Heuchera villosa

Flower color	white, pink
Bloom time	midsummer to early fall
Size	1.5–3 ft. × 1.5–2 ft.
Light	sun, part shade
Zones	Z4–8

HAIRY ALUMROOT New York to Georgia, west to Missouri and Arkansas. Rounded basal clumps to 2 ft. high and wide of velvety, hairy leaves to 5 in. across, with seven to nine triangular, sharply toothed lobes. Flower stalks are also hairy, rusty brown, to 3 ft., bearing tiny (0.25 in.), white or pinkish blossoms in showy, airy panicles, to 18 in. long. Blooms latest of any species. Prefers a well-drained, organic-rich soil; drought tolerant and more forgiving of summer heat and humidity than other heucheras; best choice for hot, humid gardens. All the following selections (some are hybrids) have *Heuchera villosa* bloodlines.

'Autumn Bride' has light green foliage and white fall flowers. Well adapted to hot, sticky summers. To 36 in. **'Blackout'** has near black leaves and creamy-white flowers. 18 in. **'Citronelle'** has chartreuse foliage. Beautiful against winter snow. 2 in.

'Frosted Violet' has dark-veined, pink-purple foliage; light pink flowers in late spring. 12 in. Introduced by Charles Oliver, PA. **'Tiramisu'** has chartreuse leaves tinged with red and overlaid with silver. When nights are cool, leaves turn amber-red edged with chartreuse. 8–10 in. tall.

Other Notable Cultivars

Most of the following are derived mainly from interbreeding *Heuchera americana*, *H. micrantha*, and *H. sanguinea*. These hybrids are sometimes classified as types of *H. ×brizoides*, but this label is less often applied to newer cultivars whose descent also includes other parents. Leading *Heuchera* breeders have included the late Alan Bloom of Blooms of Bressingham, Dan Heims of Terra Nova Nurseries, Charles and Martha Oliver of The Primrose Path, PA, and French breeder Tierry Delabroye. The following are hardy in Z4–9.

'Blackcurrant' is part of the Dolce Series. Its frilly, deep purple leaves have a metallic overlay. 12 in. **'Caramel'** has glowing apricot young growth that fades to soft amber by summer; white flowers. To 18 in. **'Electra'** has golden, red-veined leaves; white flowers in late spring. 10 in. **'Key Lime Pie'** has bright lime-green foliage year-round. Stunning flecked with snow, and great in containers. 10 in. **'Lime Rickey'** is similar, with slightly ruffled edges. White flowers. 12–18 in. **Little Cuties Series** from Terra Nova is comprised of miniature varieties bred for multiple locations. They have great year-round foliage color. 'Blondie' has caramel leaves, 5 in. × 8 in. Pink-flowered 'Peppermint' is 5 in. × 9 in. **'Obsidian'**. The glossy near-black leaves hold their color well. Insignificant flowers. 10 in. **'Petite Pearl Fairy'** is a miniature with deep plum leaves no larger than a quarter. Purple stems support airy spikes of pink flowers in spring. An Oliver introduction. 10–14 in. tall. **'Purple Petticoats'** has well-ruffled, purple foliage, wine colored beneath. 12 in.

COREOPSIS | TICKSEED

Coreopsis | ASTERACEAE

DESPITE ITS UNAPPEALING COMMON NAME, this genus has become a perennial garden standby, an easy-to-grow group of plants that tolerates a range of soils and climates and bears colorful, showy daisy blossoms through a prolonged season of bloom. Heights vary considerably: some may reach 4 ft. tall and are useful for the back of a border or for interplanting with ornamental grasses; others are mounded and more compact at 18–30 in., ideal for midborder; still others top out at 12–15 in. tall and are perfect for containers or for edging. Most species are native to North America. They attract pollinating insects and butterflies and resist deer browsing. Most also tolerate dry soils and hot, sun-drenched sites, though in droughty situations irrigation helps to increase and prolong bloom.

Coreopsis flowers are daisy-like, 1.5–2.5 in. or more across, and are commonly colored in warm hues of yellow and red, though pinks and whites are increasingly available. The leaves are lance shaped, oval, or thread-like; the small, flat seeds do indeed resemble ticks.

Many of the species and older cultivars are relatively short-lived, flourishing for just a few years before succumbing to old age. This, however, is less of a problem than it might seem, as tickseeds commonly self-sow in hospitable sites, providing their own replacements. Newer hybrids—of which there are a host—are generally less fertile and persist longer.

Full sun and well-drained soil are essential for most tickseeds, though some types tolerate partial shade. They partner well with other drought-tolerant sun lovers such as salvias, yarrows, and daylilies, and with other grassland natives including echinaceas, baptisias, and the shorter native warm-season grasses. Tickseeds are naturals for native plant and butterfly gardens, meadow plantings, and cottage gardens; they furnish outstanding cut flowers.

Stake taller types with cut brush or pea sticks to prevent sprawl, and deadhead fading flowers to prolong bloom. Cut stems back by half after the first flush of bloom to encourage rebloom. Be sparing with fertilizer; to maintain vigor, divide mature plants every few years in spring as new growth begins. Tickseeds are susceptible to powdery mildew—in cooler climates where this might be a problem, choose resistant cultivars.

Propagate by seed, or division in spring, or by basal softwood cuttings.

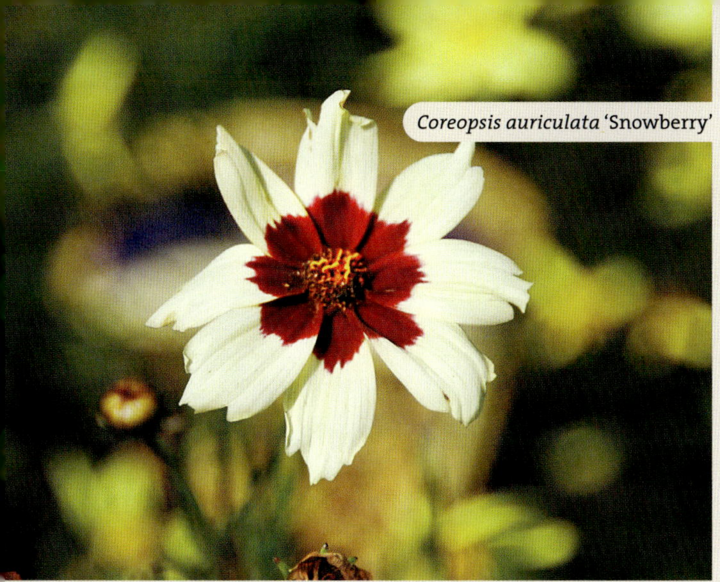

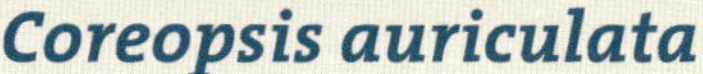

Coreopsis auriculata 'Snowberry'

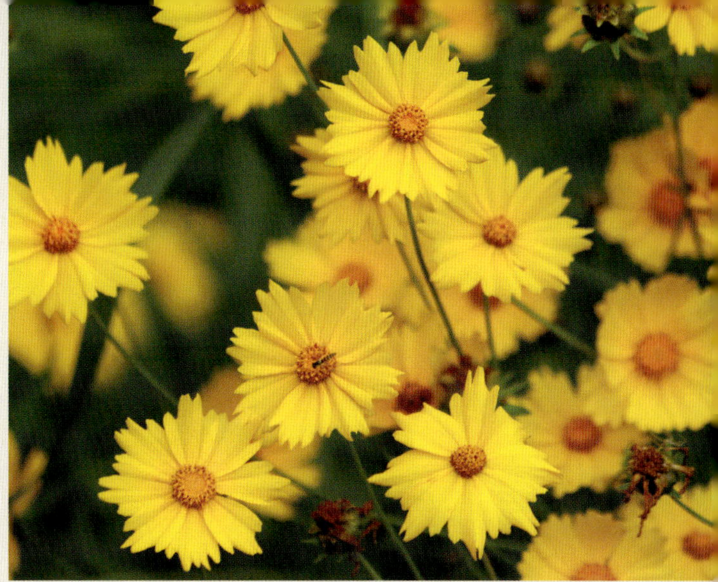

Coreopsis auriculata

flower color	yellow
bloom time	midspring to summer
size	12–36 in. high and wide
exposure	sun, part shade
zone	Z4–9

MOUSE-EAR TICKSEED, LOBED TICKSEED Woodland edges and openings throughout the southeastern United States. This hardy, low-growing species bears small, hairy, lobed leaves in lush basal rosettes and along stems; in mild climates the foliage persists through most of the winter. The 1- to 2-in. flowers are bright yellow, and appear through early summer and then sparsely until frost.

'Nana' is dwarf, forming a mat of foliage with bright yellow flowers. 2–4 in. **'Snowberry'** is more cold-tolerant than the species. It has creamy-white flowers with burgundy-red centers. 32 in. × 24 in. Z3–8.

Coreopsis grandiflora

flower color	yellow
bloom time	late spring to early fall
size	1–3 ft. × 2–3 ft.
exposure	summer
zone	Z4–9, HT

BIGFLOWER TICKSEED Meadows, grasslands, and roadsides throughout eastern North America and in the south as far west as New Mexico and California. A short-lived perennial that reseeds to provide its own replacements. Spatulate to lanceolate leaves; lower basal leaves are mostly entire, smaller stem leaves are often pinnately lobed. Flowers are solitary; deadheading is essential to prolong season of bloom and control prolific reseeding. Thrives in a range of well-drained soils, including poor, sandy, or rocky ones. Tolerant of heat, humidity, and drought; resistant to rabbits and deer.

'Domino' bears single, 2-in., yellow daisies with maroon centers. Comes true from seed. **'Early Sunrise'** bears semi-double, 2-in.-wide, bright yellow flowers. 18–24 in. high and wide. **'Sunray'** produces prolific crops of large, bright yellow, double and semi-double flowers on 18-in. plants. Hardy to zone 3.

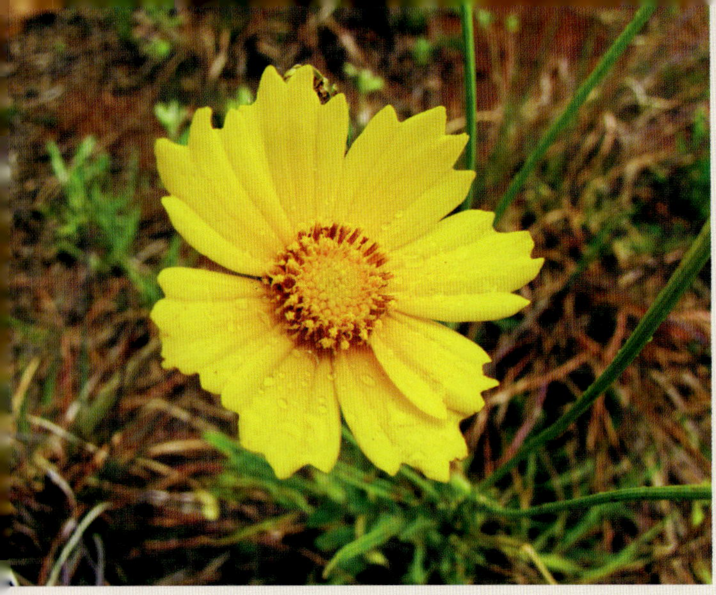

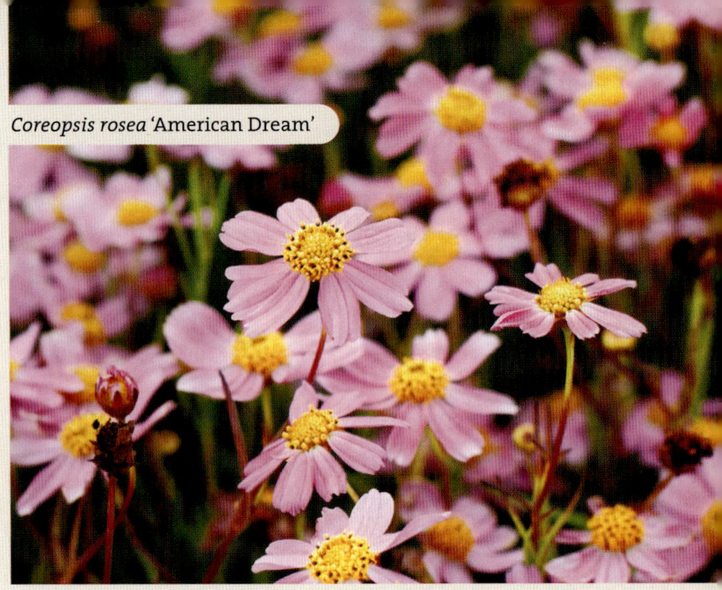

Coreopsis rosea 'American Dream'

Coreopsis lanceolata

Flower color	yellow
Bloom time	midspring to early summer
Size	1–2 ft. × 1.5–2 ft.
Light	sun
Zones	Z4–9

LANCELEAF COREOPSIS Longer lived but similar to the preceding species. Prairies, fields, and roadsides in central and southeastern United States; another tough, drought- and heat-tolerant species that flourishes on poor and rocky, well-drained soils. The 1- to 2-in., composite flowers have eight petal-like rays, toothed at the tips, borne singly atop slender erect stems. Self-seeds prolifically and can be a nuisance in formal settings; reserve for wild, native, and meadow gardens where it forms large, showy colonies. Conscientious deadheading prolongs bloom time.

'Baby Sun' has golden-yellow blooms. To 1.5 ft. **'Brown Eyes'** has golden daisies marked with maroon-brown centers. To 2 ft. **'Double Sunburst'** has semi-double, golden-yellow flowers with prominent centers. Comes true from seed. To 1.5 ft. **'Goldfink'** is compact, to 10 in.; single, golden-yellow blooms. **'Sterntaler'** produces double, golden blooms marked with showy brown centers. 1–1.5 ft.

Coreopsis rosea

Flower color	pink
Bloom time	early summer to early fall
Size	1–2 ft. × 1.5–2.5 ft.
Light	sun
Zones	Z3–8, HS

PINK TICKSEED Nova Scotia to Maryland; requires a consistently moist but well-drained soil. This rhizomatous perennial forms dense, bushy clumps. Light green, grassy, linear leaves are borne in whorls, giving the plants an attractive, airy texture. Daisylike, 0.5- to 1-in. flowers have toothless pink rays and yellow central disks. They are borne profusely and singly on short stalks for a lengthy bloom time. Does not tolerate heat and humidity well. Hardiness is sometimes a problem in cold winters.

'American Dream' bears abundant 1-in., golden-centered pink flowers on compact 18-in. plants. **'Heaven's Gate'** has yellow-centered, pink flowers with a purple eye. **'Sweet Dreams'** bears yellow-centered, white flowers with a raspberry eye.

Coreopsis verticillata 'Moonbeam'

Coreopsis verticillata

Color	yellow
Bloom time	late spring to late summer
Size	1–3 ft. high and wide
Light	sun
Zones	Z3–9

THREADLEAF COREOPSIS, WHORLED TICKSEED Eastern North America. Another heat- and drought-tolerant species that flourishes even on poor, rocky soils. The dark green, thread-like leaves provide a beautiful setting for bright yellow, daisy-like flowers borne singly in loose clusters. It spreads by rhizomes as well as seed and sometimes can be aggressive.

'Moonbeam' is compact, with creamy-yellow, golden-centered, 1- to 2-in. flowers. These are sterile, eliminating the threat of reseeding, thus making this cultivar a superior choice for borders and beds. Deadheading is tedious but extends bloom time. Demands full sun. To 2 ft. **'Zagreb'** is more compact, to 12–15 in. high and wide, with 1- to 2-in.-wide, bright yellow, golden-centered flowers.

Other Notable Cultivars

'Autumn Blush' has pastel yellow blossoms with wine-red eyes. 32 in. × 24 in. Z4–9. Pastel yellow blossoms with wine-red eyes. 32 in. × 24 in. Z4–9. **The Big Bang Series** are exciting hybrids, bred by Darrell Probst, featuring well-branched plants that bear striking flowers from early summer into fall. Excellent for containers and edging or at the front of a border. 'Cosmic Eye' has yellow flowers with a wine-colored ring surrounding the orange center. Compact at 12–15 in. × 12 in. 'Full Moon' bears single, 3-in.-wide, canary-yellow flowers with orange centers. Foliage is glossy green. 24–30 in. × 30 in. 'Galaxy' produces double, yellow flowers on compact plants to 12 in. high and wide. 'Redshift' displays yellow flowers with crimson eyes in summer, turning all red as weather cools in fall. 12 in. high and wide. **'Sienna Sunset'** flowers have soft orange petals streaked with yellow and orange centers. 16–20 in. × 12–24 in. **'Crème Brulée'** is similar to 'Moonbeam' but more vigorous, with larger, deeper yellow inflorescences, and brighter green leaves. Resistant to powdery mildew. **Limerock Series** are perennial in zones 8–10, where they tolerate heat and humidity well. Extraordinarily floriferous, covering mounds of ferny green foliage with a solid sheet of flowers from early summer to midfall. Exceptional for containers or edging. Prefers moist soil. 'Limerock Dream' bears apricot-pink flowers in spring, turning coppery-orange in midsummer. 12–16 in. × 24–30 in. 'Limerock Passion' flowers are pinkish lavender. 16 in. × 30 in. 'Limerock Ruby' has 1.5-in.-wide, ruby-red flowers. 12 in. tall. **'Little Sundial'** is dwarf with bright yellow blooms with maroon centers. 10 in. high and wide. **'Pinwheel'** has light yellow, petal-like ray flowers, curled like the vanes of a pinwheel. Sterile, does not reseed. Blue-green, mounded foliage. 24 in. × 30 in. **'Tequila Sunrise'** blooms with orange-centered, yellow daisies above variegated yellow-and-green foliage. 12–16 in. high and wide. Z5–9.

CRANESBILL | HARDY GERANIUM

Geranium

GERANIACEAE

ALTHOUGH CRANESBILLS ARE OFTEN called "hardy geraniums," it should be noted that they do not belong to the same genus as the popular bedding plants (actually *Pelargonium*) that most people refer to as "geraniums."

Whatever you call them, the cranesbills are, typically, undemanding and long-lived, requiring little maintenance in return for a vibrant floral display. They tolerate a wide range of soils, though they do not prosper in winter wet. They generally prefer sunny positions, although several species do well in part shade or direct sun for just part of the day. Alpine species and many of the hybrids grow best in full sun and a free-draining soil well enriched with compost.

In general, cranesbills form low mats or mounds of foliage and flowers, although some have a more erect, if sprawling, habit. Long-stemmed basal leaves and leafy, branched, flowering stems combine to present bold masses of handsome and long-lasting foliage. Often aromatic and mostly rounded in outline, the leaves are hand shaped, divided into segments, and often further lobed and toothed along the edges. Clusters or pairs of five-petaled flowers in white, pinks, purples, blues, violets, and dark maroon mostly bloom above the foliage mass. The beak-like fruits ripen, then dry and split to release their seeds.

Rabbits and deer seldom bother cranesbills, but mildew can be a problem, especially among plants suffering from drought.

Species easily propagated by seed sown as soon as it is ripe. Hybrids and cultivars must be divided, or increased by basal cuttings in spring. Selections with thick fleshy roots strike well from root cuttings taken in fall, and protected over winter in a spot with minimal heat.

Geranium ×cantabrigiense 'Karmina'

Geranium cinereum 'Ballerina'

Geranium ×cantabrigiense

Color	pink
Bloom time	late spring to early summer
Size	6–12 in. × 18 in.
Exposure	sun, part shade
Zones	Z5–8

CAMBRIDGE GERANIUM This sterile hybrid (*G. dalmaticum* × *G. macrorrhizum)* has bright rosy pink or sometimes white, flattened flowers with inflated calyces, on trailing stems. Glossy light green, lobed and toothed leaves, to 3.5 in. across.

'Biokovo' has white flowers flushed with pink; red calyces. A single clump may reach 3 ft. across. Red fall foliage. 6–8 in. tall. Was named Perennial Plant of the Year in 2015. **'Cambridge Blue'** ('Cambridge') has pale lavender-blue flowers. Makes an excellent groundcover to 18 in. across. 8 in. tall. **'Karmina'** ('Biokovo Karmina'). Vibrant rosy flowers from late spring into summer. Aromatic foliage provides red fall color. 6–10 in. tall.

Geranium cinereum

Color	pink
Bloom time	late spring to early summer
Size	4–6 in.
Exposure	sun, part shade
Zones	Z5–9

GRAYLEAF CRANESBILL, ASHY CRANESBILL Pyrenees Mountains of southern Europe. Often grown in rock gardens, grayleaf cranesbill makes low, evergreen rosettes of deeply divided, grayish leaves, about 2 in. across, each of the five to seven segments further lobed. Clusters of upward facing, 1-in., white or pale pink flowers, often etched with purple. Demands free drainage. Provide light afternoon shade in hot areas; best in cooler climates.

'Ballerina' has purplish red, 2-in. flowers veined with dark pink, with a maroon eye. Grayer foliage than the species. Long blooming. 4–6 in. Similar, but smaller **'Laurence Flatman'** has darker-colored flowers. 3–6 in. tall. **'Purple Pillow'** has dark-veined, purplish red flowers over a mound of gray leaves. 6 in. Z3–8 **'Splendens'** has screaming magenta flowers, striped and centered with purple. Dramatic in rock gardens. 8 in. Z4–8.

Geranium endressii

color	pink
bloom time	early summer to early fall
size	15–18 in. × 18 in.
light	sun, part shade
zones	Z4–7

ENDRESS'S CRANESBILL, FRENCH CRANESBILL French Pyrenees. Mounding clumps of glossy deep green, deeply divided leaves. Long-blooming, deep pink, cup-shaped flowers; cut back hard after the first flush to encourage further bloom. Shade from intense sun. Reliable as filler in flower borders, perhaps to replace dormant spring ephemerals. Tolerates dry shade.

'Wargrave Pink' (syn. *Geranium* ×*oxonianum* 'Wargrave's Pink') has larger flowers, often veined with deep pink. Butterflies, bees, and birds seem to love it. Seeds about in good conditions. 18–24 in. Z3–8.

Geranium himalayense

syn. *G. grandiflorum, G. himalayense* var. *meeboldii, G. meeboldii*

color	violet-blue
bloom time	late spring to late summer
size	1–2 ft. × 1.5 ft.
light	sun, part shade
zones	Z4–10, HS

HIMALAYAN GERANIUM Himalayan Mountains. Masses of 2-in.-wide, white-centered, intensely blue flowers, above dense mounds of lobed, 4-in. leaves. Appropriate for beds, borders, and beneath shrubs, or as a dense groundcover. Drought tolerant; excellent in dry and coastal climates, but not in those with summer heat and humidity.

'Baby Blue' has violet-blue, 1.5-in. flowers, white centered and veined with purple. Long blooming till midsummer. Red and gold fall color. 12 in. Z4–8. **'Birch Double'** ('Plenum') has ruffled, fully double, lilac-blue, 1- to 2-in. flowers till midsummer. Good groundcover, especially on the edge of woods, and in containers. 18–24 in. Z4–7.

Geranium maculatum 'Espresso'

Geranium macrorrhizum

flower color	cerise
bloom time	spring
size	15–18 in. × 18 in.
light	sun, part shade
zones	Z4–8

BIGROOT GERANIUM, BULGARIAN GERANIUM Southern Europe, particularly Bulgaria. Easy to grow, tolerates most conditions including dry shade (even under maples). Large, sticky, lobed, light green leaves, 4–8 in. across; soft to the touch, highly aromatic, vibrant red and maroon fall color. Flowers flattish, usually a deep cerise with dark red, inflated calyces, and prominent red stamens. Spreads by succulent underground stems.

'Bevan's Variety' is a superior groundcover for shaded places. Deep magenta flowers accented with red calyces bloom from spring to late summer. 12 in. Z5. **'Ingwersen's Variety'**. A superior cultivar with very pale pink flowers. 12–18 in. **'White-Ness'** ('Snow Sprite'), collected from the slopes of Mt. Olympus. Marble-white flowers and stamens, pale green foliage. This is worth looking for. 8–10 in.

Geranium maculatum

flower color	pink
bloom time	spring
size	1–2 ft. × 1 ft.
light	part shade, shade
zones	Z3–8

SPOTTED GERANIUM, WILD GERANIUM, WOOD GERANIUM Woodlands and clearings of eastern North America. This slight, clump-forming woodlander bears clusters of upward-facing, saucer-shaped, 1.5-in. flowers in varying shades of pink, over pairs of deeply lobed and toothed stem leaves. Seeds may be ejected from dehiscing fruits more than 20 feet. Pest and disease free, but not the showiest of the genus. Attractive to butterflies; appropriate for native plant and wild gardens.

'Espresso' has dramatic non-fading, reddish brown leaves beneath pink flowers. Excellent as a groundcover, especially for dry places. ***G. albiflorum*** is a white-flowered form.

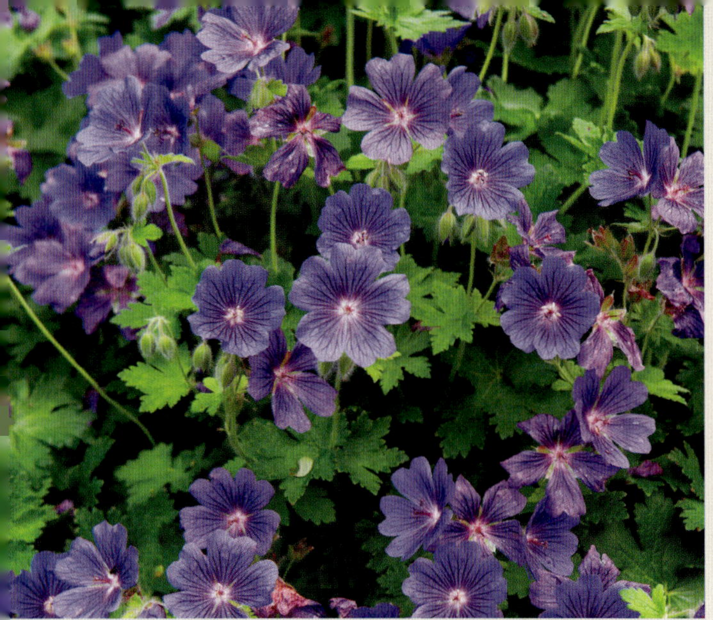

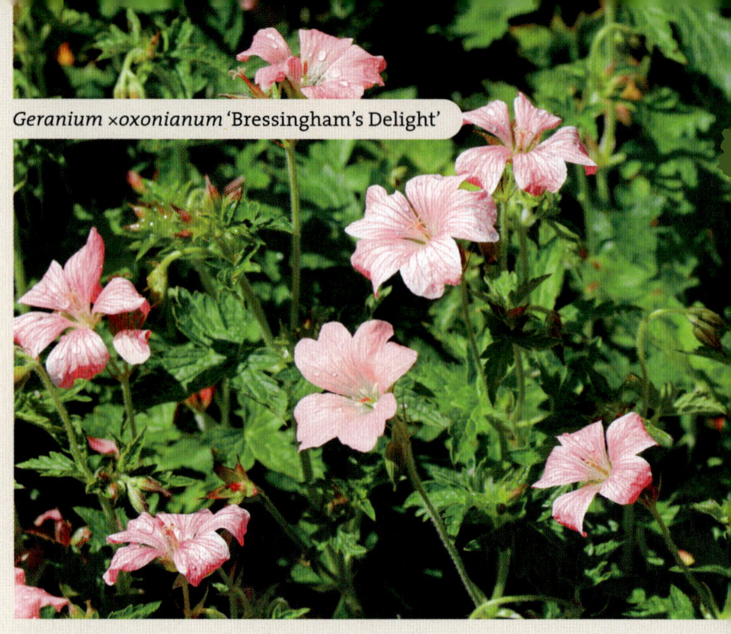

Geranium ×oxonianum 'Bressingham's Delight'

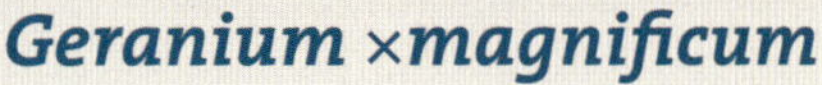

Geranium ×magnificum

Flower color	violet-blue
Bloom time	late spring to early summer
Height/Spread	18–24 in. × 24 in.
Light	sun, part shade
Zones	Z4–8

SHOWY GERANIUM, PURPLE GERANIUM Of garden origin (*G. ibericum* × *G. platypetalum)*. Sterile, vigorous, with abundant bloom. Soft, divided basal leaves, to 6 in. wide. Vivid 1.5-in., violet-blue flowers veined with purple. Mass along pathways and border edges, or use as a focal point in large rock gardens.

Geranium ×oxonianum

Flower color	pink
Bloom time	spring
Height/Spread	1–2 ft. × 2 ft.
Light	sun
Zones	Z4–8

HYBRID GERANIUM Of garden origin (*G. endressii* × *G. versicolor*).

'A. T. Johnson' has dark-veined, silvered pink flowers. Shear after bloom time to promote a possible second crop. Long blooming. Light green, lobed foliage, semi-evergreen in mild climates. 12–18 in. **'Rose Clair'** and **'Claridge Druce'** are similar. **'Bressingham's Delight'**. Soft pink flowers from spring to fall. Deeply lobed, rounded leaves. 1–1.5 ft. Z5–8. **'Katherine Adele'** has very pale pink flowers 0.75 in. across veined with purple. Leaves are marked with bronze in the centers. A seedling of **'Walter's Gift'**. 15 in. tall.

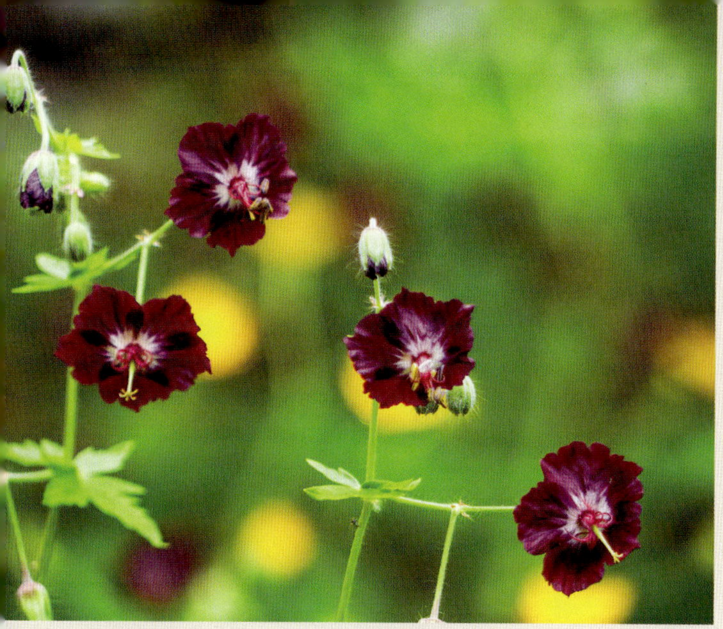

Geranium phaeum

Color	maroon
Bloom	late spring to early summer
Size	18–24 in. × 12 in.
Light	sun, part shade
Zones	Z3–7

MOURNING WIDOW, DUSKY CRANESBILL Native to damp meadows of Europe. Erect stems rise from thick roots that ensure survival during drought. Deeply divided leaves, 4–8 in., are spotted with purple at their base. The unusual pendent, almost black but variable, 0.75-in. flowers are more curious than showy, with pointed, slightly reflexed petals and strongly exserted stamens.

'Album'. Flowers are white or faintly pink blushed. **'Lily Lovell'** has large, purple-mauve flowers to 1.5 in. across, and light green leaves. **'Raven'** is a selection with unblotched, pale green foliage. 18 in. **'Samobor'** has deep burgundy flowers above variably marked purple leaves. May self-seed. Shear after bloom for fresh foliage. 18 in. Z6–8.

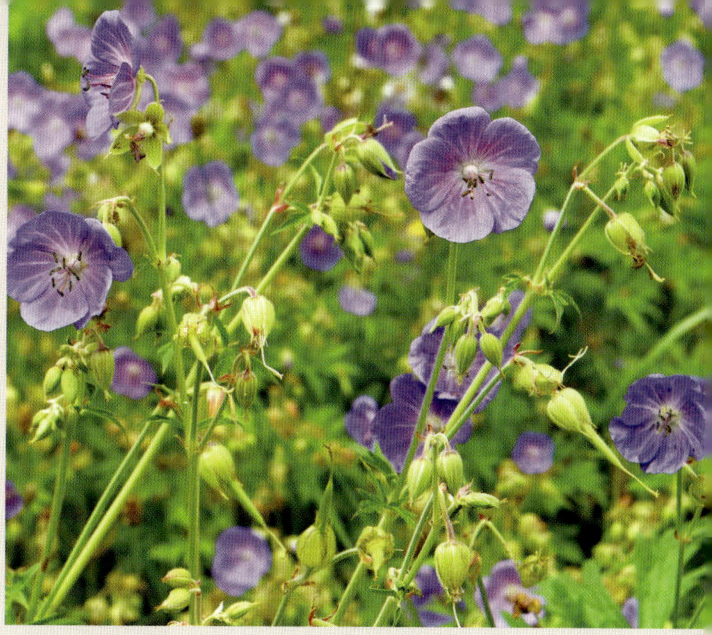

Geranium pratense

Color	white, blue, violet
Bloom	late spring to midsummer
Size	24–36 in. × 24 in.
Light	sun, part shade
Zones	Z5–7

MEADOW CRANESBILL Northern Europe, Asia. Crowded inflorescences of blue, violet-blue, or white, saucer-shaped flowers, 1–2 in. across. Deeply divided leaves are jaggedly lobed and toothed. May need staking, especially in warm climates. Seeds freely. Prefers acid soil but tolerates lime.

'Laura' has masses of sterile, double, white flowers. Very long blooming. Mounds of cut leaves; suitable for cottage gardens or borders. 24 in. **'Midnight Reiter'**. Deep burgundy foliage, non-fading, dark lilac flowers. A gem for plant collectors, selected from the Pacific Northwest. Appropriate for rock gardens and troughs. 6–8 in. × 12–16 in. Z5–7. **'Plenum Violaceum'** is sterile, with rosette-like, 1-in., double, deep violet flowers, centered with dark purple. Clumps of divided, irregularly lobed, and toothed leaves rise from stout, fleshy roots. 18 in. Z3.

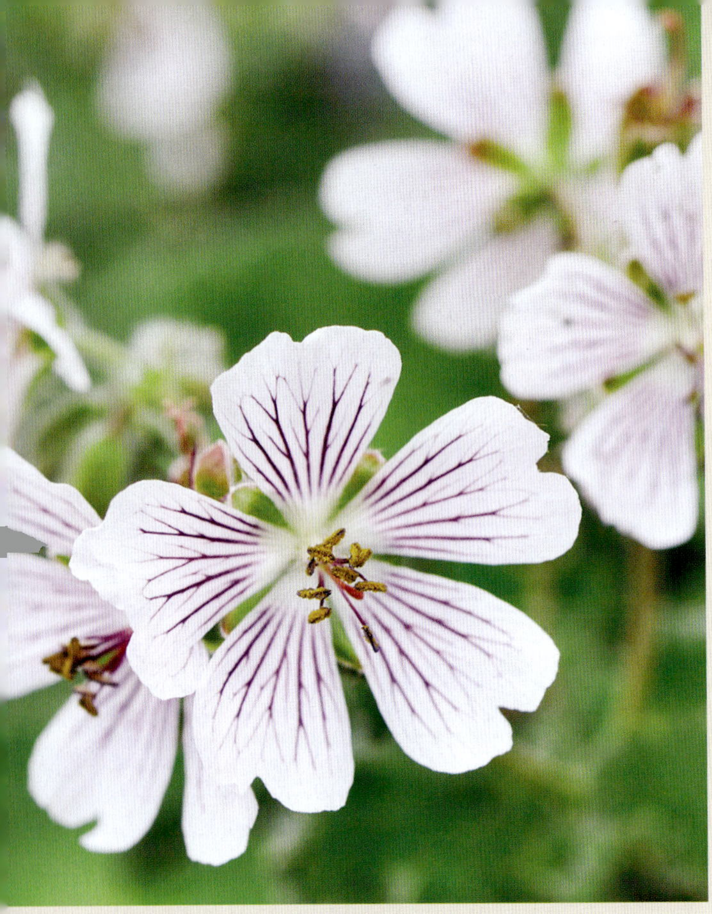

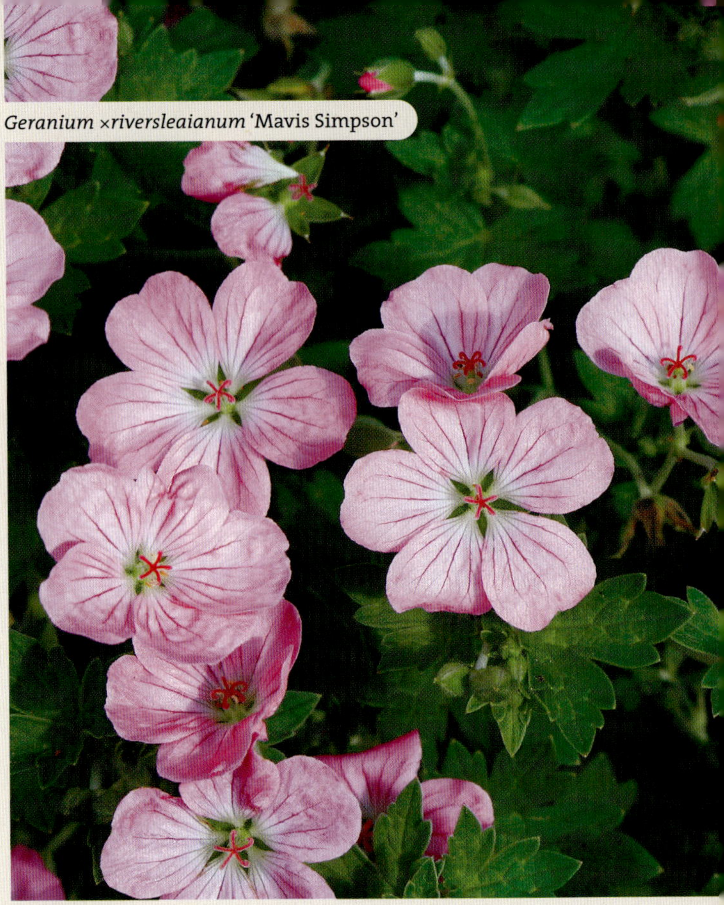

Geranium ×riversleaianum 'Mavis Simpson'

Geranium renardii

color	white
bloom time	late spring to early summer
size	1 ft. high and wide
light	sun, part shade
zones	Z6–8

DWARF CRANESBILL Caucasus Mountains. Low clumps of wrinkled, grayish leaves to 4 in. across. These are as soft as a kitten's ear, and are split halfway into blunt, barely lobed divisions. The white or lavender-flushed, 1-in. flowers cluster in dense umbels, but bloom is sometimes sparse. Grown for its wonderful foliage. Lovely in rock gardens, and where soil is poor.

Geranium ×riversleaianum

color	pink, magenta
bloom time	summer
size	10–12 in. × 24 in.
light	sun, part shade
zones	Z6–8, HS

CRANESBILL Of garden origin (*G. endressei* × *G. traversii*). Long, trailing, branching stems bear deeply divided, gray-green leaves 2–4 in. across. Funnel-shaped, dark-veined, bright pink or magenta flowers, 1.5 in. across, and with notched petals, bloom in summer.

'Mavis Simpson' sports 1-in.-wide, light pink flowers with cream eyes and purple veins. 18 in. **'Russell Pritchard'** bears intense magenta flowers above lobed and sharply toothed, grayish green leaves. 9 in.

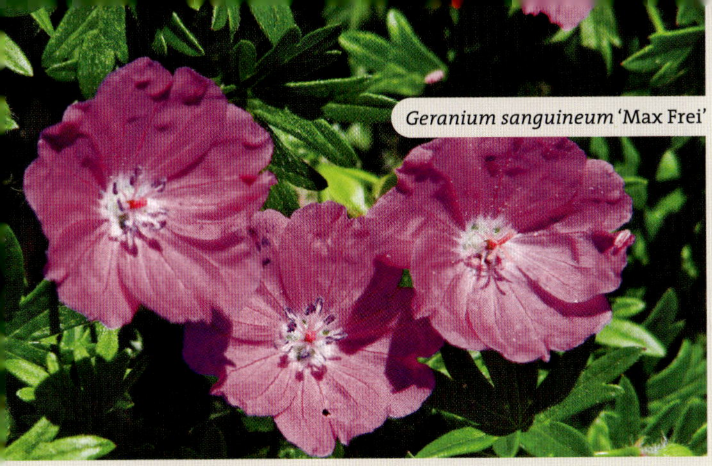

Geranium sanguineum 'Max Frei'

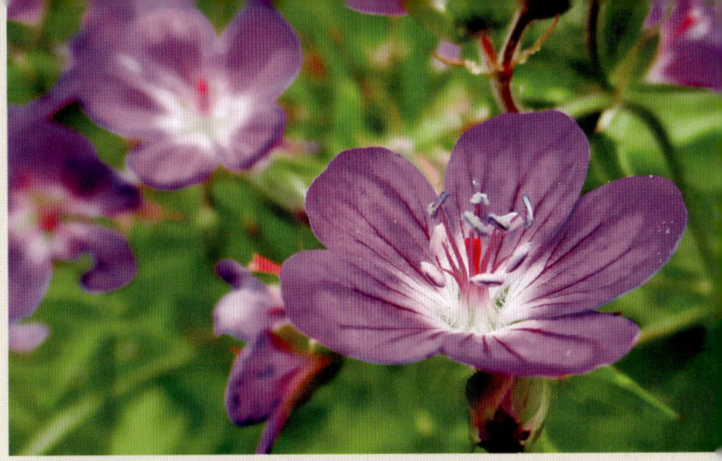

Geranium sanguineum

Color	magenta
Bloom time	spring
Size	9–12 in. × 12 in.
Light	sun, part shade
Zones	Z4–8

BLOODY CRANESBILL Europe, northern Turkey. Dense, clumping perennial with far-reaching rhizomes. Few basal leaves; deeply divided into several segments, dark green, 2- to 4-in. stem leaves are seldom toothed. Good fall color in sun. Abundant upward-facing, cup-shaped, vibrant magenta, 1.5-in. flowers with notched petals, purple veining, and white eyes that face upward.

'Album' has pure white flowers; a loose billowy habit. 18 in. **'Alpenglow'** displays bright reddish rose blooms on clumps 8 in. tall and to 24 in. across. **'Cedric Morris'** has slightly softer deep pink, 1-in. flowers; long blooming. To 24 in. **'Max Frei'**. The reddish purple flowers attract butterflies in summer. Fine groundcover with good fall color. Cut back to revitalize the plant if foliage becomes shabby. 6–9 in. **Var. *striatum*** (syn. *Geranium sanguineum* var. *lancastriense*, *G. sanguineum* var. *prostratum*), striped cranesbill, has light pink flowers with a deeper pink eye and darker veining. Excellent as a groundcover, edging, or a rock garden plant. 4 in. **'Splendens'** is taller with similar flowers to 1.75 in. across. 18 in. Do not confuse with shorter *G. cinereum* 'Splendens'.

Geranium sylvaticum

Color	pink, white, violet
Bloom time	mid- to late spring
Size	1–2 ft. high and wide
Light	part shade
Zones	Z5–8

WOOD CRANESBILL, WOODLAND CRANESBILL Damp meadows of Europe, particularly Iceland, northern Turkey. Early blooming, with usually purple-violet (sometimes pink or white), white-eyed, 1-in. flowers appearing with tulips and late daffodils. Deeply cut, roundish leaves, 6–7 in. across.

'Mayflower'. Mats of deeply cut leaves; light blue-violet, 1.5-in. flowers, white at the base. 2–2.5 ft.

Geranium wallichianum

(color)	pink
(bloom time)	early summer to early fall
(size)	9–12 in. × 18 in.
(light)	sun, part shade
(zone)	Z4–8

WALLACH'S GERANIUM Northeastern Afghanistan to Kashmir. Trailing, non-rooting stems make this prostrate geranium easy to control. Scrambling and weaving through taller plants or tumbling over walls or rocks, this species and its cultivars make a showy splash of color. Pairs of somewhat wrinkled, marbled, and coarsely divided leaves measure 2–6 in. long. White-eyed, purple-veined, flattish, 1- to 1.5-in. flowers are deep pink, purple, or blue.

'Buxton's Variety' ('Buxton's Blue'). Superior and more compact than the species. Purple-veined, brilliant blue flowers accented with a central white halo. Sprawling carpets of slightly mottled leaves. Perfect at the front of beds and borders, perhaps backed by dark coleus, *Coreopsis* 'Moonbeam', or *Salvia* 'East Friesland'. **'Crystal Lake'** has glowing crystal blue flowers prominently etched with dark purple veins. Palm-shaped, marbled foliage. Long blooming and easy care. 18 in. Z5–9.

Other Notable Cultivars

'Ann Folkard' is a superior hybrid with deeply cut, yellowish green foliage on trailing stems that scramble and weave through sturdier companions.. Rich magenta flowers are punctuated with a black eye. Best in cool-summer regions in part shade. 8 in. × 3–4 ft. **'Brookside'** is very long blooming with bowl-shaped, white-eyed, sapphire-blue flowers from spring into midsummer; it repeats as weather cools. Cut back after the first flush of bloom. Heat tolerant. Good fall foliage color. 12–18 in. Z5. **'Cheryl's Shadow'** develops a slowly spreading, compact mound of dark maroon foliage that remains attractive all season. Light pink flowers in spring. 6–10 in. Z7–10. **'Johnson's Blue'** has 2-in.-wide, periwinkle-blue flowers. Finely cut leaves become red and gold in fall. Cut back after the first flush. Slightly sprawling (more so than 'Rozanne') but a good weaver. 18 in. Z4–10. **'Nimbus'**. Possibly superior to 'Johnson's Blue'. Violet-eyed, lavender-blue flowers above mounds of dissected leaves. Good in containers, coastal gardens, and for edging beds, borders, and paths. 20 in. Z4–8. **'Orion'** is a seedling of **'Brookside'**. Abundant large, lilac-blue, purple-veined flowers all summer above finely dissected foliage. 18–24 in. **'Rozanne'** ('Gerwat'; syn. *Geranium wallichianum* 'Buxton's Variety' × *G. himalayense*) is certainly among the best of the hardy geraniums for beds and borders. Very long blooming with cupped, brilliant violet-purple, white-eyed flowers, to 2.5 in. across. Good-looking foliage. Heat tolerant. Perennial Plant Association Plant of the Year for 2008. Strikingly similar 'Jolly Bee' may be a synonym. 18–24 in. Z5–8.

CYCLAMEN

Cyclamen

PRIMULACEAE

THE MOST FAMILIAR of the cyclamens is *Cyclamen persicum*, the Persian, florist's, or greenhouse cyclamen that is often forced into flower for the holiday season and sold by the millions as decorative houseplants or to be planted out in frost-free areas. They have been hybridized extensively for compact growth, attractively marked foliage, diminutive size, jewel colors, and more attributes. However, as beautiful as they are with their attractive heart-shaped foliage and brightly colored, swept-back petals, few succeed outdoors year-round in colder gardens. Fortunately, the same beauty is also found in hardier species that also hail from the eastern Mediterranean.

Cyclamen grow from corm-like tubers that gradually expand with age. From these emerge plain or variously silver-marked, rounded or heart-shaped leaves borne on succulent stems, above which rise swept-back flowers in reds, pinks, and white, mostly blotched at the nose with deep red. Cyclamens grow best in a slightly alkaline, well-drained soil. They go dormant after blooming and should then be allowed to rest; ideally, keep the soil barely damp. All parts of the plants are mildly toxic if ingested, but are still acceptable to browsing deer. Sometimes known as sow bread, alluding to the fact that pigs root for the tubers in the wild.

If flowers are pollinated, seed capsules develop at the tips of spiraling stems and split when seed is mature. Sow as soon as ripe. Protect seedlings and young plants from digging squirrels.

Cyclamen cilicium

color	white, pink
bloom	fall
size	2–3 in. × 6–8 in.
light	sun, part shade
zone	Z6–9

HARDY CYCLAMEN Evergreen woodlands of the mountains of southern Turkey. Pale pink to rosy flowers blotched with purple on the nose. Deep green, rounded or heart-shaped leaves, boldly marked with silver, appear with or just after the flower buds in fall. Bloom lasts for several weeks; the foliage persists into spring. There is a white-flowered form. Add composted pine needles to the soil to raise acidity and increase drainage. Excellent in dry shade under deciduous trees and shrubs. Good for containers.

Cyclamen coum

color	white, pink
bloom	winter to early summer
size	2–3 in. × 6–8 in.
light	part shade, shade
zone	Z4–9

EASTERN CYCLAMEN Western Black Sea coast of Bulgaria, east to Iran, Turkey, Lebanon, and Israel. Rounded, deep green leaves patterned with silver, or plain but lustrous. After the leaves have appeared, flowers bloom in several shades of pink, rimmed with white at the snout and stained purple red. Provide a site with diffuse light, especially under tall deciduous trees where soil is humus rich and moisture retentive but not waterlogged. Tolerates drought well. Plant tubers shallowly, slightly above soil level; appreciates a winter mulch. Sometimes catalogs separate clones with different leaf markings into groups such as the "Pewter Group."

'Album' (f. *albissimum*) has white flowers marked with carmine at the nose. **'Silver Leaf'** bears exquisite heart-shaped, silvery leaves with a dark green center.

Cyclamen hederifolium

syn. *C. hederifolium* 'Rosenteppich', *C. neapolitanum, C. immaculatum*

flower color	white, pink
bloom time	late summer to early fall
size	4–5 in. × 6–8 in.
light	sun, part shade, shade
zones	Z4–8

IVY-LEAVED CYCLAMEN Grows wild from southern France to the Balkans, and along the northern Mediterranean and Aegean Sea to western Turkey. The hardiest species, it does best in soil generously enriched with humus to improve soil tilth and moisture retention. Mulch in summer, and in regions with intense sunlight protect from midday rays. Excellent under high deciduous trees, where a colony may increase and thrive for many years; in time, the tubers may grow to 3 in. or more across. Nodding flowers and foliage appear at the same time, or the pointed flower buds may precede the foliage that then persists through the winter months into the following spring. Gray-green leaf blades are usually marked with purplish silver and held at an angle on long pedicels (stalks). Plant the tubers as soon as you receive them, less than 1 in. deep. Plants are very variable. Suitable for container culture.

'Album' ('Perlenteppich') has all-white flowers.

Cyclamen purpurascens

syn. *C. europaeum*

flower color	red, purple
bloom time	summer to fall
size	4–5 in. × 6–8 in.
light	part shade, shade
zones	Z5–9

PURPLE CYCLAMEN Central and southern Europe. This woodlander is happy in alkaline soil amended with plenty of composted leaf mold; less tolerant of summer drought than some other species. The dark reddish purple flowers are fragrant and start to bloom at the same time as the leaves emerge in mid- to late summer and into early fall. The foliage remains evergreen, sometimes for ten or so months. Not a great seed producer, except in very favorable conditions. A sugary coating envelops the seed coat to attract ants that serve as seed disseminators.

DAYLILY

Hemerocallis | XANTHORRHOEACEAE

THIS GENUS EPITOMIZES ONE of the greatest challenges facing the perennial gardener today: How do you make choices when the menu has become so huge? Currently, there are some 60,000 hybrids registered with the American Hemerocallis Society, and more are added daily.

Fortunately, it isn't necessary to review every alternative. Nursery workers divide hybrid daylilies into several classes based on characteristics including the size of the plant and the form, color, and blooming season of the flowers. Becoming familiar with this system enables you to identify which class will suit the aesthetics of any garden spot. Consider the cultural conditions within your garden and weed out all but those groups of hybrids adapted to it. An abundance of choices will remain, but by applying these two sets of criteria, any selection you make will be successful.

Evergreen daylilies (cultivars that maintain foliage year-round) tend to be the best choices for hot-climate gardens. Dormant daylilies have foliage that dies down in fall prior to winter dormancy and usually are the best choices for cold-climate regions.

Hemerocallis foliage is strap shaped, long, and narrow. Leafless stems (scapes) carry the flowers; they have parts in threes. Hybridizers have added a range of new flower forms to the genus, including many doubles. There are three basic flower size categories: "dwarf" is a compact daylily that produces scapes under 12 in. tall (like 'Black-Eyed Stella'); "miniature" has flowers 3 in. in diameter or less (as in 'Peach Fairy'); and "tetraploid" describes daylilies with double the normal number of chromosomes. These tend to be more vigorous than diploids; flowers are usually larger, more intensely colored, and with heavier substance, on sturdier scapes. 'Chicago Apache' is an example.

There are many flower types and forms:

- Single flowers retain their original, wild type configuration. Popular cultivars include 'Hyperion' and 'Rosy Sunset'.
- Double flowers have modified, petal-like stamens that create the appearance of extra petals. Examples include 'Siloam Double Classic' and 'Prester John'.
- Circular flowers are rounded in outline with overlapping petals and sepals. Examples include 'Sir Francis Drake' and 'Stella De Oro'.
- Triangular flowers have sepals that recurve (curve backward) more than the petals. Examples include 'Barbara Mitchell' and 'Shaka Zulu'.
- Star-shaped flowers are closed at the throat, with long, sometimes pinched petals, and recurving narrow sepals. Examples include 'Burgundy Star' and 'Cream Giant'.
- Spider and spider variants have attenuated petals and sepals, much longer than normal in proportion to their width. Examples include 'Aabachee' and 'Tarantula'.

Single flowers

Double flowers

Circular flowers

Triangular flowers

Star-shaped flowers

Spider and spider variants

Typically individual flowers don't last longer than a day, but so many buds are produced that a single plant may bloom for 30 to 40 days.

Early-season daylilies typically bloom in late spring to early summer. Midseason daylilies bloom in early to midsummer. Late-season bloom is usually four to six weeks after peak season. There are also repeat bloomers (also known as "remontant" and "recurrent") that produce more than one flush, or bloom several times over the course of a growing season. Brassy golden 'Stella De Oro' begins flowering with the early season cultivars and continues blooming almost continuously until fall.

The color range among the hybrids is extraordinary, with hues from pale cream and yellow through gold and orange to red, pink, and purples, even near blacks; only true whites and true blues are lacking. The yellow and oranges are particularly showy when intermixed with blue delphiniums and hydrangeas, for example. White Shasta daisies provide an effective foil to colorful daylily blossoms. Massed or planted in drifts, daylilies shine against an evergreen background.

Average garden soil suits most daylilies, but they will tolerate poor, well-drained soils that retain moisture; drought tolerant when established. A site with full sun to part shade is perfect; with less than six hours of sun, daylilies survive but bloom sparsely. Daylilies have a well-deserved reputation as low-maintenance perennials, but the hybrids vary in vigor; the less vigorous often show greater susceptibility to pests. Remove spent blooms daily to maintain a neat appearance; divide congested clumps every few years to maintain vigor and enhance bloom.

Common pests include aphids, spider mites, and thrips, but they rarely pose a serious threat to healthy plants. Slugs and snails can be a problem. Rabbits are seldom troublesome, but daylilies are at the top of the gourmet menu for deer.

Divide in spring or fall; start your own seeds and see what results.

Hemerocallis citrina

	yellow
	late spring to early summer
	3–4 ft. × 1.5–2 ft.
	sun, part shade
	Z3–9

CITRON DAYLILY Northeastern China. Thick clumps of arching, narrow leaves to 40 in. long. Fragrant, 6-in., trumpet-shaped flowers are borne on scapes to 45 in.; blooms open at sunset and close the following morning. Tolerates a range of soil types.

Hemerocallis dumortieri

	yellow
	midspring
	18–24 in. × 24 in.
	sun, part shade
	Z3–9

DUMORTIER'S DAYLILY Japan, Korea, Manchuria, eastern Siberia. This very early bloomer may flower six to eight weeks earlier than most other daylilies. The leaves are narrowly strap-shaped; 3- to 4.5-in. flowers are lemon yellow, streaked with brown on the back. Delicately fragrant.

Hemerocallis lilioasphodelus

syn. *H. flava*

Color	yellow
Bloom time	midspring to late spring
Size	2–3 ft. × 1.5–2 ft.
Exposure	sun, part shade
Hardiness	Z3–10

LEMON DAYLILY China. Trumpet-shaped, 4-in.-wide, lemon flowers are very fragrant; borne on erect, 3-ft.-tall scapes. One of the earliest to bloom. Similar to *Hemerocallis citrina*, this species is tough and exceptionally tolerant of poor soils and summer heat and humidity.

DEAD NETTLE

Lamium

LAMIACEAE

DEAD NETTLES ARE AMONG the most popular plants for groundcovers for North American and Canadian gardens. Like their mint family relatives—mints, sages, and thymes—they are square stemmed with pairs of more-or-less evergreen leaves and two-lipped, hooded flowers. Although many of the 50 or so species of *Lamium* are weedy and unsuitable for ornamental gardens, those mentioned here are valuable, mannerly perennials.

In large part, this outstanding clan is grown for its foliage, borne on stoloniferous stems. Leaves are mostly kidney shaped or triangular, coarsely toothed, wrinkled, and often attractively marked with silver or white. Flowers are white, yellow, or pink-purple, some marked with darker speckles on the lower lip. The uppermost petal forms a protective hood over the pollen-bearing stamens.

Dead nettles are easily grown in average to fertile, moderately moist soils; the sprawling stems root at the nodes. They adapt to sun, part shade, or even shaded sites. They are challenged by combined heat and humidity.

Space dead nettles closely as groundcover, to fill in quickly and smother weeds. Valuable at the front of borders, to face down low shrubs, in rock gardens; they also thrive in containers with other shade lovers such as Chinese astilbe 'Pumila', lungworts, and coral bells. The most showy-foliaged specimens can stand alone in interesting containers. Mostly pest and disease free, but watch for slug and snail damage. Seldom browsed by deer.

To propagate, detach rooted plantlets, or take cuttings in early summer. Some cultivars come true from seed.

Lamium galeobdolon

syn. *Lamiastrum galeobdolon*

Color	yellow
Bloom	spring
Size	8 in. × 18 in.
Light	part shade, shade
Zone	Z4–8, HT

YELLOW ARCHANGEL, FALSE LAMIUM Europe, western Asia. Often seen as a neglected groundcover, yellow archangel provides a handsome, weed-proof blanket only if plants are cut back hard before new growth appears in spring and after bloom; pinch back straggling shoots to encourage bushiness. This otherwise low-maintenance perennial tolerates dry and alkaline conditions well; can be aggressive in rich soil. Round-toothed, mid-green, 2.5-in. leaves often marked with silver; mostly evergreen. Hairy, brown-spotted, bright yellow flowers cluster in whorls in the upper stem nodes. Heat tolerant. Mostly grown for foliage.

'Herman's Pride' makes neat mounds of dark green, metallic leaves, flecked with silver; yellow flowers. **'Variegatum'** ('Florentinum'). Foliage has broad splashes of silver; yellow flowers. A fine groundcover.

Lamium maculatum

	red, pink, white
	spring to fall
	8–12 in. × 18 in.
	sun, part shade, shade
	Z4–8

SPOTTED DEAD NETTLE, SPOTTED HENBIT Native to moist grasslands and light woodlands in Europe, northern Africa to Lebanon, Syria, and Turkey. Erect to sprawling stems, usually well branched at the base. Opposite, triangular or heart-shaped, toothed leaves are softly hairy, often striped or blotched with white or silver. Flowers cluster in verticillasters in the upper leaf axils; mostly pink or purplish, with darker freckles on the two lower lobes. Bloom time is extended: the first flush appears in midspring, tapers off in summer heat, but reblooms as weather cools, usually lasting until the first hard frost. Excellent planted close as an evergreen groundcover. Pinch straggling shoots to keep compact.

Other Notable Cultivars

'Anne Greenaway', a British selection, has small, green-and-silver leaves, irregularly edged with chartreuse. Mauve-pink flowers. Exciting planted solo in a black container. **'Aureum'** ('Gold Leaf') has bright lemon-yellow leaves, striped with white down the middle. Pink flowers. **'Beedham's White'** is similar but with white flowers. **'Beacon Silver'** has green-rimmed silver leaves, red-flushed stems, and pinkish purple flowers. **'White Nancy'** has white flowers, light green stems, and green-rimmed silver leaves. Supplies a cool clean look in shade. **'Red Nancy'** has rosy red flowers. Intolerant of heat and humidity. **'Pink Chablis'** blooms from spring until hard frost in fall. Silver leaves edged with dark green. Flowers in shades of pink. A superior selection from Garry Grueber. **'Purple Dragon'** has silver leaves edged with green; large, purple flower clusters. Silver leaves edged with green; large, purple flower clusters.

DELPHINIUM | LARKSPUR

Delphinium | RANUNCULACEAE

THE HYBRID DELPHINIUMS that are cultivated to such perfection in English mixed borders, with their head-high, regal spires of vividly colored blossoms, are rightfully iconic. However, they are also finicky plants that in the United States perform well only in such cool, moist regions like the Pacific Northwest, and even here require plenty of nurturing. This has led too many American gardeners to dismiss delphiniums out of hand. In fact, this remarkably diverse genus offers hardy species adapted to almost every region of our country. Indeed, many are native to this continent. Additionally, in recent years breeders have introduced new strains of hybrids that offer many of the assets of their English relatives, but combine them with a more vigorous, self-sufficient constitution.

Few perennials are as effective as delphiniums in providing a vertical accent in beds or borders. Although the pattern of growth varies somewhat with the species, delphiniums typically produce clusters of upright, sometimes branching stems, crowned in season with flowers borne in spikes or racemes, sometimes in panicles. Each flower consists of five petal-like sepals surrounding a "bee" of two to four smaller true petals at the center, and commonly with a spur projecting from the back. Although blue is the color associated with delphinium flowers in the popular imagination, delphinium blossoms include pigments for red and yellow as well; depending upon the balance of pigments, flowers can range from pale cerulean to deep blues and violets to pinks, reds, yellows, and white. Delphinium leaves may be basal or alternate on the stem, and are palmately lobed or divided.

Delphiniums prefer a well-drained, humus-rich soil and thrive in full sun to light shade. Recommended care includes regular deep watering during spells of rainless weather, feeding in early spring and fall with a balanced (avoid high-nitrogen products) slow-release fertilizer, and staking to support the individual flower spikes of taller hybrids. Cut spent spikes back to their bases to encourage rebloom of laterals.

Pests and problems are legion, and include slugs and snails on succulent young growth, and black-spotted foliage caused by cyclamen mites; curled and distorted leaves are usually a symptom of aphids; yellow and stunted plants may indicate nematodes. Black, foul-smelling decay at the base of plants is caused by bacterial crown and root rot; powdery mildew can disfigure stems and foliage, and stunt growth. The flowers attract butterflies, bees, and hummingbirds, but they resist deer and rabbits.

Delphiniums are poisonous in all or some of their parts, and cause skin irritation in some people. Protect your hands with gloves. Never decorate food plates with these flowers.

Plants can be started from seed or propagated by dividing healthy plants. Cuttings of young shoots root readily in spring.

Delphinium ×*belladonna*

	various
	spring to summer
	3–4 ft. × 2 ft.
	sun
	Z3–10, HS

BELLADONNA DELPHINIUM Of garden origin. A group of hybrids that derives principally from crosses between *Delphinium elatum* and *D. grandiflorum*. Characterized by finer foliage and somewhat smaller stature than the classic border delphiniums, the belladonna hybrids require less staking than their loftier relatives. They bear loose racemes of single or double, 1.5- to 2-in. flowers on branching stems over an extended season; deadheading promotes another flush in late summer. Mildew resistant.

'Belladonna' bears light blue, single flowers. **'Bellamosum'** ('Bellamosa') has dark blue blossoms. **'Casa Blanca'** has pure white, single flowers. **Connecticut Yankee Hybrids** produce single flowers in shades of white, blue, lavender, and purple on numerous branched stems. Seldom need staking; ideal for small gardens. Compact at 24–30 in. × 10–14 in.

Delphinium cardinale

	red
	spring to summer
	6 ft. × 2 ft.
	sun
	Z7–10, HS

SCARLET LARKSPUR This Californian thrives on well-drained soils in hot, dry areas, with occasional deep irrigation. Palmately divided leaves, with 1-in., vivid scarlet flowers with yellow bees. Plants become semi-dormant after bloom; withhold water until growth resumes. Propagate from seed.

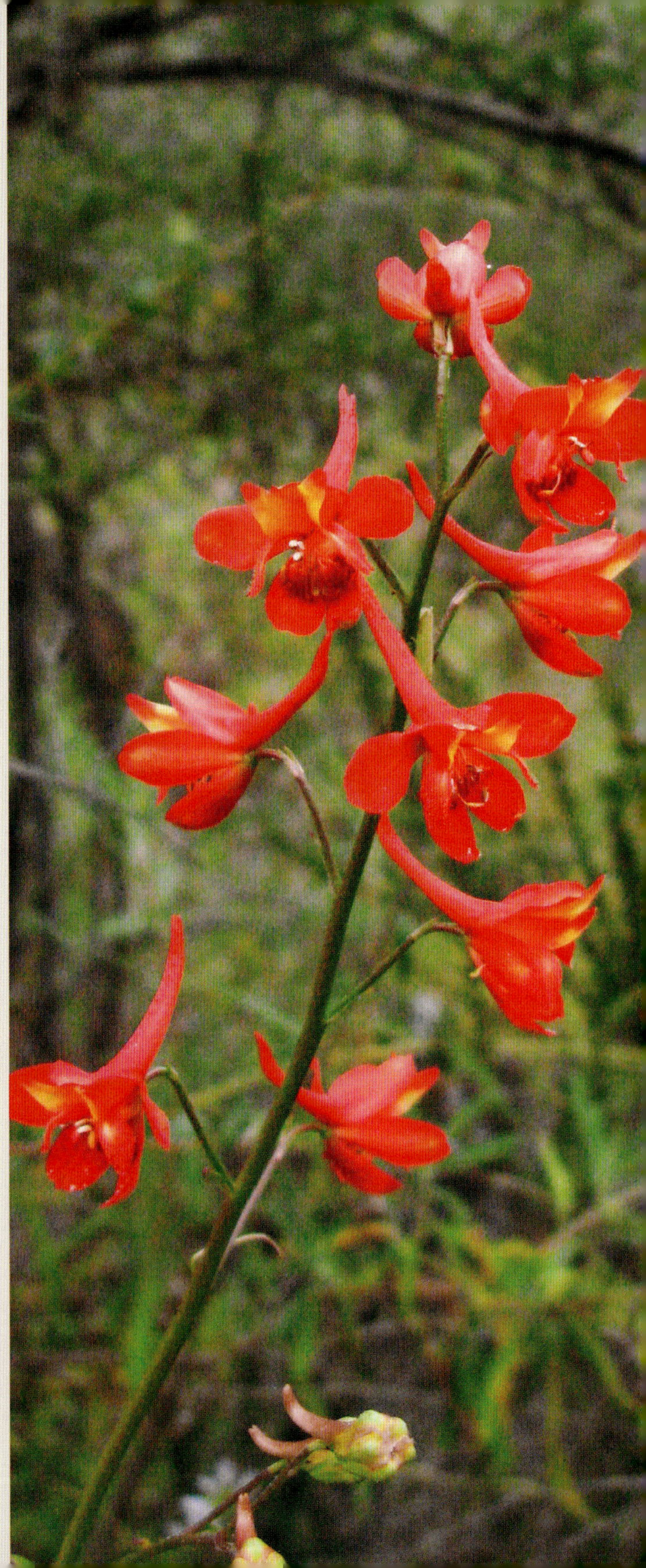

Delphinium ×*elatum* 'Red Caroline'

Delphinium ×*elatum*

	various
	late spring to early summer
	3–6 ft. × 2 ft.
	sun, part shade
	Z3–7, HS

TALL HYBRID DELPHINIUM Of garden origin. The quintessential English border delphiniums were bred by crossing Siberian *Delphinium elatum* with *D. exaltatum* and *D. cheilanthum*. This hybrid group comes with double and single flowers in shades of white, yellow, pink, blue, and purple.

Such tall, imposing flowers require adequate support. Install three stakes as tall as the ultimate projected height in a triangle around each plant, early in the growing season; tie in stems periodically as they extend upward. Propagate from soft cuttings or start from seed.

Blackmore and Langdon Strain, long a favorite from California, has exceptionally large flower spikes that reach a height of 5 ft. or more; blossoms in hues ranging from creamy yellows through blues and purples to pink, often with a contrasting bee at the center of each flower. Usefulness in North American gardens is limited by sensitivity to humid heat. **Blue Fountains Strain** is dwarf at 2.5–3 ft. tall in shades of blue. Available as seed. **New Millennium Series** is a collection of 14 color-themed strains of delphiniums bred by Terry Dowdeswell of Dowdeswell's Delphiniums, Wanganui, NZ. Double or single flowers, often with a contrasting bee. They are winning popularity for their superior hybrid vigor and improved resistance to disease and environmental stress. Available as seed; each strain offers subtly different expressions of the basic type. 3–5 ft. 'Blue Lace' has light, sky-blue petals with a pinkish tinge. 'Innocence' sports fluffy, fully double, pure white flowers. 'Pink Punch' has frilled flowers in pink and purple shades, with striped bees. 'Royal Aspirations' is deep sapphire to navy blue with contrasting white bees. **Pacific Giant Strain** is another favorite. True to their name, in perfect conditions these California-bred cultivars can reach a height of 8 ft. Semi-double, 3-in. blossoms in white, pink, lavender, and blue. Garden favorites since their introduction in the 1930s, the Pacific Giants have, according to experts, degenerated over the decades, losing vigor and the purity of their colors. **'Princess Caroline'** has pink flowers. 24 in. tall. **'Red Caroline'** represents a breeding color breakthrough, a border delphinium with double, true-red blossoms. Stems are 4- to 6-ft. Propagate vegetatively.

Delphinium grandiflorum 'Blue Mirror'

Delphinium grandiflorum

	blue
	spring to summer
	1–2 ft. × 1–1.5 ft.
	sun
	Z3–8

CHINESE OR SIBERIAN DELPHINIUM, SIBERIAN LARKSPUR Russia and China. Forms compact, bushy mounds of deeply palmately divided, dark green leaves and loose, airy racemes of blue or white flowers. Typically short-lived but self-seeds readily.

'Blue Mirror' bears gentian-blue flowers over a prolonged season.

Delphinium nudicaule

	red
	spring to summer
	1–2 ft. × 1 ft.
	sun, part shade
	Z4–10, HS

DWARF SCARLET LARKSPUR California and Oregon. Single or double, long-spurred, orange-red flowers. Intolerant of winter damp as well as summer humidity. Often short-lived.

'Laurin' has bright scarlet flowers.

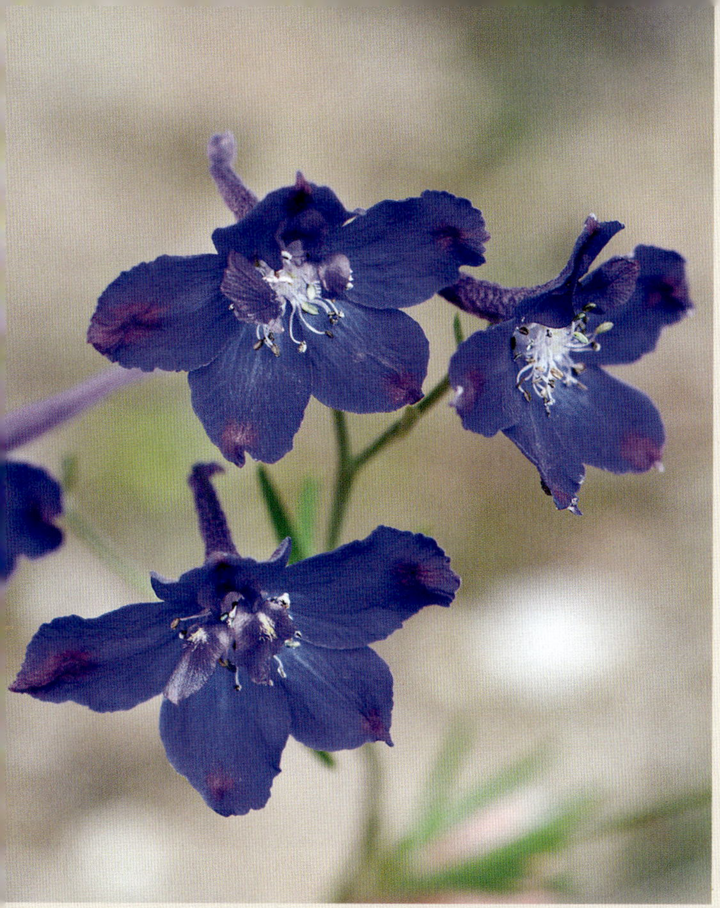

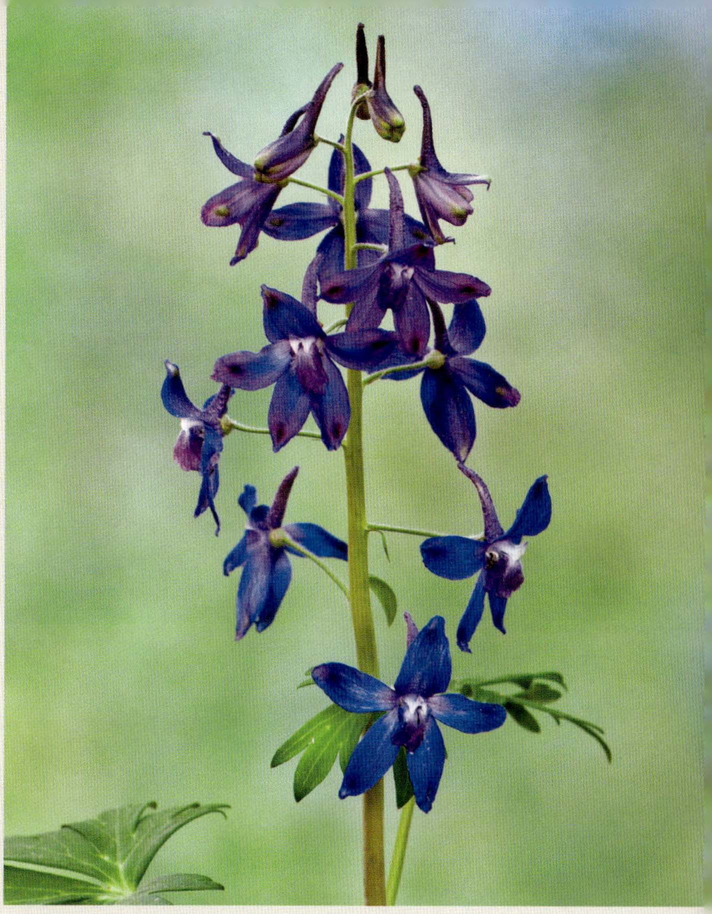

Delphinium tatsienense

Color	blue, white
Bloom time	spring to summer
Size	1.5–2 ft. × 1–1.5 ft.
Light	sun
Zones	Z6–10, HS

CHINESE DELPHINIUM Western China. This bushy, compact species is suited to the front of a bed or border, or containers. Hirsute leaves are divided into three segments; 1.25-in. flowers borne in branched racemes. Start from seed.

Sky Lights Strain bears white, pale blue, or deep blue flowers. Blooms the first year from seed. 10–12 in. tall.

Delphinium tricorne

Color	white, blue-purple
Bloom time	early spring
Size	18–24 in. × 9 in.
Light	sun, partial shade
Zones	Z4–7

DWARF LARKSPUR Native to eastern and midwestern North America, this species blooms for three weeks in early spring. It bears 0.75- to 1-in., lavender-blue to dark purple flowers with white bees, with occasional all-white-flowered specimens. Prefers average to moist, humus-rich soils; self-sows readily before going dormant with summer's onset. Attracts bees and butterflies, and ideal for wildlife or native plant gardens, and on the edge of light woods. Combine with wild sweet William seed.

FAIRY BELLS

Disporum | CONVALLARIACEAE

THIS GENUS OF ASIAN WOODLAND NATIVES offers a number of fine garden perennials. Until recently, it also included half a dozen North American natives as well, and though botanists have renamed these as *Prosartes* and reclassified them as members of the lily family, these species are still commonly sold under their former names, so we've kept them here.

These are not flamboyant plants; their attractions, though considerable, tend more to the discreetly elegant. Their bell-shaped or star-shaped blossoms are modest, but they are combined with attractive foliage and berries; their adaptation to shade makes them very useful for shady borders and woodland gardens. When selecting a site for fairy bells, dappled sunlight is ideal, but they do tolerate full shade. They prefer humus-rich, moist but well-drained soils with a somewhat acid pH—they do not tolerate drought. Thanks to their rhizomatous root systems, fairy bells tend to spread once established, although they do so at a manageable rate, making them valuable groundcovers. They are natural companions for other shade lovers such as hostas, astilbes, and ferns.

Propagation is by seed, sown in the fall and overwintered in a cold frame or other protected spot, or by division of mature plants in early spring.

Disporum cantoniense

(flower color)	white
(bloom time)	midspring to early summer
(size)	4–6 ft. × 2–3 ft.
(exposure)	part shade, shade
(zone)	Z5–9

CANTONESE FAIRY BELLS A highly variable Chinese species that has upright or arching stems bearing lanceolate, green, variegated, or even purple leaves, typically 5 in. long and 2 in. broad. White, pale yellow, or even red flowers. Noted plant explorer Dan Hinkley has introduced two outstanding cultivars:

'Green Giant' produces bamboo-like shoots that emerge in shades of pink, white, and green, before maturing to deep green. Fragrant, creamy-white, bell-shaped flowers followed by black fruit in fall. 6 ft. Z7–9. **'Night Heron'**, whose leaves open a lustrous deep red-burgundy in spring before fading to greenish purple in summer. Creamy, bell-shaped flowers are borne in terminal clusters atop 5- to 6-ft. stems, and are followed by glistening black-purple fruit. Z5.

Disporum flavens

syn. *D. uniflorum*

(flower color)	yellow
(bloom time)	early to midspring
(size)	24–30 in. × 9–12 in.
(exposure)	part shade, shade
(zone)	Z5–8

FAIRY BELLS A Korean species that forms a slowly spreading clump. Lanceolate leaves may reach 6 in. long; flower buds appear at the stem ends with the new growth in spring, opening into small clusters of tubular, 0.5- to 1-in.-long, soft yellow flowers. Berries that ripen to black in late summer follow the flowers; fall foliage color can be an attractive yellow.

Disporum lanuginosum

syn. ***Prosartes lanuginosa***

yellow

early to late spring

1–3 ft. × 1 ft.

part shade, shade

Z4–7

YELLOW FAIRY BELLS, YELLOW MANDARIN Native from Ontario south through Appalachian region to Alabama. Forms patches of delicately branched, zigzagging stems bearing ovate, glossy green leaves to 6 in. long and 2 in. wide, with prominent veins from base to tip. Flowers, which may reach up to 0.8 in. long, are yellow-green, nodding, and bell shaped, flaring at the mouth. Bright red berries follow in fall.

Disporum sessile

white

early to midspring

2 ft. × 3 ft.

part shade, shade

Z5–8

JAPANESE FAIRY BELLS This eastern Asian native requires an evenly moist, rich, acid soil. Where these conditions are met, growth tends to be rapid, developing into dense clumps of stemless, lanceolate, bamboo-like foliage. Showy, white, bell-shaped flowers dangle from stems. Good for the front of the border and edgings as well as woodland gardens.

'Variegatum' is compact, with white-and-green-striped flowers and foliage. To 16 in. tall.

FALSE INDIGO | WILD INDIGO

Baptisia | FABACEAE

ALTHOUGH WELL-KNOWN TO Native Americans who used false indigo as a source of blue dyes, this genus has only recently found a major place in US gardens. Native to eastern and midwestern North America, baptisias vary in stature and flower color, but in general bear pea-like flowers in showy spikes in spring, and trifoliate, commonly blue-green leaves. The leaves are arranged alternately on stems that cluster in dense, shrub-like groups. Baptisias' naturally neat form and tolerance for poor soils, even clays and rocky ones, as well as drought, has made them staple plantings over the last decade. As their popularity has grown, they've attracted interest from plant hybridizers, especially at the Chicago Botanic Garden and North Carolina Botanical Garden. A steady stream of refined and floriferous cultivars and hybrids have appeared in recent years, with flowers in novel colors and bicolored combinations.

False indigos perform best on sunny sites, though they also tolerate partial shade. They are taprooted and difficult to transplant: container-grown specimens are easier to establish in the garden than bare-root stock. However, their long taproots equip baptisias to reach deeper than many plants, making them exceptionally drought tolerant. Shear and shape the plants after flowering (unless saving the seed pods) to encourage compact growth and eliminate the need for staking. Seldom attacked by pests and diseases; resistant to deer.

Baptisias are attractive in beds and borders as single specimens or in groups of several plants. The larger types can be imposing and are useful for adding structure to perennial or mixed plantings, or even planted among low shrubs. Their season of bloom coincides with Siberian irises and peonies, both of which make fine companions. A blue-flowered baptisia energizes a predominantly yellow planting; the blue-green foliage common to many harmonizes nicely with silver-foliaged plants like lavenders. These tough plants work well in prairie plantings, native gardens, and meadows, and their combination of striking flowers and handsome foliage makes them useful additions to cottage gardens. Baptisias attract butterflies. If left unsheared, the plants produce plump black seedpods that are popular elements of dried flower arrangements.

Propagate the species by seed; scarify seed to allow water to penetrate the hard seed coat. Sow in containers to avoid transplant shock when planting out later. Propagate named cultivars by stem cuttings taken in spring while still green and soft.

Baptisia albescens

syn. *B. alba*

Color	white
Bloom	early spring to midspring
Size	2–4 ft. × 2–2.5 ft.
Light	sun, part shade
Zone	Z5–8

WHITE FALSE INDIGO Southeastern United States. Multiple small, white, pea-like flowers, to 0.5 in. long, carried in numerous 12-in. spikes or racemes atop charcoal-black flower stems; these rise above a mound of clover-like, trifoliate, bluish green leaves that remain attractive for most of the season.

Var. *alba* (syn. *Baptisia pendula*) reaches a height of 3–4 ft., with pendent, large, black seed pods. **Var. *macrophylla*** (syn. *B. leucantha*, *B. lactea*) has white flowers on 5- to 7-ft. stems.

Baptisia australis

Color	indigo blue
Bloom	mid- to late spring
Size	3–4 ft. high and wide
Light	sun, part shade
Zone	Z3–9

BLUE FALSE INDIGO Rich woods, thickets, and stream banks from Pennsylvania, south to North Carolina and Tennessee. Upright bushes of leafy stems bear bold spires of blue pea flowers. May need support in less than full sun. Prune after bloom to shape as a shrub "wannabe," although this forfeits the rattling, black seedpods. Excellent naturalized in meadows or used to control erosion on difficult banks. 2010 Perennial Plant of the Year.

Var. *minor* (syn. *Baptisia minor*) is more compact than the species, reaching half its height and spread.

Baptisia sphaerocarpa 'Screamin' Yellow'

Baptisia sphaerocarpa

color	yellow
bloom time	mid- to late spring
size	2–3 ft. × 2–3 ft.
light	sun, part shade
zone	Z5–8

YELLOW WILD INDIGO Missouri to Oklahoma, south to Louisiana and Texas. Yellow flowers (to 0.5 in. long) in abundant 12- to 15-in. spikes borne atop yellow-green stems above a mound of blue-green foliage. Spherical seedpods to 0.75 in. ripen to tan and then brown.

'Screamin' Yellow' may reach 5 ft. Bears a profuse crop of yellow flowers above mounds of yellow-tinged, green foliage. From Larry Lowman's program.

Other Notable Cultivars

Several of these were introduced by Jim Ault at Chicago Botanic Garden and Rob Gardner at the North Carolina Botanical Garden in Chapel Hill.

'Dutch Chocolate' bears chocolate-purple flowers over mounded, blue-green foliage. Late spring to early summer. 2.5–3 ft. × 2 ft. Z4–9. **'Midnight Prairieblues'** bears 24-in.-long spikes of violet-blue flowers over three to four weeks in early summer. 48 in. × 48–54 in. Z4–9. **The Prairieblues Series**, from the Chicagoland Grows program, was bred especially for regions with very cold winters and hot summers, although they thrive in most parts of the country: 'Solar Flare Prairieblues' is golden yellow. 36 in. × 36–48 in. 'Starlite Prairieblues' has soft blue flowers; 'Twilite Prairieblues' has bicolored burgundy-and-lemon flowers. 5 ft. high and wide. Z4–8. **'Purple Smoke'** carries black stems with smoky violet flowers in midspring. 3–4 ft. Z4–9.

FLAX | PERENNIAL FLAX

Linum

LINACEAE

Common flax (*Linum usitatissimum*), the source of linen and of flax seed, is the best-known member of this genus, which also includes some garden-worthy perennial species. Perennial flax are long blooming, and supply some of the garden's most vivid blues. Individual blooms open early on sunny days but often are spent by late afternoon. Flax prefers lean, well-drained soils. They may self-seed.

Propagate by seed, by cuttings of young basal shoots in spring, or divide mature plants.

Linum flavum

flower color	yellow
bloom time	summer
size	10–12 in. × 8–12 in.
exposure	sun
zone	Z5–7

GOLDEN FLAX, YELLOW FLAX Native to central and southern Europe. Upright clumps, sometimes woody at the base, are clothed with dark, spoon-shaped foliage. Funnel-shaped, upward-facing, bright yellow flowers to 1 in. across are arranged in dense terminal cymes.

'Compactum' is only 6 in. tall.

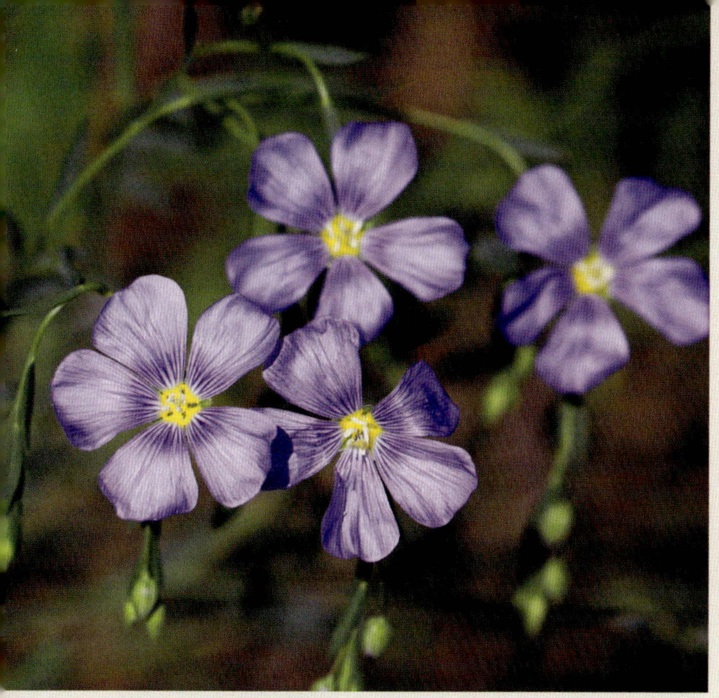

Linum lewisii

syn. *L. perenne* subsp. *lewisii*

- blue
- late spring to early summer
- 12–24 in. × 8–12 in.
- sun
- Z3–9

PRAIRIE FLAX, LEWIS'S BLUE FLAX, WESTERN BLUE FLAX Native to grasslands, meadows, and disturbed soils throughout the United States west of the Mississippi River. Species named for its discoverer, Meriwether Lewis, co-leader of the Lewis and Clark Expedition. This short-lived native bears needle-like, blue-green leaves and five-petaled, 2-in.-wide, sky-blue flowers that open fully only on sunny days. Deer tolerant, but slugs, snails, and aphids may be troublesome; attracts butterflies. Susceptible to stem rot, rust, damping off, and other fungal and bacterial problems. Appropriate in dry, sunny meadows, prairie and perennial plantings, open woodlands, rock gardens, and containers.

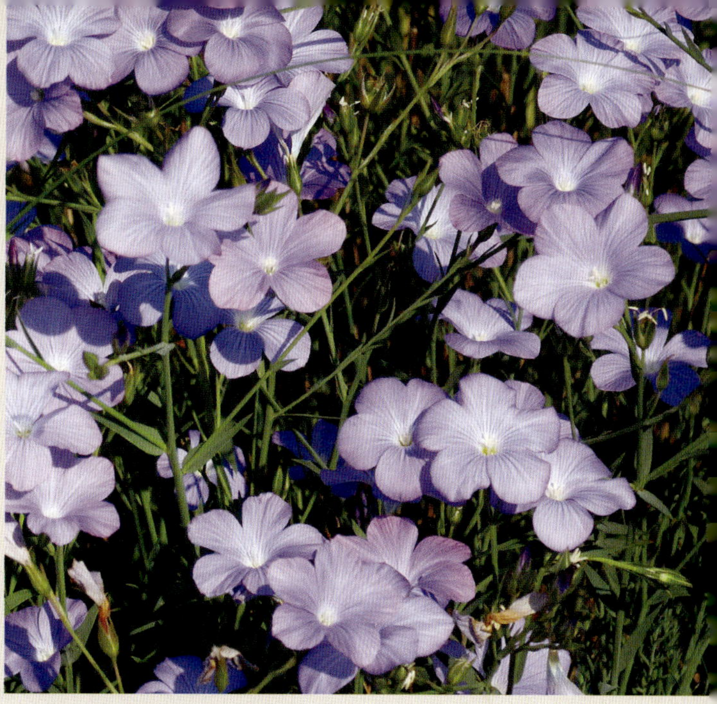

Linum narbonense

- blue
- late spring to early summer
- 18–24 in. × 15–18 in.
- sun, part shade
- Z5–9

SPANISH BLUE FLAX Native to northern Spain. Narrow, gray-green leaves arranged in whorls around the stems, topped by cymes of about ten saucer-shaped, five-petaled, 1-in., sky blue flowers accented with white eyes. Supposedly longer lived than more common *Linum perenne*. Ideal along paths, among rocks on sunny slopes, and in dry gardens.

'Heavenly Blue' has deep blue, white-eyed flowers. 18 in.

Linum perenne

color	blue
bloom time	late spring to early summer
size	1–2 ft. × 9–18 in.
exposure	sun, part shade
zones	Z5–8

PERENNIAL FLAX, BLUE FLAX, PERENNIAL BLUE FLAX Europe, temperate Asia. Short-lived, tufted perennial with wiry stems and narrow, linear leaves to 1 in. long. Funnel-shaped, sky blue flowers, borne prolifically for eight weeks or more, are five-petaled, to 0.75 in. across. Tolerates dry, shallow, and rocky soils; naturalizes where conditions are suitable. Mass for best displays in rock gardens, meadows, and herb gardens.

'Appar' has outstanding vigor, a long season of bloom, and is a strong reseeder that mixes well with grasses and other wildflowers in erosion control mixes. **'Nanum Diamond'** shows off clean white flowers. 10–12 in. **'Nanum Sapphire'** bears bright blue flowers on 8–10 in. stalks.

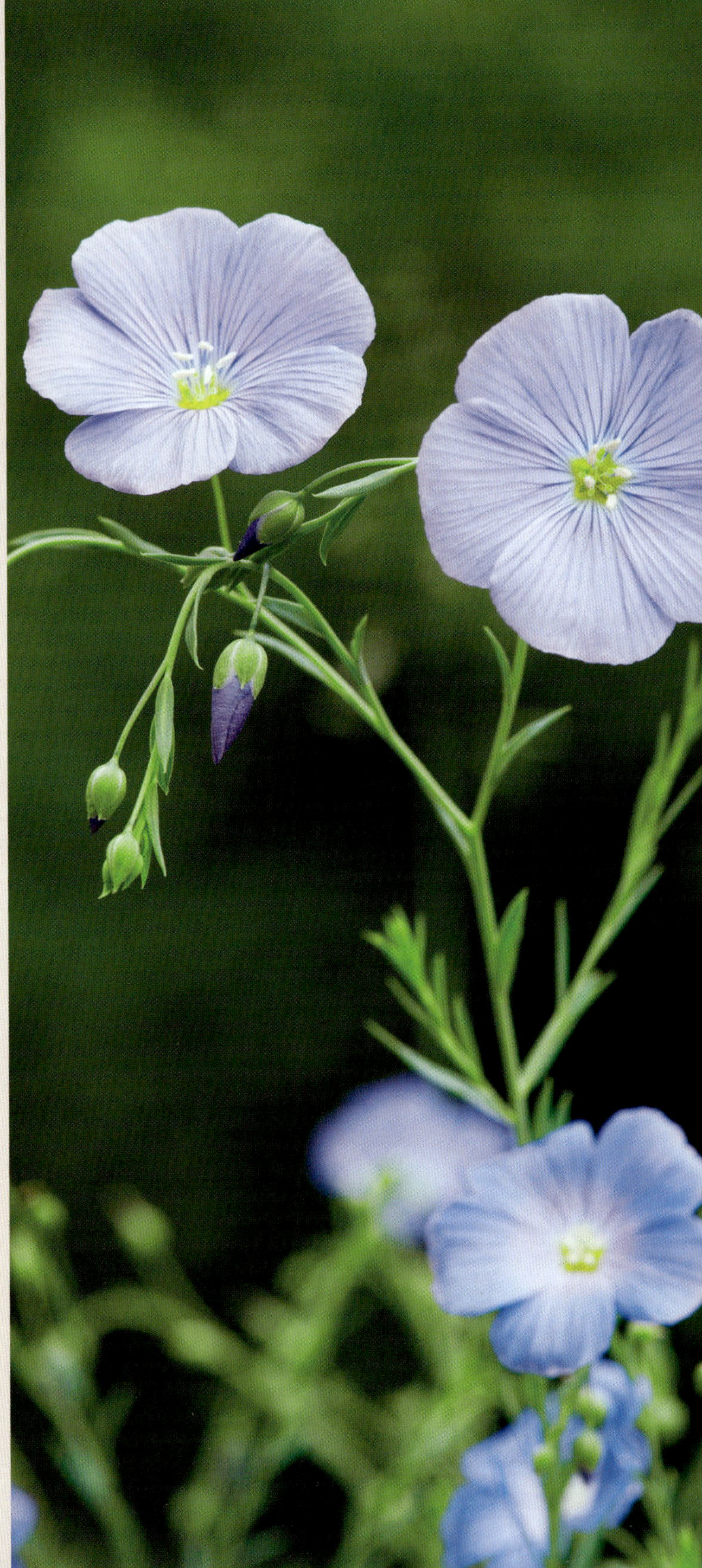

FLEABANE | SEASIDE DAISY

Erigeron

ASTERACEAE

THESE UNFORTUNATELY NAMED PERENNIALS are easy to grow, tolerant of most soils and sites, good for cutting, and (reputedly) repel fleas. Furthermore, they are long blooming, bearing charming aster-like flowers, each with two or more rows of ray flowers surrounding yellow disk florets.

Found throughout the temperate zone, this genus includes many North American natives. Several, such as *Erigeron philadelphus* and *E. canadensis*, are considered weeds, although the former is sometimes included in wild, native, or meadow gardens. The showiest fleabanes are mostly hybrids with parentage that often includes orange fleabane, *E. aurantiacus*, and daisy or showy fleabane, *E. speciosus*. Though aster lookalikes, fleabanes mostly bloom prior to the aster season in spring and summer. Flowerheads may be single or semi-double, and either solitary or clustered in flat-topped inflorescences. Basal leaves are petioled, but the stem leaves are alternate and often clasping.

Well-drained soil is a must, and once established, plants tolerate dry soils well. Taller selections—which may require staking—make fine cut flowers; harvest when the flowers are fully open. Only occasionally browsed by deer, more often by rabbits.

Divide in spring or start from seed for bloom the following season.

Erigeron aurantiacus

- orange
- summer to late summer
- 12 in. high and wide
- sun
- Z4–8

ORANGE FLEABANE Turkestan native. Basal rosettes of spatulate, softly downy, 3- to 4-in. leaves; stem leaves clasp the stem. Flowerheads are 1–2 in. across, bright orange with green disks, and borne singly atop slender, upright stems. Short-lived, but easy to start from seed in spring; early seedings usually bloom the first season.

Erigeron glaucus

color	mauve
bloom	spring to summer
size	10–12 in. × 12 in.
light	sun
zone	Z3–9

SEASIDE DAISY, BEACH FLEABANE, BEACH ASTER Ocean bluffs and ravines in coastal California and Oregon. Evergreen, gray-green leaves are glaucous, spoon-shaped, and blunt at the tips, to 6 in. long, sometimes rimmed with teeth. Slender-rayed, semi-double flowerheads bloom for several weeks. Excellent in free-draining sandy soils in cottage and rock gardens, as edging plants, between pavers, atop stone walls, and in containers. Salt tolerant; an important plant in seaside gardens. Attracts insects and butterflies. Deadhead to extend bloom time, and cut back hard every couple of years to maintain vigor. Provide light midday shade and extra water in inland gardens.

'Bountiful' is compact, with very long-blooming, 3-in., lavender flowerheads. 6–10 in. **'Cape Sebastian'** has whitish foliage and violet flowerheads. 12 in. **'Roger Raiche'** is upright with purple flowers. Long bloom time. To 18 in. **'Sea Breeze'** produces 1.5-in.-wide, pinky-mauve blooms in abundance in midspring and continues through summer if deadheaded routinely. 8–12 in. Z7.

Erigeron karvinskianus

color	white, pink
bloom	spring to fall
size	6–24 in. × 36–60 in.
light	sun
zone	Z7–11

MEXICAN DAISY, BONYTIP FLEABANE, SANTA BARBARA DAISY Mexico to Venezuela. Excellent as a trailing groundcover, Mexican daisy is covered with small white or pink-flushed daisies all summer. Prefers sandy, free-draining soil and full, but not intense, sun. Blooms the first season if seed sown in early spring, and self-seeds abundantly. Can become aggressive and is difficult to eradicate. Delightful tumbling over rocks and walls, and in containers. Tough but charming pink Santa Barbara daisy, *Erigeron* × *moerheimii*, is very similar but sterile, and more compact. Both are great attractors of beneficial insects.

'Profusion' bears white flowers that fade to pink. Spreads freely. 6–8 in.

Erigeron speciosus

color	lilac
bloom time	summer
size	12–30 in. × 24 in.
exposure	sun, part shade
zone	Z2–7

DAISY FLEABANE, SHOWY FLEABANE, OREGON FLEABANE, ASPEN FLEABANE Western United States. From woody rootstocks rise multiple stems clothed with clasping leaves and branching at the top. Each branch is topped with narrow-rayed but showy 2-in.-wide flowerheads. Tall selections may require staking. Best in temperate climates where summers are cool. Cut back after blooms are spent to encourage rebloom and help the new basal growth overwinter successfully. Seldom cultivated outside of native plant gardens. One of the dominant parents of the showy hybrid group (*Erigeron* ×*hybridus*), along with *E. alpinus*, *E. aurantiacus*, *E. speciosus* var. *macranthus*, and sometimes *E. glaucus*.

Other Notable Cultivars

Erigeron hybrids were formerly more popular in American gardens than they are today, especially the series bred by famed British plantsman Alan Bloom. These and others are still offered by mail from British nurseries. The following are available in the United States as of this writing.

'Darkest of All' is one of the best and most popular selections with deep violet flowers. 24 in. **'Pink Jewel'** produces masses of semi-double, 1.5-in., orchid-pink flowers. Excellent cut flower. 24 in. Z4. **'Prosperity'** is getting more difficult to find in the marketplace, but is well worth growing for its large, semi-double, lavender-blue daisies on 18-in. stems. Good cut flower. **'Rotes Meer'** ('Red Sea') has several layers of shocking pink ray flowers encircling a yellow center.

FOAMFLOWER | SUGAR SCOOP

Tiarella

SAXIFRAGACEAE

THIS GROUP OF EXTRAORDINARY woodlanders offers outstandingly handsome foliage, ethereal bloom, and two patterns of growth—spreading and clump forming—to satisfy a diversity of needs. Most are natives of North America and require little care if given a shady site with moist, organic-rich soil. Depending on the species and type, the leaves are divided into three to nine lobes, rounded like columbine or lobed like a red maple; they are often highlighted with black or red patterning, and the foliage commonly takes on a reddish cast during cool weather. Borne in airy racemes in spring, the tiny flowers are white with very long stamens, creating the frothy effect referred to in the plants' common name.

Closely related to heucheras, with which they have been interbred to create so-called ×*Heucherella*. In recent years, breeders have also crossed different species to create a host of fine new hybrids. Whereas the species bloom for just three to six weeks, some hybrids may remain in flower for months. The spreading species provide shade-loving, handsome, and dependable groundcovers; the clump formers provide valuable foliage interest and texture to shady borders and woodland displays.

No serious pest or disease problems; deer resistant. Wet soil in winter is usually fatal. Divide hybrids in spring; sow seed of species and overwinter outdoors with protection.

Tiarella cordifolia

Flower color	white, pink
Bloom time	mid- to late spring
Size	9–12 in. × 12–24 in.
Light	part shade, shade
Zone	Z4–9

HEARTLEAF FOAMFLOWER Nova Scotia and Ontario to Georgia and Mississippi, west to Minnesota. Spreads rapidly by stolons to form clumps to 2 ft. wide. Green, medium glossy, three- to five-lobed, heart-shaped leaves to 4 in. wide, red along the veins. Evergreen where winters are mild, commonly becoming reddish bronze in cold weather. Racemes of white or light pink flowers bloom for six weeks in spring on mostly leafless stems above the foliage.

Tiarella trifoliata

syn. *T. trifoliata* subsp. *unifoliata*, *T. trifoliata* var. *unifoliata*

Flower color	white
Bloom time	early summer
Size	4–20 in. × 8–24 in.
Light	part shade, shade
Zone	Z6–10

SUGAR SCOOP Damp coniferous forests, Alaska south through California, east to Montana and Idaho. Broadly heart-shaped, three- to five-lobed, scallop-edged leaves, 2–4 in. wide. Small, white, starry flowers gather in spikes, followed by little, scoop-shaped pods. Removing spent flower stalks may prompt rebloom. Moderately moist, well-drained soil; irrigate every 10 to 14 days in dry weather during growing season.

Tiarella wherryi

flower color	white
bloom time	midspring to fall
size	12–18 in. × 12 in.
exposure	part shade, shade
hardiness	Z5–8

FOAMFLOWER Woodlands of southeastern United States. Forms non-spreading clumps of slightly fuzzy, maple-like, lobed leaves, evergreen in mild winters; green accented with purple, burgundy in winter. Creamy-white flowers in 1- to 6-in. spikes for six weeks, with occasional rebloom in fall.

Other Notable Cultivars

'Crow Feather'. Bright green leaves traced with purple-black turn pink, red, purple, and blackish in winter. Light pink spring flowers. 8–12 in. × 12 in. Z4–9. **'Elizabeth Oliver'** is semi-spreading. Deeply cut, maroon-streaked, 2- to 3-in.-wide leaves turn purple in fall and winter. Light pink flowers. 12–15 in. × 12 in. Z4–8. **'Pink Skyrocket'**. Deeply cut, medium green leaves with central black blotch, shiny black in fall. Pink flowers in 12-in.-long spikes. 6–12 in. × 12 in. Z4–9. **'Sugar and Spice'** has mounds of colorful, pinnately divided foliage boldly marked with red. Bottlebrush racemes of pink flowers. 8–12 in. Z4–9.

FORGET-ME-NOT

Myosotis

BORAGINACEAE

NOTHING SAYS NOSTALGIC CHARM like forget-me-nots, and very few perennials are as easy to grow. If you can provide a moist, organic-rich soil in sun or part shade, forget-me-nots of one kind or another will flourish in your garden from Alaska to zone 9 on the West Coast. These mid- to late-spring bloomers display a range of flower colors from the namesake forget-me-not blue to pink and white. The five-lobed flowers are individually small but are borne in natural nosegays, and commonly spread seed to form increasing colonies. Almost mandatory for cottage gardens, forget-me-nots combine well with astilbes, bergenias, and coral bells in woodland gardens, and are naturals for moist meadows, streambanks, or pondsides. Deer resistant; attracts butterflies.

Propagate by seed or division.

Myosotis asiatica

syn. *M. alpestris* subsp. *asiatica*

flower color	blue
bloom time	midspring to midsummer
size	6–12 in. × 4–6 in.
exposure	sun, part shade
zones	Z3–8, HS

MOUNTAIN FORGET-ME-NOT, ASIAN FORGET-ME-NOT Native to northern regions of the world, including from Alaska through the Pacific Northwest and the Rocky Mountains to Colorado. Commonly sold in the nursery trade as *Myosotis alpestris*, under which name it serves as the state flower of Alaska. Bloom season varies with the climate, being delayed in northern regions or at high altitudes. Leafless clusters of yellow-eyed, blue flowers to 0.3 in. Leaves oblanceolate to elliptic, to 5 in. long at base, shorter as they ascend the stems. Grows best on well-drained moist to wet soils with neutral pH. Ideal for rock gardens and containers. Susceptible to red spider mites, powdery mildew, and leaf rot, especially in hot summer weather.

'Ultramarine' produces prolific flushes of intensely deep blue flowers. **Victoria Series** offers cultivars with blue, pink, or white flowers.

Myosotis scorpioides

syn. *M. palustris*

bloom color	blue
bloom time	late spring to midsummer
size	6–12 in. × 9–12 in.
exposure	sun, part shade
zones	Z5–9

TRUE FORGET-ME-NOT, WATER FORGET-ME-NOT Temperate North America. Glossy, oblong to lanceolate, bright green leaves to 4 in. long; yellow-eyed, light sky-blue flowers are 0.25 in. across, borne in scorpioid cymes that uncoil as flowers open (like a scorpion extending its sting). Adapts to growing in shallow water to 3 in. deep; good for margins of water gardens, streams, and ponds, where it covers the ground (not aggressively) by creeping rhizomes. Pinch young growth to encourage bushiness. Insect and disease resistant, with the exception of mildew and rust.

Var. *semperflorens* is dwarf with heavier, longer bloom than the species. Repeat blooms sporadically to frost. 6–8 in. **'Southern Blues'** grows to only 6 in. but spreads vigorously. Sky-blue flowers. Exceptionally tolerant of sultry summers. **'Unforgettable'** has variegated, cream-edged foliage; bright blue flowers.

Myosotis sylvatica

bloom color	blue, pink
bloom time	mid- to late spring
size	6–12 in. × 6–9 in.
exposure	sun, part shade
zones	Z3–8

FORGET-ME-NOT European native that flourishes as a garden escapee in many parts of North America. Tufts of hairy, green, oblong-lanceolate leaves 1–3 in. long; dense cymes of yellow- or white-eyed, blue flowers, to 0.4 in. in diameter. Short-lived perennial, persists through self-seeding. Provide afternoon shade where summers are hot. Refined enough for borders or beds but also appropriate when naturalized at woodland edges or pond and stream margins. Excellent and traditional interplanting for spring bulb displays, forget-me-not foliage provides cover as bulbs fade into dormancy. Susceptible to mildew and rust.

'Bluesylva', part of the Sylva Series, has bright blue flowers and a compact growth habit. 6–8 in. × 12–18 in. The series also includes bright pink, white- or light yellow-eyed 'Rosylva', and white, yellow-eyed 'Snowsylva'. These are especially good for edging. **'Royal Blue Compact'** has sky-blue flowers, accented with white or yellow eyes. Compact. 6–8 in. × 4–6 in.

FOXTAIL LILY | DESERT CANDLE
KING'S SPEAR | *Eremurus* | ASPHODELACEAE

LOOKING FOR A DRAMATIC vertical focal point for your flowerbeds and borders? Foxtail lilies never fail to attract comment with their imposing, statuesque habit and bold bloom. The flower stems rise naked from octopus-like roots to bear at their tips dense, long, "bottle-brush" racemes of starry flowers, with prominent exserted stamens. Flowers open in succession from the bottom upward, ensuring a long bloom time; they serve as butterfly attractors and are excellent when cut. Arranged in a basal rosette, the thick leaves are broadly strappy and often become shabby, even during flowering, and retreat underground in summer; camouflage with attractive foliage of companion plants (bronze fennel works well) or plan to overplant with shallow-rooted annuals. Apply a winter mulch of leaves, compost, or straw after the ground freezes in fall to insulate from winter thaws and refreezes. Deep, rich, well-drained soil is essential for good results. It is best to plant the tubers in fall, 2–3 in. deep on a hillock or cone of soil (sand in heavy soil) with the pointed crown pointing up and the "fingers" spreading out and down 2–3 in. If the roots appear dried up upon receipt, soak them for a few hours before planting.

Foxtail lilies are ideal companions for flowering shrubs and show up well against a background of evergreens. Plant in groups between shrubby St. John's worts, hydrangeas, spireas, potentillas, or dwarf evergreens. They are also spectacular against a hedge or at the back of flowerbeds and borders, perhaps behind the bluish leaved false indigo (*Baptisia*). Reports differ as to the deer resistance of foxtail lilies; protect from slugs that attack the new growth.

Once established, do not disturb the brittle roots, except to divide the crowns in spring or fall carefully every few years to reinvigorate the plants and increase stock. Stratify seed before sowing; seedlings may require six years to reach blooming size.

Eremurus ×isabellinus 'Isobel'

Eremurus himalaicus

Flower color	white
Bloom time	late spring to early summer
Size	3–8 ft. × 3 ft.
Light	sun
Zones	Z3–8

FOXTAIL LILY, HIMALAYAN FOXTAIL LILY Temperate regions of the Himalayas and Afghanistan. Probably the hardiest species of *Eremurus*. Grayish green foliage to 2 ft. long, and white, 1-in. flowers clustered into tapering flower spikes up to 4 in. wide and 2 ft. or more long. Plant in a wind-protected spot, in front of a dark-colored solid fence, hedge, or other sheltering background; support in windy sites.

Eremurus ×isabellinus

Flower color	white, yellow, pink, red
Bloom time	early summer
Size	6 ft. × 2 ft.
Light	sun
Zones	Z5–8

FOXTAIL LILY This catch-all group includes many of the most sought-after and elegant flowers, resulting from crossing *Eremurus olgae* × *E. stenophyllus*. Soaring above their green, 6- to 12-in.-long leaves, tall, naked stems carry 6- to 18-in.-long racemes of starry, 1-in. flowers in various colors.

'Cleopatra' has orange flowers striped with red. 4–5 ft. tall **'Isobel'** is rosy pink flushed with orange. 5–6 ft. **'Pinocchio'** has bright yellow flowers. 3–6 ft. **'Romance'** has pale pink flowers with yellow stamens. 3–4 ft. **'White Beauty'** is pure white. 4–5 ft. tall.

Eremurus robustus

	pink
	early summer
	6–9 ft. × 3 ft.
	sun
	Z6–9

FOXTAIL LILY, GIANT DESERT CANDLE Rocky alkaline hillsides of Turkestan. This huge plant demands plenty of room and commands attention wherever it is grown. Smooth gray-green foliage is about 2 in. wide and up to 4 ft. in length. Columnar, 2- to 3-ft. racemes composed of countless fragrant, 1.5-in., peachy pink flowers with orange stamens, top ramrod-like scapes in early to midsummer. Attractive to honeybees seeking pollen. Requires a cold period in winter to induce blooming. Attractive companions include hardy geraniums, euphorbias, and species roses.

Eremurus stenophyllus

syn. *E. bungei*

	yellow
	late spring to early summer
	3–6 ft. × 3 ft.
	sun
	Z5–8

FOXTAIL LILY Central Asia, Iran. Tufted with grayish green, sometimes hairy leaves, to 10 in. Deep yellow, 0.75-in. flowers in dense racemes atop tall stems.

FUMEWORT

Corydalis | FUMARIACEAE

THIS GENUS WAS ALMOST UNKNOWN in American nurseries until the latter part of the twentieth century, but in the years since it has assumed a prominent place in our gardens. It deserves even wider planting. The generic name means "crested lark," a reference to their exquisite spurred flowers; these can illuminate partially shaded parts of the landscape with an invaluable burst of color. Note that two popular species formerly included in this genus, *Corydalis lutea* and *C. ochroleuca*, have recently been reassigned to their own genus, *Pseudofumaria.*

Corydalis roots are fleshy or tuberous, and their leaves are finely divided; depending on the species they may be yellowish, bronzy, or light green, often infused with a bluish cast. Flowers are tubular and spurred, usually held in dainty loose clusters at the tips of succulent stems. Corydalis requires a consistently cool, moist soil high in organic matter; in cold areas, mulch the plants well in winter. Few species tolerate muggy heat and humidity in summer. Where they flourish, they make excellent companions for small bulbs, ferns, epimediums, lungworts, lilyturf, and other shade lovers in woodlands, along pathways, and in rock gardens. Deer resistant; tubers are sometimes dug and devoured by squirrels and chipmunks.

Propagate by seeds sown outdoors in fall or indoors with stratification followed by bottom heat (65–75°F).

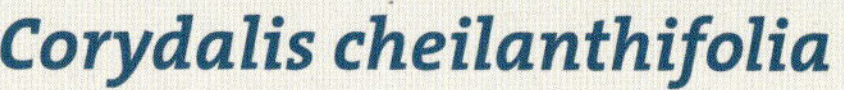

Corydalis cheilanthifolia

flower color	yellow
bloom time	spring
size	6–18 in. × 6–12 in.
light	sun, part shade
zones	Z3–8, HS

FERNLEAF CORYDALIS China. Very finely divided foliage, bronzy green with stronger bronze hue when young. Flower clusters held above the leaves and on separate stems. Fleshy rooted. Seeds about; collect seed when ripe (black) and sow in place. Resents transplanting. Beautiful with early miniature narcissus.

Corydalis elata

flower color	blue
bloom time	late spring to early summer
size	16 in. × 12 in.
light	part shade
zones	Z6–8, HS

BLUE CORYDALIS, BLUE FALSE BLEEDING HEART Sichuan Province, China. Cobalt-blue flowers appear after the foliage has emerged. This species is easier to grow and more heat tolerant than most *Corydalis flexuosa* selections, and not as prone to going dormant in summer heat.

Self-seeds once established. Be alert for rust, slugs, and aphids.

Corydalis flexuosa

Color	blue
Bloom time	late spring to summer
Size	12–15 in. × 12 in.
Light	part shade
Zones	Z5–8, HS

BLUE CORYDALIS Western Sichuan Province, China. Summer dormant growing from small bulbs. Light green foliage, sometimes flushed with purple, is twice divided into three. Long-spurred, bright blue flowers, white at the throat, crowd into terminal and axillary racemes. Humus-rich soil that drains freely is ideal.

'Blue Panda'. Spurred, elongated, light blue flowers, pinkish and yellow tipped at the mouth. Summer dormant but fall rebloom. 10 in. **'China Blue'**. Fragrant, dark blue flowers, purple at the mouth. Often summer dormant; mulch to cool soil and retain moisture. 16 in. **'Père David'** has clear blue flowers and divided leaves touched with red or purple. 12 in.

Corydalis solida syn. *C. halleri*

Color	red-purple
Bloom time	spring
Size	6–12 in. × 8 in.
Light	part shade
Zones	Z4–8

PURPLE CORYDALIS, FUMEWORT Eastern Europe. Gray-green, ferny, 3-in. leaves emerge early in the spring from tuberous roots. Spikes of as many as 20 narrow-spurred, 1-in., tubular blossoms cluster at stem tips. After a brief bloom time, the foliage yellows and disappears tidily.

'Beth Evans' is very floriferous with pink flowers accented with white throats. Z6–8. **'George Baker'** has red flowers. Z6–8.

Other Notable Cultivars

'Berry Exciting' is well named with its bright purple-red flowers set against golden leaves. Summer dormant. 10 in. Z5–9. **'Blackberry Wine'** has lacy, bluish green foliage and fragrant, deep maroon flowers from late spring to early summer. 10 in. Z5–8. **'Canary Feathers'** has upright spikes of bright yellow flowers set against bluish foliage. Blooms in spring into summer and sporadically as the temperatures cool. Great in rock gardens or along woodland paths. 7–8 in. Z6–9.

GAS PLANT

Dictamnus

RUTACEAE

THIS GENUS IS COMPOSED of a single species. Its common names refer to a phenomenon often described but seldom actually witnessed: reportedly, the inflammable oil that gives the foliage its lemon scent volatilizes in hot weather, and on a still summer afternoon may supposedly erupt in a flash if ignited with a lit match. Fortunately, this is the least of the plant's attractions.

Gas plant is easygoing, growing in any average, well-drained garden soil, though it prefers a moist, fertile, and organic-rich one. Best adapted to full sun, it also tolerates light shade, and though slow to mature—it may take several years for a seedling to reach the flowering stage—once established in the garden it is very long-lived and requires little maintenance.

Planted singly or massed in a border, herb, or cottage garden, it makes an imposing statement; it blends well with daylilies, campanulas, and irises. Pests, including deer, and diseases rarely afflict gas plant seriously. Contact with its foliage may cause a rash in some individuals.

Propagate by seed, planting the new seed as soon as it ripens. Once this taprooted plant is established, it resents disturbance, making division and even the transplanting of mature plants risky.

Dictamnus albus

syn. *D. fraxinella*

color	white, pink, red, lilac
bloom time	late spring to early summer
size	2–3 ft. × 1.5–2.5 ft.
light	sun
zones	Z3–8

GAS PLANT Native to southwestern Europe, and southern and central Asia to China and Korea. Upright clumps of erect, rigid stems that typically don't require staking. The foliage is light green, glossy, and pinnate with an elegant appearance, and releases a lemon scent when bruised or crushed. Showy five-petaled, 1-in. flowers have prominent wispy, upcurving stamens, and are borne in racemes at the stem tips; they may be mauve, pink, or white, etched with purple veins. Attractive star-shaped seedheads follow.

Var. ***purpureus*** bears flowers that are pale to deep purple-pink, with darker veins.

GAURA

Gaura | ONAGRACEAE

THIS GENUS INCLUDES ONLY ONE garden-worthy perennial species. Its open structure, slender stems, and cloud of delicate, fluttering blooms makes that particular gaura an exceptional plant for leavening and enhancing the texture of a border, and a natural companion for ornamental grasses, purple coneflowers (*Echinacea*), and other taller summer bloomers. It's also well suited to native plant gardens, meadows, and wildflower gardens. This plant tolerates urban pollution well and also has exceptional heat and humidity tolerance; if given sufficient irrigation during dry spells, it will continue to bloom right through the peak of summer.

Gaura tolerates a wide range of soils, from well-drained, fertile ones to those that are dry and acid. When grown in rich soils, gaura tends to sprawl; cutting stems back by half in mid- to late spring helps keep growth more compact and sturdy. Deadheading the spent flowers helps to control prolific self-seeding.

Generally pest and disease free, though subject to root rot on heavy, poorly drained soils. This species is also deer resistant.

The easiest way to propagate this plant is by seed, as gaura forms taproots and is difficult to transplant once established. Start seed in containers to avoid transplant shock when planted out. Named cultivars, however, must be multiplied by division, which can be undertaken after two to three years of growth.

Gaura lindheimeri

(flower color)	white, pink
(bloom time)	late spring to early fall
(size)	3–5 ft. × 1–2 ft.
(light)	sun
(zone)	Z5–9

BUTTERFLY GAURA Texas and Louisiana. Despite its southern origins, butterfly gaura is surprisingly hardy. Forms a vase-shaped, airy cluster of wiry stems from which sprout stemless, narrowly lanceolate, 1- to 3-in. leaves; the reddish stems and the foliage are occasionally spotted with maroon. The common name refers to the delicate, butterfly-like appearance of the four-petaled flowers, which are borne in long, open, terminal panicles with the blooms opening a few at a time over an extraordinarily long season.

'Blushing Butterflies' ('Benso') is compact, to 24 in. high and wide, with dark green foliage, and light pink-and-white flowers; **'Crimson Butterflies'** has crimson new growth and hot-pink flowers: **'Sunny Butterflies'** has leaves edged with white, pink flowers. 24 in. tall. **'Whirling Butterflies'** has pink-tinged white flowers. **'Pink Cloud'** bears unusually heavy crops of bright pink flowers over an extra-long season. 30 in. **'Siskiyou Pink'** was the first strong pink cultivar. Introduced by Baldassare Mineo of Siskiyou Rare Plant Nursery. **'Snow Fountain'** bears all white flowers on 18- to 24-in. plants.

GENTIAN

Gentiana

GENTIANACEAE

A TRADITIONAL FAVORITE of rock gardeners, gentians have much to offer also for other horticultural applications. Indigenous to every continent except Antarctica, this genus furnishes native species no matter where you garden. Their flowers include some of the most intense blues found in the plant kingdom. They are popular as food sources, especially for native bees, butterflies, and hummingbirds. These are not aggressive plants, but their sparkling floral colors make them ideal for use as visual accents singly or in small groups. The intense dot of blue contributed by a single gentian blossom energizes any yellows in the surrounding border, and provides elegant contrast to silver foliage.

With some exceptions, gentians are native to mountain areas, and like most peak-dwelling plants they prefer moist but very well-drained soils and are notably cold hardy. Like most alpines, gentians as a group have low tolerance for heat when combined with humidity, though a few, included here, are more tolerant than most. Gentians are outstanding in their traditional home, the rock garden, but also show up beautifully when displayed in containers, and can be quite useful in the front of a border. Deer resistant, but bothered by slugs and snails. Foliage is subject to rust and foliage spots, but is seldom a nuisance.

Propagate most species by division or use freshly ripened seed.

Gentiana andrewsii

	blue
	fall
	1–2 ft. × 1–1.5 ft.
	sun, part shade
	Z3–7, HS

CLOSED-BOTTLE GENTIAN Colorado, eastward to Virginia and north into Canada. Unlike other members of this genus, *Gentiana andrewsii* is a lowland plant that flourishes in moist fields and prairies, woodland edges and thickets, and low, wooded areas near streams and ponds. Its dark blue flowers never open voluntarily; borne in clusters at the top of the main stem, the flowers retain their bud form, expanding into 1.5-in.-long, pleated tubes whose tips remain closed until a bumblebee forces its way in to steal the nectar. Medium green, glossy, ovate leaves are held in opposing pairs and in a whorl beneath the floral cluster. Best in moist but well-drained, cool, organic-rich, and mildly alkaline soil, but tolerant of slightly acid, well-dug and amended clay; tolerates seasonal drought once established. A star of all woodland gardens or shady borders, as well as moist meadows or the banks of a stream or pond.

Gentiana asclepiadea

	blue
	late summer to early fall
	24–30 in. × 24 in.
	sun, part shade
	Z5–7, HS

WILLOW GENTIAN Mountain meadows of Europe and western Asia. Its common name refers to its slender, willow-like leaves and graceful, arching growth; the 2-in. flowers are rich blue, flaring trumpets borne in pairs and sprouting from the upper leaf axils. Requires a moist but well-drained, moderately fertile, acid or neutral soil. Well suited to woodland edges where it pairs well with small ferns, heucheras, heucherellas, and variegated Solomon's seal. Does not thrive in hot, humid summers.

'Alba' is a white-flowered cultivar. **'Pink Swallow'** bears intense pink flowers and dark green leaves.

Gentiana dahurica

syn. *G. gracilipes*

color	purple-blue
bloom time	summer
size	6–12 in. × 12 in.
exposure	sun, part shade
zone	Z4–7

DAHURIAN GENTIAN An Asian native that forms a loose mound of narrow, deep green, glossy, lanceolate leaves, from which arise lax stems bearing clusters of white-throated, deep blue, trumpet-shaped flowers. Requires moist, gritty, and well-drained soil with acid to neutral pH. Excellent for rock gardens.

Gentiana lutea

color	yellow
bloom time	summer
size	3–4.5 ft. × 2 ft.
exposure	sun
zone	Z6–9, HS

GREAT YELLOW GENTIAN, BITTERWORT Europe, western Asia. Erect stiff stems carry opposite pairs of glaucous, ribbed leaves to 12 in. long. Tiered clusters of yellow, starry flowers emerge from leaf axils. Seldom seen in US gardens but available as seed, and well worth seeking out. Raise container-grown plants to avoid root damage at transplanting time. Valuable medicinally and appropriate for herb gardens as well as borders.

Gentiana makinoi 'Royal Blue'

Gentiana makinoi

(flower color)	blue
(bloom time)	midsummer to early fall
(size)	18–24 in. × 6–12 in.
(exposure)	sun, part shade
(zone)	Z3–7

ROYAL BLUE GENTIAN Mountains of Japan. Upright perennial with semi-evergreen, dark green, ovate leaves. Intensely blue, 2-in.-long flowers borne in the upper leaf axils of the stems; never fully open, retaining a close-ended tubular shape like that of a Christmas tree light bulb. Requires an acid, humus-rich, moist but well-drained soil. Generally pest and disease free, but attractive to deer.

Encourage a more compact, less sprawling habit by pruning stems back by half in late spring to early summer. This species contributes a bright note of color to late summer borders, and combines well with acid-loving shrubs such as blueberries and rhododendrons. Very attractive as a cut flower.

'Marsha' has blue-purple flowers and is compact, to 20 in.; a good choice for containers. **'Royal Blue'** grows to 24 in. bearing royal violet-blue flowers.

Gentiana scabra

	blue
	late summer to early fall
	6–8 in. × 8–12 in.
	sun, part shade
	Z4–8

JAPANESE GENTIAN Japan. Low-growing, evergreen species whose flowers, borne at the stem ends, are bell shaped and a rich, sapphire blue. Excellent for rock gardens, borders, and in open woodlands. Prefers an acid, humus-rich, moist, well-drained soil. Compatible with ericaceous shrubs such as blueberries, heaths and heathers, and rhododendrons.

'Zuikorindo' bears deep pink flowers.

Gentiana septemfida

	blue
	mid- to late summer
	6–12 in. × 12–18 in.
	sun, part shade
	Z4–9

SUMMER GENTIAN Caucasus Mountains. Forms a trailing mound of deep green foliage that in summer glows with deep blue, trumpet-shaped blossoms, sometimes with white throats. Easier to cultivate than the fall-blooming gentians, it tolerates heat and humidity if there is some afternoon shade.

Var. *lagodechiana* has cobalt-blue trumpets. A fine rock-garden plant, suitable for edging or for planting into a retaining wall, and well suited to container cultivation. 4–8 in. Z4–7.

GEUM | PRAIRIE SMOKE | AVENS

Geum ROSACEAE

IF YOU ARE LOOKING FOR A SHOW STOPPER, you won't find it among the geums; what you will find, though, are reliable, low-maintenance, and consistently rewarding perennials, real workhorses that combine attractive foliage with bright and long-lasting blooms.

Geums are closely related to potentillas, and like their kin they make useful fast-growing groundcovers. The medium green leaves are fuzzy, usually lobed, and borne typically in neat, clumping mounds. The flowers are medium sized, usually 1.5 in. or so in diameter, cup shaped, and most often composed of single rounds of petals; many of the cultivars and hybrids bear showier double or semi-double flowers. The colors run to bright oranges and reds.

Due to their naturally compact, mounded habit, geums are handy for lending substance to the front of a border. Here they complement more vertical plants such as dwarf irises, delphiniums, and perennial salvias. Their bright blossoms are particularly striking when the plants are massed. Although the main period of bloom is from late spring through early summer, these plants often rebloom intermittently if deadheaded. Geums are also a good source of cut flowers.

Intolerant of the combination of heat and humidity, geums prefer a moist but well-drained soil—they adapt well to rock gardens but do not persist long in dense clays and don't tolerate wet soils in wintertime. Rarely troubled by pests and diseases; deer and rabbit resistant.

Divide established plants every three years or so in fall or spring to help maintain plant vigor and increase your stock. Plants can also be started from seed, although most species hybridize promiscuously and character of seedlings is unpredictable.

Geum coccineum

color	red
bloom time	late spring to early summer
size	12–18 in. × 9–12 in.
light	sun, part shade
zones	Z5–7, HS

AVENS Balkans. Forms a 6-in. mound of hairy, irregularly lobed leaves consisting of five to seven leaflets; evergreen in the warmer parts of their range. Five-petaled, brick-red flowers borne on wiry, branching stems that rise several inches above the basal foliage mound. Deadheading encourages rebloom in cool-summer regions; where summers are hot the plants benefit from afternoon shade. Leave some flowers on the plant to serve as a source of the attractive, fluffy seedheads that follow.

'Borisii' grows to a height and spread of 6–12 in.; orange flowers. **'Cooky'** is 6–12 in. tall and spreads 6–9 in.; brilliant orange flowers with orange-yellow stamens. Foliage persists in spite of summer heat. **'Koi'** has bright orange flowers above a compact, 4-in. mound of glossy green leaves. 8 in. Z4–7.

Geum quellyon syn. *G. chiloense*

color	yellow, orange, red
bloom time	late spring to early summer
size	2 ft. high and wide
light	sun, part shade
zones	Z5–9, HS

CHILEAN AVENS Chile. Forms a cushion of fuzzy, dark green, strawberry-like leaves that are semi-evergreen or even evergreen in the warmer parts of the plant's range. Branched stems carry the single, 1.5-in.-wide, cup-shaped flowers; those of cultivars are usually semi-double or double, and may be slightly larger. Prefers a rich, well-drained, neutral to slightly acid soil. Short-lived.

'Georgenberg' has soft orange flowers with hints of apricot, peach, and salmon. Repeat bloomer. 15 in. **'Lady Stratheden'** ('Goldball') has yellow, semi-double flowers. 16–24 in. **'Mrs. J. Bradshaw'** ('Feuerball', 'Fireball') is a profuse bearer of large, orange-yellow, semi-double flowers. Leaves turn burgundy color in fall. 16–24 in. **'Red Dragon'** bears scarlet, double flowers. 16–20 in. **'Starker's Magnificum'** has double, apricot-tangerine flowers. 15–18 in.

Geum rivale

Color	orange, purple, white
Bloom time	late spring to early summer
Size	6–24 in. × 6–18 in.
Light	sun, part shade
Zones	Z2–7

PURPLE AVENS, WATER AVENS, CHOCOLATE ROOT Bogs and wet meadows across northern North America and south into New Mexico, as well as northern Europe and central Asia. The North American population produces large plants with small flowers, whereas the European and Asian plants are more compact with much larger flowers; the blooms of both are nodding and bell shaped, pinkish apricot in color. Leaves pinnate, measuring to 8 in. long and 2 in. across; basal leaves have five to seven leaflets, the upper ones have three. Individual leaflets are coarsely serrated, slightly hairy, rough textured, and medium green; terminal leaflet is sometimes divided into three lobes. Flowers are borne in cymes on dark purple, hairy stems; individual blooms measure 0.75–1 in. across, and are composed of five dull red to pale purple petals and five dark purple sepals. Prefers a consistently moist, neutral to mildly acid soil, tolerates garden soils with more than average moisture. Best suited for growing in bog gardens or at the margins of water gardens.

'Flames of Passion' bears semi-double, scarlet-red flowers from spring well into summer, followed by feathery prairie smoke–like seed pods. 12 in. × 18 in. Z5–9. **'Leonardii'** ('Leonard's Variety') blooms with copper-pink flowers. 8–12 in. **'Lionel Cox'** has yellow-tinged pink flowers. 12 in. **'Marika'** is compact with creamy-peach flowers. 9–12 in. tall. **'Snowflake'** is compact, to 9 in., with pure white flowers. Holds its flowers outward rather than nodding as in **'Album'**.

Geum triflorum

syn. *Erythrocoma triflora*

color	reddish pink, purple
bloom time	late spring to early summer
size	6–18 in. × 6–12 in.
light	sun
zones	Z3–7, HS

PRAIRIE SMOKE, PURPLE AVENS Prairie native, Pacific Coast inland as far as New Mexico and northward into Canada, east across the upper Midwest into New York. Hairy, rhizomatous plant with pinnately divided, fern-like green leaves with 7 to 19 leaflets. The reddish pink to purplish, nodding, globular flowers (usually borne in clusters of three) are attractive, but the distinctive beauty of this plant lies in the fruiting heads that follow: as the flowers age, the protruding styles lengthen to form a cluster of 2-in.-long, feathery, gray tails, giving the whole the look of a miniature feather duster.

Prefers a dry, well-drained soil in a sunny location, though it benefits from some afternoon shade in hot-summer regions. Tolerant of moist but well-drained soils, though likely to prove short-lived in such conditions. Typically free of pests and problems. This soft-textured plant is effective at the front of a border, but is most striking when massed in a meadow or prairie setting.

Other Notable Cultivars

'Banana Daiquiri', an introduction of Illinois's Intrinsic Perennial Gardens, has semi-evergreen leaves below long-stemmed, semi-double, pale yellow flowers. Beautiful, slightly frilly blooms. 18–24 in. × 15–18 in. Z4–8. **'Blazing Sunset'** grows 18–24 in. high and wide, with double, scarlet flowers 50 percent larger than those of other geums. Flowers all summer. Z5–7, HS. **'Cherry Cordial'** is compact, with single, red blossoms followed by fluffy seedheads. 9–12 in. Z5–7, HS.

GIANT HYSSOP

Agastache | LAMIACEAE

AN OLD-FASHIONED FAVORITE, *Agastache* is ideally suited to modern gardens. The various species have much of the vigor and toughness of their mint relatives but with little of the invasiveness that make the mints so problematic. The flowers are pretty and sweet scented but for the most part modest. Although they don't grab the eye like some of their more flamboyant fellows, they are borne over a long season, typically from midsummer to early fall when blooms of any kind are scarce in perennial gardens. They also attract a steady stream of hummingbirds, butterflies, and other pollinators. Foliage is usually aromatic on sturdy stems that rarely require staking. They fit easily into a wild or meadow garden.

Though occasionally subject to powdery mildew, agastaches are typically pest free and notably resistant to grazing deer and rabbits. They flourish in a wide range of well-drained soils, though are likely to live short lives on damp clays. Small wonder then that this traditional standby is receiving renewed attention from plant breeders, who have introduced a host of fine new cultivars in recent years.

A natural for butterfly gardens, agastaches also make good companions for roses—the fragrances are complementary and the well-furnished foliage of giant hyssops masks the rose's leggy stems. Likewise, their spires of blossoms make agastaches useful as visual punctuation for summertime mixed borders. The drought tolerance of the western US species makes these North American natives perfect for xeriscapes. Encourage rebloom by routine deadheading.

Propagate by seed or division, or by taking semi-hardwood and softwood cuttings just as flowering is about to begin.

Agastache cana

Color	pink
Bloom time	early summer to midfall
Size	24–36 in. × 18 in.
Light	sun, part shade
Zones	Z5–9, HS

TEXAS HUMMINGBIRD MINT Texas and New Mexico. Long-blooming spikes of fragrant, raspberry-pink flowers borne above aromatic, gray-green foliage. Drought tolerant but will not stand wet feet or humidity.

Agastache foeniculum

Color	lavender, purple
Bloom time	midsummer to early fall
Size	2–4 ft. × 1.5–3 ft.
Light	sun, part shade
Zones	Z4–8

GIANT BLUE HYSSOP Native to fields, prairies, and woodland openings throughout the upper half of North America. This perennial grows well on moist, well-drained soils, but once established also tolerates dry soils. Unlike most agastaches, giant blue hyssop copes well with humidity. The flowers are borne in whorls around the square stems, stacked one on top of the other in tall spikes. The anise-scented foliage may be dried for use in teas; flowering stems add color as well as fragrance to cut-flower arrangements.

'Golden Jubilee' bears young foliage that is yellow to chartreuse, maturing to lime green.

Agastache rugosa 'Honey Bee Blue'

Agastache rugosa

flower color	violet-blue
bloom time	midsummer to early fall
size	4 ft. × 1.5 ft.
exposure	sun, part shade
zone	Z5–9

KOREAN HYSSOP Introduced into the nursery trade by plant collector Dan Hinkley, this Asian native balances its long-blooming, violet-blue flowers with glossy, deep green, intensely mint-scented foliage. Like *Agastache foeniculum*, this species tolerates humidity.

'Honey Bee Blue' bears blue flowers with gray-green foliage.

Agastache rupestris

flower color	orange
bloom time	midsummer to early fall
size	1–3 ft. high and wide
exposure	sun
zone	Z5–9, HS

ROCK ANISE HYSSOP West Texas and Mexico. A combination of orange and yellow blooms edged with magenta and pink and licorice-scented, silvered foliage makes this species the showiest of the bunch. It is notably drought tolerant, but is likely to fall prey to fungal infections where summers combine heat with humidity.

Other Notable Cultivars

'Acapulco Salmon and Pink' bears mint-scented foliage and spikes of large, bicolored orange-and-pink flowers. 24–30 in. × 15 in. Z5–10. **'Black Adder'** displays spikes with stacked whorls of smoky red-violet blossoms all summer and into early fall. 2–3 ft. × 1.5–2 ft. Z6–9. **'Blue Fortune'** produces tall spikes of powder-blue flowers. 3–4 ft. × 1.5 ft. Z5–9. **'Firebird'** has spikes of mixed copper, coral, and red flowers. 4 ft. × 2 ft. Z6–9. **'Heatwave'** has plenty of deep hot-pink spikes on tight, clumping plants. Tolerates heat and humidity. 36 in. in bloom. Z5–10.

GLOBE DAISY

Globularia | PLANTAGINACEAE

BEST KNOWN TO ROCK GARDEN AFICIONADOS, globe daisies deserve a wider application. They are excellent in troughs and can be tucked into small cracks in walls or between pavers, as well as serving as slow-growing groundcovers. In spite of their common name, they are not related to the daisy family; formerly they were given their own taxonomic family: Globulariaceae.

Mostly ground-hugging, globe daisies produce mats of good-looking, leathery, evergreen leaves topped by dense, rounded heads of flowers borne on perky stems. The creeping stems, woody at their base, root where they touch soil, but this colonization is easily controlled. A sharp, well-drained soil is essential for most species, as is a sunny spot. Alkaline soil is preferable; dress with lime chips where soil tends to be acid. Tolerates droughty conditions well. Deadhead for neatness after bloom time.

Globe daisy is a larval food for some species of butterflies and moths. It is resistant to deer and gophers, but may be attacked by slugs.

Difficult to divide; heeled cuttings (softwood stems with a piece of woody tissue attached) can be separated in summer and then rooted. Seeds need a chilling for two months before they will germinate.

Globularia cordifolia

	blue
	spring
	2–5 in. × 12 in.
	sun, part shade
	Z5–8

HEART-LEAVED GLOBE DAISY Scree and rocky mountainous areas of the Mediterranean region. Makes tight rosettes of evergreen, shiny, spoon-shaped leaves 1–2 in. long and notched at the tip. Flower stems shrouded in tiny flattened leaves poke their heads above the foliage in late spring topped with 1.75-in., powder-puff heads of lavender flowers. Most attractive as a slow-growing groundcover.

Globularia meridionalis

syn. *G. bellidifolia, G. cordifolia* subsp. *bellidifolia, G.cordifolia* subsp. *meridionalis*

	blue
	summer
	6–12 in. × 12 in.
	sun, part shade
	Z5–7

GLOBE DAISY Southeast Alps and Mediterranean region. Mats of lustrous evergreen, 3-in. leaves usually lance shaped and rounded at the tips. In summer upright stems clothed with smaller leaves rise to 12 in. or so, topped with showy button-like, globular heads of small flowers in varying shades of lavender-blue. Low dianthus, lewisias, and other unthirsty perennials are excellent companions.

GLOBE MALLOW

Sphaeralcea | MALVACEAE

WITH THEIR TOUGH CONSTITUTION and flowers like mini hollyhocks, globe mallows are certain to please. They bloom abundantly and tolerate dry, poor soil, where other species may falter, growing naturally in deserts and dry riverbeds as found in gardens of the western United States. Globe mallows may also be cultivated under glass. Some species are covered with star-shaped hairs that irritate sensitive skins; never touch your eyes after tending globe mallows.

Although they survive in poor, dry conditions, globe mallows are more vigorous when grown in average garden soils and kept thirsty. Full sun is essential. Grow in a gritty, free-draining potting soil under glass or sunroom for indoor display. Be alert for white flies. Globe mallows are food plants for some species of caterpillar, including painted ladies; checkerspots and others visit for nectar; also attractive to birds and bees. Globe mallows are an important food for deer, rabbits, and rodents. Perfect to decorate wildflower and wildlife gardens, native plant gardens, or other informal areas.

Sow seed in spring in containers, or divide plants in spring. Stem cuttings root well in spring and summer.

Sphaeralcea ambigua

	pink, orange
	late summer to fall
	2–3 ft. × 2 ft.
	sun
	Z7–10

DESERT MALLOW, DESERT HOLLYHOCK, WILD HOLLYHOCK Native to dry parts of the southwestern United States. A very variable species that hybridizes promiscuously; mostly covered with stellar, white or yellowish hairs. Clumps of stems spirally clothed with fuzzy, fleshy, 0.75- to 2.5-in., broadly ovate, three-lobed leaves; these are ruffled or scalloped around the edges. Showy, cupped, 2-in., pink or orange flowers bloom in loose spikes in the upper leaf axils almost all season. Ideal for xeric, wildflower, and desert gardens. Height dependent on rainfall; in wet seasons the plants get to 4–5 ft. or so in the wild; perhaps only 12 in. in arid sites. Tolerates alkaline soil well. Where their ranges overlap, desert mallows often hybridize with smaller, orange *Sphaeralcea fendleri*.

'Louis Hamilton' (Louis Hamilton apricot mallow) is free blooming with scarlet-coral flowers for much of the summer. 30 in. Z7–10.

Sphaeralcea munroana

	red, orange
	summer to fall
	1–3.5 ft. × 2 ft.
	sun
	Z4–9

MUNRO'S GLOBE MALLOW Idaho to British Columbia and California. This very tough plant adapts to inhospitable sites and tolerates poor soil and low water with aplomb. Upright, unbranched stems, grayish with hairs, are furnished with alternate, silver-green foliage. Toothed, broadly ovate leaves are shallowly three lobed (sometimes five lobed), 1–2 in. long. Long wands of 1-in.-wide, apricot-orange to red flowers bloom for several weeks in terminal and axillary clusters. Spreads by underground runners, but is seldom invasive.

Several notable cultivars have resulted from a cross of this species with *Sphaeralcea fendleri* var. *venusta*: **'Wild Blush'** has pale pink flowers, **'Wild Sherbet'** has orange flowers, **'Wild Pale Pink'** is pale pink.

GOAT'S BEARD

Aruncus

ROSACEAE

OFTEN CONFUSED WITH SIMILAR ASTILBES, goat's beards are vigorous, clump-forming perennials with airy, plume-like blooms that inject a note of lightness into the garden. The loose, feathery, branched wands of tiny blossoms rise high above the leaves and are valued as cut flowers. Masses of dark green, divided foliage are handsome and sometimes display fall color.

Grow in partly shaded spots where the soil does not dry out readily—drought may cause leaves to become crispy and brown. The sides of streams and ponds and similarly damp places are ideal locations if the soil is rich in humus. The taller of the two species, *Aruncus dioicus*, is effective under trees and shrubs or as a backdrop at the back of the border. Partner with foxgloves, columbines, and late-blooming bulbs, including camassias. In native plant gardens woodland phlox, blue cohosh, and wild geranium are appropriate companions. Pest and disease free; seldom browsed by deer.

Propagate by division in early spring or fall, or by seed sown in fall and overwintered in a protected spot.

Aruncus aethusifolius

syn. *A. sylvester* var. *sylvester*

Color	white
Bloom time	early to midsummer
Size	10–16 in. × 12 in.
Light	sun, part shade, shade
Zones	Z3–9

DWARF GOAT'S BEARD This Korean species develops clumps of very finely divided, dark green leaves that in sunny spots become reddish in fall. Astilbe-like, creamy-white flowers bloom above the leaves. Great as a foliar contrast for small hostas in rock gardens, troughs, or at the front of partly shaded borders. Carefree and cute.

Aruncus dioicus syn. *A. sylvestris*

Flower color	cream
Bloom time	late spring to early summer
Size	4–6 ft. × 2–4 ft.
Light	sun, part shade
Zones	Z3–7

GOAT'S BEARD, WHITE GOAT'S BEARD, BRIDE'S FEATHERS Europe to eastern Siberia, eastern North America. This bold clumping perennial prefers high-humus woodland soils and should not be allowed to dry out. Tolerant of sun, but intense sun burns the foliage even with extra irrigation. Erect and shrub-like, the branching stems bear an abundance of two- or three-times divided leaves with oval leaflets, doubly serrated along their edges. Tall, feathery plumes of creamy-white flowers, up to 20 in. long, rise well above the foliage mass. Male and female flowers are borne on separate plants; the male flowers tend to be showier and fluffier. Appropriate for native plant, wild, and meadow gardens, along stream banks, and around ponds. Mass, group, or grow as a specimen. The rootstock becomes very tough and woody with age—if you plan to increase stock by division, you may need a machete.

'Kneiffii' has much more deeply cut, almost thread-like foliage. Good for smaller spaces in moist soil. 2–3 ft.

Other Notable Cultivars

'Guinea Fowl' (*Aruncus dioicus* × *A. aethusifolius*) makes neat, compact clumps of leaves, more dissected than those of *A. aethusifolius*. Inflorescence a delicate spray of tiny white flowers. Best in light shade. 12–18 in. Z5–7. **'Misty Lace'**, also a hybrid of *A. dioicus* × *A. aethusifolius*, tolerates full sun and is somewhat hardier than 'Guinea Fowl'. This hybrid displays intermediate characteristics of its parents. Better than others for hot and humid gardens. An Allan Armitage introduction. 18–24 in. Z4–7.

GOLDENROD

Solidago | ASTERACEAE

EUROPEAN GARDENERS HAVE LONG esteemed native American goldenrods, but until recently they were ignored, at least horticulturally, on this side of the Atlantic, possibly due to the mistaken but enduring belief that they cause hay fever. What they actually provide is a long lasting and remarkably hardy, perennial source of late summer and fall color, as well as invaluable late-season nectar sources for butterflies and bees.

A few species of goldenrods are native to Central and South America, and Eurasia, but the overwhelming majority, more than 60 species, originated in the fields and prairies of North America. Typically, they form an aggressive network of rhizomes or woody subterranean stems (caudices). From these rise upright or sprawling stems, 6–60 in. or more tall, depending upon the species. Alternate leaves are linear to lanceolate, commonly serrated along the margins. Tiny, golden yellow (or sometimes white) flowerheads cluster into parasol-like, plume-like, or branched sprays. They bloom in late summer to fall.

Adaptable and undemanding, goldenrods thrive in lean to moderately fertile soils in full sun; some tolerate part shade. Use the aggressive species in meadows, native and prairie plantings, or at woodland edges; the hybrids shine in late-season borders, and contrast dramatically with blue and violet asters. Choose late selections to harmonize with fall fruits, berries, and ornamental grasses. Staking is seldom needed; deadhead to extend bloom. Foraging bees, butterflies, and insects flock to collect the waxy pollen and nectar; deer resistant. Rust and powdery mildew may be a nuisance.

Propagate by division in spring or fall. Sow seed of species in late fall or early spring.

Solidago caesia

color	yellow
bloom time	late summer to midfall
size	18–36 in. high and wide
exposure	sun, part shade
zone	Z4–8

BLUE-STEMMED GOLDENROD, WREATH GOLDENROD Woods and fields of central and eastern North America. Arching, greenish purple stems bear toothed, lanceolate, 2- to 5-in. leaves. Bright yellow flowerheads cluster loosely in leaf axils along the stems. Clump forming, not an aggressive spreader. Fine cut flower.

Solidago odora

color	yellow
bloom time	late summer to early fall
size	2–4 ft. × 1–2 ft.
exposure	sun, part shade
zone	Z3–9

SWEET GOLDENROD Dry, sandy, open woods, eastern and central United States. Sessile, anise-scented, lanceolate, 3- to 4-in., dark green leaves on smooth or downy stems. Yellow flowerheads cluster in one-sided plumes. Tolerates poor, dry soils; does not spread aggressively but may self-seed. Good for butterfly gardens, meadows, borders, fragrance, and cottage gardens.

Solidago rugosa 'Fireworks'

Solidago rugosa

yellow
late summer to midfall
3–5 ft. × 1.5–2.5 ft.
sun
Z4–8

ROUGH GOLDENROD Moist fields and wetlands from Newfoundland, west to Michigan, south to Texas and Georgia. Recessed veins give the 3- to 4-in., lanceolate leaves a wrinkled appearance. Erect, arching, hairy stems rise from low mounds with showy panicles of yellow flowerheads. Spreads slowly by rhizomes and seed; good for rain gardens, meadows, and prairies.

'Fireworks', introduced by North Carolina Botanical Garden, has long, arching sprays of golden-yellow flowerheads. Attractive mingled with the orange hips of *Rosa glauca*. Mass for best effect. 3–4 ft.

Solidago speciosa

yellow
midsummer to early fall
1–3 ft. high and wide
sun, part shade
Z3–8

SHOWY GOLDENROD Dry soils in open woods, fields, and prairies throughout central and eastern United States. Narrowly lanceolate, 4- to 6-in., oblong-elliptic leaves become smaller as they ascend stiff, erect, reddish stems. Very showy, erect, pointed clusters of tiny, bright yellow flowerheads at stem tips. Tolerates poor, dry soils.

Solidago sphacelata

syn. *Brachychaeta sphacelata*

flower color	yellow
bloom time	late summer to midfall
size	12–24 in. × 12–18 in.
light	sun
zone	Z4–8

AUTUMN GOLDENROD Virginia to Georgia, west to Illinois and Tennessee. Compact, with low-growing mats of heart-shaped, toothed leaves. Stiff, arching stems branch at tips with plumes of small, yellow flowerheads. Tolerates dry, rocky, and clay soils. A useful groundcover; an asset in cottage and rock gardens.

'Golden Fleece' produces lavish displays of bright yellow flowerheads in arching, cylindrical plumes. A Dick Lighty introduction. 15–18 in. **'Wichita Mountains'** has gold flowers. Introduced by Steve Bieberich. 30 in.

Other Notable Cultivars

'Baby Gold' has large sprays of gold flowers. 2–2.5 ft. **'Crown of Rays'**. Erect plumes of bright yellow flowers from mid- to late summer. 2–3 ft. **'Little Lemon'** is exceptionally compact and well branched, with racemes of pale lemon flowers. Mid- to late summer. 8–12 in. Z5–8. **'Peter Pan'** bears extra-large, spreading clusters of warm yellow blooms. Late summer to late fall. 24–28 in. Z3–9. **'Solar Cascade'** has abundant golden flowerheads cluster in leaf axils along reflexed stems from late summer to late fall. Not an aggressive spreader. 2–3 ft. Z3–9.

HELLEBORE | CHRISTMAS ROSE

Helleborus

RANUNCULACEAE

"SCHNEEROSE" (SNOW ROSE) is a German name for hellebores, and it underlines one reason for these plants' surging popularity: their ability to bloom during adverse seasons when most other perennials are still hiding underground. In fact, it is quite common to find hellebores poking their flowers and foliage up through a carpet of snow. Depending on the species, they may bloom as early as midwinter in mild climates, or in very early spring where winters are harsher. This, however, is far from the only virtue of these plants. They offer beautiful long-lasting flowers and striking evergreen foliage. Though hellebores respond best to a well-watered and well-drained, rich, humus soil, once established on a site they are notably tough, withstanding both drought and neglect, and commonly surviving as last evidences of some abandoned garden. Originally cultivated for their medicinal qualities, hellebores are permeated with toxic compounds that make them notably resistant to grazing by deer and rabbits, though also less-than-ideal choices for a landscape with young children.

Some 20 species of hellebores inhabit various areas of Europe and Asia. Most are cultivated only by specialist collectors, but just four species, *Helleborus argutifolius, H. foetidus, H. niger,* and *H. orientalis,* together with the dozens of fine hybrids derived from them, are sufficient to satisfy the rest of us. Those who are fascinated by hellebores should consult the websites of specialist growers—be aware though, the fancy new selections and cultivars are not inexpensive. Hellebore authority Graham Rice (writing for the Royal Horticultural Society) suggests combining hellebores in the landscape with early-blooming spring bulbs, such as *Crocus tommasinianus, Scilla mischtschenkoana,* and snowdrops, or setting them against a backdrop of the brilliant red twigs of red stem dogwood. Hellebores also provide a handsome complement, both in foliage and flowers, to such broad-leaved evergreens as hollies and camellias.

Propagation is by seed or division; in either case, the offspring is likely to take at least two to three years to attain flowering size. Hellebores do not tolerate waterlogged soils; be sure to provide them with good drainage. Potential problems include crown rot when grown on wet or poorly drained soils, and leaf spot.

Helleborus argutifolius

syn. *H. corsicus, H. lividus* subsp. *corsicus*

Flower color	green
Bloom time	late winter to early spring
Size	24–48 in. × 24–36 in.
Light	sun, part shade
Hardiness	Z6–9

CORSICAN HELLEBORE Corsica and Sardinia. Glossy, evergreen leaves are each composed of three leaflets with strongly serrate margins, light green with tints of blue and pearl. Nodding, bowl-shaped flowers, pale green in color, measure 1–2 in. across, and are borne in profusion above the foliage on stout flower stems. Sensitive to cold, though plants will survive brief dips to 0°F; tolerates a range of soils as long as they drain well.

'Janet Starnes' has green-and-cream variegated foliage. **'Pacific Frost'** has foliage abundantly frosted with an overlay of cream and pale green. A favorite in the damp maritime regions. **'Silver Lace'** has pewter-silver foliage.

Other Notable Cultivars

Hybrids and strains are numerous and growing. This is just a sampling: ×***ballardiae*** (*Helleborus lividus* × *H. niger*) **'Cinnamon Snow'**. Bright cinnamon-red stalks support outfacing, white blooms that age to pink in late winter to early spring. 12 in. × 18 in. **Brandywine Strain** has a mix of colors, many spotted; single, semi-double, and double flowers. Bred by David Culp. ×***ericsmithii*** **'HGC Champion'** ('Winter's Bliss'). Dark green, prickly edged leaves and rosy buds; outfacing cream flowers with pink reverse. 15 in. × 24 in. Z4–8. **Golden Lotus Strain** bears large, double, yellow flowers, often with pink edging and reverse. Z4–8. **Heronswood Double Strain** has double flowers in pinks and roses, cream, purple, and lilac. ×***nigersmithii*** **'Walhelivor'** (Ivory Prince) has burgundy-petioled, silver-veined, glossy green leaves. Reddish buds open to white flowers in midspring. To 10 in. Z5–8. **Royal Heritage Strain**, introduced by John Elsley, includes vigorous growers with variously colored flowers with overlapping petals.

Helleborus foetidus

Flower color	greenish white
Bloom time	late winter to early spring
Size	1–2 ft. × 1–1.5 ft.
Exposure	part shade, shade
Zones	Z5–9

BEAR'S FOOT HELLEBORE, STINKING HELLEBORE, STINKING BENJAMIN A native of western and central Europe, this species boasts dark green, evergreen leaves that are deeply lobed, divided into seven to ten narrow, lanceolate to elliptical, tooth-edged segments; the overall effect is celebrated by the nickname "bear's foot." Clusters of pale green flower buds appear early in the New Year; shortly thereafter, nodding, bell-shaped, greenish white flowers tipped with purple, up to 1 in. across, open. When bruised, flowers and foliage release an unpleasant skunk-like odor that is rather exaggerated by the names "foetidus" and "stinking."

Provide plants with a moisture-retentive, organic-rich, slightly alkaline soil that drains well. Cut back flowering stems after blooming to encourage new growth. Plants may self-seed in favorable habitats. Protect from winter winds—a blanket of evergreen boughs is recommended in zone 5.

'Gold Bullion' has bright golden young foliage. Try it with *Mukdenia*. **'Krenitsky'** (Krenitsky's bear claw hellebore) has dark green, very serrate leaves; 2-ft.-tall stalks of light green flowers. **'Piccadilly'** (12–18 in.) and **'Sienna'** (24 in.) both have blackish green foliage. **Red Silver Strain** has leaves with a silvery sheen, with reddish stems and leaf bases; chartreuse flowers, heavily rimmed with red-purple. This is a variable seed strain. **'Wester Flisk'** has red-stemmed, finely divided foliage, and bell-shaped, light creamy-green flowers rimmed with purple. 2 ft. Z4.

Helleborus niger

Color	white, pink
Bloom time	mid-winter to early spring
Size	9–12 in. × 12–18 in.
Light	part shade, shade
Zones	Z3–8

CHRISTMAS ROSE Europe and southwest Asia. Leaves are dark green, glossy, composed of seven to nine leaflets, to 8 in. long by 2.5–3 in. across; evergreen in milder climates, but deciduous where winters are severe. The large, bowl- to cup-shaped flowers may reach 3 in. wide, with five tepals (petals) surrounding a boss of yellow stamens. They are borne singly or in threes, on thick stems, white shading to pink as they mature; bloom may begin as early as December where winters are mild, and may persist for two months. This species prefers a humus-rich, well-drained soil, and a spot protected from winter winds. Christmas roses establish slowly, generally taking several years to bloom size; they grow best if left undisturbed. May self-seed where conditions are good.

'HGC Josef Lemper' (Josef Lemper Christmas rose) grows to just 9 in. Large, white flowers over a prolonged season. Z3–8. **'Potter's Wheel'** has rounded, large, white flowers accented with a green eye. A parent of several hybrids.

Helleborus orientalis

Color	white, pink, purple
Bloom time	late winter to midspring
Size	12–18 in. × 15–18 in.
Light	part shade, shade
Zones	Z4–9

LENTEN ROSE Native from northeastern Greece through Turkey to the Caucasus Mountains. Large leaves are palmate, leathery, glossy green, and 8–16 in. wide, 12 in. or more in length; evergreen where winters are mild. The large flowers are 3–4 in. in diameter, nodding or outfacing and cup shaped, ranging in color from white to pink, light pinkish purple to deep purple-black, with a contrasting boss of yellow stamens. Prefers organic-rich, well-drained soils, with a location protected from winter winds. Faster to establish and easier to grow than *Helleborus niger*; more tolerant of division. Self-seeds in hospitable sites.

HIBISCUS | ROSE MALLOW

Hibiscus

MALVACEAE

HIBISCUS MAKE A SPLASH wherever they are planted. This genus contains small trees and shrubs, perennials, and annuals; here, the focus is on perennial species, all of which bring a strong tropical attitude to the garden.

Unusually large flowered, hibiscus have wide-mouthed, trumpet-shaped flowers borne singly or in clusters in the upper leaf axils. The colors are primarily reds, pinks, and white, sometimes yellow or purple, and most have a conspicuous, contrasting eye. Stamens cluster in a prominent column around the male parts (pistil), a typical characteristic of the mallow family. Foliage is large, alternately arranged on the stems, and mostly palmately lobed or maple-like.

Excellent in damp soils, hibiscus also thrive in average to rich soil in beds and borders. A natural component of waterside gardens, especially in warm areas, they are valuable for rain gardens or native plant and wildlife gardens. Shorter selections work well in containers and planter beds. Good companions include cardinal flower, milkweeds, tall asters, and Indian poke (*Veratrum viride*). Interesting with ornamental grasses in containers.

Maintenance is low, except for removing the Japanese beetles that may otherwise shred the flowers and leaves. The stems may die back in winter; if so, remove them prior to the appearance of new growth. Staking may be necessary in windy places, but usually the base of the stems becomes woody, making that chore superfluous. Deadhead to avoid unwanted seedlings and to encourage further bloom.

As noted, Japanese beetles are the most serious threat, but mealybugs, scale, and white flies can also become a nuisance. Diseases include stem and root rots, viruses, rust, and fungal leaf spot. Protect from deer.

Increase stock by dividing established plants or by seed. Seeds should be scarified (nicked) or soaked overnight prior to sowing; this allows water to penetrate the seed coat and initiate germination.

Hibiscus coccineus

(color)	red
(bloom time)	summer
(size)	5–7 ft. × 3 ft.
(exposure)	sun
(zone)	Z7–9

SWAMP HIBISCUS, SCARLET ROSE MALLOW, RED SWAMP MALLOW Coastal swamps of Georgia and Florida. Sparsely clothed with maple-like leaves, tall stems become woody at the base. Bright crimson flowers 3–6 in. across with five spoon-shaped petals, borne singly in upper leaf axils. Each flower lasts just a single day, but is nevertheless eye popping. Effective in damp soils at pond sides, but also in large borders. Seldom damaged by Japanese beetles. Late to break ground in spring.

'Alba' has pure white flowers. To 10 ft. Z6–11.

Hibiscus grandiflorus

syn. *Thespesia grandiflora*

color	pink
bloom time	fall
size	6–7 ft. × 6 ft.
light	sun
zones	Z7–9

VELVET MALLOW, MAGA COLORADA, PUERTO RICAN HIBISCUS Coastal plains of southern Louisiana to Florida. This bold perennial has huge (to 10 in. across), velvety gray leaves on tall stems, woody at the base. With age, crowns increase to 2 ft. or more across. Fragrant, 7- to 8-in.-wide, soft pink flowers are marked with crimson at the base—these are the largest blossoms of any North American species, and remain open overnight. Moist but average soil; does not tolerate droughty conditions. Seldom attacked by Japanese beetles. Sometimes hybridizes with *Hibiscus coccineus* where natural ranges overlap.

Hibiscus moscheutos

(flower color)	white, pink, red
(bloom time)	midsummer to early fall
(size)	3–5 ft. × 3 ft.
(light)	sun
(zone)	Z3–9

ROSE MALLOW, SOUTHERN ROSE MALLOW, SWAMP ROSE MALLOW Texas to the eastern United States and into Canada, along streams, and beside ponds and lakes. These imposing plants, woody at the base, spread slowly to develop into large colonies that are a sight to behold. Alternate leaves are more or less heart shaped, grayish green above, white and hairy underneath. Large, open flowers accented with crimson at their bases. Brown seed capsules follow. Susceptible to Japanese beetles, although some selections reputedly less than others; deer resistant in some regions, but vulnerable in others. Hummingbird attractor. Very late to emerge in spring. Dramatic in damp places beside water features, but tolerates average garden soil well. Combine with Joe-Pye weed, tall ornamental grasses, and asters at the back of borders.

Other Notable Cultivars

Selections and cultivars abound, with more introduced annually. This is a small selection.

'Blue River II' displays pure white, 10-in. flowers on 5-ft.-tall stems; foliage a deep, slightly bluish green. Z5–10. Disco Belle series includes **'Disco Belle'**, **'Disco Belle Red'**, and **'Disco Belle White'**, all compact with 9-in.-wide flowers. Japanese beetles love these. Seed propagated strain, available in separate colors. 20–24 in. **'Kopper King'**, bred by Nebraska's Fleming Brothers, has dinner-plate-sized, very pale pink flowers veined and centered with crimson. Copper-colored, maple-like leaves, burnt orange beneath. 3.5–4 ft. Z4–9. **'Lady Baltimore'** has deep pink, slightly ruffled blooms, with a red eye. 4–6 ft. Z5–9. **'Lord Baltimore'** has 10-in.-wide flowers like cherry-red dinner plates. 4 ft. Z5–10. **'Luna Red'** bears bright crimson flowers to 8 in. across. Reputedly deer resistant. 3 ft. **'Luna Pink Swirl'** has crimson-eyed, pale pink and red flowers. 24–36 in. Z4–9. **'Peppermint Schnapps'**, from the Cordials Collection, has 8- to 10-in., candy pink flowers splashed and centered with red. 4–6 ft. Z5–9.

HIMALAYAN POPPY

Meconopsis

PAPAVERACEAE

A GEOGRAPHICAL PUZZLE, this genus includes one species native to the British Isles and almost 40 more indigenous to the Himalayas. These poppy relatives—annuals, biennials, and evergreen or herbaceous perennials—all prefer cool, moist climates and seldom flourish in regions with hot, humid summers. Typically they form rosettes of hairy leaves and four-petaled, bowl-shaped flowers, reminiscent of related poppies.

Best where summers are cool, with moisture-retentive, well-drained, acid soil; they rot out in winter with wet feet. Organic mulch helps to maintain consistent soil moisture. The strong taproots resent disturbance.

All make fine additions to cottage gardens, wildflower meadows, or rock gardens; the blue poppies, for those who master their cultivation, also provide a choice ornament for sunny, well-drained borders and containers. Prone to attack by slugs and snails; deer resistant.

Propagate by fresh seed.

Meconopsis betonicifolia

color	blue
bloom time	late spring to early summer
size	24–48 in. × 18–24 in.
exposure	part shade
zones	Z7–8, HS

BLUE POPPY Himalayas. Basal rosette of 6-in., toothed leaves covered with rusty hairs; 2- to 3-in.-wide, sky-blue flowers borne singly or in terminal cymes. Not difficult to grow in suitable climates. If soil is not sufficiently acid, colors may be muddy mauve instead. A border and rock garden gem.

'Hensol Violet' has lilac-rose flowers.

Meconopsis cambrica

syn. *Parameconopsis cambrica*

Color	yellow, orange
Bloom time	late spring to early summer
Size	18 in. × 12 in.
Exposure	sun, part shade
Zones	Z5–9, HS

WELSH POPPY Britain, Ireland, western part of northern Europe. The easiest to cultivate, this species produces basal rosettes of divided, deeply toothed, pale green leaves, from which rise upright, bristly stems that carry solitary, 2- to 3-in., bowl-shaped, yellow to orange blooms; occasionally reblooms after initial flush of flowers. Plants are short lived but reseed prolifically, even sometimes becoming weedy. Particularly attractive naturalized in open woodland settings with forget-me-nots or grape hyacinths. Fresh seed is essential.

'Flore Pleno' bears double, yellow flowers. **'Muriel Brown'** bears double, orange-red flowers. **'Rubra'** has single, red flowers, 3 in. in diameter.

Meconopsis grandis

Color	blue
Bloom time	late spring to early summer
Size	2–4 ft. × 1–2 ft.
Exposure	part shade
Zones	Z5–7, HS

BLUE POPPY, ASIATIC POPPY Western Himalayas, northern Burma, and Yunnan. Basal rosettes composed of bristly, entire or coarsely toothed, wedge-shaped, medium green leaves, to 12 in. long. Upright stems bear cupped, deep sky-blue flowers, 4–5 in. across. Requires climate and soil similar to those favored by *Meconopsis betonicifolia*: best adapted to mild coastal regions, or higher altitudes. Appropriate for open woodlands or rock gardens. A heartbreaker, but a triumph for those who bring this treasure to bloom.

Other Notable Cultivars

***×sheldonii* 'Lingholm'** (*M. betonicifolia* × *M. grandis*) is bristly, 6- to 10-in. leaves, rich blue, 1.25-in. flowers from late spring. Treat as *M. betonicifolia* or *M. grandis*; hybrid vigor reputedly makes 'Lingholm' easier to cultivate. 48 in. × 18 in. Z3–7. **'Slieve Donard'** is vigorous with pointed, rich blue flowers. To 36 in.

HOLLYHOCK

Alcea | syn. *Althaea* | MALVACEAE

NO COTTAGE GARDEN IS COMPLETE without hollyhocks, which are known for their graceful, stately spires of blossoms and are among the best loved and most evocative of flowers. The cup-shaped, sessile, or nearly stalkless flowers arrange themselves in racemes around a central stem that in ideal conditions—full sun, good air circulation, moist, well-drained soil, and a dry climate—may soar to a height of 10 ft.

In less-than-ideal conditions, however, especially in moist, humid climates, hollyhocks are likely to prove martyrs to rust, a fungal infection. Prevention of rust is easier and more effective than controlling an outbreak; buy only disease-free plants, or start rust-resistant types from seed. Clean up thoroughly in late fall to prevent rust spores from overwintering onsite.

Hollyhocks are also subject to attack by slugs, snails, and spider mites, as well as Japanese beetles, but they are seldom browsed by deer. Staking is necessary to support the taller cultivars. Though not long-lived, hollyhocks are more persistent if cut to the base after blooming; leave a stalk or two to set seed to be assured of volunteer seedlings the next spring.

With this minimal care, hollyhocks provide a spectacular backdrop to shorter perennials and make dramatic cut flowers. One of the few plants that flourish in the root zone of black walnut trees. The blooms attract hummingbirds and butterflies.

Propagate by seed.

Alcea ficifolia

	various
	midsummer to early fall
	6–8 ft. × 2–3 ft.
	sun
	Z3–9

FIG-LEAF HOLLYHOCK, RUSSIAN HOLLYHOCK Siberia. As the name indicates, the leaves of this species are deeply cut, "fingered" like the leaves of a fig. The white, yellow, copper, pink, or red flowers are single, to a diameter of 3 in. Rust resistant.

Happy Lights is a seed strain in the full range of flower colors; late-winter-sown seeds produce plants that bloom the first year.

Alcea rosea

syn. *Althaea rosea*

Color	various
Bloom time	midsummer to early fall
Size	6–8 ft. × 1–2 ft.
Light	sun
Zones	Z3–10, HS

HOLLYHOCK Turkey, Asia. The classic hollyhock of Old World cottage gardens. Only those in dry, sunny climates should expect good results.

Countless strains and cultivars are available, including:

Chater's Double Hybrids include double powder-puff flowers in a full range of mixed or individual colors. **'Crème de Cassis'** bears 3- to 4-in., single or semi-double, black currant–colored flowers edged with paler rose. 4–6 ft. **Majorette Mix** is a dwarf strain. Double or semi-double flowers in whites, yellows, pinks, and reds. 24–30 in. × 12 in. **Powder Puffs Mix** has white, yellow, rose, or red, fully double flowers to 4 in. across. **'Sunshine'** has large, single flowers of sunny yellow. 5–6 ft. Z3–9.

Alcea rugosa

Color	yellow
Bloom time	midsummer to early fall
Size	6–8 ft. × 2–3 ft.
Light	sun
Zones	Z3–9

RUSSIAN HOLLYHOCK Ukraine. Furrowed, gray-green leaves are cleft into five lobes. Hairy stems carry single, 4-in., butter-yellow flowers. Rust resistant.

HOSTA | PLANTAIN LILY

Hosta

ASPARAGACEAE

THIS GENUS REGULARLY lists at or near the top in perennial popularity polls, and no wonder. Hostas flourish from USDA zones 3 through 8.

Hostas' chief attraction is their foliage, borne in neat circular clusters of broad leaves with parallel veins that may be colored gold or blue as well as green, and striped, edged, or splashed with white or some other contrasting color. Foliage texture varies from shiny and smooth to pleated, puckered, and waxy, and individual leaves may measure 1–20 in. long and 0.75–12 in. wide. The flowers of most species and cultivars are unremarkable, borne in summertime in terminal racemes atop erect scapes. The blossoms are lily-like, typically pendulous, 0.75–2 in. long, with six petal-like tepals, in shades of white, lavender, or violet. One exception to the rule is *Hosta plantaginea*, whose white flowers are not only fragrant—it's the only species with this characteristic—but also measure up to 6 in. long. Plant breeders are currently focusing on hosta cultivars with more attractive and fragrant flowers.

Often categorized as a "shade plant," hostas offer some of the best choices for lower-light situations, though most prefer partial shade, and none flourish in deep, unrelieved shade, especially the dry shade found beneath conifers and shallow-rooted deciduous trees such as maples. In fact, many cultivars require a couple of hours of direct sunlight daily if they are to look their best. The best exposure for hostas is one with morning sun and afternoon shade. Noontime and early afternoon shade is particularly important where sun is intense.

For best growth, provide a nutrient-rich, organic soil that is moisture-retentive but well drained. Hostas should receive an inch of water a week, either from natural precipitation or irrigation, throughout the growing season.

Hostas are subject to a number of fungal and viral diseases; be sure to start with healthy, disease-free plants from a reliable grower. Notched leaf margins are a sign of black vine weevils. Yellowing of the leaves in June followed by chocolate-brown streaks or blotches between the veins are symptoms of foliar nematodes, and plants infested with them are best removed and disposed of off-site. Mice and voles sometimes attack the roots and crowns; slugs, snails, and deer relish hosta foliage. Cultivars with thick-textured, waxy, blue foliage appear less palatable to deer.

With their expansive foliage, hostas furnish a uniquely luxuriant effect to partially shaded beds and borders, presenting a visually soothing contrast to such brightly colored, shade-tolerant annuals as impatiens, coleus, and wax begonias. They provide an attractive edging for shade-tolerant shrubs such as azaleas, viburnums, and hollies, and under a deciduous canopy make an outstanding follow-up for snowdrops, crocus, tulips, daffodils, and other spring-blooming bulbs. Hostas mingle easily in woodland gardens, where their bold foliage provides attractive contrast to finer-leaved neighbors including ferns, hellebores, lungworts, and wild gingers.

Propagate named cultivars by division, ideally in late summer about 30 days before the first fall frost. Hosta seed germinates readily, though the offspring of cultivars may not possess the desirable traits of their parents. Sow outdoors in fall or stratify seed in the refrigerator and start indoors in early spring.

Hosta fortunei 'Francee'

Hosta crispula

syn. *H. sieboldiana* var. *sieboldiana*

Flower color	lavender
Bloom time	early summer
Size	1–1.5 ft. × 2.5 ft.
Light	part shade
Zones	Z3–9

CURLED-LEAF HOSTA Native to Japan. Traditionally treated as a species, but recent research has revealed it to be a form of *Hosta sieboldiana*. Forms cushions of long-stemmed, dull green, 5- to 7-in., ovate leaves with irregular, white margins. Racemes of 1.75-in., pale lavender flowers borne on 3-ft. scapes; as many as 40 flowers per raceme. Sensitive to hot sun; mass in shade as ground cover.

Hosta fortunei

Flower color	lilac
Bloom time	summer
Size	1–1.5 ft. × 2 ft.
Light	part shade, shade
Zones	Z3–9

FORTUNE'S HOSTA Japan. Treated as a species by horticulturists, but recently revealed as a form of *Hosta sieboldiana*. Somewhat waxy, gray-green, ovate leaves, 6–12 in. long, borne in 2-ft. mounds. Racemes of pale lilac, 1- to 1.5-in. flowers carried on 3- to 4-ft. scapes. Genetically variable, and a parent to many selections including:

'Albopicta' ('Golden Spring') has young leaves pale yellow with irregular, dark green margins; leaves become all green as they mature in summer. **Var. *hyacinthina*** (syn. *H. fortunei* 'Hyacinthina', *H.* 'Hyacinthina') has blue-gray, greenish leaves with thin, gray rim. **'Francee'** has dark green, heart-shaped leaves rimmed with a white band. Sun tolerant; a perennial favorite.

Hosta gracillima

syn. *H. longipes* var. *gracillima*

Flower color	purple
Bloom time	late summer
Size	12 in. × 30 in.
Exposure	part shade
Zones	Z3–8

SMALL ROCK HOSTA ("HIME IWA GIBOSHI") Native to mountain valleys in Japan's Kochi Prefecture. Narrow, glossy green leaves, 4 in. long and 2 in. wide, with wavy margins. Fast growing, a gem for troughs, rock gardens, or the fronts of borders.

Hosta lancifolia

Flower color	lilac
Bloom time	late summer
Size	1 ft. × 1.5 ft.
Exposure	part shade, shade
Zones	Z3–9

NARROW-LEAVED PLANTAIN LILY Japan. Another traditional "species" in horticulture that is probably more correctly treated as a cultivar of garden origin. Forms a mound of long-stemmed, glossy deep green, lanceolate leaves 2–6 in. long. Scapes, 2 ft. tall and spotted purple at the base, bear racemes of 1.5- to 2-in., flaring, pale flowers flushed with purple. Good for edging.

Hosta plantaginea

Flower color	white to lilac
Bloom time	mid- to late summer
Size	12–18 in. × 18–24 in.
Light	part shade, shade
Zones	Z3–9

AUGUST LILY Native to China and Japan. Erect and spreading, this medium-sized hosta has glossy, rounded, heart-shaped, light yellow-green leaves and large, 3- to 6-in.-long, trumpet-shaped, white, heavily fragrant flowers borne on scapes up to 30 in. The common name refers to this species' late blooming season. Attracts hummingbirds.

Var. *japonica* (var. *grandiflora*, 'Grandiflora') is exceptionally vigorous, to 26 in. tall and 46 in. wide. **'Royal Standard'** is a cultivar of long standing with very fragrant white flowers. Tolerates full sun as long as it is not intense. Carefree and reliable.

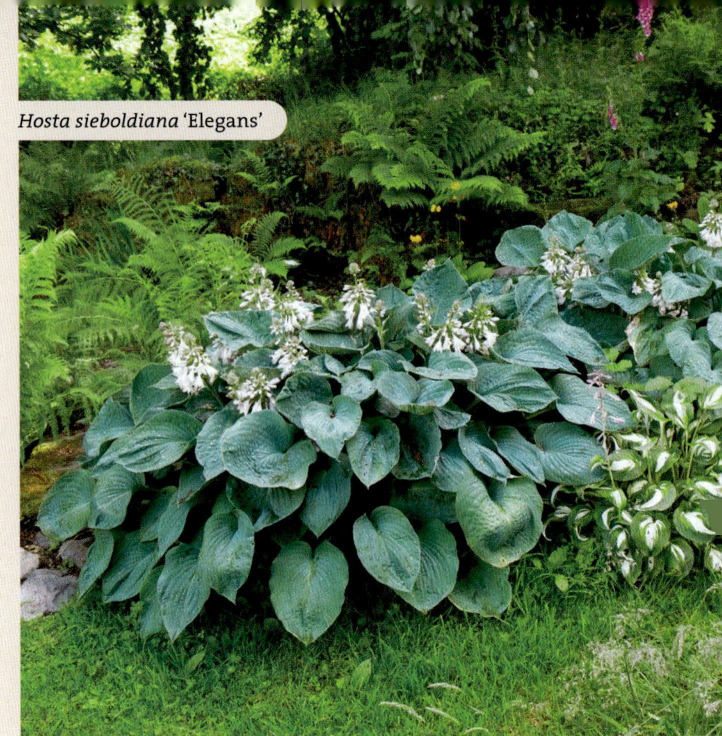

Hosta sieboldiana 'Elegans'

Hosta sieboldiana

Flower color	white
Bloom time	early summer
Size	2–3 ft. × 3–4 ft.
Light	part shade, shade
Zones	Z4–8

SIEBOLD'S HOSTA The species is native to Japan, and is usually available in the nursery trade in the form of the cultivar *Hosta sieboldiana* 'Elegans' (sometimes listed as var. *elegans*; more correctly var. *sieboldiana*). Thick textured and corrugated, the large 13 in. × 10 in., blue-green leaves are heart shaped; funnel-shaped flowers, 1–1.5 in. long, are white with a violet tinge, and borne on 36-in. scapes. An exceptionally shade-tolerant hosta, but slow growing. The blue color is due to a wax on the leaf surface that rapidly degenerates in hot climates.

'Frances Williams' has large, rounded and cupped, bluish green leaves irregularly bordered with gold. White flowers.

Hosta sieboldii 'Kabitan'

Hosta undulata 'Albo-marginata'

Hosta sieboldii

syn. *H. albomarginata*, *H. lancifolia* var. *marginata*

lilac
late summer
1 ft. high and wide
part shade, shade
Z3–9

SEERSUCKER'S HOSTA Native of Japan with undulate, lanceolate, dark green, 4- to 5-in. leaves, matte above and shiny beneath. Racemes of nodding, bell-shaped, 1.5- to 2-in., white flowers veined with purple.

'Kabitan' has pale yellow-green leaves with green margins and violet flowers.

Hosta undulata

syn. *H. lancifolia* var. *undulata*, *H. media-picta*, *H. variegata*

lilac
early summer
1.5 ft. × 1–1.5 ft.
part shade, shade
Z3–9

WAVY-LEAF PLANTAIN LILY Of horticultural origin. Wavy, sometimes contorted leaves with elliptic to ovate, green blades 5–6 in. long, marked with a broad cream central stripe and edged with darker green.

'Albo-marginata' ('Silver Rain') has tapering, elliptic leaves, gray-green at the center, margins rimmed with cream. Fast growing, spreads, a handsome groundcover. **'Variegata'** ('Undulata'), to 10 in., has smallish leaves irregularly streaked with white at the center and undulating green margins, twisted leaf tips.

Hosta ventricosa

color	purple
bloom time	summer
size	4 in. × 12 in.
light	part shade, shade
zones	Z3–9

DARK PURPLE–FLOWERED HOSTA ("MURASAKI GIBOSHI") Native to China and Korea. A natural dwarf with heart-shaped, glossy dark green leaves with twisted tips and vivid blue-purple flowers.

Hosta venusta

color	violet
bloom time	early summer
size	4 in. × 1 ft.
light	shade, part shade
zones	Z3–9

HANDSOME PLANTAIN LILY China, Korea. Diminutive, 1- to 2-in. leaves with long petioles; 10- to 12-in. scapes bear sparse racemes of 1–1.5 in., funnel-shaped flowers that are violet marked with darker veins.

'Variegated' has leaves with cream centers and wavy margins in various shades of green.

Other Notable Cultivars

Because hostas hybridize readily, professional and amateur breeders have created a dizzying number of cultivars—some 6000 were in commerce at last count. Within this plethora, there is considerable variation in adaptation to climate and conditions.

For starters, leaf color can provide a clue as to light requirements. In general, hostas with yellow or golden leaves (like **'Gold Regal'**) can stand more sun than hostas with green, blue, or white-variegated leaves. Unless they receive at least a couple of hours of full sun daily, preferably in the morning or after midafternoon, the yellow-leaved hostas take on an unattractive greenish tint. Blue-leaved hostas such as **'Blue Mouse Ears'** may tolerate such sunnier sites in cooler, northern climates, but their blue color is likely to fade to green unless protected from direct afternoon sun, especially where it is very strong. White-variegated hostas also tend to prefer shadier sites, though cultivars with thicker leaves (such as 'Francee') are more sun tolerant. Bleached patches on the leaves that turn brown and then fall away usually indicates sunburn.

In terms of climatic adaptation, as a rule, hostas that bear fragrant flowers, like the species *Hosta plantaginea* and its hybrid descendants such as **'Fragrant Bouquet'**, **'Fragrant Dream'**, and **'Summer Fragrance'**, are the most tolerant of heat and humidity. Typically, fragrant-flowered hostas also share golden-leaved hostas' requirement for extra sunlight, and seem to be extra attractive to deer.

Visit the American Hosta Society's directory of outstanding hosta display gardens (americanhostasociety.org/community/display-gardens) for regionally oriented cultural information and selections.

ICE PLANT

Delosperma | AIZOACEAE

THESE SOUTHERN AFRICAN succulent plants are easy to grow, requiring little care, and provide a convenient as well as attractive solution for troublesome hot and droughty areas of the landscape. They are also promiscuous: there are 100 or so species and they interbreed freely in the wild, causing considerable debate among botanists trying to sort out the ice plant family tree. Be sure not to confuse these plants with *Carpobrotus edulis*, which is also known as iceplant and is highly invasive.

Ice plants provide vivid splashes of color in the landscape, and their mats of jellybean-like foliage are often seen blanketing steep banks and hillsides beside highways, where they generally flourish without any care. They actually prefer rocky, average to poor soil, as long as it drains well. The drainage is non-negotiable: ice plants will surely die in their first winter if planted in waterlogged clay or any other soil that remains persistently wet. Even where the drainage is good, a gravel topdressing or mulch is beneficial to facilitate water runoff around the crowns of the plants.

Although ice plants tolerate partial shade, their bloom is most abundant when grown in full sun. Partner them with other succulents such as sedums, sempervivums, opuntias, crassulas, and red hot poker aloes in crevices between rocks, in raised beds, on dry, nutrient-poor banks, or in containers. Deer resistant.

Propagate from seed at about 70°F, or take stem cuttings in spring or summer. Increase cultivars vegetatively.

Delosperma cooperi

syn. *Mesembryanthemum cooperi*

Flower color	magenta
Bloom time	early summer to late fall
Size	3–5 in. × 24–36 in.
Light	sun, part shade
Zones	Z5–9, HS

HARDY ICE PLANT, COOPER'S ICE PLANT, TRAILING ICE PLANT Native to rocky slopes of central southern Africa, hardy ice plants are adapted to very well-drained but average soils. This fleshy creeper has cylindrical, light green leaves 1–2 in. long; these may become red in cold temperatures. Showy solitary, daisy-like, 2-in., hot-pink flowers with white anthers cover the plants all summer until frost. Very tolerant of drought, and invaluable in xeric gardens; excellent as a groundcover on difficult dry, sunny banks, as well as being well suited to rock gardens, containers, and raised beds. Fast growing and can be aggressive in some areas. Excellent in coastal gardens.

Delosperma dyeri

Flower color	orange, coral
Bloom time	spring to fall
Size	2–3 in. × 18–20 in.
Light	sun
Zones	Z5–9

RED MOUNTAIN ICE PLANT Native to the mountains of South Africa's Eastern Cape. A prolific bloomer, red mountain ice plant covers itself with shiny, white-eyed, coral- and watermelon-red starry flowers for a period of several months. Provide a sunny spot with very free drainage. Drought tolerant. Especially handsome in rock or raised gardens.

'Psdold' has scarlet flowers.

Delosperma nubigenum

	yellow
	spring
	4 in. × 24 in.
	sun
	Z6–9

YELLOW ICE PLANT Found at high altitudes of the Lesotho Mountains of South Africa, this species tolerates more humidity than most. Low, succulent, evergreen mats of pointed, oval, bright green leaves become watery green (like green grapes) in winter, sometimes tinged with red. They thrive in poor, rocky soil with little water, so are excellent for dry and even xeric gardens as groundcover, on walls, as edgings, or in rock gardens. Do not irrigate. In spring these easy-to-grow plants are covered with bright yellow, orange-eyed daisies that attract butterflies.

'Basutoland' produces masses of bright yellow flowers in late spring into summer. Oval, lettuce-green leaves. Tolerates bright shade as well as sun. Great for raised beds and containers. 2–4 in. Z5–9

Other Notable Cultivars

'Beaufort West' sports small, light pink daisies above cushions of fat, succulent, 1-in. leaves. Z5–7, HS. **'Eye Candy'** belongs to a group of smaller-flowered, white-eyed ice plants bred in Japan. Carmine-red flowers, maturing to orange. Spring blooming. Z5–7, HS. **'Fire Spinner'** is exceptionally hardy with white-eyed, brilliant orange-and-magenta flowers, 1.5 in. across. Z5–8. **'John Proffitt'** (Table Mountain) is considered superior to similar *Delosperma cooperi*. Long-blooming, glistening, bright magenta daisies. Z6–8. **'Kelaidis'** (Mesa Verde) has salmon-pink daisy flowers on compact plants from spring to fall. Tolerates light shade. Z4–8. **'Pink Ribbon'** is bicolored pink-and-orange. All summer bloom. Z5–11.

INULA

Inula

ASTERACEAE

IF YOU'VE SEEN ONE YELLOW DAISY, have you seen them all? Not really. Leopard's bane, arnica, and inula are superficially similar flowers, but each has its own charm, strengths, and weaknesses. Inulas offer bold, if sometimes coarse, rough foliage, typically with large basal leaves, the upper ones diminishing in size. Flowerheads are solitary or grouped, flattish, with slender, yellow ray flowers surrounding darker-colored, tubular disk flowers.

Provide a sunny site with average, well-drained soil that remains moist during dry spells. Outstandingly cold hardy. The low-growing species are appropriate for rock gardens and the edges of beds and borders; mass larger species between shrubs to dramatic effect. Deadhead for a long bloom season.

Propagate by seed or division in spring.

Inula ensifolia

color	yellow
bloom time	late spring to early summer
size	1–2 ft. × 1 ft.
light	sun
zones	Z3–7, HS

SWORDLEAF INULA, ELECAMPANE, HORSEHEAL Caucasus region of Europe. This easy, compact perennial branches freely and is topped with solitary or groups of slender-rayed, 1- to 2-in., orange-yellow daisies. Coarse, willow-like leaves are sessile, alternate, and parallel veined, hence "ensifolia," which means "leaves like swords." Their bloom time may last six weeks or so; excellent cut flowers. Prone to powdery mildew.

'Compacta' grows to only 6 in.; charming in rock gardens. **'Sunray'** produces its golden-yellow daisies in summer. 1.5 ft. Z3–9.

Inula helenium

	yellow
	midsummer
	2–6 ft. × 3 ft.
	sun, part shade
	Z3–7

ELECAMPANE, HORSEHEAL, MARCHALAN Britain, Europe, to western Asia; naturalized in the United States. These large and rather coarse but impressive plants have huge lower leaves, 2–3 ft. in length; stem leaves are smaller and sessile. The foliage is rough-hairy on the upper surfaces, downy-soft beneath. The 2- to 3-in.-wide flowerheads may be solitary or borne in groups. Keep soil moist. Best confined to herb gardens. Valued as a medicinal herb for centuries. Sweet candy cakes were formerly made from elecampane.

Inula royleana syn. *I. racemosa*

	yellow
	late summer
	24–30 in. × 18 in.
	sun
	Z3–7, HS

HIMALAYAN ELECAMPANE Western Himalayan Mountains region, especially Kashmir. Clump forming and erect, with black flower buds that open to shaggy, orange-yellow, 5-in. blooms on unbranched stems. Basal leaves are ovate, 6–10 in. long, furry beneath and with winged petioles; upper leaves are elliptic, to 8 in., with enlarged, stem-clasping bases. Excellent cut flower. This plant has a long history of medicinal use; the roots have been used to make an expectorant, among other things.

IRIS

Iris | IRIDACEAE

NOTABLE FOR ITS MYRIAD of floral colors, iris is appropriately named for Iris, Greek Goddess of the Rainbow. This huge genus of about 300 species is native throughout northern temperate regions of the world, where it grows in chilly mountain areas as well as in meadows, on hillsides, and beside streams in North America, Europe, Africa, and Asia. Various forms have been cultivated for centuries and many are depicted in art (think Vincent van Gogh and George Gessert) and in emblems, particularly the fleur-de-lis of French kings and of Scouting, and on the flags of St. Louis, Missouri, and Quebec, Canada.

The genus is often divided according to whether the particular species grow from bulbs, rhizomes, or fleshy rhizomatous roots. Foliage is mostly sword-shaped, narrow or broader according to type, and sometimes arranged in fans. The flowers, solitary or several per stem, have floral parts in trios; three inner "standards" that are generally upright, three outer "falls" that are often reflexed; the three-branched style has stigmas on the underside and covers the anthers, an adaptation to expedite pollination by flying insects and ants, or others seeking nectar. A three-part fruiting capsule follows; sometimes these are valued for dried winter floral arrangements.

Most irises require a sunny position to thrive, although some tolerate afternoon shade; crested irises do well in woodland shade. A few types, such as the Louisiana irises, thrive in wet soils, but most irises prefer well-drained soils of average to good fertility. Soil pH is seldom critical, except in the case of Japanese iris, which demands lime-free soil. Note that *Iris pseudacorus*, native to Europe, western Asia, and northwest Africa, though often found in nurseries, has proven invasive.

There is an iris for almost every spot in the garden. Tall species mix well with shrubs and other tall perennials toward the back of borders, while the slightly lower-growing bearded, Siberian, and Japanese types are colorful mid-border plants, contrasting well with more rounded spurges, bleeding hearts, ornamental sages, and peonies. Bulbous netted and Danford irises are suitable for rock gardens and small spots where color is needed. They force well for early indoor displays. Bulbous Dutch irises are popular cut flowers. Japanese roof iris, *I. tectorum*, and winter iris, *I. unguicularis,* deserve mention for iris fanciers.

Deer seldom browse irises, though they occasionally nip off the blossoms of crested types, generally leaving behind the decapitated blossoms. Other pests include iris borers on rhizomatous types and thrips that attack the flowers. Both can become seriously destructive if not controlled.

Propagate by division. Start species from seed, though seedlings take a couple of years to reach blooming size. Check out specialist nurseries for the most recent introductions.

Iris cristata

color	blue, purple
bloom	spring
size	3–9 in. × 15 in.
light	part shade, shade
zone	Z3–8

CRESTED IRIS, DWARF CRESTED IRIS Native to woodlands of the eastern United States, from Maryland to Oklahoma and Georgia. Slender, creeping, woody rhizomes spread widely along the surface, and function effectively as groundcovers. Fans of narrow, sword-shaped, 4- to 8-in.-long leaves; fragrant, almost stalkless flowers 1–1.5 in. across are held on 1.5- to 2-in. perianth tubes. Flowers may be solitary or paired, have upright monochrome standards, spreading falls decorated with a cream or yellow crest, and a large central white blotch or signal usually rimmed with purple or violet. Be alert for slugs that shred the foliage and damage the blooms too. Spectacular when allowed to naturalize in light woods or clearings, or on shaded rocky slopes and in rock gardens.

'Eco Bluebird', one of several cultivars introduced by Eco-Gardens, has dark blue flowers crested with orange and a white throat. **'Powder Blue Giant'** has large, open flowers of pale lavender and purple-rimmed white blotches. **'Shenandoah Sky'** has deep lilac flowers, a yellow crest, and purple-rimmed white blotches on the falls. **'Tennessee White'**, selected by Don Shadow, is vigorous with white flowers decorated with a yellow crest. Possibly the best white. **'Vein Mountain'**, introduced by We-Du Nursery, has very light blue flowers, with orange crests outlined with deep purple.

Iris ensata syn. *I. kaempferi*

(flower)	various
(calendar)	summer
(size)	2–3 ft. × 1.5–2 ft.
(sun)	sun
(zone)	Z4–9

JAPANESE IRIS, JAPANESE WATER IRIS Native to Japan, China, Korea, India, and eastern Russia. Grassy leaves to 2 ft. long, each with a conspicuous raised midrib, emerge from stout rhizomes. Two to four flowers, usually 4–6 in. across, in white, blues, purples, and reddish violet are borne on sparsely branching stems; some modern cultivars may have flowers to 10 in. across. Blooms appear flat with arching falls blotched with yellow, and slightly smaller, almost flat standards. Requires an acid, humus-rich soil, moist but not necessarily boggy. Never apply lime. Plant about 2 in. deep as soon as possible without the roots drying out. Divide in fall or just after bloom time.

Superb for rain gardens, beside water gardens, and in shallow ponds. However, Japanese irises also thrive in ordinary garden soils, and provide magnificent displays among astilbes and hostas.

There are countless cultivars; the following is a small selection:

'Dragon Tapestry' is white-splashed, dark burgundy. **'Eleanor Perry'** has deep lilac flowers traced with violet. **'Great White Heron'** is semi-double and pure white. **'Lion King'** has frilly, purple-edged white falls flashed with yellow. **'Pink Frost'** is lightly ruffled with lavender-pink flowers, yellow at the center.

Iris foetidissima

(color)	mauve
(bloom time)	spring to summer
(size)	1.5–2.5 ft. × 1.5–2 ft.
(light)	sun, shade
(zone)	Z6–10

STINKING IRIS, GLADWYN IRIS, FOETID IRIS Britain, southern and western Europe, northern Africa. This unusual iris is grown predominantly for its colorful seeds. Evergreen, 2- to 4-ft.-long, sword-like leaves have a very slight, unpleasant odor when bruised. Growing from slow-spreading rhizomes, the two- to three-times-branching flower stalks, flattened on one side and shorter than the leaves, each bear up to three, pale grayish, 2.5-in. flowers with bronzy yellow falls. Blossoms open consecutively, but many-stemmed plants may flaunt a dozen simultaneously. Seedpods similar to Brazil nuts follow; these split into three sections, each revealing two rows of round, scarlet, sometimes yellow or white ('Fructo-alba') seeds. Sow fresh seed when possible; slow to establish. Remove shabby leaves after winter. Use seedpods for dried arrangements. Tolerates coastal gardens, and almost pure sand, as well as tree roots in shaded spots.

'Citrina' has pale yellow flowers veined in purple. A superior cultivar. **'Holden Clough'** (probably *Iris foetidissima* × *I. chrysographes*, or *I. pseudacorus*) is vigorous, with golden flowers overlaid with purple veining and yellow-blotched falls.

Iris ×germanica 'Beverly Sills'

Iris ×germanica

(color)	various
(bloom time)	early summer
(size)	8–36 in. × 9–24 in.
(light)	sun
(zone)	Z3–10

BEARDED HYBRID IRIS, GERMAN IRIS Of hybrid origin, probably the largest and most popular type of irises in cultivation. Named for the hairy "beard" that decorates the falls. The plants arise from thick rhizomes that lie close to the soil surface, sprouting fans of broad, sword-shaped gray-green leaves. Several flowers are borne on each stem. In addition to the bearded falls, the standards are erect, usually wide, and often frilly. Flower color varies from white through pastel pinks, blues, and yellows, to deep saturated bronzy golds, blues, and purples, with standards and beard often of contrasting hues. Some cultivars are fragrant, many repeat bloom, and most make lovely cut flowers. Spectacular additions to early summer beds and borders; low-growing cultivars are appropriate for rock gardens and the front of the border; tall ones bring grace to the back of borders and fit in well among shrubby cinquefoil, roses, weigelas, and other shrubs.

Plant in free-draining soil, with the rhizome half-buried or just at the soil surface; in very hot regions, slightly deeper. Divide every three to four years. Be alert for iris borers, which lay eggs in the rhizomes to emerge as larvae with a built-in food supply; the larvae are pinkish white with black heads. Destroy infected plants and rhizomes, which often become mushy from bacterial or fungal infections that gain entry through the borer tunnels. Traditionally the leaf fans have been cut to about 9 in. in late summer to allow sun ripening of the rhizomes.

There are innumerable cultivars; here are a few: **'Beverly Sills'** is slightly ruffled with pale coral-pink flowers; apricot beard. May rebloom. 32–38 in. tall. **'Champagne Elegance'** has apricot falls; very pale pink standards. Reblooms. 28–34 in. **'Immortality'** ('Immortelle') has very wide, slightly ruffled, white falls; buttercup-yellow beards. Reblooms. 30–36 in. **'Raspberry Blush'** is pale crushed-raspberry color with darker patches on the falls; orange-raspberry beards. 18–24 in. **'Superstition'** is so deep purple as to appear almost black. 32–38 in.

Louisiana iris 'Black Gamecock'

Louisiana Iris

Color	various colors
Bloom time	summer
Size	3–4 ft. × 3 ft.
Light	sun
Zones	Z4–9

This group of distinct species is found wild in marshes and wetlands along the Gulf Coast of Texas and Florida, and in the Mississippi basin. Species include: brick-colored *Iris fulva* (syn. *I. cuprea*), blue-flowered *I. brevicaulis* (syn. *I. foliosa*), blue-violet *I. giganticaerulea*, purple and white-flowered *I. hexagona*, and reddish purple or yellow *I. nelsonii*. Breeding programs have produced several notable hybrids. Elegant, beardless, and crestless flowers, with slender falls and floppy standards, come in an astonishing range of colors. Louisiana irises thrive in moist beds and borders and are excellent cut flowers. Plant 2 in. deep in fall and mulch heavily. Easily divided.

Iris pallida

Color	lavender
Bloom time	late spring
Size	2–4 ft. × 2 ft.
Light	sun
Zones	Z4–9

SWEET IRIS, ORRIS, DALMATIAN IRIS Northern Italy, Croatia. Long, fat rhizomes support sword-shaped, glaucous, almost evergreen leaves to 1.5 in. wide. Sparsely branched, leafless stems bear several flowers enclosed in papery silver spathes, well above the foliage. The pale lavender, yellow-bearded flowers smell deliciously of vanilla, orange blossom, or grape jelly depending upon your nose. All variants have excellent, good-looking foliage that persists through summer and contrasts with the rounded form of the plants. Fine in rock gardens, beds and borders, and fragrance and herb gardens.

'Argenteo-variegata' ('Alba-variegata') has blue-gray leaves striped longitudinally in creamy white. Powder blue flowers. **'Variegata'** ('Zebra', 'Aurea-variagata') has glaucous leaves striped with yellowish cream. Similar flowers and perhaps more vigorous than the white-striped selection. **Var. *dalmatica*** is a superior selection with more saturated color. Yellow beards.

Iris sibirica 'Pink Haze'

Iris sibirica

color	blue
bloom	late spring
size	24–36 in. × 24 in.
light	sun, part shade
zone	Z3–9

SIBERIAN IRIS Central Europe to southern Russia, northern Asia. Easily grown, makes dense, upright clumps of bright green, narrowly lance-shaped leaves that remain handsome through the season. Branched stems carry up to five beardless flowers, each about 3 in. across, usually well above the foliage mass. The species has blue-violet flowers with dark veining and white throats. Slow spreading but persistent. There are countless cultivars in assorted colors; the following are a few popular ones:

'Butter and Sugar' has white standards, creamy-lemon falls. 3–3.5 ft. Z5–10. **'Caesar's Brother'**, an old cultivar, is very upright with deep purple flowers. 1.5–3 ft. **'Pink Haze'** has soft pale lavender falls, rimmed with white, dark throat. 30 in. **'Super Ego'** has soft light blue flowers; wavy falls etched with deep blue. 32 in. **'White Swirl'** has white flowers, yellow at the throat. 24–30 in.

Iris tuberosa

syn. *Hermodactylus tuberosus*

color	yellow-and-deep purple
bloom	late winter to early spring
size	12–15 in. × 6 in.
light	sun
zone	Z6–8

SNAKE'S-HEAD IRIS, BLACK IRIS, HERMES FINGERS Greece, Spain, Turkey. Evergreen clumps of sword-shaped, gray-green leaves, to 12–15 in. long, arranged in two ranks. Very early blooming; fragrant, 2- to 3-in. flowers with spatulate, glassy green falls, dramatically blotched with very deep purple. The erect, 1-in., pea-green standards surround a greenish yellow, conspicuously three-forked style.

JERUSALEM SAGE

Phlomis

LAMIACEAE

Phlomis IS A GENUS OF SAGE-LIKE PLANTS grown for both their attractive foliage and eye-catching flowers. Large leaves are corrugated, and covered with white or grayish woolly hairs. The typical mint family flowers are two-lipped, the upper providing a protective hood over the three-lobed lower. Lavender-pink, yellow, or white flowers are arranged in dense, several-flowered verticillasters.

Drought-resistant phlomis prefers a sunny spot where soil is fertile and drains well. They are sensitive to extreme temperature fluctuations and they do not enjoy muggy conditions. Cut to the ground before spring growth emerges. Easy care, but leafhoppers may be troublesome. Eminently suitable for wildlife gardens, where they attract birds, butterflies, and bees; resistant to both rabbits and deer. In beds and borders phlomis provides architectural impact and color over a long season.

Divide in spring, or take soft cuttings of young growth.

Phlomis cashmeriana

Color	lilac pink
Bloom time	midsummer
Size	2–4 ft. × 2 ft.
Light	sun, part shade
Zone	Z5–9

KASHMIR SAGE Native to drier areas of Kashmir and the Western Himalayas, this species is impressive in dry gardens where humidity is low. Upright, stately plants clothed with pairs of soft, gray-woolly leaves. Basal leaves are 4–10 in. long, stem leaves smaller. Numerous bold verticillasters of 1-in., deep lavender-lilac flowers on the upper stems. Sculptural seedheads maintain winter interest. Good as cut flowers; dried stems are attractive in winter bouquets.

Phlomis fruticosa

Color	yellow
Bloom time	early to midsummer
Size	2–4 ft. × 3 ft.
Light	sun
Zone	Z6–10

JERUSALEM SAGE Eastern Mediterranean. Widely grown in California, this underused plant should gain acceptance elsewhere. Bushy plants, often woody below, are covered with coarse, elliptical to lanceolate, 2- to 3-in., gray-green leaves, white-woolly with hairs beneath; hairy stems appear slightly yellow. Flower buds cluster in tight, tiered whorls in the upper leaf axils and open to hooded, butter-yellow, 1- to 1.25-in. blooms. In cool climates Jerusalem sage is dormant in winter, but erupts from the base in spring. Attractive in borders with 'Big Blue' sea holly, lavender, or salvias.

Phlomis tuberosa 'Amazone'

Phlomis russeliana

	yellow
	late spring to early fall
	3–4 ft. × 2.5 ft.
	sun
	Z3–9

JERUSALEM SAGE, STICKY JERUSALEM SAGE Syria, Turkey. Evergreen, with sage-green foliage, softly fuzzy beneath. Ovate basal leaves, heart-shaped at the base, may reach 6–8 in. long. Smaller upper-stem leaves have scalloped or undulating rims. Ball-like clusters of pale yellow, hooded, 1- to 1.5-in. flowers arranged up the stem, topiary like.

Phlomis tuberosa

syn. *Phlomoides tuberosa*

	pink
	early to late summer
	2–5 ft. × 3 ft.
	sun, part shade
	Z5–8

TUBEROUS JERUSALEM SAGE Central and southeastern Europe to central Asia. Bushy, with vigorous, upright stems arising from tuberous roots. Arrow-shaped, crumpled, 8- to 10-in. leaves are variably hairy, coarsely toothed along the margin, and decrease in size as they ascend deep purple stems. Deep purple calyces contrast well with pink, 1-in. flowers.

'Amazone' (Sage-leaf Mullein) has rosy-mauve flowers on burgundy stems. Mostly evergreen; toothed leaves, grayish with downy hairs. 4–5 ft. Z5.

JOE-PYE WEED | BONESET

Eupatorium, Eupatoriadelphus, Eutrochium | ASTERACEAE

THIS GLOBE-TROTTING GENUS is found all over the Northern Hemisphere—in Europe, northern Africa, and central Asia—but it is the North American species, natives of the eastern half of the continent, that are the horticultural stars. (Similar *Eupatoriadelphus* is another recently reclassified genus that has been broken away from *Eupatorium*.) These garden-worthy types earn their keep with their strong presence: they are large, exuberant plants that contribute foliage mass and texture, as well as flowers. Individually the flowers are small and most often subdued in color, but they are borne on substantial to huge, parasol-like heads. Furthermore, their bloom season commonly comes in late summer or fall, when the perennial garden most needs additional color. The flowers attract butterflies and other insect pollinators, and the seedheads that follow provide late-season food for a variety of birds.

The taller ones—they can stand head-high or even higher—require staking in a wind-swept site. Alternatively, pinch back the stems in mid- to late spring to about half their height to promote more compact, bushy growth; this treatment also leads to a slightly later bloom season. These plants appreciate a rich, organic soil, and require moderate but regular irrigation while young, as well as for the best bloom. However, they tolerate drought once established.

Combine Joe-Pye weed with other late bloomers such as goldenrods (*Solidago*), swamp hibiscus (*Hibiscus coccineus*), asters, and the taller ornamental grasses. The native species are ideal for native, meadow, or prairie plantings, as well as at the back of borders and among shrubs. Butterflies and bees are frequent visitors and pollinate the flowers. Typically they are healthy plants, but are susceptible to leaf miners, mildew, and leaf spots. Only *Eupatorium fistulosum* is reportedly browsed by deer; others are left alone.

Propagate by dividing mature clumps in late winter or spring, by seed, or by stem cuttings taken in spring.

Eupatorium altissimum

syn. *Ageratina altissima*

Flower color	white
Bloom time	late summer to early fall
Size	3–4 ft. × 2–3 ft.
Light	sun, part shade
Zone	Z3–9

TALL BONESET This tough and adaptable species is native throughout the eastern half of North America, inhabiting dry to mesic prairies, meadows, woodland openings, pastures, and even vacant lots. It forms a group of upright, hairy stems that branch only at their tips in the flower clusters. Dark green, pubescent leaves are opposite, lanceolate to narrowly ovate, and up to 5 in. long and 1 in. wide. Inflorescence is a flat-topped cluster of tiny, white flowers that bloom for four to six weeks. Not particularly showy, but hardy and versatile, growing equally well on loams, clays, and gravelly soils of assorted pH levels. Withstands drought well and competes successfully with most neighbors in meadow plantings or wild gardens.

'Prairie Jewel' has variegated cream-and-green, mottled foliage. More compact than the species, reaching a height of 3 ft. Z4–9.

Eupatorium capillifolium

Flower color	white
Bloom time	midsummer to early fall
Size	4–8 ft. × 3–4 ft.
Light	sun, part shade
Zone	Z4–10

DOGFENNEL Roadsides and disturbed sites from Massachusetts to Florida, westward to Missouri and Texas, as well as Cuba and the Bahamas. Spreads by rhizomes and can be weedy. Forms a clump of hairy stems with aromatic, finely dissected, feathery foliage ("capillifolium" means "hair-leaf"), somewhat similar to that of fennel (*Ferula*). Individual flowers are small, but borne in large, loose plumes. A tall and striking plant, though not distinguished enough for most borders; better for meadows and native plant areas.

'Elegant Feather' is more refined, forming narrow, upright plumes of finely textured foliage. Sterile, does not self-seed as does dogfennel. Z7–10

Eupatorium coelestinum

syn. ***Conoclinium coelestinum***

color	blue
bloom time	late summer to early fall
size	2–3 ft. high and wide
exposure	sun, part shade
zone	Z4–9

HARDY AGERATUM Eastern half of North America. Red stems bear heads of fuzzy, blue flowers that are closely similar to those of the familiar annual ageratum or floss flower. Tolerant of most soils, but best suited to clays and organic-rich ones. Prefers moist to average conditions; grows best in full sun, but tolerates light shade. Naturalizes readily, making an attractive tall groundcover.

'Cory' is upright, with crinkled leaves and more abundant, showier blooms on purple stems.

Eupatoriadelphus dubium

syn. ***Eupatoriadelphus dubius, Eupatorium dubium***

color	pink
bloom time	midsummer to early fall
size	2–5 ft. × 1 ft.
exposure	sun, part shade
zone	Z4–8

EASTERN JOE-PYE WEED East Coast of North America from Nova Scotia to South Carolina. Typically 3- to 4-ft.-tall, purple-flecked stems clothed in whorls of lanceolate, toothed leaves. Small, purplish pink flowers carried in domed heads 4–7 in. across. Prefers moist soils but tolerant of drought. A compact alternative to its better-known relatives *Eupatorium purpureum* and *Eupatorium maculatus*.

'Phantom' is extra compact, with wine-colored, sweet-scented flowers. 2–3 ft.

Eupatoriadelphus maculatus 'Gateway'

Eupatoriadelphus maculatum

syn. *Eupatoriadelphus maculatus, Eupatorium maculatum, Eutrochium purpureum* subsp. *maculatum*

Flower color	purple
Bloom time	midsummer to late summer
Size	4–7 ft. × 3 ft.
Light	sun, part shade
Zones	Z5–9

SPOTTED JOE-PYE WEED Manitoba south to Georgia eastward. Solid purple or purple-spotted stems bear toothed, lanceolate leaves in whorls of three to five. Small, light purple flowers borne in branched, usually flat-topped clusters to 8 in. across. Flowers are lightly scented and very showy when planted in mass. Prefers an organic-rich, moist soil; leaf edges liable to browning and crisping when subjected to drought. Especially valuable for foraging bees.

'Atropurpureum' (syn. *Eupatoriadelphus purpureum* var. *atropurpureum*) has purplish black stems and reddish purple flowerheads to 18 in. wide. **'Gateway'** is relatively compact with wine-colored stems; it bears huge, pink flowerheads, 12–18 in. across. 3–5 ft. tall.

Eupatorium purpureum

syn. *Eutrochium purpureum*

Flower color	pink, purple
Bloom time	midsummer to early fall
Size	5–7 ft. × 2–4 ft.
Light	sun, part shade
Zones	Z3–9

SWEET-SCENTED JOE-PYE WEED Wet meadows, stream banks, and wooded slopes throughout the eastern half of the United States and Ontario. Erect clumps of sturdy stems furnished with whorls of three to four serrated, lanceolate, dark green leaves to 12 in. long. Domed, mauve flowerheads are vanilla scented, to 8 in. across; they give way to attractive seedheads that persist into winter. Prefers a moist, fertile, richly organic soil; tolerates average soils unless subjected to drought, which causes browning of leaf edges. Plant in groups or mass at the back of borders, cottage gardens, meadows, and at the water's edge.

'Little Red' has pink-purple flowers. Compact at 3–4 ft. × 2–3 ft.

JUPITER'S BEARD | VALERIAN

Centranthus | CAPRIFOLIACEAE

THOUGH THIS GENUS INCLUDES a dozen or so species, only *Centranthus ruber* is popular with gardeners. Easy to grow and extremely undemanding, Jupiter's beard was a favorite of old-time cottage gardeners. It is an ideal beginner's plant, very forgiving and flourishing even in poor, infertile, and droughty soils, and yet its rewards are sophisticated enough to please connoisseurs.

Jupiter's beard prefers a slightly alkaline pH, but succeeds in any average, well-drained garden soil; its tolerance for drought makes this an excellent choice for xeriscapes and coastal gardens. Unless saving seed, remove fading flowers to promote a second flush of bloom; Jupiter's beard tends to be short lived so it is wise to have replacement seedlings handy. Cut stems back to 6 in. in late summer to stimulate new vegetative growth for overwintering. Attractive to butterflies and bees; seldom browsed by deer, and mostly reported resistant to rabbits. A good groundcover for sunny banks; seeds itself into crevices between pavers or in walls. Commonly found seeded into the mortared walls of European castles and ruins.

A traditional choice for cottage gardens, Jupiter's beard partners well with other alkaline-loving, old-fashioned flowers such as baby's breath, pinks, and pincushion flower. Useful source of cut flowers.

Propagate by seed, by division of mature plants in early spring or fall, or by spring basal cuttings.

Centranthus ruber 'Coccineus'

Centranthus ruber

syn. *Valeriana rubra*

Flower color	red, pink, white
Bloom time	late spring to late summer
Size	1.5–3 ft. × 2–3 ft.
Light	sun, part shade
Zones	Z5–8

JUPITER'S BEARD, FOX'S BRUSH, KEYS-OF-HEAVEN
Native of Europe, northern Africa, and the Middle East, this plant has naturalized in our Pacific Coast states, Arizona, Utah, and Hawaii. The fleshy leaves are bluish green and lance shaped, borne on ascending, often sprawling stems. Dense cymes of fragrant, small, star-shaped flowers.

'Albus' bears creamy-white flowers. Compact to 2 ft. **'Atrococcineus'** flowers are deep brick red. **'Coccineus'** has carmine flowers. To 2 ft. **'Roseus'** has rosy-pink flowers.

LADY'S MANTLE

Alchemilla

ROSACEAE

LADY'S MANTLES, PARTICULARLY *Alchemilla mollis*, are among those cottage-garden perennials that people often remember with nostalgia from their childhood. Indeed, the softly hairy, lobed, and pleated leaves that hold a drop of rain or dew like a pearl, and the froth of tiny chartreuse flowers are irresistible. The name of the genus refers to the belief that the beads of water held by the leaves were "celestial water," pure enough to be used by alchemists trying to turn base metals into gold.

Only a few species are cultivated. Alchemillas do best in shade or part shade; avoid planting sites in intense sun. Soil should be humus rich and moisture retentive; leaves may burn if allowed to dry out. Low maintenance, except for deadheading to control promiscuous self-seeding. Cut back shabby foliage to the crown; fresh new growth will appear in a few weeks. The flowers can be enjoyed as fresh cuts or dried for later use; the leaves serve as attractive filler in flower arrangements. Air-dry flower sprays by hanging them upside down in bunches in a cool, well-ventilated place.

Lady's mantle is excellent as edging along pathways or massed as a groundcover, perhaps broken up with sweeps of hardy geraniums, hostas, or lilyturf. It is valued in partly shaded beds and borders; appropriate partners include grape hyacinths, daffodils and other spring bulbs, astilbes, toad lilies, and Japanese anemones. Partner smaller species in rock gardens with rock cress, perennial candytuft, and low-growing herbs such as thymes. Deer and rabbits seldom browse, but slugs and snails attack young seedlings; a light scattering of gravel deters them.

Divide established or overgrown plants in early spring every three to five years as growth commences; discard worn out pieces. Sow seed in spring.

Alchemilla alpina

Color	green
Bloom time	early summer
Size	3–8 in. × 20 in.
Exposure	sun, part shade
Zone	Z3–7

MOUNTAIN LADY'S MANTLE Alpine regions of Europe. A diminutive plant with 2-in., deeply lobed, sharply toothed leaves, rimmed with silvery hairs that also blanket the underside. Loose sprays of frothy flowers rise on 3-in. stems. Excellent in rock gardens or between pavers. *Alchemilla conjuncta* is similar but may reach 16 in.; *A. ellenbeckii* (Z5–7) rises only a few inches with deeply lobed, 1-in. leaves, hairy on both sides. Plant with creeping thymes and mazus.

Alchemilla erythropoda

syn. *A. serbica*

Color	yellow green
Bloom time	late spring to late summer
Size	6–12 in. × 8 in.
Exposure	sun, part shade
Zone	Z3–7

RED-STEMMED LADY'S MANTLE Mountains of Turkey and Russia. This "mini-mollis" gets a red tinge to its stems in full sun. The leaf stems or petioles are covered with fine hairs, and both sides of the bluish green, shallowly lobed leaves are also velvety. Excellent for troughs, rock gardens, and where space is limited.

Alchemilla mollis 'Robusta'

Alchemilla mollis

(color)	green-yellow
(bloom time)	late spring to early summer
(size)	18–24 in. × 24 in.
(exposure)	sun, part shade
(zones)	Z3–8

LADY'S MANTLE Turkey and Carpathian Mountains. This, the most widely grown of the lady's mantles, has light green, velvety leaves to 6 in. across, pleated into 7 to 11 lobes, and serrated along the rim. Airy sprays of 0.25-in., greenish yellow, petal-less flowers in early summer. Deadhead routinely to prevent copious self-seeding, which can cause it to become weedy. Note that this plant is difficult to remove once planted. Keep soil moist. Lady's mantle is charming as an underplanting for pink roses, and a fine companion for cottage garden flowers: foxgloves, hollyhocks, irises, and bellflowers. *Alchemilla mollis* is possibly a synonym for common lady's mantle, *A. vulgaris*; reportedly *A. vulgaris* has a somewhat looser habit.

'Robusta' is an upright clumper, more full-bodied and with larger leaves than the species. Yellowish green flowers in early summer, repeating later in the season. Tolerates heavy clay soil and drought when established. 15 in. × 36 in. **'Senior'** grows to about 10 in. × 28 in. **'Thriller'** is more compact. Green-flowered inflorescences to 9 in. across. 14 in. × 30 in.

LAVENDER

Lavandula

LAMIACEAE

FEW OTHER PERENNIALS OFFER such a concentration of sensual gratifications as the lavenders. With their deliciously scented, silver-hued, evergreen foliage, lavenders reward eye, nose, and touch. Not surprisingly, they find many applications in the home as well as the garden. Lavenders have a reputation among gardeners for being finicky, but if a few basic cultural needs are met, they are reliable, relatively undemanding plants. Best of all, they are rarely molested by deer or rabbits.

Nearly all species of lavender originated around the Mediterranean. To grow them successfully, match the conditions in which they evolved as closely as possible: a well-drained, lean, sweet soil, with bright sunlight in an airy location; with excellent drainage, lavenders can thrive in regions with cooler summers and cold winters; summer heat and humidity are problematic for most, as are heavy, water-retentive soils. Grow lavenders in raised beds or containers if necessary to enhance drainage; a lime chip or gravel mulch creates a drier microclimate at the crown, and aids surface runoff. Different species of lavender vary in their climatic adaption—selecting the type best suited to your conditions is particularly important with this genus. Once established, lavenders are notably drought tolerant.

Where soils are heavy, improve drainage with coarse sand or grit, along with compost before planting. Avoid an overly rich diet that encourages soft, disease-prone growth and reduces the foliage fragrance, as the essential oils do not intensify. Maintenance includes an annual barbering just after new growth has appeared: cut back by a third to encourage compact, vigorous growth. Beware of pruning too early, as soft young growth may get frosted.

Lavender is an obvious choice for herb gardens; elsewhere they are outstanding planted as low hedges along pathways or to define garden spaces perhaps in containers, to furnish color and contrast in perennial and mixed borders, in rock gardens, or in fragrance gardens, especially those for the visually impaired. Dramatic when massed, lavenders respond well to the regular severe clipping demanded by topiary. Foraging bees and butterflies flock to the flowers; lavender honey is a gourmet item. The oils are used not only in toiletries, but are important in aromatherapy. Sachets of dried lavender retain their fragrance for several years, providing a pleasant aroma to clothing, and also deter clothes moths. In the kitchen, flavor scones, cookies, and ice cream with the dried flowers.

Propagate hybrids and named cultivars by spring tip cuttings, or by mound layering; start species from seed sown indoors seven to ten weeks before the last spring frost.

Lavandula angustifolia 'Hidcote'

Lavandula angustifolia

syn. *L. latifolia*

flower color	lavender, pink, white
bloom time	early to midsummer
size	2–3 ft. × 2–4 ft.
exposure	sun
zones	Z5–8, HS

ENGLISH LAVENDER Not of English origin but rather native to stony hillsides of the Mediterranean. Semi-woody, English lavender bears narrow, needle-like, gray-green leaves to 2.5 in. long on square stems. Tiny but abundant flowers are arranged in tight terminal spikes; corollas and calyces are frequently of contrasting hues. Both foliage and flowers are highly aromatic. Tolerates air pollution well.

There are many cultivars in the marketplace, mostly 18–24 in. This is a selection:

'Compacta' is well suited to low hedges. Extra-silver foliage; purple-and-violet flowers. **'Hidcote'** ('Hidcote Blue') makes compact mounds; very dark purple-and-violet flowers. Slow growing; suitable for hedges. **'Irene Doyle'** has especially fragrant, light purple-and-violet flowers; fall rebloom. Tolerates clipping well; good for hedges. **'Loddon Blue'** has purple-blue flowers. **'Munstead'** is compact with purple-and-violet flowers. Common in the nursery trade, but most plants sold under this name are seed propagated, and not uniform or true to type. Paler than 'Hidcote'. Popular for culinary use. **'Nana Alba'** is exceptionally compact, with pure white flowers. 1 ft. × 2 ft.

Lavandula dentata

Color	violet-blue
Bloom time	early summer to fall
Size	2–3 ft. × 4 ft.
Light	sun
Zones	Z8–10, HS

FRENCH LAVENDER Not a French native, but from southern and eastern Spain, northwestern Africa, Ethiopia, Israel, Jordan, and the Arabian Peninsula. The bright green, 1- to 1.5-in. leaves are velvety, deeply toothed along the edges. Short, fat spikes of pale lavender-blue flowers are topped with light purple bracts. Fragrance is strong and herbal, intermediate between typical lavender and rosemary. Evergreen, blooms almost yearround in the southern part of its range.

'Linda Ligon' has white-and-green variegated foliage; mauve flowers. Unusual for hedges. **Var. *candicans*** has more silvery foliage than the species.

Lavandula ×*intermedia*

Color	pale lavender
Bloom time	early to midsummer
Size	2–3 ft. high and wide
Light	sun
Zones	Z5–8, HS

LAVANDIN A hybrid group originating from crosses of *Lavandula angustifolia* and *L. latifolia*. These highly fragrant plants form shrubby mounds of gray-green, needle-like leaves with 3- to 4-in. spikes of flowers. Some growers report a better tolerance to heat and humidity than most other lavenders.

'Alba' is white flowered. 1–1.5 ft. × 1.5 ft. **'Grappenhall'** has blue-purple flowers. Dries well. 3 ft. × 5 ft. Z5–11. **'Grosso'**. Silver-green foliage in 2- to 3-ft. mounds. Large, plump spikes of exceptionally fragrant, lavender flowers bloom above the foliage. Valued for its oil. Z5–11. **'Phenomenal'** makes uniform mounds of silvery foliage that does not die back in winter. Resists foliar diseases and drought. 24–32 in. high and wide. Z4–8. **'Provence'** is particularly aromatic; light lavender flowers on upright stems. 24–36 in.

Lavandula latifolia

syn. *L. spica*

Color	blue, purple
Bloom	late spring to late summer
Size	3 ft. × 4 ft.
Light	sun
Zones	Z6–8, HS

SPIKE LAVENDER, PORTUGUESE LAVENDER Native to central and eastern Spain, southern France, northern Italy. Similar to English lavender, but with coarser foliage. Blue-gray flowers carried on long, spiky stems. Fragrance is more camphor-like. Valued in soap and perfume industries, and for aromatherapy.

Lavandula stoechas

Color	pink, purple, lavender
Bloom	late spring to summer
Size	1–3 ft. high and wide
Light	sun
Zones	Z8–9, HS

FRENCH LAVENDER, SPANISH LAVENDER, TOPPED LAVENDER Mediterranean basin, southern Europe, northern Africa. Narrow, gray-green, 0.5- to 1.5-in. leaves; short-stalked, dense, pineapple-like heads of tiny, blackish purple flowers, topped by a tuft of purple bracts. Exceptionally heat and drought tolerant.

'Lemon Leigh' is lemon scented; white flowers topped with showy yellow bracts. 20–28 in. × 18–36 in. Z7–9. **'Madrid Blue'** has sky blue flowers accented with upright white bracts. Early and compact; perfect for containers. 1–2 ft. **'Mulberry Ruffles'** is part of the Ruffles Series. Deep pink flowers. 2 ft.

Lavandula viridis

color	yellow
bloom time	early to late summer
size	2–3 ft. high and wide
exposure	sun
zones	Z8–10, HS

YELLOW LAVENDER Mediterranean. Bright green foliage with a pine fragrance; flowers similar to *Lavandula stoechas* in form, but with creamy-yellow corollas and greenish yellow bracts. A striking contrast planted among other lavenders.

LAVENDER COTTON

Santolina ASTERACEAE

THESE DWARF, AROMATIC, EVERGREEN subshrubs are invaluable for edging beds and paths. Tolerant of clipping, they lend themselves for use as compact hedges to provide garden structure. Fine-textured, entire or pinnately dissected leaves, bluish silver-gray or green, are borne densely on woody, branching stems. Button-like, yellow, 0.75-in. flowerheads on slender stems are abundant in summer, 4–10 in. above the foliage. Santolina foliage has a resinous, herbal scent; traditionally used as a moth and insect repellant.

Originating in the Mediterranean region, these plants prefer full sun and average to dry, well-drained soil; tolerant of alkaline and poor soils, but not of wet, rich ones. Once established, the plants endure drought, but dislike hot, humid weather. Cut back in spring to encourage compact, healthy new growth. Santolinas perform well as formal, clipped hedges, but do not flower if sheared regularly.

Insect, rabbit, and deer resistant, but vulnerable to root rot on damp soils. Propagate by layering or division, by half-ripe stem cuttings in summer, or by seed; germination is slow.

Santolina chamaecyparissus

Flower color	yellow
Bloom time	early to midsummer
Size	1–2 ft. × 2–3 ft.
Light	sun
Zones	Z6–9

LAVENDER COTTON Western and central Mediterranean region. Forms dense mounds of evergreen, silver-gray foliage. Drought tolerant once established; prefers gritty or sandy soils. Vigorous but not invasive; may be grown as an annual where not hardy. An asset to herb and rock gardens, border fronts, knot gardens, xeriscapes. Good groundcover for sunny slopes.

'Pretty Carol' has deep yellow flowers. 12 in. × 24 in. Z7–10. **'Lemon Queen'** is 18 in. × 24 in., with pale, lemon-yellow flowers; silver-gray foliage. **'Weston'** is a dwarf form, to 12 in.

Santolina rosmarinifolia

Flower color	yellow
Bloom time	late spring to midsummer
Size	1.5–2 ft. × 2–3 ft.
Light	sun
Zones	Z7–9

GREEN LAVENDER COTTON Dense, neat mounds of evergreen, fragrant foliage; leaves alternate, 1- to 2-in.-long, smooth, narrow, and finely divided. Long-stalked, button-shaped flowers are solitary. Uses and cultural requirements similar to those of *Santolina chamaecyparissus.*

'Lemon Fizz'. Foliage is yellow in full sun, chartreuse in part shade. 18 in. × 24 in. **'Morning Mist'** is reportedly more damp-tolerant than the species.

LEOPARD PLANT

Farfugium

ASTERACEAE

VETERAN GARDENERS MAY KNOW the leopard plants by their former botanical names as members of the genus *Ligularia*. More recently, however, certain leopard plants were given their own genus, Farfugium, as befits such bold, intriguing perennials.

These eastern Asian plants are grown mainly for their handsome evergreen, long-stalked leaves that are held well above the crown. Valuable in wet places beside ponds and streams, or as dramatic accents in beds and shrub borders. They are good companions for astilbes and Japanese irises. The variegated cultivars are most popular, particularly as dynamic container plants to decorate sunrooms. All bear loose, long-stemmed clusters of yellow daisies late in the season; many gardeners feel these detract from the foliar display and remove them.

Leopard plants do best in average soil that is moist but not waterlogged. Most prefer morning sun, but accept light shade; some tolerate full sun. Foliage may droop or flag during midday sun, but regain its turgidity in the cool of the day. Mulch well where soil tends to dry out. Protect from slug damage; usually ignored by deer.

Increase by dividing clumps in spring, or start from seed with protection in winter.

Farfugium japonicum 'Aureomaculatum'

Farfugium japonicum

syn. F. *tussilaginea, Ligularia tussilaginea*

(flower color)	yellow
(bloom time)	fall
(size)	18–24 in. × 24 in.
(light)	sun, part shade
(zone)	Z6–11

LEOPARD PLANT Rocky cliffs along the coasts of Japan and Korea. This clumping perennial has glossy, long-stalked, 6- to 10-in.-wide leaves, kidney shaped with wavy, toothed, or entire margins. Bright yellow daisies, 2 in. or so across, cluster on long stems well above the foliage in fall and into winter. An excellent contrasting companion for fine-textured ferns. The cultivars are more often grown than the species.

'Argenteum' ('Albovariegatum', 'Variegatum'). The 10-in.-wide leaves are thick and cupped, irregularly rimmed with wide, white streaks, held on purple stems covered with woolly hairs. Yellow flowerheads. 15–24 in. Z7–8. **'Aureomaculatum'** (syn. *Ligularia tussilaginea* 'Aureomaculata') has 8- to 10-in.-wide, dark green leaves, irregularly and conspicuously marked with yellow spots. Yellow, daisy-like flowers. Do not allow to dry out or become waterlogged. 20 in. Z6. **'Cristata'** ('Crispatum', syn. *L. tussilaginea* 'Cristata') has bold, glossy, heart-shaped, 1-ft.-wide leaves twisted from the stem like a snail. The leaves have frilly edges and are woolly hairy beneath. Yellow flowers. 2 ft. Z6–8.

LEOPARD PLANT | GOLDEN GROUNDSEL

Ligularia

ASTERACEAE

THESE STATUESQUE, DRAMATIC PLANTS are especially well suited to damp, partly shaded sites, such as rain gardens and watersides. They develop large clumps of rounded, heart-shaped, or arrowhead-shaped leaves, often held on dark stems. Several are grown especially for their amazing foliage; others also have attractive floral displays.

These water-loving plants demand soil that remains moist constantly, preferably enriched with humus or compost; avoid standing them in water. Ligularias are extremely sensitive to hot sun, even when the roots are damp; on sunny days, the large leaves often droop like elephant ears, only to recover at dusk. This is stressful for the plant. Select a growing spot with protection from noonday sun, ideally with light, dappled shade. Apply organic mulch to help retain moisture during the summer.

Good companions for ligularias (especially in deer country) include cinnamon and ostrich ferns, water irises, cardinal flower, and snakeroot. Boggy areas and open woodlands are ideal places for ligularias; shady north-facing beds and borders are appropriate if irrigation is available. Smaller sorts are ideal for the margins of miniature water gardens.

The conditions favored by ligularias are also ideal for slugs and snails that attack the young growth, disfiguring the foliage badly. Otherwise serious pests or diseases are few. All species resist deer browsing.

Sow seed in spring or fall; divide species and selections before bloom in spring or after flowering.

Ligularia dentata

syn. *Senecio clivorum*

color	orange
bloom time	early to midsummer
size	3–4 ft. × 3 ft.
exposure	part shade
zones	Z3–8

LEOPARD PLANT, BIG LEAF LIGULARIA China, Japan. Basal clumps of long-stalked, leathery foliage is the main attraction of this plant. Dark green and coarsely toothed leaves, to 1 ft. long. Thick, fibrous stems carry loose clusters of untidy, yellow-orange, 3-in. daisy flowers. Largely replaced by superior cultivars.

'Britt-Marie Crawford'. Shiny, kidney-shaped leaves of blackest purple, to 7 in. long. Yellow-orange flowers rise above the foliage mass. More sun tolerant than some. 2–3 ft. Z4–8. **'Dark Beauty'**. Very deep purple leaves on purple stems. Gold flowers. 3–4 ft. Z3–8. **'Desdemona'**. Serrated, kidney-shaped leaves are red, but mature to green with persistent purple undersides. Purple-stemmed, ragged, yellow-orange daisies. 2–3 ft. Z3–8. **'Othello'** is similar.

Ligularia przewalskii

syn. *Senecio przewalskii*

color	yellow
bloom time	mid- to late summer
size	5–6 ft. × 3 ft.
exposure	part shade
zones	Z4–8

SHAVALSKI'S LIGULARIA Northern China. Black stems clothed with triangular, palmately lobed, 12-in.-long leaves, deeply and irregularly cut. Narrow, loose racemes of yellow flowerheads rise on dark greenish purple stems.

'Dragon's Breath'. Exotic-looking clumps of very deeply cut, dark leaves. Spikes of bright yellow flowers on purple stems, early. 24–30 in. Z4–9.

Ligularia stenophylla

syn. *L. stenocephala*, *Pojarkovia pojarkovae*

Color	yellow
Bloom time	early to late summer
Size	4–5 ft. × 5 ft.
Light	part shade
Zone	Z5–8

NARROW-SPIKED LIGULARIA Northern China, Japan. This species is similar to *Ligularia przewalskii*, but has heart-shaped leaves and paler stems. Tall, slender racemes of few-rayed, yellow flowerheads, to 1.5 in. across.

'Chinese Dragon' has bold, deeply cut leaves, serrated along the edges. Clusters of few-rayed yellow flowers top each stem. Very attractive to butterflies. 3–4 ft. Z4–8. **'Little Rocket'** is a dwarf form of 'The Rocket'. Slender racemes of yellow flowers. Late summer. 3–4 ft. Z4–8. **'The Rocket'**. Early summer spikes 18–24 in. long held above the mass of dark green, jagged-edged leaves on black stems. 4–5 ft. Z5–8.

Other Notable Cultivars

'Gregynog Gold' (*Ligularia dentata* × *L. veitchiana*). Substantial green, heart-shaped leaves, rimmed with sharp teeth. Broadly conical clusters of orange daisies. 4–6 ft. Z4–9. **'Last Dance'** is compact with bold, heart-shaped, dark green foliage beneath loose clusters of dark-centered yellow daisies. The last to bloom. 12–18 in. Z4–8. **'Osiris Café Noir'** has thick, serrated olive, purple, or brown leaves topped by yellow daisy flowers. Introduced by Serge Fafard. Z4–8. **'Osiris Fantaisie'**. Clumps of rubbery, dark green, heart-shaped leaves with undulating jagged edges, on purple stems; undersides are burgundy. Sturdy branching stems hold 2- to 3-in., double, deep yellow daisies just above. Mid- to late summer. 2–3 ft. Z3–8.

LEWISIA | CLIFF MAIDS

Lewisia

PORTULACACEAE

THIS NORTH AMERICAN GENUS of flowering succulents is named for the famed Meriwether Lewis, co-leader of the Lewis and Clark expedition. Lewisias are found in the wild in well-drained sites in the mountains of the northwest United States. They are much sought after, especially by alpine plant specialists who enjoy the challenge of nurturing them as much as for the beautiful flowers. Many species are very difficult to grow, but those outlined here are less temperamental. Wild populations of some species are under stress from overenthusiastic collectors and are now protected by law.

Typically, lewisias form basal rosettes of succulent, deciduous or evergreen leaves that arise from a fleshy taproot. The deciduous species, including *Lewisia rediviva* and *L. longipetala*, die back just after flowering and must remain dry while dormant, until the following spring.

Grow lewisias in rock gardens, between rock crevices, or, where the climate is unsuitable, in containers in alpine houses. They demand free-draining soil and a dry situation during the winter; quick to rot if roots remain wet. Gritty loam, lightly amended with coarse leaf mold or compost, is best for container-grown plants, and a similar mix is ideal for plants grown outdoors; pack the mix into vertical crevices and between rocks to ensure perfect drainage. Accelerate rain runoff with gravel mulch around the plant collars. Many do well with part shade, although a mostly sunny spot is usually fine.

Pests and diseases are few, apart from stem rot; slugs, snails, and aphids may become a problem. Deer tolerant, but destroyed by voles.

Lewisia columbiana

Color	pink
Bloom	spring to summer
Size	6–10 in. × 6 in.
Light	part shade
Zones	Z4–8, HS

COLUMBIAN LEWISIA Mountain regions of British Columbia, Washington, and Oregon. Evergreen and succulent, the leaves are linear to spatulate, to 3 in. long. Open sprays of pink-striped white or lavender to magenta, 0.5-in. flowers rise above the basal rosette.

'Rosea' has deep crimson-mauve flowers. Makes relatively large plants. 6–8 in.

Other Notable Cultivars

'Bright Eyes' has flowers in the usual colors, but with a conspicuous pale eye. 6–8 in. **Rainbow Dazzlers Strain** has white, yellow, orange, pink, or purple blooms. 8–10 in. **Sunset Strain** produces 1-in. flowers in a range of colors from apricot and tangerine, through yellow to cream and pink. 6 in. tall. **'Yellow Shades'** has flowers in various shades of pale lemon to gold. 8 in.

Lewisia cotyledon

syn. *L. finchiae, L. purdyi*

Color	white, yellow, orange, pink
Bloom	spring to early summer
Size	9–12 in. × 8 in.
Light	part shade
Zones	Z3–9, HS

CLIFF MAIDS, SISKIYOU LEWISIA Siskiyou Mountains of Oregon and south to northern California coastal ranges. This is the most widely grown species for its ease of cultivation outside its natural range. It hybridizes freely and many selections are available. Evergreen basal rosettes of 1- to 5-in.-long, fleshy, spoon-shaped leaves give rise to thick, branching stems topped with compact clusters of brilliantly and variably colored, open, funnel-form flowers, to 1 in. across.

The **Cotyledon Hybrids Strain** comes in assorted colors; evergreen. 6–12 in. **'Little Plum'** (*Lewisia longipetala × L. cotyledon*), a hybrid, has succulent, evergreen leaves that reportedly are rot and pest resistant. Deep carmine-flushed pink flowers. 3–4 in. **'Regenbogen'** ('Rainbow') has salmon and pink flowers.

LILYTURF | MONKEY GRASS

Liriope | ASPARAGACEAE

PROBLEM SOLVERS RATHER THAN garden stars, the lilyturfs nevertheless can be attractive when used in the right spot and the right way. These low, grass-like plants from eastern Asia combine glossy foliage with grape hyacinth–like spikes of late-summer flowers in purples, blues, or white. Evergreen in hot and humid climates, but elsewhere foliage browns—refresh by mowing on a high setting in early spring.

Lilyturfs prefer moist, fertile soils in part shade but will grow in any average, well-drained soils, in full sun. Tolerates heat, humidity, and drought and air pollution; resistant to rabbits, but susceptible to slugs and snails. Deer resistance is spotty; reports stating that deer devour liriope are countered by others reporting no damage at all.

Lilyturfs have a naturally neat, almost dapper, appearance that makes them perfect for edging paths or beds in formal landscapes, as well as a handsome and durable groundcover.

Propagate by division.

Liriope muscari 'Variegata'

Liriope spicata 'Silver Dragon'

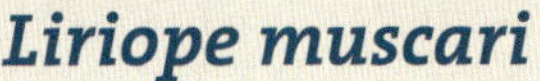

Liriope muscari

Flower color	lavender
Bloom time	late summer
Size	12–18 in. × 9–12 in.
Light	sun, part shade
Zones	Z6–10

LILYTURF China and Japan. Tuberous rooted, forms slowly expanding clumps of strap-like, arching, glossy dark green leaves to 1 in. wide. Erect spikes with tiered whorls of violet-purple flowers similar to those of grape hyacinths emerge above foliage in late summer. Persistent black berries follow. Survives in sheltered locations in zone 5.

'Big Blue' has 15- to 18-in.-long leaves; violet flowers. **'Monroe White'** has white flowers. **'Pee Dee Gold Ingot'** produces yellow young foliage that deepens to gold or chartreuse, holding color year-round. Lavender flowers. **'Silvery Sunproof'** has green-and-white-striped foliage; lavender flowers. More sun tolerant than other cultivars. **'Variegata'** has green-and-white-striped leaves; lavender flowers.

Liriope spicata

Flower color	blue, white
Bloom time	late summer
Size	9–18 in. × 1–2 ft.
Light	sun, part shade
Zones	Z4–10

LILYTURF China, Vietnam. Forms grass-like clumps of narrow, arching, glossy dark green leaves to 0.25 in. wide; erect spikes of small, pale lavender to white flowers borne among the leaves; blackish berries follow. Spreads quickly by underground rhizomes and can be aggressive. Outstanding as a groundcover under shallow-rooted trees, along streams and ponds, and for stabilizing soil on erosion-prone banks and slopes.

'Silver Dragon' has leaves striped with green-and-silver-white; pale purple flowers; whitish green berries.

LUPINE | LUPIN

Lupinus

FABACEAE

THE NAME LUPINE DERIVES from the Latin word for "wolf," recalling an old-time belief that these plants devoured the richness of a soil. In fact, the opposite is true: lupines are found mostly on poor, sandy soils, but their roots have the ability to convert atmospheric nitrogen into plant nutrients. This trait is common to pea family members.

These desirable, though often short-lived, perennials combine handsome, typically fingered, palmately divided leaves with spires of colorful, pea-type flowers. The species are best grown on loose, very well-drained, lean soils similar to those of their native habitats. The showier and somewhat longer-lived garden hybrids, however, perform best on humus-rich, moderately fertile, well-drained soils. Avoid excessive fertility, which when combined with winter wet is likely to prove fatal.

In addition to perennial species, *Lupinus* includes some annuals (notably Texas bluebonnet) and shrubs. The perennial hybrids are ideal for creating rhythms of late spring color and texture, providing a pleasant contrast to bulbs or other perennials; the dense foliage remains attractive all season. The species are better suited to meadow or prairie plantings—care should be taken, however, to keep them out of pastures as they are toxic to grazing animals. Lupines are not trouble-free, though the reward is worth the extra effort. In wetter climates, they are prone to slugs and snails when young, and susceptible to powdery mildew and aphids as well; serious infestations should be dealt with by cutting plants back almost to the ground. Stake taller types. Attracts butterflies; deer resistant.

Propagation by seed is most successful: scarify seeds and soak overnight before sowing.

Lupinus arboreus

(color)	yellow, blue
(bloom time)	late spring to early summer
(size)	3–5 ft. high and wide
(exposure)	sun, part shade
(zone)	Z8–10

BUSH LUPINE, TREE LUPINE Western North America. Fast-growing, semi-evergreen, shrubby perennial with palmate leaves and erect, 10-in. racemes of fragrant, yellow flowers. Drought resistant; excellent for dry and coastal gardens. A parent of many garden hybrids.

Lupinus perennis

(color)	blue, purple
(bloom time)	late spring
(size)	1–2 ft. × 1 ft.
(exposure)	sun
(zone)	Z3–8

SUNDIAL LUPINE, WILD LUPINE Maine to Florida. Dense mounds of palmately divided leaves, each with seven to eleven leaflets, to 2 in. long. Terminal, 8-in. racemes of light blue to purplish flowers; 2-in., bean-like, seed-filled pods follow. Flourishes on sandy, nutrient-poor and drought-prone soils; dislikes clays and loams.

Lupinus polyphyllus

(flower color)	blue, purple, reddish, white
(bloom time)	late spring to early summer
(size)	3–5 ft. × 2–2.5 ft.
(exposure)	sun
(zones)	Z4–7, HS

BIGLEAF LUPINE Western North America. Robust, with bold, rich green, palmate leaves, each with 5 to 18 leaflets to 6 in. long, and imposing 12- to 28-in.-long racemes of 0.5-in. flowers on mostly unbranched stems. Best adapted to cool summers. A parent of many garden hybrids.

Other Notable Cultivars

'Chandelier' has yellow flowers; repeat blooms if deadheaded. 40 in. × 18–24 in. Z4–8. **'Chatelaine'** has dense racemes of bicolored, pink-and-white flowers on 3- to 4-ft. stems. Z3–7. **Gallery Strain** is compact, 15–18 in., with white, blue, pink, red, and yellow flowers. Z3–7. **'My Castle'** has fragrant, scarlet flowers: repeats if deadheaded. 40 in. × 18–24 in. Z4–8. **Russell Hybrids** bear spikes of flowers in shades of pink, red, yellow, blue, and white, often bicolored, in early and midsummer. 2.5–3 ft. × 1–1.5 ft. Z4–8. **Tutti Frutti Mix**, possibly superior to Russell hybrids, has large robust flower spikes in a range of bicolors. 3–3.25 ft.

MALLOW | MUSK MALLOW

Malva | MALVACEAE

IN FRENCH "MAUVE" MEANS MALLOW, and in fact the flowers of many mallows are a soft lilac-lavender hue. This genus includes three species of perennials of special interest to gardeners.

All have alternate, palmately lobed leaves and bear five-petaled flowers in pinks or white as well as mauve. The blooms bear a strong family resemblance to those of related hollyhocks and hibiscus, and bloom over a long period. Although perhaps not as refined as tall, slender hollyhocks, they are less trouble-prone.

Moderately moist, well-drained soils are ideal; mallows are somewhat drought tolerant. Japanese beetles and hollyhock rust attack the foliage, but mallows seldom suffer serious damage. Attracts butterflies; rarely browsed by deer.

Often short lived, mallows commonly reseed. Deadhead to encourage rebloom unless saving seed.

Propagate by seed or divide in spring.

Malva sylvestris 'Zebrina'

Malva alcea

color	pink
bloom time	summer to early fall
size	2–4 ft. × 1.5–2 ft.
exposure	sun, part shade
zones	Z4–7, HS

GREATER MUSK-MALLOW, HOLLYHOCK MALLOW Native to southwestern, central, and eastern Europe, and southwestern Asia. Hairy stems bear palmately lobed leaves 0.75–3 in. long and wide; basal leaves are shallowly lobed, while those on the upper stems are deeply divided and fingered. Flattened clusters of flowers emerge from the upper leaf axils and stem tips; each is bright pink, 1.3–2.3 in. across; no fragrance. To control height, cut back stems in spring. Good for borders and cottage gardens.

'Fastigiata' (var. *fastigiata*) grows upright, with a narrow form. 12–18 in. wide.

Malva sylvestris

syn. *M. sylvestris* var. *mauritiana*

color	mauve-and-purple
bloom time	midsummer to early fall
size	3–4 ft. × 1.5–2 ft.
exposure	sun, part shade
zones	Z5–8

TALL MALLOW, FRENCH HOLLYHOCK Fields and hedgerows of western Europe, northern Africa, and Asia. Erect or decumbent branching stems carry coarse, hairy, maple-like leaves with five to seven shallow lobes; foliage is deep green when young but fades and becomes ragged as the season advances. Bright mauve, 1- to 2.5-in. flowers, striped with darker purple, have notched petals. Short lived but reseeds vigorously. Tolerates heat and humidity better than most mallows or hollyhocks; good for muggy climates.

'Braveheart' has dark purple–veined, deep rose flowers. **'Primley Blue'** grows to 18–24 in., with powder blue, violet-veined flowers. **'Purple Satin'** has ruffled, burgundy-violet flowers with deeper purple veins. **'Zebrina'** has satiny, mauve flowers striped with dark maroon.

MARSH MARIGOLD

Caltha

RANUNCULACEAE

JUST HOW THIS GENUS acquired the common name of marigold isn't clear, but it's a misnomer, for its flowers are clearly close relatives of buttercups. The most widely cultivated species is *Caltha palustris*, which the Royal Horticultural Society describes as "an essential plant to brighten up the margins of a pond or a boggy area with sunny yellow flowers."

All parts of marsh marigolds are toxic—even the sap may raise a rash in sensitive individuals. This makes these perennials a poor choice for a landscape with children but endows the plants with resistance to deer. Marsh marigolds thrive in a wide range of soils, so long as they are rich in organic matter and consistently moist.

Propagate by dividing mature plants or by seed collected as soon as it is ripe; sow in late summer and overwinter in a cold frame or other cool but protected spot.

Caltha palustris

	yellow
	early to midspring
	10–12 in. × 12–18 in.
	sun, part shade
	Z3–7

YELLOW MARSH MARIGOLD, KINGCUP Bogs and other wet locations throughout the northern and coastal parts of North America, and northern temperate regions worldwide; flourishes inland if given sufficient moisture. Mounds of glossy, heart- or kidney-shaped leaves with stout, hollow, branching stems. Buttercup-like, waxy, bright golden-yellow flowers are 1.5 in. across, with five petal-like sepals, carried on upright stems 12–18 in. Sometimes reblooms in late summer or fall. May spread by seed on consistently damp soils.

Var. *alba* bears single, white flowers. **'Flore Pleno'** (possibly 'Multiplex', 'Monstrosa', 'Monstrosa-Plena'), sometimes known as May blob, bears double yellow pompon-like flowers with green-yellow centers, similar in appearance to a florist's ranunculus. Sterile and longer-blooming.

MILKWEED | BUTTERFLY WEED

Asclepias

APOCYNACEAE

IT MAY SEEM COUNTERINTUITIVE to include a plant in your garden because of its ability to attract insects, but for many, that is the most persuasive argument for planting milkweeds. Several species do bear attractive, even showy flowers, and most are hardy and reliably perennial given an appropriate site. But what makes them really special is that they serve as nurseries for the caterpillars that metamorphose into monarch butterflies.

The common name for this genus refers to the milky appearance of its sap, which in many species is toxic. By feeding on milkweed leaves, monarch butterfly larvae (caterpillars) make themselves poisonous, thus protecting themselves against birds and other predators. The toxicity of asclepias plants makes them resistant to deer, rabbits, and squirrels. Some species have been esteemed as medicinal, although all parts of the plant are toxic in quantity unless cooked. Gardeners with sensitive skin should protect themselves with gloves when working around these plants.

Milkweeds form clumps of sturdy, fibrous stems with ovate to blade-shaped, generally leathery, green leaves, and dense, rounded, or flat-topped clusters of flowers at stem tips and leaf axils. The flowers attract many different butterflies in addition to monarchs. Prolong bloom time of individual plants by deadheading before seed set; to encourage a second crop of flowers, cut plants back after the first flush of bloom. The fat or skinny, spindle-shaped seedpods that follow split when ripe to release seeds equipped with gossamer parachutes that aid dispersal by wind.

With the exception of a few species adapted to wetland habitats, milkweeds thrive in full sun in almost any well-drained garden soil, even nutrient-poor ones. Pinch off the tips of new shoots when they are 5 in. tall to encourage bushiness. Fungal and bacterial leaf spots may attack milkweeds in hot and humid conditions.

An obvious choice for butterfly and wildlife gardens, milkweeds are also at home in meadow gardens, while the more refined cultivars hold their own in mixed borders. They make bright and long-lasting cut flowers; sear the base of the stem with a flame to seal in the sap.

Propagate in containers to obviate root disturbance at planting time. Sow scarified seed outdoors in fall, or stratify and start indoors in early spring. Spring basal cuttings root readily in sand; milkweeds are taprooted and do not respond well to division.

Asclepias curassavica

Color	scarlet, orange
Bloom time	early summer to fall
Size	2–3 ft. × 1.5–2 ft.
Light	sun
Zone	Z9–11

BLOOD FLOWER, MEXICAN BUTTERFLY WEED Tropical Central and South America. Not winter-hardy in colder zones. Showy flowers borne over a long season attract hummingbirds and bees as well as butterflies. A valuable cut flower.

Asclepias incarnata

Color	pink, white
Bloom time	early to late summer
Size	4–5 ft. × 2–3 ft.
Light	sun
Zone	Z3–6

SWAMP MILKWEED Across the United States as far west as the Rocky Mountain states. A wetland species that is ideal for rain gardens, or pond and stream banks, but which also tolerates better-drained soils in garden borders. Clusters of small, fragrant flowers, usually pink to mauve but occasionally white, followed by interesting long pods. Attracts hummingbirds, butterflies, and bees.

'Cinderella' bears exceptionally large clusters of pink, vanilla-scented flowers from midsummer to early fall. **'Ice Ballet'** has pure white flowers that contrast dramatically with butterfly visitors. 3- to 5-ft. tall.

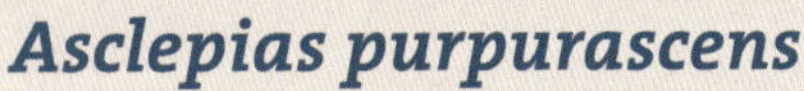

Asclepias purpurascens

	pink, purple
	late spring to midsummer
	2–3 ft. × 1–3 ft.
	sun, part shade
	Z3–9

PURPLE MILKWEED Eastern North America from New Hampshire to North Carolina, west to Minnesota and Arkansas. Tolerates poor, dry, and rocky soils. A vigorous spreader, it often forms large colonies; not suitable for flower borders but an asset in native plantings, meadows, or open woodlands. Rose pink to purple flowers.

Asclepias tuberosa

	orange, yellow
	midsummer to early fall
	1–2.5 ft. × 1–1.5 ft.
	sun
	Z3–9

BUTTERFLY WEED, PLEURISY ROOT Eastern and southwestern North America. The showiest of the milkweeds, bears clusters of brilliant orange or yellow flowers from midsummer. Butterfly weed performs well in ordinary garden soils, but once established, this tough plant also thrives on poor, dryish soils that do not become waterlogged. Not an aggressive spreader. Named the 2017 Perennial Plant Association Plant of the Year.

'Gay Butterflies' is a hybrid mix with blooms in red, orange, or yellow. Especially good for cut flowers. 24–30 in. **'Hello Yellow'** has lively yellow flowers. 24–30 in. tall.

MONKSHOOD

Aconitum

RANUNCULACEAE

THIS GENUS OF 250 OR MORE species has accumulated a wealth of common names, including wolf's bane, leopard's bane, helmet flower, and devil's helmet, most of which refer to the plants' poisonous qualities or the helmet-like shape of the flowers. All parts of the plants are toxic; the sap (containing the poison, aconitine) has found use as a poison to tip arrows for hunting and war. Even so, a number of species and hybrids are definitely garden-worthy, though they should never be planted where children play or near vegetable or herb gardens. *Aconitum* nomenclature is very confusing; locating a recommended species may involve searching under the synonyms included in the following descriptions.

Monkshoods usually have tuberous roots that give rise to upright stems clothed with attractive, alternate foliage, deeply cut, dissected, or lobed. The 1- to 2-in. flowers are hooded or helmet shaped with a large sepal that protects the sexual parts. Blooms are borne in long racemes or panicles, up to 20 in. long, raised well above the mass of foliage.

Although they prefer part shade, monkshoods accept full sun where summers are temperate, as long as the soil does not dry out. Ideally, soils should be fertile, cool, and moisture retentive but not waterlogged. Maintenance is minimal; deadhead spent flower spikes to their bases only, as lateral branches will bloom later. Some species may require staking. Always wear protective gloves when working with aconitum and avoid exposing open wounds or eyes to the sap. Never decorate a plate of food with the blooms. In beds and borders, summer phlox, assorted daisies, and daylilies are good companions; avoid placing the blue-flowered monkshoods against a dark background as the flowers tend to disappear.

Resistant to deer and rabbit browsing. Bumblebees pollinate the flowers and suck nectar from the end of spurs under the hood.

Divide the tuberous roots in fall or early spring every three years or so to maintain vigor and to increase. Start from seed in spring.

Aconitum ×cammarum 'Bicolor'

Aconitum ×cammarum

syn. *A. napellus* var. *bicolor*, *A. ×bicolor*

flower color	various
bloom time	summer to fall
size	3–4 ft. × 2 ft.
light	sun, part shade
zones	Z3–7, HS

BICOLOR MONKSHOOD Of garden origin. Probably a cross between *Aconitum napellus* and *A. variegatum*. Habit varies from stiffly erect to more relaxed. Lustrous, deeply five- to seven-fingered, dark green, 2- to 3-in. leaves.

'Bicolor' (syn. *A. ×bicolor*) bears wide, loosely branched panicles of 1.5-in., white, helmet-shaped flowers edged with blue; midsummer. May need staking. 4 ft. tall. **'Bressingham Spire'** has narrow wands of violet-blue flowers on sturdy stems that seldom need staking. 2–3 ft. tall.

Aconitum carmichaelii

flower color	deep blue
bloom time	late summer to early fall
size	2–5 ft. × 2 ft.
light	sun, part shade
zones	Z3–7, HS

AZURE MONKSHOOD, AUTUMN-FLOWERING MONKSHOOD Central and western China, North America. Tuberous roots give rise to erect stems to 5 ft. tall under ideal conditions; more often 2–3 ft. Handsome leathery, dark-green foliage is deeply cut into three to five lobes. Dense, 8-in.-long panicles of large, violet or deep blue flowers. Prefers consistently moist soils; a fine choice for wet soil beside water features, in damp woods, and rain gardens.

'Arendsii' (syn. *Aconitum ×arendsii*). Branched panicles of large, strong azure-blue helmet flowers in fall. Stout stems seldom need staking. Introduced by Georg Arends of Germany. 2–4 ft. tall. **'Barker's Variety'** has loose spikes of deep violet flowers in fall. Start from seed. To 6 ft. tall. **'Cloudy'**, a mutation of 'Arendsii', is upright, with thick stems and lots of bicolored, light blue-and-white flowers. 34 in.

Aconitum henryi 'Spark's Variety'

Aconitum henryi

color	indigo blue
bloom	summer
size	4–5 ft. × 2 ft.
light	sun, part shade
zones	Z3–7

HENRY'S MONKSHOOD Western China. Sturdy lower stems, but upper ones are thin and may even semi-twine. Foliage is not as leathery as *Aconitum carmichaelii*'s, but is divided into three to five lobes almost to the leaf base. Loose clusters of flowers. Usually needs support.

'Spark's Variety' (syn. *A.* 'Spark', *A.* 'Spark's Variety', *A.* ×*cammarum* 'Spark's Variety'), autumn monkshood, is summer blooming with branched clusters of amethyst-blue flowers on slender stems. 4 ft. Z5.

Aconitum napellus

color	blue
bloom	mid- to late summer
size	2–4 ft. × 1 ft.
light	sun, part shade
zones	Z3–8

COMMON OR ENGLISH MONKSHOOD, HELMET FLOWER Europe. Variable, but leaves are usually divided into five to seven lobes, and further cut into lance-shaped segments. Terminal racemes of indigo-blue flowers.

'Album' (syn. *Aconitum napellus* var. *albidum*) has spires of white flowers in midsummer. 3–4 ft. Z5–8. **'Carneum'** (syn. *Aconitum compactum* 'Carneum') has blush-pink flowers that intensify in color in cool, damp climates. 4–5 ft. Z2–8. **'Rubellum'**. Dark foliage shows off the spires of light pink flowers well. Best in part shade; may fade in intense sun. Good cut flower. 36 in. Z4–8.

Aconitum vulparia

syn. *A. lycoctonum*

Flower color	yellow
Bloom time	summer to early fall
Size	3–5 ft. × 1.5 ft.
Light	sun, part shade
Zones	Z3–6

YELLOW WOLFSBANE, BADGER'S BANE Central and southern Europe. Long-stalked basal leaves diminish in size as they ascend the stem. Foliage is dark green, paler beneath, rounded or kidney shaped and cleft into five to nine divisions, each toothed and three lobed. Pale yellow, 0.75-in. flowers crowd into terminal racemes; blossoms rounded at the top and narrowed at the middle.

Other Notable Cultivars

'Blue Lagoon' is compact with bright blue flowers that open from the bottom up. Excellent as cut flowers. Mid- to late summer bloom. 10–12 in. Z4–8. **'Blue Scepter'** is excellent for cutting and adapts well to shaded borders. Branching spires of white flowers broadly edged with purplish blue. 28 in. Z4–8. **'Ivorine'** is compact, bushy, and erect with short, dense spikes of small, creamy-white flowers in early to midsummer. Best in part shade. 36 in. Z4–8. **'Newry Blue'** has navy-blue flowers on erect stems. Comes true from seed. 4–5 ft. Z3–7. **'Pink Sensation'** is a Piet Oudolf introduction with silvery pink flowers accented with a dark throat. No staking required. Best in sun. 36–40 in. Z3–8. **'Stainless Steel'** bears metallic-blue flowers from early to late summer, with complementary grayish foliage. 40 in. Z2–9.

ORNAMENTAL ONION

Allium AMARYLLIDACEAE

THIS ENORMOUS AND COSMOPOLITAN genus ranges throughout temperate regions of the Northern Hemisphere, with a handful of species from Central and South America, and also Africa. Within this range, alliums have adapted to habitats as diverse as sandy uplands and lowland swamps, though most prefer well-drained, even droughty sites.

Alliums include several staples of the kitchen garden, including onions, garlics, shallots, leeks, and chives. Their blooms may be less familiar in the flower garden, but they are, nonetheless, as essential in their own way as their edible relatives. Their ability to store energy in their bulbs makes alliums nearly invulnerable to seasonal drought—many species grow best where summers are hot and dry—and helps them weather all sorts of other adverse conditions. Furthermore, the sulfur-based chemicals that give alliums their pungent aroma act as repellents to deer, rabbits, and rodents, even many insect pests. Be alert for onion flies and thrips, however. Wet soils, especially during dormancy, may cause bulbs to rot.

Typically allium leaves are long and cylindrical (think chives) or strap shaped (think leeks), and though attractive enough when fresh and green, they grow tattered and flop as the season progresses. Accordingly, plant alliums in fall among bushy flowers or ornamental grasses that will hide the alliums' aging foliage; such neighbors will also help to support the alliums' naked scapes (flower stalks). Small individual flowers are borne in umbels, radiating clusters that collectively look like bright, botanical starbursts. Most bloom is in late spring or early summer, neatly bridging the June gap, the temporary dearth of bloom that afflicts perennial gardens after most spring bulbs are spent and before the summer perennials do their stuff.

Planted in groups along the length of a border, alliums' sculptural flowers add a visual rhythm to any design. Allium flowers attract nectar-foraging butterflies and bees; many ornamental onions make elegant cut flowers.

To propagate alliums, lift and divide the clumps of bulbs when dormant, or start from seed—many alliums are prolific seed producers and surround themselves with hosts of volunteer seedlings without any encouragement from the gardener.

Allium aflatunense 'Purple Sensation'

Allium aflatunense

	purple
	late spring
	3–4 ft. × 6 in.
	sun
	Z3–8

PURPLE ORNAMENTAL ONION Iran. Baseball-sized heads of brilliant purple, tiny, starry flowers rise on tall scapes. Typical bluish, strappy foliage that begins to die back at bloom time. Pastel-colored German irises and silvery catmints are compatible bedfellows; a skirt of lady's mantle camouflages fading leaves.

'Purple Sensation' is more widely grown than the species; plant in groups of 10 to 12 for a real impact. Fortunately, the bulbs are not expensive.

Allium atropurpureum

	dark purple
	late spring
	12–24 in. × 4 in.
	sun
	Z3–8

ORNAMENTAL ONION East Asia to northern India. So dark is the purple of this allium's star-shaped flowers that the densely packed, tennis-ball-sized umbel looks almost black. They pose a dramatic contrast to the blossoms of lighter colored relatives such as hybrid 'Mont Blanc' and a complement in form as well as color to the simultaneous flowers of 'Sooty' sweet William.

Allium bulgaricum

syn. *A. siculum* subsp. *dioscoridis*, *Nectaroscordum siculum* subsp. *bulgaricum*

cream, maroon

late spring to early summer

24–36 in. × 6–8 in.

sun, part shade

Z5–10

SICILIAN HONEY LILY This Mediterranean native requires regular irrigation through its period of growth until the end of bloom time, but thereafter prefers a drier soil. The parasol of pendulous, 0.5- to 1-in. flowers measures 4 in. or more across, with individual cream flowers, striped with maroon and touched with green. Baptisias and tall bearded irises, which bloom at the same time, make good companions.

Allium caeruleum syn. *A. wallichii*

blue

early summer to summer

12–36 in. × 6–12 in.

sun

Z3–9, HS

BLUE GLOBE ONION This Asian native blooms a couple of weeks later than *Allium atropurpureum* or *A. bulgaricum*, and provides one of the few true blues of the early summer perennial garden. The flowers are borne in 1-in., spherical clusters; the leaves die back before the flowers emerge. An asset to cottage, meadow, and rock gardens, this onion blooms simultaneously with herbaceous peonies; its exquisite flowers contrast handsomely with the peonies' lush blooms.

Allium cernuum

Color	pink
Bloom time	early to late summer
Size	12–18 in. × 6–8 in.
Light	sun, part shade
Zones	Z3–9

NODDING ONION, LADY'S LEEK Dry clearings, rock outcroppings, and prairies in mountainous regions from Canada to Mexico. Nodding onion produces its loose umbels of drooping, pink or white flowers atop scapes that bend downward at the top, possibly to restrict the variety of pollinating insects. The strappy leaves are flattened and solid, with a small ridge along the length. Very easy to grow, nodding onion seeds about unless deadheaded, but never becomes aggressive. The bulbs sometimes produce offsets, creating clumps. Tolerates a wide range of well-drained soils; drought tolerant when established. Attractive with beebalms, black-eyed Susans, and milkweeds in native, meadow, or wild gardens.

Allium moly

Color	yellow
Bloom time	late spring
Size	9–18 in. × 6–9 in.
Light	sun, part shade
Zones	Z3–9, HS

LILY LEEK Southern Europe. Starry, greenish yellow flowers are borne in loose, 2-in.-wide clusters. In average, well-drained soil and full sun (avoid intensely sunny spots) this species naturalizes, forming extensive colonies readily, though it isn't an aggressive invasive.

'Jeannine' is a superior selection that bears two scapes per bulb, topped with golden yellow flowers.

Allium senescens 'Glaucum'

Allium schubertii

color	rose-purple
bloom time	late spring
size	12–36 in. × 12–18 in.
light	sun
zones	Z7–9

SCHUBERT ONION This native of the eastern Mediterranean and central Asia bears spherical, starburst heads of flowers, 1 ft. or more in diameter, which are guaranteed to stop traffic. *Allium schubertii* overwinters successfully in zones 5–6 given well-drained soil and tucked in with an insulating mulch of straw or evergreen boughs in late fall. Enjoy the blooms in your garden, allow them to go to seed and dry, then bring them indoors to serve as focal points of dried arrangements.

Allium senescens

color	pink
bloom time	mid- to late summer
size	9–24 in. × 12 in.
light	sun
zones	Z4–10

GERMAN GARLIC, BROADLEAF CHIVES Europe, northern Asia. Bulbous with short rhizomes that make vigorous, but not invasive, clumps. Strappy basal leaves, 2–12 in. long; dense, 0.75-in. umbels composed of 20 or more fragrant, cup-shaped flowers last for several weeks. Suitable for rock gardens and atop retaining walls.

'Blue Twister' was selected for its unusual bright blue, twisted leaves. Deadhead routinely to extend bloom. 12 in. Z3–8. **'Glaucum'** (subsp. *glaucum*) has interesting clumps of twisted, bluish gray foliage. Lavender-pink heads of flowers rise above the foliage mass. Decorative even when not in bloom.

Allium thunbergii

	reddish violet, white
	fall
	18–24 in. × 10 in.
	sun, part shade
	Z5–8

JAPANESE ONION Japan. This underused species deserves a wider audience, if only for its late bloom time. Through the season, slightly untidy tufts of mid-green, grassy foliage, triangular in cross section, mark their spot. In late summer, sturdy, 8- to 9-in. scapes are topped with small, green buds the shape of dunce caps; these enlarge and open to 1- to 2-in.-wide globes of numerous reddish violet flowers with slender exserted stamens and styles that produce a dainty appearance. Foliage takes on orange hues after the first hard frost. Flowers dry well and if left on the plant remain decorative as the flowers fade to deep pink. Drought tolerant. Divide in spring.

'Ozawa' sports heads of many reddish violet flowers. 12–20 in. **'Alba'** is white flowered. Not as robust as 'Ozawa'. 12–15 in.

Allium tuberosum

	white
	late summer to early fall
	12–30 in. × 12 in.
	sun, part shade
	Z4–8

GARLIC CHIVES, CHINESE CHIVES Southeast Asia. Rhizomatous clumps of bulbs produce a mass of bluish green, flattened leaves, keeled at the base; these are edible and can serve as a substitute for garlic. In late summer, tall scapes topped with heads of small, starry, fragrant, white flowers appear that attract numerous pollinating insects. Deadhead to prevent widespread self-seeding, which may become a nuisance. Holds its own with white garden phlox 'David', spider plants, and panicle hydrangeas (*Hydrangea paniculata*) in white combinations in beds and borders. Seeds about too much for planting in rock gardens, but valuable in herb garden containers.

PEONY

Paeonia

PAEONIACEAE

AS CLOSE TO FOOLPROOF as any perennial can be, peonies offer spectacular, fragrant bloom combined with handsome foliage, and a lifespan that may last half a century or more. The Chinese, who brought peonies into their gardens as early as the seventh century CE, first recognized the ornamental potential of this genus. Contemporary gardeners will find peonies useful when planted singly for adding substance as well as color to mixed borders, and fine material for low, informal hedges.

Peonies are unmatched as cut flowers. Shasta daisies, flax, and bearded irises all make good companions for them. Easy and generally pest free; susceptible to foliar diseases, botrytis blight, and phytophthora blight, especially where air circulation is poor. Deer and rabbit resistant.

Peonies are another genus that offers an embarrassment of riches; there are many hundreds of cultivars from which to choose. Fortunately, identifying those that suit your conditions and taste is a relatively simple process.

Garden peonies are commonly divided into three groups:

Herbaceous peonies behave as perennials, dying back to the ground every fall. The older cultivars, which descend from Chinese garden peonies, are mostly selections of the species *Paeonia lactiflora*. Many modern breeders continue to work within that group, but in the twentieth century a number of hybrid groups, descended from crosses of two or more species, appeared; hybrids represent an increasing proportion of the new introductions. Herbaceous peonies form multi-stemmed clumps, 1.5–3 ft. high and wide, with shiny green leaves that persist throughout the summer. They bloom during the transition from spring into summer, with each individual cultivar blooming for an average of seven to ten days. Flower colors of herbaceous peonies range from white to yellow to coral to pink to red to maroon. There are no blues, and true yellows are rare: the species *P. mlokosewitschii* bears lemon-yellow flowers, and a handful of hybrids, including 'Claire de Lune', 'Prairie Moon', and 'Goldilocks', also have pale yellow flowers.

Tree peonies, despite their name, are deciduous, woody-stemmed shrubs. A mature tree peony in full flower is one of the most dramatic sights of spring gardens, and provides a magnificent focal point in a mixed border. As shrubs, however, they are outside the scope of this guide.

Itoh peonies, or intersectional peonies, are crosses between herbaceous and tree peonies. These hybrids behave like herbaceous perennials, but exhibit the larger blossom type of their shrubby parent, with flowers 8–10 in. in diameter. They are outstandingly floriferous; mature plants may bear 30 to 50 blossoms apiece. Flower color range is similar except that the intersectionals include more bright yellows. Their height and spread is similar to that of herbaceous peonies, typically 2–3 ft. Disease-resistant foliage. Mostly hardy to zone 4.

Peonies are further categorized by their flower form:

Single. Flowers with a single ring of petals.

Japanese/anemone type. Flowers whose pollen-bearing stamens have become more-or-less transformed into staminodes or narrow petaloids, resulting in slightly fuller blossoms.

Semi-double. Flowers with more than one row of petals emerging from the crown of the flower; the central cluster of pollen-bearing anthers is visible during bloom.

Full double. Flowers with multiple rows of petals, with so many of the floral stamens and stigmas converted into petals that no trace of the flower's sexual parts are visible.

Bombs. A type of double peony; the central petals form a globular cluster that rests on a "halo" of flattened outer "guard" petals; guard petals are often differently colored from the central petals.

Growers also commonly categorize herbaceous peonies by indicating when a cultivar blooms within the four- to five-week herbaceous peony season. Intersectional peonies have a prolonged period of flowering; individual plants typically remain in bloom for three to four weeks, peaking near the end of the herbaceous peony season.

Peony flowers are famous for their intoxicating fragrances, from sweet to citrusy and spicy. Not all peonies are fragrant; the perfume intensity varies markedly even among fragrant types. Double-flowered selections tend to be more fragrant than single ones; pink- or white-flowered types have more fragrance than red-flowered ones. A light but pronounced citrus or spicy fragrance is common among the intersectionals.

Paeonia lactiflora cultivars are mostly hardy through zone 2. Other species and many hybrids may be less cold hardy, but commonly overwinter successfully through zone 3. The intersectional peonies are hardy to zone 4.

Peonies require between 500 to 1000 winter chilling hours (between 32–40°F) to flower successfully; zone 8 is the southern edge of their range. Gardeners in warmer areas find that early-blooming cultivars are best adapted to their climate; the onset of very hot weather in late spring causes the buds of late-blooming cultivars to abort. Furthermore, single or Japanese types generally perform better in such areas than do doubles.

Most peonies prefer full sun. If summer sun is intense, partial shade is beneficial. Several species tolerate moderate shade, especially *P. anomala*, *P. mlokosewitschii*, and *P. obovata* (*P. japonica*).

Paeonia anomala

red
late spring
18–24 in. high and wide
sun, part shade
Z2–7

ANOMALOUS PEONY Native to coniferous woods, dry grasslands, rocky hillsides, from northern Russia through central Asia. Striking deep green leaves, deeply divided into long, narrow leaflets, on sturdy stems; foliage turns orange-yellow in fall. Upward-facing, sweetly perfumed, single, intense rose-red flowers to 3 in. wide, with central bosses of golden anthers. Provide well-drained, moderately fertile soil. More shade tolerant than *Paeonia lactiflora* types; good for woodland edges. Usually blooms about three weeks ahead of most garden cultivars. Reportedly resistant to botrytis. Good for rock gardens, borders, and among other shrubs in woodland clearings.

Paeonia brownii

reddish brown with green
late spring to early summer
8–20 in. × 12–18 in.
sun, part shade
Z5–7

WESTERN PEONY Native to chaparral, sagebrush, and pine forests from eastern Washington, south through the northern two-thirds of California; east to Utah, western Wyoming, and Idaho. Clusters of stems bear fleshy, twice-divided leaves with oval leaflets covered with white to blue, waxy powder. Flowers solitary at stem tips, pendulous, and single, with reddish brown petals edged with greenish yellow. Drought tolerant; intolerant of wet winters. Good for rock gardens.

Paeonia mlokosewitschii

syn. *P. daurica* subsp. *mlokosewitschii*

	yellow
	late spring to early summer
	18–24 in. high and wide
	sun, part shade
	Z4–9

GOLDEN PEONY, MOLLY-THE-WITCH Caucasus Mountains. Soft blue-green leaves, each with three to seven round-tipped leaflets; emerging foliage is purplish, and retains purple margins, stems, and petioles well into growing season. Early-blooming, pale yellow, shallowly cupped, 3- to 5-in. flowers are single; yellow anthers cluster around central yellow-green carpels (ovaries). Mildly fragrant, shade and drought tolerant, prefers fertile, well-drained, average to moderately moist soil. When seeds ripen, the enclosing receptacle splits, exposing a shiny red or pink interior, set with scarlet and shiny blue-gray seeds. A superb accent plant in borders, cottage gardens, or at woodland edges.

Paeonia obovata

	white, red, purple
	late spring to early summer
	1–2 ft. high and wide
	sun, part shade
	Z5–8

WOODLAND PEONY Native to woodlands from Siberia through Manchuria, northern China and Japan. Gray-green leaves divided into oval to broad-elliptic leaflets, with terminal leaflets obovate. Single, cup-shaped flowers are rose-purple centered with yellow stamens; mildly fragrant; midseason. Receptacles split when seeds ripen in late summer, revealing red interiors studded with glossy black seeds. Blends well in bright woodland settings with hostas, astilbes, and other woodland flower and foliage perennials. Single, white-flowered *Paeonia japonica* is now considered a variant of *P. obovata*.

'Alba' has white flowers.

Paeonia tenuifolia

Color	red
Bloom time	mid- to late spring
Size	12–24 in. × 9–18 in.
Exposure	sun, part shade
Hardiness	Z4–8

FERNLEAF PEONY Southeastern Europe, Turkey, Caucasus. Persistently attractive foliage is feathery, deeply divided, and lobed. Midseason; 2- to 3-in., crimson flowers. Provide rich, moderately moist, well-drained soil. Well adapted as accent plants in perennial borders, for low hedges, and as edgings along walkways.

PERENNIAL FORGET-ME-NOT

Brunnera

BORAGINACEAE

THIS GENUS CONTRIBUTES one species with a number of notable selections to the garden. Since the foliage remains attractive throughout the growing season, plants are effective in flowerbeds as specimens or grouped as a foil for colorful summer perennials and annuals. Variegated cultivars—ideal for containers in light shade—are especially susceptible to leaf burn when exposed to intense sun.

Provide moisture-retaining fertile soil for best results; the leaf edges tend to crisp if allowed to dry out, especially where temperatures are higher. Brunneras contrast well with spring bulbs, including daffodils, grape hyacinths, and summer snowflakes. Barrenworts, lungworts, and ferns are good companions in light shade, massed under trees and shrubs, or in drifts. Deer resistant, but protect from slug damage. Pests and diseases are seldom serious. Foliage of variegated forms may revert to all green; remove such reversions at their base.

This low-maintenance perennial self-seeds freely, but propagate selections vegetatively by division in spring. Increase the species by root cuttings in winter.

Brunnera macrophylla 'Jack Frost'

Brunnera macrophylla

syn. *Anchusa myosotidiflora*

(flower color)	blue
(bloom time)	late spring to early summer
(size)	1–2 ft. × 18 in.
(exposure)	sun, part shade
(zones)	Z3-9, HS

SIBERIAN BUGLOSS, HEART-LEAVED BRUNNERA, PERENNIAL FORGET-ME-NOT Moist, open woodlands from eastern Europe to western Siberia. Rough-textured foliage held aloft on long petioles rises from the crown to form handsome clumps that mature after the plants bloom; young leaves expand into heart-shaped blades 6–8 in. across. The 0.25-in., yellow-eyed, blue flowers are carried in loose, terminal panicles atop slender, hairy stems.

'Dawson's White' has irregular cream margins to its leaves. Similar to **'Variegata'** but reputed to be less susceptible to sunburn. Foliage may revert. To 18 in. **'Emerald Mist'** bears mid-green leaves widely blotched with silver toward the edges. 18 in. tall. **'Hadspen Cream'** has leaves irregularly bordered with cream. 12–15 in. **'Jack Frost'** has predominantly silver leaves etched with emerald veins below blue flowers. **'Mr. Morse'** is similar but white flowered. 15–18 in. Named the 2012 Perennial Plant of the Year. **'Langtrees'** ('Aluminum Spot') sports pairs of large, silver ditto marks around the leaves. To 12 in. **'Looking Glass'**, a sport from 'Jack Frost', has more silvery leaves and less green veining. Not as hardy as other cultivars. 6–15 in.

PERUVIAN LILY | PRINCESS LILY

Alstroemeria

ALSTROEMERIACEAE

THESE SOUTH AMERICAN PERENNIALS are best known to the wider public as particularly long-lasting cut flowers. Indeed, to satisfy the appetite of the floral industry, millions of alstroemerias are raised in the fields and greenhouses of South America, Holland, and Israel, as well as California. They are often seen as symbols of friendship and devotion and are quite common in gift bouquets.

The genus *Alstroemeria*, named by Swedish botanist Carl Linnaeus for his friend, Baron Klaus von Alstroemer, includes some 60 species, a few of which are appropriate as garden flowers. Some, such as A. pygmaea, are highly ornamental, but are so demanding to grow that they are confined mainly in alpine greenhouses.

Alstroemerias arise from fleshy rhizome-like tuberous roots (invasive in some species) that generally form clumps up to 2 ft. or so across. Their stems are well clothed with narrow, mid-green leaves, grayish beneath and 3–5 in. in length; the petioles (leaf stalks) are twisted so that they invert the leaves. Showy, even gaudy flowers are tubular and held in loose, simple or compound umbels at the stem tips. Each flower is six-tepaled (petals and sepals are not differentiated) and grows from 1.5–4 in. long. Attracts hummingbirds and butterflies.

Plant Peruvian lilies carefully, avoiding damage to the tuberous roots, in moisture-retentive, fertile, well-drained soil. Add organic matter at planting time and mulch with compost or well-rotted leaves annually to reduce water loss. The tuberous roots suffer if allowed to dry out. Evergreen in mild-winter areas, alstroemerias go dormant in fall where winters are cold; protect clumps with evergreen boughs in winter. As alstroemerias brighten a floral arrangement, so too do they introduce more vivid hues into perennial and mixed borders. An obvious choice for cutting gardens, but a number of selections have been bred for planting in containers and at the front of borders. Tall selections look cheerful planted among evergreens such as rhododendrons, azaleas, and Japanese andromeda. Deadhead to extend bloom time.

Be alert for virus diseases and gray mold that mar the flowers and leaves. Slugs dine on young foliage and flowers, but deer and rabbits mostly ignore them. Those with sensitive skin may react to the sap of alstroemerias; protect hands with gloves when working with these plants.

Increase by division in spring or fall, or start seed in containers to avoid disturbing the tubers at transplanting time. Seed germinates readily.

Alstroemeria aurea

syn. *A. aurantiaca*

color	orange
bloom time	summer
size	30–36 in. × 18 in.
light	sun, part shade
zone	Z7–10

PERUVIAN LILY Chile. Clumps of running tuberous roots produce erect, well-foliaged stems. The tepals are bright orange, the upper pair freckled and splashed with red; exserted stamens are drooping.

'Luna' is clear yellow.

Alstroemeria huemulina

color	orange
bloom time	summer to late summer
size	24 in. × 18 in.
light	sun
zone	Z8–11

PERUVIAN LILY South America. Easy to grow, with clumps of non-running roots. Medium-size blooms are brown splashed, with brilliant deep orange tepals. First flush of bloom is repeated a few weeks later.

Alstroemeria psittacina

(flower color)	red
(bloom time)	summer to fall
(size)	2–3 ft. × 3 ft.
(exposure)	sun, part shade
(zone)	Z7–10

PARROT FLOWER Brazil. Clusters of exotic-looking brownish red flowers tipped with green. Mauve-spotted stems bear 3-in.-long, lance-shaped leaves. Roots spread widely and can become more than a nuisance. Best protected from intense afternoon sun. Very long-lasting as cut flowers.

'Variegata' has clean white–edged leaves. Red flowers are speckled with maroon and green. Summer dormant after bloom time. Z6–9.

Other Notable Cultivars

Alstroemerias are bred for the cut-flower trade but perfect for residential gardens. Most are well-behaved hybrids with amazing, sparkling flowers borne over a long season. This is a tiny sampling of what is available:

'Casablanca' has pink-flushed, white flowers flecked with maroon. 40 in. Z6–9. **'Freedom'** is clump forming with reddish peach flowers blotched with cherry-sprinkled white on the upper petals. An introduction from Mark Bridgen's Cornell breeding program. 30 in. Z5–8. **'Glory of the Andes'** is a variegated selection derived from 'Sweet Laura' . 24–30 in. Z6. **Inca Series**, from Dutch breeder Könst, includes several superior introductions for compact, non-invasive growth and long bloom (early summer to fall). 'Inca Adore' ('Koadore') has red flowers accented with a wide band of yellow with brown freckles. 'Inca Ice' ('Koice') has whitish flowers, yellow at the throat and speckled with deep maroon dashes. Mostly 24 in. × 36 in. Z6–9. **Princess Lilies Series**, bred by Van Zanten Plants in Holland, is superior for window boxes and planters, and at the front of cottage garden borders. Though frost sensitive, they are especially heat tolerant. 'Princess Oxana' ('Staprioxa') is deep rose splotched with yellow and dashes of maroon. 10 in. Z7–8. 'Princess Ivana' ('Staprivane') has 2-in.-wide, yellow-throated, cherry-red flowers. Mounding habit, great for containers and in the landscape. 12–15 in. Z8–11. **'The Third Harmonic'** (*Alstroemeria* 'Peach Harmony' × *A. aurea*), introduced by George Hare, has large, orange flowers speckled with purple at the lip, and claret-flushed beneath. Tolerates heat and humidity. 48 in. Z6–9.

PHLOX

Phlox

POLEMONIACEAE

"ESSENTIAL" MEANS INDISPENSABLE, but it also indicates that anything labeled this way is of the essence—as a perennial for American gardens, phloxes qualify in both respects. The genus is almost entirely native to this continent, from the edge of the Alaskan tundra to the Gulf Coast of Florida.

Phlox leaves, typically entire and generally lanceolate or linear, are borne in opposing pairs; tubular, often fragrant flowers flare into five lobes at their mouths. Individual flowers, though modest in size, are abundant, grouped in large panicles or solitary in blankets that almost hide the foliage. The color palette is inclusive, lacking only yellow, unmixed oranges, and true blues to complete the spectrum.

Phlox fanciers can enjoy bloom from midspring through early fall by growing different species; summer phloxes (*Phlox paniculata*) have a particularly generous bloom time that may extend over two months with assiduous deadheading. Creeping phloxes serve as groundcovers in rock gardens and on sunny banks, compact species decorate the front, and tall phloxes shine as border backdrops; several contribute to cottage and cutting gardens. The species are appropriate in native, wild, and meadow gardens, and sometimes in open woodland gardens. Many excellent cultivars and hybrids are offered in nurseries, with more arriving annually.

The cultural requirements of phloxes vary between species, but most prefer sunny or lightly shaded sites, with six hours or so of direct sunlight daily (*P. divaricata* is the exception; see its entry for details). Creeping and mat-forming types prefer leaner, very well-drained, even gritty soils; upright border and meadow phloxes require moderately moist, fertile, humus-rich soils. Few species thrive in high heat and humidity; timely irrigation is usually critical for good flowering.

Carefully select the phlox species suited to your climate, soil, and conditions. Fungal root rot may be a problem, but some species are resistant. In hot, dry conditions spider mites are serious; susceptibility to powdery mildew varies, and it is wise to select resistant species and cultivars. Thinning to increase air circulation is also helpful. Butterflies and hummingbirds flock to phlox; deer and rabbits devour them.

Other reliable and attractive species include *P. bifida*, *P. nivalis*, *P. adsurgens*, *P. pilosa*, *P. ×procumbens*, and numerous hybrids that are well worth seeking out.

Divide cultivars in spring or early fall, or take stem cuttings in early midsummer. Start species from seed.

Phlox divaricata 'Chattahoochee'

Phlox carolina

color	white, pink, purple
bloom	early to midsummer
size	24–30 in. × 18–24 in.
light	sun, part shade
zone	Z3–8

CAROLINA PHLOX, SUMMER PHLOX, THICKLEAF PHLOX Native to woodland edges and openings from North Carolina to southern Illinois, and south to the Gulf of Mexico. Groups of slender, erect, red-streaked stems with leathery, oval leaves. Loose, dome-shaped clusters of fragrant, lavender to pink flowers. Prefers moisture-retentive but well-drained soil. Powdery mildew resistant.

'Gypsy Love' (syn. *Phlox carolina* var. *angusta* 'Gypsy Love') has fragrant, bright pink flowers from late spring. Lustrous foliage. 24 in. × 18 in. **'Miss Lingard'**, often listed as a *P. carolina* cultivar, is probably a hybrid with *P. maculata*. Showy clusters of fragrant, white flowers in early summer with intermittent rebloom. Outstanding resistance to powdery mildew. 2–3 ft. × 2–3 ft. **'Kim'** has bright pink flowers in summer to autumn. 12–18 in. × 12–24 in.

Phlox divaricata

color	blue
bloom	mid- to late spring
size	9–12 in. high and wide
light	part shade, shade
zone	Z3–8

WOODLAND PHLOX, WILD SWEET WILLIAM Native to rich woods, fields, and streamsides throughout central United States northward into Quebec. Spreading mounds of sticky, hairy stems clad with 1- to 2-in., lanceolate to elliptic leaves. Sprawling stems root at the nodes to establish spreading colonies. Fragrant, 1.5-in., blue, lilac, or pink flowers in loose clusters at stem tips. Provide humus-rich, moderately moist, well-drained soil; mulch in summer. Susceptible to powdery mildew—cut back stems after flowering to force clean, healthy new growth; watch for spider mites and rabbits; mostly deer tolerant. Shallow-rooted, woodland phlox makes a good cover for early spring bulbs. Lovely in native and woodland gardens, rock gardens, and shady borders where coral bells, hostas, and lungworts are appropriate companions.

'Chattahoochee' has fragrant, maroon-eyed, bluish lavender flowers. Probably a hybrid. Rabbit and deer resistant. **'Eco Texas Purple'** has violet-purple flowers with reddish centers. **'Fuller's White'** is white flowered. **'London Grove'** has powder-blue flowers. **'Montrose Tricolor'** has silvery-mauve flowers; foliage striped and edged white and pink.

Phlox glaberrima

	pink, purple, white
	midspring to late spring
	2–4 ft. × 2–2.5 ft.
	sun, part shade
	Z3–8

SMOOTH PHLOX Wet woods, meadows, and prairies throughout the southeastern United States. Similar-looking to *Phlox paniculata* but spring blooming and very resistant to powdery mildew. Upright stems bear thin, 5-in., lanceolate leaves. Fragrant, tubular, and five-lobed flowers, to 1 in. across, congregate in large, pyramidal clusters at stem tips. Tolerates moister soils than other species. Seldom needs staking, deadhead to prolong bloom; mulch in summer. Watch for spider mites, especially in hot, dry weather. Deer tolerant. A gem for spring borders, meadow plantings, and cutting gardens.

'Morris Berd'. White-eyed, rose-pink flowers. Long blooming. 18–24 in. **'Triple Play'**. Creamy white–edged leaves; pink-lavender flowers. 1 ft. × 2 ft.

Phlox maculata

	pinkish purple
	early summer to late summer
	2–3 ft. × 1–2 ft.
	sun, part shade
	Z3–8

MEADOW PHLOX, WILD SWEET WILLIAM Moist meadows, low-lying woods and riverbanks throughout the eastern United States. Rhizomatous clumps of upright, red-spotted stems with dark, thin, finely toothed, lanceolate leaves to 5 in. Sweetly scented, tubular five-lobed flowers to 0.5 in. across, carried in 10- to 12-in.-long, cylindrical panicles at stem tips. Thrives in average, moderately moist, well-drained soils in airy, open positions. Intolerant of drought; apply a summertime mulch. Resists powdery mildew; spider mites attack especially in hot, dry conditions. Seldom needs staking; deadhead to prolong bloom. Spreading rhizomes and self-seeding may result in large colonies. Good for summer borders, cottage and meadow gardens, and cut flowers.

'Natascha' has bicolored pink-and-white, very fragrant flowers. Compact. 2 ft. **'Omega'** is white, accented with a pale pink eye.

Phlox paniculata 'Peppermint Twist'

Other Notable Cultivars

×***arendsii*** (*Phlox divaricata* × *P. paniculata*) is a large group of hybrids from the Arends Nursery. At their best they combine the compact habit of woodland phloxes, and the large flowerheads of summer phloxes; early to midsummer bloom. Outstanding examples with mildew resistance include: **'Ping Pong'**, with large clusters of mildly fragrant, red-eyed light pink flowers. 1.5–2 ft. × 1–1.5 ft. Z3–8. **'Sabine'** has soft, bluish pink, fragrant flowers. 20 in. Z4–8. **Spring Pearl Series** bears domed flower clusters, often but not uniformly fragrant, in white, pink, fuchsia, magenta, and bicolors; all cultivars have feminine names, like 'Miss Jill', 'Miss Karen', 'Miss Margie', and 'Miss Mary'. Compact at 16–24 in. × 14–18 in. Z4–8.

Phlox paniculata

	various
	midsummer to early fall
	3–6 ft. × 1–3 ft.
	sun, part shade
	Z4–8

SUMMER PHLOX, BORDER PHLOX Open woods, meadows, and moist roadsides from central New York to Missouri and Kansas, south to North Carolina, Tennessee, and Louisiana. Somewhat demanding, but glorious when its needs are met. Clumps of stiff stems, unbranched below, clothed with 1-in.-wide, ovate to ovate-oblong leaves to 6 in. long; rounded, 4- to 6-in. panicles of fragrant, tubular, five-lobed flowers. Self-seeds, producing mostly magenta flowers; cultivars bloom in shades of white, coral, pink, red, lavender, and violet; often bicolored with contrasting eyes.

Provide good air circulation, and protect from intense midday sun to avoid foliage yellowing. Maintain soil moisture with summer mulch; few cultivars embrace heat and humidity. Stake taller types early, at 6–8 in., to prevent flopping; extend bloom time with routine deadheading. Powdery mildew is the curse of summer phlox; seek resistant selections.

There are hundreds of cultivars; the following are resistant to powdery mildew and mites, and have notably fragrant flowers:

'Delta Snow' has 1-in.-wide, purple-eyed, white flowers. Exceptional heat tolerance; good for areas with high humidity. 2–4 ft. × 2–3 ft. **'Nora Leigh'** has light green foliage irregularly margined with cream. Dark pink–eyed, white flowers. 30 in. **'Orange Perfection'** has 1-in., salmon-orange flowers with magenta eyes. 36 in. × 20 in. **'Peppermint Twist'** has flowers like 1.25-in.-wide pinwheels of pink and white. Very compact. 16 in. × 12–15 in. **'Robert Poore'** has deep magenta flowers on 3- to 5-ft. stems. **'Shortwood'** ranked most resistant to powdery mildew at Chicago Botanic Garden trials. Hot-pink flowers with darker pink eyes. 42–48 in. × 24–30 in.

Phlox stolonifera 'Sherwood Purple'

Phlox stolonifera

- lavender, white
- late spring to early summer
- 6–12 in. × 9–18 in.
- sun, part shade
- Z5–9

CREEPING PHLOX Woodlands and stream banks of southern Appalachians. Creeping stems form 3-in.-high mats of oblong to oval, 3-in.-long leaves. Fragrant, 0.75-in. flowers are commonly lavender but sometimes white, borne in loose clusters. Tolerates light shade, deer, and some drought; vulnerable to rabbits and powdery mildew. Good groundcover for native, shade, and woodland gardens, border fronts, and rock gardens; a good "cover-up" for fading spring bulbs.

'Blue Ridge' has violet-blue flowers. **'Bruce's White'** is vigorous with fragrant, white flowers. **'Home Fires'** has dark pink flowers. **'Sherwood Purple'** has medium purple flowers.

Phlox subulata

- pink, purple, white
- early to midspring
- 3–6 in. × 1–2 ft.
- sun
- Z3–9

MOSS PHLOX Native to dryish, rocky soils in open woodlands and slopes from Michigan, Ontario, and New York, south to Tennessee and North Carolina. Spreading carpets of semi-evergreen, 1-in., needle-like leaves are blanketed with loose cymes of fragrant, 0.5- to 0.75-in. flowers by midspring. Provide humus-rich soil in full sun in cold climates, and dappled midday shade where sun is intense. Prone to spider mites, but powdery mildew resistant; shear after flowering to stimulate modest rebloom. Deer resistant, but beware of rabbits. Showy in rock gardens and for edging, good groundcover for sandy, sunny south- or west-facing banks. Cultivars include:

'Allegheny Smoke' has pale, grayish blue flowers. **'Dirigo Arbutus'** has lavender flowers with darker eyes. **'Red Wings'** has rose-red flowers with darker red eyes. **'Snowflake'** is compact with white flowers.

PINK | DIANTHUS

Dianthus

CARYOPHYLLACEAE

ALTHOUGH THIS GENUS OF 350 species includes many with exquisitely beautiful and often sweetly scented flowers, until recently American gardeners have made little use of dianthus. Carnations (*Dianthus caryophyllus*) might be standbys in the cutting garden, and alpine gardeners have long prized the neat, cushion-forming species for their rock gardens, but the demanding nature of most cultivated dianthus—older types tolerated neither poor drainage nor summer heat and humidity—and their relatively short season of bloom made them infrequent choices for perennial gardens. Over the last couple of decades, however, plant breeders have successfully addressed these two limitations in their new introductions. As a result, dianthus is claiming increased space in our gardens.

The common name for these flowers—pinks—may seem to derive from the rosy hues so common among dianthus blossoms, but actually it is a reference to the petals' frilly edges, which look as if they've been cut or "pinked" with a tailor's pinking shears. Another old name is "clove pink"—the deliciously spicy scent common to these flowers formerly made them a popular ingredient for potpourri, and for flavoring wines and ales. Modern cooks garnish salads and other cold dishes with edible dianthus petals. Scent, fortunately, is one of the qualities emphasized by contemporary dianthus breeders who have introduced a number of hybrids with outstanding perfumes.

Borne singly or in few or many-flowered panicles, cymes, or heads, dianthus flowers are usually colored in shades of white and pink to red, often with a contrasting central eye. Pairs of grassy, often glabrous, blue-gray or gray-green leaves form dense mats or cushions that are commonly evergreen or semi-evergreen.

Dianthus require a well-drained soil, ideally with a neutral to alkaline pH; mulch with limestone chips if soil is acid. Poor drainage promotes root rot and rust. They grow best in full sun, though light afternoon shade can be beneficial where the sun is intense. Many of the new hybrids can be raised from seed and often bloom their first year. Deadhead routinely for possible bloom later.

Deer resistant and generally pest free, dianthus may suffer from powdery mildew in humid weather, especially where air circulation is poor. Compact forms provide neat edgings for the front of a border or bed, and they flourish if tucked into a soil-backed stone wall; mat-forming cultivars thrive if set into the cracks of a dry-laid stone pavement. Taller species make long-lasting cut flowers.

Propagate named cultivars by taking 2- to 3-in.-long cuttings from side shoots stripped off with a bit of the main stem (a heel) or from "pipings," shoot tips snapped off at a node. Dianthus also layer easily.

Dianthus ×allwoodii 'Alpinus'

Dianthus amurensis 'Siberian Blue'

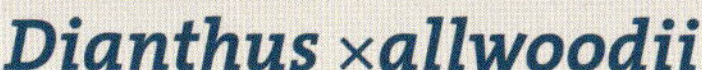

Dianthus ×allwoodii

various

late spring to late summer

10–18 in. high and wide

sun

Z3–10

COTTAGE PINK, BORDER CARNATION, ALLWOOD PINK Of hybrid origin: *Dianthus caryophyllus* × *D. plumarius*. Tufted plants with grass-like, grayish green foliage. Solitary, single, semi- or fully double, 1.5- to 2-in.-wide flowers with pinked petals are often bicolored.

'Agatha' is compact, long-lived, and cold hardy; semi-double, pink flowers with darker eye, and outstanding fragrance. 10 in. high and wide. **'Alpinus'**. Extra-compact plants form neat mounds of blue-green foliage beneath strongly perfumed, single flowers in shades of pink and red, often with contrasting darker eye. Early summer to frost. Available as seed. 6–9 in. tall. **'Aqua'** has 12-in. stems bearing fragrant, double, white flowers. **'Doris'** bears perfumed, semi-double, salmon-pink flowers with a deep rose eye. **'Frosty Fire'** bears cherry red, double flowers flecked with white. Fragrant, drought and heat resistant. 12 in.

Dianthus amurensis

lavender

late spring to late summer

6–12 in. × 12–15 in.

sun, part shade

Z3–8

AMUR PINK This compact species displays the toughness one would expect of a Siberian native. Long-lived and drought tolerant once established.

'Siberian Blue' bears lavender-blue, 0.5- to 1-in.-wide blooms in small but abundant clusters over blue-green foliage; the flowers offer the closest to true blue found in this genus. Unscented, best in gritty soils, and ideal for rock gardens or containers.

Dianthus barbatus 'Indian Carpet'

Dianthus barbatus

	various
	late spring to early summer
	1–3 ft. high and wide
	sun
	Z3–10

SWEET WILLIAM Southern Europe, Asia. A short-lived perennial or biennial that is often grown as an annual (especially in regions with hot summers). This cottage gardening favorite is useful for cutting and in sunny mixed borders. It bears dense, many-flowered, flat or domed clusters of single, semi-double, or double flowers in white through shades of pink to crimson; commonly multicolored. Often fragrant, individual flowers measure 0.5–1 in. in diameter. They attract bees, hummingbirds, and butterflies. Dark green, glossy, strap-shaped leaves. A source of long-lasting, strong-stemmed cut flowers; encourage prolonged bloom and preserve vigor of plants by cutting stems of fading flowers off at ground level to prevent seed set. Best in cool climates but tolerates heat where summers are dry.

'Dunnett's Dark Crimson' has deep crimson flowers with a white eye. **'Heart Attack'**, one of the best cultivars for heat and humidity, bears dark red, almost black, carnation-like flowers on 12- to 18-in. stems from early spring through summer. May persist for many years; unusually long-lived for this species. Z4–8. **'Indian Carpet'** is a dwarf strain, with flowers in white through shades of pink to red, often with contrasting bands. Late spring to summer. 6–12 in. Z3–9. **'Newport Pink'** produces fragrant, single, coral-pink flowers that bloom from late spring through early summer. 18–24 in. × 2 ft. Z4–11. **'Sooty'** has mahogany foliage and maroon flowers from spring through early summer. Fragrant. 12–18 in. × 9–12 in.

Dianthus deltoides 'Zing Rose'

Dianthus deltoides

(color)	various
(bloom time)	late spring to early summer
(size)	6–18 in. × 12 in.
(light)	sun, part shade
(zones)	Z3–10, HS

MAIDEN PINK Northern Europe. Among the cold-hardiest dianthus, maiden pinks are exceptional for this genus because they thrive in partial shade. Forming loose mats of evergreen, narrowly linear to lance-shaped leaves, these plants are covered with 0.75-in., slightly fragrant flowers. Blossoms of unimproved specimens are typically deep pink with a darker band at the base of the petals. Shear off fading flowers for neatness, to prevent seed set, and to encourage rebloom in fall. Cover with evergreen boughs through winter in cold climates; crown rot may afflict plants grown on poorly drained soils. Excellent for rock gardens, edgings, and containers.

'Confetti Cherry Red' bears a profusion of candy apple–red flowers. Deadhead for fall rebloom. 6 in. tall. **'Zing Rose'** bears deep rose-red blossoms in late spring and, if deadheaded, again in fall. 6–12 in. **'Zing Salmon'** is similar but with bright salmon-pink flowers.

Dianthus gratianopolitanus 'Feuerhexe'

Dianthus gratianopolitanus

syn. *D. caesius*

various

spring to summer

6–12 in. × 12 in.

sun

Z3–10, HS

CHEDDAR PINK Western and central Europe. Another cold-hardy dianthus that is sensitive to summer humidity, though some cultivars are more tolerant than others. Grassy, gray-green to blue-gray, evergreen foliage spreads in dense mats, making this species an outstanding choice for border edging, tucking in between the stones of a wall, or spilling down a sunny bank. Bears an abundance of solitary, single or double flowers in spring; shear off fading flowers and pinch back straggling foliage to promote dense growth and intermittent summer rebloom. **'Bath's Pink**' bears clove-scented, single, pink flowers marked with magenta ring; heat and humidity tolerant. 1994 Herbaceous Perennial Georgia Gold Medal Winner. 8 in. **'Feuerhexe'** ('Firewitch') grows 3–6 in. tall and to 12 in. wide. Cold hardy, but tolerates heat and humidity. Bears heavy crops of single, clove-scented, hot-pink blossoms in late spring. 2006 Perennial Plant of the Year. **'Tiny Rubies'**. Dense mats of deep green foliage, 10–12 in. across, covered with 4-in.-tall, tiny, double, unscented, deep pink blossoms. Tolerates heat and humidity. Beautiful as a groundcover or to edge a path. **'Wicked Witch'** is a sport of 'Feuerhexe' that bears cherry-red flowers.

Dianthus knappii

yellow

late spring to midsummer

12–18 in. × 9–12 in.

sun

Z3–9

HAIRY GARDEN PINK Eastern and central Europe. The only yellow-blooming dianthus has 0.5- to 1-in.-wide flowers with no fragrance. Lanky stems, with an open growth habit, support fine-textured, pubescent, grayish foliage. Blooms during its first year from seed.

'Yellow Harmony' offers larger flowers and tidier, more upright growth than the species.

Dianthus plumarius

color	various
bloom time	summer to fall
size	6–12 in. × 8–24 in.
light	sun
zones	Z3–10, HS

COTTAGE PINK, GRASS PINK This heirloom flower, brought to the United States from Europe in Colonial times, was a favorite of old-time cottage gardeners. Cottage pinks form loose tufts or mats of evergreen, blue-green foliage; in season it bears clusters of single or double, usually fragrant flowers, elevated 12 in. above the leaves. Long blooming, especially if deadheaded. A nostalgic addition to bouquets, cottage pinks make fine edgings for beds and borders, and thrive in sunny rock gardens. Requires a moist, humus-rich soil.

'Birmingham' bears fragrant, double, white flowers. Heat and humidity tolerant. Z4–8. **'Cyclops'** has single flowers in red, pinks, and white. 12 in. **'Mrs. Sinkins'** has exquisitely perfumed, fully double, white flowers. Largely replaced by modern selections; the calyx tends to split causing the flower to "blow." **Romance Mix** produces single flowers in a wide range of pinks, many bicolored. **Sweetness Mix** blooms the first year from seed, bearing sweet-scented flowers in shades of rose, pink, carmine, and white. Compact, excellent for containers and bedding. 4–6 in.

Dianthus superbus

color	various
bloom time	late spring to early summer
size	12–30 in. × 24 in.
light	sun
zones	Z4–8, HS

LILAC PINK This Eurasian native performs as a short-lived perennial or biennial. Grass-green tufts of narrow, evergreen leaves are borne on lax, branching stems. Fragrant, lacy-edged, 1.5- to 2-in., single flowers, paired or solitary, range in color from pink to mauve. Prefers a rich, moist soil. Reseeds readily.

'Crimsonia' is more compact than the species with fragrant, crimson blossoms on 20-in. stems. **'Primadonna'** bears bright pink, perfumed flowers with lacy-edged petals.

POPPY

Papaver | PAPAVERACEAE

A GOOD NEWS, BAD NEWS GENUS, poppies offer glorious flowers and robust growth, two qualities that have made them traditional garden favorites. First cultivated ornamentally roughly 7000 years ago in Mesopotamia, withered poppy blossoms have been found in Egyptian tombs. On the negative side, several perennial poppies, including Oriental poppies, become summer dormant. Soon after spring bloom time, the foliage becomes unsightly before disappearing altogether, leaving a gap in the border. Partner poppies with expansive, later-blooming perennials to fill the hole, or plug in summer-blooming annuals. Oriental poppies, the showiest and most popular of the perennial species, have a short season of bloom: this lasts but a week or two, though at their peak these flowers eclipse any others in the garden.

Species poppies have four to six petals, commonly red or orange, often with a black blotch at the base, encircling a knot of stamens and a compound pistil. Cultivars and garden hybrids include many double forms and a color palette of oranges, reds, yellows, lilacs, and purples, as well as white. Fertilized flowers display characteristic salt cellar–like, bulbous seed capsules; when ripe and shaken by the wind, tiny seeds escape through pores just below their circular caps. Basal clumps of alternate, commonly petioled, pinnately divided leaves; stem leaves sessile. Foliage and stems are usually hairy.

Native to open, sunny habitats on rocky hillsides and colonizers of disturbed soils, poppies thrive as agricultural weeds. In cultivation they prefer fertile, humus-rich, moderately moist, well-drained soils in full sun. Where summers are hot, provide light afternoon shade; poppies thrive in cool summer areas and struggle with heat and humidity. They strongly resent root disturbance and once established should not be moved.

The pharmaceutical potency of poppies varies with the species, but common sense dictates avoiding consumption. They are handsome as cut flowers; seal the stem ends with a flame immediately after harvesting.

Propagate by seed sown directly or in peat pots. Increase cultivars by root cuttings.

Papaver alpinum

syn. *Oreomecon alpina*

flower color	orange, white, yellow, red
bloom time	late spring to early summer
size	6–10 in. × 6–8 in.
light	sun
zone	Z3–7, HS

ALPINE POPPY Mountains of western and central Europe, Balkans. Low rosettes of fern-like, olive-green leaves; satiny, cup-shaped flowers, 1–3 in. wide carried on upright stems in assorted colors. Short-lived in zone 5 to 7, but a self-seeding annual or biennial elsewhere. Best adapted to troughs, rock gardens, and cottage gardens; drought tolerant. Deadhead to prolong bloom.

Papaver atlanticum

flower color	orange, red
bloom time	spring to fall
size	12–24 in. × 9–12 in.
light	sun, part shade
zone	Z5–10

ATLAS POPPY, ATLANTIC POPPY Morocco. Low rosettes of hairy, 1-in.-wide, blue-green leaves to 4 in. long. Flowers to 3 in. across, followed by club-shaped seed capsules. Drought tolerant; requires well-drained soil. Reblooms, without summer dormancy; reseeds freely. Rock gardens, containers, or gravel gardens.

'Flore Pleno' has semi-double apricot flowers.

Papaver nudicaule

syn. *Oreomecon nudicaulis*

flower color	orange, pink, red, yellow, white
bloom time	late spring to early summer
size	12–24 in. × 9–12 in.
light	sun
zones	Z2–7, HS

ICELAND POPPY, ARCTIC POPPY Mountains of Asia, Arctic regions. Basal clumps of pinnately lobed, blue-green leaves. Solitary flowers top naked stalks; delicately scented, saucer shaped with crinkled petals, to 4 in. across. Short-lived; prefers cool summers, elsewhere best treated as winter annuals. A rock-garden gem, handsome in containers. Susceptible to powdery mildew.

Wonderland Mixture offers flowers in shades of yellow, orange, white, and red.

Papaver orientale

flower color	red, orange
bloom time	late spring to early summer
size	40 in. × 30 in.
light	sun
zones	Z3–8, HS

ORIENTAL POPPY Mountain meadows and screes of Armenia, northeast Iran, Turkey. Bristly, serrate, grayish green leaves to 12 in. long are pinnately dissected into lance-shaped segments. Summer dormant shortly after bloom. Single, 4- to 6-in. flowers are orange or red blotched with blackish purple at the base of each crepy, ruffled petal; large, black seedpods follow. Drought tolerant once established. Very long-lived.

Other Notable Cultivars

Many cultivars are hybrids resulting from complex crosses with other species, particularly *Papaver orientale* and very similar but slightly taller *P. bracteatum*. The following notable selections are all distinguished by dark blotches at the bases of the four petals.

'Beauty of Livermere' has 4- to 6-in., scarlet flowers. 4 ft. **'Patty's Plum'** displays plum-purple flowers, 4–5 in. across. **'Pink Ruffles'** has 4- to 6-in., pink flowers with deeply fringed petals. 24 in. **'Royal Wedding'** bears 5- to 8-in.-wide, white flowers that sway majestically above 30- to 35-in. plants. **'Salmon Glow'** displays salmon, many-petaled, almost double flowers. 30 in.

PRAIRIE MALLOW | CHECKER BLOOM

Sidalcea | MALVACEAE

LOVE WHAT HOLLYHOCKS DO for your garden but tired of watching them fall to rust? Try rust-resistant *Sidalcea*. These western North America natives are closely similar to related hollyhocks with tall, clustered spikes of five-petaled, star- or saucer-shaped flowers in pinks, white, or purple. Sharply toothed, deeply lobed leaves rise from basal clumps. They commonly bloom for years without problems, even self-seeding in favorable conditions.

Full sun or partial shade, in moist but well-drained neutral to acid soils are suitable conditions. Tall selections may require staking; cut stems back after initial flowering to promote rebloom; flowering can last all summer. Prairie mallows provide good punctuation or vertical accents for borders, with a picturesque simplicity ideal for cottage and cutting gardens. Attracts bees, butterflies, and, unfortunately, Japanese beetles; deer and rabbit resistant.

Divide selections and hybrids; start species from seed.

Sidalcea malviflora

	pink
	spring to midsummer
	36–48 in. × 18–24 in.
	sun, part shade
	Z5–9, HS

PRAIRIE MALLOW, CHECKER BLOOM Moist meadows from southern Oregon to Mexican border. Dense tufts of dark green, fleshy, palmately lobed leaves rise from rhizomatous roots. Clusters of stems lined with pink to purple flowers; blooms open in the morning and twist closed at night. Reliable and easy to grow; excellent additions to grasslands or meadow plantings. Summer dormant in response to drought but thrives with moisture; tolerates moderate to low water once established.

'Elsie Heugh' has satiny, pinkish purple flowers in summer. 30–36 in. × 12–18 in. Z5–7. **'Little Princess'** is compact with satiny, pink flowers in summer; cut back for later rebloom. 18–24 in. × 12 in. Z5–7.

Sidalcea oregana

(flower color)	pink
(bloom time)	late spring to early summer
(size)	2–4 ft. × 1–3 ft.
(exposure)	sun, part shade
(zones)	Z5–10, HS

OREGON CHECKER MALLOW British Columbia, south through California, east into Wyoming and Montana. Taprooted; rounded, toothed basal leaves are palmate and shallowly lobed; stem leaves more deeply lobed. Coarse, bristly stems with loose spike-like racemes of pink to deep rose flowers, 1–1.5 in. across.

'Brilliant' has deep rose flowers with a central white halo. 24–36 in. Z5–7.

Other Notable Cultivars

'Party Girl' has bright green leaves, rounded below but deeply lobed on the stems. Deep pink, 2- to 3-in.-wide, hollyhock-like flowers. Prefers full sun. 2–3 ft. × 1.5–2 ft. Z5–7. **Stark's Hybrids** produce flowers from pale pink to deep purple-pinks. 24–36 in.

QUEEN OF THE PRAIRIE | MEADOWSWEET

Filipendula | ROSACEAE

A SELECT GENUS OF JUST 12 species, queen of the prairie offer a range of attractions: perfumed, eye-catching flowerheads and handsome foliage, combined with the ability to flourish in a variety of climates, typically without significant pest or disease problems; they are deer tolerant as well. These hardy, rewarding plants thrive in deep, organically rich, moist soils in full sun or partial shade. Summer drought may cause their leaves to scorch; cut the stems back when the dry spell breaks; fresh foliage soon replaces the old.

Depending on the stature of the species you select, queen of the prairie can serve at the back or middle of a border. The taller, more robust species hold their own as part of meadow plantings, especially where soils are moist. Their airy, pastel-hued flowers and bold foliage complement the finer textures and more subdued colors of the grasses. Queen of the prairie show up especially well when planted in drifts, and furnish excellent cut flowers. Propagate in spring or fall by seed or by division.

Filipendula glaberrima

flower color	white
bloom time	mid- to late spring
size	36 in. × 24 in.
exposure	sun, part shade
zones	Z5–8

NAKAI KOREAN MEADOWSWEET Northeastern Asia. This underappreciated species is seldom found in the nursery trade, yet makes a fine garden perennial. In mid- to late spring, clumps of grape-like leaves give rise to stalks bearing corymbs of small white or pink flowers.

Filipendula purpurea

flower color	pink, white
bloom time	late spring to midsummer
size	36–48 in. × 24–36 in.
exposure	sun, part shade
zones	Z3–8

JAPANESE MEADOWSWEET Japan. Upright and clump forming, bears rich green, maple-like leaves that measure 4–8 in. across, and fluffy corymbs of astilbe-like flowers that are white with red stamens (appearing pink from a distance) or purple. Easily cultivated in average, well-drained garden soil, but performs best on those that are fertile, organic rich, and kept consistently moist. Benefits from some afternoon shade in hot, sunny areas. Susceptible to powdery mildew, rust, and leaf spot, but usually without serious damage.

'Alba' is white flowered. **'Elegans'** is more compact, with flowers similar to those of the species, but with evident red stamens. 18–24 in. tall. **'Purpurascens'** has purple-tinted foliage.

Filipendula rubra

syn. *Spiraea lobata, S. palmata*

Color	pink
Bloom	early to midsummer
Size	6–8 ft. × 3–4 ft.
Light	sun, part shade
Zone	Z3–8

QUEEN OF THE PRAIRIE, FALSE SPIREA Wet grasslands and fens from Missouri to North Carolina, northward into Canada. This plant offers an unusual characteristic: both its flowers and foliage are fragrant. Forms an imposing, upright clump of sturdy, often reddish stems that rarely need staking. Leaves compound, to 2 ft. long, composed of one to seven bright green, deeply palmately cut leaflets as much as 6 in. long. Fluffy, sweet-scented, pink flowers are individually tiny but borne in dense, astilbe-like panicles, 6–9 in. wide. Flourishes in moist or even wet, well-drained soils, especially those that are fertile and humus rich. Does not tolerate drought, but free from serious insect or disease problems. A good planting for pond sides or stream banks, this species self-seeds freely in a hospitable site. Spectacular, especially when grown in a mass, outstanding for wild or naturalized areas, wet meadows, or the back of a border.

'Albicans' ('Magnificum Album') has white flowers and is shorter. 5–6 ft. **'Venusta'** ('Magnifica', 'Venusta Magnifica', syn. *Filipendula venusta*) has deep pink flowers on 4 ft. stems.

Filipendula vulgaris

syn. *F. hexapetala, Spiraea filipendulina*

Color	white
Bloom	late spring to early summer
Size	16–20 in. × 12–18 in.
Light	sun, part shade
Zone	Z3–9

FERN-LEAF DROPWORT Pastures of Europe, much of central and northern Asia. Much more tolerant of dry soils than other members of the genus. Forms a low mound of finely cut, dark green, fern-like leaves, from which arise upright stems bearing panicles of creamy-white flowers. Useful for edging, for the front of a border, or for containers. Foliage smells of wintergreen when crushed.

'Multiplex' ('Flore Pleno') has drooping panicles of 0.25–0.40 in., double, white flowers like tiny rosebuds. **'Plena'** bears double flowers; outstanding for cutting and formerly a staple of wedding bouquets.

Other Notable Cultivars

'Kahome' is a dwarf that attains a height and spread of just 6–12 in. Astilbe-like corymbs of tiny, fragrant, rosy pink flowers in summer to early fall. The bright green, fern-like foliage is as attractive as the blooms.

RED HOT POKER | TORCH LILY

Kniphofia

ASPHODELACEAE

THESE FLAMBOYANT EXOTICS won an enthusiastic following among nineteenth-century gardeners before the tastemakers of the day branded them as vulgar, and they fell out of fashion. Today their popularity is on the rise and once again they are sought after as dramatic players for mixed and perennial beds. Extensive breeding programs, involving *Kniphofia galpinii*, *K. uvaria*, *K. praecox*, and *K. macownii*, have produced plants with more than red-and-yellow torches; cream, lime green, yellow, and varied coral flowers are not unusual.

This genus includes natives from temperate regions around the world, but especially from southern Africa and Madagascar. Deciduous (evergreen, especially in mild climates), torch lilies are tough and long lasting. They arise from dense mats of cord-like fibrous roots that produce tufts of grassy leaves of varying widths—some quite handsome. Strong upright scapes carry usually dense "pokers" of stemless, tubular flowers, which open from the bottom up. The pokers vary in shape with the species or selection.

Plant in spring in open, sunny or partly shaded sites, in well-drained soil high in humus. The crowns should not be deeper than 2–3 in. deep. The roots require plenty of water during bloom time; if allowed to dry out, the flower buds may abort. Winter wet causes crown rot.

Torch lilies provide colorful focal points, especially among shrubs; group together to make a statement. In beds and borders, designs benefit from the addition of these vertical plants to contrast and complement rounded coneflowers, baptisia, asters, and hydrangeas. A planting of torch lilies marching down the edge of a driveway is unforgettable. Long lasting as cut flowers. Seldom browsed by deer; a nectar source for butterflies and other insects.

Leave roots undisturbed once established, except for division in springtime to relieve overcrowding or multiply stock. New plants may be started from seed, though seedling growth is slow. In marginal zones, traditionally the leaves have been tied up to cover and protect the crown.

Kniphofia caulescens

Color	coral
Bloom time	late summer
Size	3–4 ft. × 2 ft.
Light	sun, part shade
Zone	Z5–10

BLUE-LEAF RED HOT POKER High grassy slopes in South Africa's Drakensberg Mountains. This dramatic plant produces tufts of fibrous, strongly blue, strappy, 36-in. leaves, wider at the base. Fat, oblong cylinders of flowers, bright coral fading to lemon, are carried on erect, short, but sturdy stems.

Kniphofia uvaria

syn. *K. aloides*, *Tritoma uvaria*

Color	red
Bloom time	summer
Size	3–5 ft. × 4 ft.
Light	sun
Zone	Z5–9

RED HOT POKER, COMMON TORCH LILY, POKER PLANT Cape Peninsula, South Africa. Evergreen plants are variable, developing heavy clumps of sword-shaped grayish leaves about 3 ft. long. Be careful working around them, as the edges of the leaves are frequently abrasive and bloody hands result. Long pokers of 1- to 2-in. flowers, red in the bud but maturing to orange or yellow, adorn stiff scapes. Largely replaced in commerce by its hybrid offspring.

Other Notable Cultivars

'Alcazar' blooms early with light terra cotta flowers. 3–4 ft. **'Earliest of All'** is among the earliest to bloom. Orange red to yellow. 2.5 ft. **'Echo Mango'** has soft apricot flowers in late spring and summer; repeats. 3.5 ft. **'Green Jade'** has long, icy lime-green cylinders of flowers, paler at the tip. Midsummer. 4–5 ft. **'Little Maid'** is excellent for containers. Long, slender spikes of creamy-white flowers. Late. A Beth Chatto introduction. 2 ft. **'Percy's Pride'**. Very large, light yellow to lime flowers cluster tightly in oval torches. Early and repeats. Strappy, 1-in.-wide leaves. 3 ft.

ROCK ROSE | SUN ROSE

Helianthemum | CISTACEAE

THEY AREN'T ROSES, but these perennial subshrubs thrive in sunny or partially shaded locations; they handle well-drained rocky or sandy soils with ease. Once rooted into a site, sun roses are very drought tolerant, and their ground-hugging foliage and colorful flowers qualify them as ideal groundcovers for dry sunny banks or rock gardens. They also thrive in hot, drought-prone areas along the edge of driveways or between a sidewalk and the street (sometimes called a "hell strip"). Additionally they can hold their own in more refined surroundings of a sunny border, where they mix well with lavenders, spurges, and oreganos. Beautiful draped over the edge of a retaining wall.

Opposite leaves are oblong or linear, and evergreen, to 1.5 in. long; they vary from soft downy grays to light or bright greens, sometimes with a crinkled texture. The flowers are mostly 1 in. or more across, five petaled, and in the species white, yellow, or occasionally pale pink; many hybrids on the market have extended the color palette to include a range of yellows, pinks, oranges, and reds. These flowers attract bees and butterflies, adding another kind of color to the garden.

Sow seed of species. Take tip cuttings of named cultivars in summer after bloom time. Shearing back plants at that time promotes compact growth, plus it forces out new shoots, an ideal source of cuttings.

Helianthemum alpestre

syn. *H. oelandicum* subsp. *alpestris*

color	yellow
bloom time	early to midsummer
size	5 in. × 8 in.
light	sun
zones	Z6–8, HS

ALPINE ROCK ROSE Native to the mountains of southern Europe, alpine rock rose forms dense, green carpets with bright yellow flowers. Prefers a gritty soil, low in nitrogen. Not for hot and humid summer climates.

Helianthemum mutabile

syn. *H. nummularium* 'Mutabile', *H. nummularium* subsp. *nummularium*

color	various
bloom time	late spring to early summer
size	6–12 in. × 24 in.
light	sun
zones	Z6–8, HS

FROSTWEED Native to the Mediterranean basin. Downy, gray foliage is set off by 1-in., white, pink, rose, red, or yellow flowers. Prolific bloom on suitable sites. Shear back after flowering to encourage rebloom. Provide well-drained, alkaline soil. Easily started from direct-sown seed. This is a useful and attractive cover for dry, sunny spots, and is excellent for borders or containers. Does not tolerate heat and humidity. Apply winter mulch in zone 5.

Helianthemum nummularium

Color	pink, yellow
Bloom time	late spring to early summer
Size	6–12 in. × 2–3 ft.
Light	sun
Zone	Z5–7

ROCK ROSE Native to Europe and Asia Minor, the species bears evergreen, grayish green, lanceolate leaves, 1–2 in. long. Five-petaled, rose-like flowers, to 1-in. in diameter, usually bloom in shades of pastel pink or yellow; terminal clusters of flowers bloom for up to two months. Individual blossoms last only a day, but the plants are so prolific that at times flowers hide the foliage entirely. Best adapted to cool summers and mild winters, this species prefers full sun and dry, alkaline, rocky or sandy, well-drained loams. Shear after flowering to promote compact growth; in zone 5, protect overwintering plants with an insulating blanket of evergreen boughs.

Other Notable Cultivars

Most cultivars are descended from *Helianthemum nummularium*, and bloom from late spring to early summer. 8–18 in. Z4–9, HS. This is a sampling.

'Ben Moore' is deep orange, with a darker eye. 5 in. **'Cheviot'** has peach-colored blossoms above gray foliage. **'Hartswood Ruby'** ('Hartswood') has red flowers above glossy green foliage. **'St. Mary's'** bears white flowers with deep green foliage. 8 in. × 24 in. **'Wisley Pink'**, rose-pink flowers with silver foliage. **'Wisley Primrose'** has soft yellow flowers above gray-green leaves.

RUSSIAN SAGE

Perovskia

LAMIACEAE

ONE SPECIES OF THIS GENUS has made its way into gardens, but this singularity has made a big impact. A premier textural plant, Russian sage's finely cut, silvery foliage glistens in the summer sun, and combined with its long-blooming clouds of tiny, blue flowers introduces an impression of lightness to the heaviest garden border. A cooling contrast to dazzling summer annuals, this plant is also remarkably tough and carefree.

Russian sage thrives on well-drained, poor soils; once established it shrugs off all except the most prolonged summer droughts. To promote compact growth, prune stems back hard into woody bases, but only after 1 in. or so of new spring growth has emerged; left uncut this plant sprawls untidily; too much fertilizer and irrigation encourages soft growth and sprawl. Like many aromatic plants, Russian sage resists deer and rabbits as well as most insect pests.

Propagate by softwood or semi-hardwood cuttings. Low-growing stems may layer themselves.

Perovskia atriplicifolia 'Blue Spire'

Perovskia atriplicifolia

syn. ***Salvia yangii***

	blue
	midsummer to midfall
	3–5 ft. × 2–4 ft.
	sun
	Z5–9

RUSSIAN SAGE Himalayas, western China. A subshrub commonly grown as an herbaceous perennial. Aromatic, deeply divided, silver-green leaves with toothed edges clothe stiffly upright, square, silver stems, woody at the bases. Light blue, tubular flowers are two lipped, borne in tiers of whorls in branched, terminal panicles 12–15 in. long. 1995 Perennial Plant Association Plant of the Year.

'Blue Spire' has larger flowerheads than the species. 4 ft. tall. **'Filigran'** is sturdier and more upright; especially fine, lacy foliage. **'Little Spire'** is compact, 2–3 ft. tall. **'Longin'** is similar to 'Little Spire' but more upright with larger, less-dissected leaves. 3–4 ft.

SAGE

Salvia

LAMIACEAE

THIS ENORMOUS GENUS is most familiar to gardeners in the form of the ubiquitous scarlet sage (*Salvia splendens*), a frost-intolerant species with spikes of hot-red flowers, commonly grown for bedding. With some 750-plus species, however, the sages also offer many fine hardy and tender perennials. These have become mainstays of beds, borders, and cottage gardens across the country. In particular, the southwestern and central US species have become invaluable in hot, dry gardens, and a critical source of color for containers, xeriscapes, and water-wise landscapes across the country. Many make fine cut flowers.

Sages exhibit the stems, square in cross section, opposite leaves, and racemes or panicles of two-lipped flowers, typical of the mints. Flower colors include blues, pinks, and reds, or less often white or yellow. Usually foliage is entire, but sometimes pinnately divided, often toothed along the margins; the leaves may be coated with hairs that protect them from water loss, and increase drought tolerance. Leaves are often aromatic. Seldom affected by pests and diseases, although occasionally infestations of whiteflies, aphids, mealybugs, spider mites, and powdery mildew occur. Grazing deer and rabbits mostly avoid sages.

Sow seed of species in spring or early fall. Increase cultivars by softwood cuttings or divide mature clumps, both in spring.

Salvia argentea

Color	white
Bloom	summer
Size	24–36 in. × 24 in.
Light	sun
Zones	Z5–8, HS

SILVER SAGE Southern Europe, northern Africa. Grown mostly for its beautiful furry, silver leaves; short-lived, behaves as a biennial. Basal rosettes of oblong, 7- to 8-in.-long, toothed leaves. Spikes of whitish flowers appear the second year in many-branched, terminal panicles. Self-seeds. A great accent plant.

Salvia chamaedryoides

Color	blue
Bloom	early summer to fall
Size	18–24 in. × 24–48 in.
Light	sun, part shade
Zones	Z7–10

GERMANDER SAGE, BLUE OAK SAGE Mexico. Broad rhizomatous mounds of woody stems and quilted, downy, sage-green leaves. Spikes of sky-blue flowers bloom heavily in early summer, then intermittently until a fall flush. This fast-growing species thrives in sun and heat, prefers loamy, moist, well-drained soil; drought tolerant once established. Attracts hummingbirds and butterflies. Good for beds and borders, container plantings, and suitable for cottage or desert gardens, xeriscapes, and rock gardens.

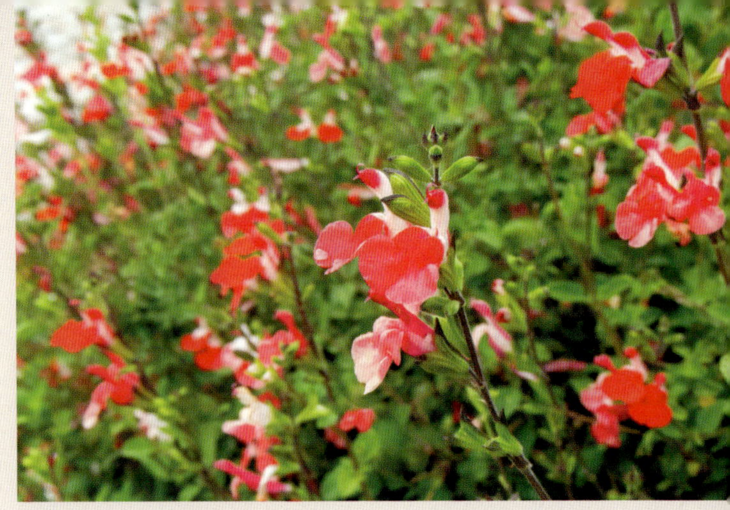

Salvia farinacea

color	blue
bloom time	late spring to early fall
size	1–3 ft. × 1–2 ft.
light	sun, part shade
zones	Z7–10

MEALYCUP SAGE Texas, Mexico. Commonly grown as a warm-weather annual, but an invaluable perennial where hardy. Shrubby, clumping with branching stems. Serrate, ovate-lanceolate, gray-green leaves, to 3 in. long. Violet-blue flowers, with white-powdered ("mealy") calyxes, are borne in 4- to 8-in., terminal and axillary racemes. Prefers evenly moist, well-drained soil, but tolerates clays, moderate drought, and dryish soils, but not winter wet. Attracts butterflies. Adaptable and valued for beds and borders, meadows, cottage and cutting gardens.

'Augusta Duelberg' blooms heavily with silvery-white flowers from late spring until frost. 2.5 ft. × 4 ft. **'Strata'** is a seed strain with blue-and-white, bicolored flowers. 18 in. × 12 in. **'Victoria Blue'** is compact with deep violet-blue flowers. 16 in. × 12 in.

Salvia greggii

color	red, pink, purple, yellow
bloom time	early spring to fall
size	1–3 ft. high and wide
light	sun
zones	Z8–10, HT

AUTUMN SAGE Upland areas of southwest Texas to central Mexico. Evergreen, upright, or mounding with stems woody at the base; medium green leaves are glabrous, simple, and elliptical to 1 in. long. Blooms over an extended season, profusely in fall, with 0.25- to 1-in. flowers. Adapts to a wide range of well-drained conditions; quite drought tolerant but bloom is best with weekly irrigation. Thrives in the hot, humid southeastern United States and the humid Pacific Northwest. Attracts hummingbirds.

'Big Pink' has large, violet-pink flowers with dark maroon calyxes. 2.5–3.5 ft. Z7–10. **'Lowry's Peach'** has yellow-throated, reddish orange blooms with creamy-peach lower lips. Glossy foliage. 3 ft. × 3 ft. Z7–9. **'Maraschino'** has bold scarlet-red flowers. Blooms almost non-stop. 3–4 ft. × 2–3 ft. Z7–10. **'Variegata'** (desert blaze Texas sage) has white-edged leaves; bright red flowers. 2 ft. × 3 ft. Z8–10. **'Wild Thing'** produces spectacular coral-pink flowers. Vigorous. Z5.

Salvia officinalis 'Tricolor'

Salvia guaranitica

Color	blue
Bloom time	summer to fall
Size	4–6 ft. × 4.5 ft.
Light	sun
Zones	Z7–10

BLUE ANISE SAGE Argentina, Brazil. Dark green, 4- to 6-in. leaves are barely hairy. Brilliant deep blue flowers in whorls of three to eight, on very long spikes. Upper flower petals appear to hover above shorter lower petals. Nectar source for hummingbirds.

'Argentine Skies' has spikes of pale blue flowers. **'Black and Blue'** produces spikes to 12 in. long; flowers are deep blue, with black calyces. 3–6 ft. **'Costa Rica Blue'** is very similar. **'Van Remsen'** is a stunning giant selection. Spikes of cobalt-blue flowers. 6–7 ft.

Salvia officinalis

Color	blue
Bloom time	late spring to early summer
Size	12–24 in. × 24–30 in.
Light	sun
Zones	Z4–8

COMMON SAGE, CULINARY SAGE Mediterranean region. Wrinkled, strongly aromatic, 3- to 4-in., gray-green leaves on woody stems. Whorls of 0.5- to 1-in., lavender-blue flowers borne in erect spikes. This standard culinary species can be used as a hardy ornamental in borders, or cottage, herb, and kitchen gardens. Prefers average, medium-moist, well-drained soils, but tolerates dry, rocky ones.

'Aurea' has leaves variegated gold and light green. 12–18 in. **'Berggarten'** has deep blue flowers; large, broad, gray-green leaves. 24 in. **'Icterina'** (golden variegated sage) has foliage irregularly splashed with gold. 8–16 in. **'Purpurascens'** has purplish leaves. 12–24 in. tall. **'Tricolor'** has marbled gray-green, white, and purple foliage edged with pink. 12–18 in.

Salvia patens 'Oceana Blue' ('Salsyll')

Salvia pratensis 'Rhapsody in Blue'

Salvia patens

flower color	blue
bloom time	summer to fall
size	18–24 in. × 12 in.
light	sun, part shade
zones	Z8–10

GENTIAN SAGE Whorls of 1-in. flowers in the most glorious shades of gentian blue. Erect, bushy stems, clothed with aromatic, ovate leaves, rise from tuberous roots. Tolerates heat and drought. May need staking.

'Oceana Blue' ('Salsyll') has deeper blue flowers. 24–36 in.

Other Notable Cultivars

'Indigo Spires' (*Salvia farinacea* × *S. longispicata*) is bushy, with twisting, 24- to 36-in.-long spikes of 0.5-in., purple flowers; late summer to fall. 3–4 ft. Z7–11. **'Mystic Spires Blue'** ('Balsalmisp') is similar in color but on much more compact plants. **'Wendy's Wish'** has dark maroon stems that bear brilliant non-fading, cherry-red flowers. Sterile, long blooming. Fine for containers. 40 in. Z9–11.

Salvia pratensis

flower color	lavender-blue
bloom time	late spring to late summer
size	1–3 ft. high and wide
light	sun
zones	Z4–8

MEADOW SAGE, MEADOW CLARY Europe. Clump forming with mildly aromatic, 6-in., dull gray-green leaves. Upright, dense, spike-like racemes of tiny, deep lavender-blue flowers, often with sporadic rebloom through summer, if cut back as first flush fades. Thrives in average, well-drained soil. Tolerates drought and very light shade. Mostly available as cultivars.

'Eveline' produces an abundance of pink-flowered spikes from early to midsummer. Glossy foliage; compact, bushy. To 24 in. **'Rhapsody in Blue'** is a prolific bearer of blue-and-violet flowered spikes. Broad, gray-green leaves; compact, bushy habit. 20–24 in. **'Swan Lake'** has wrinkled, light green leaves; 20-in. spikes of pure white flowers.

Salvia ×sylvestris 'Caradonna'

Salvia ×sylvestris

(color)	purple, white, pink
(bloom time)	early summer to fall
(size)	3 ft. × 2 ft.
(light)	sun
(zones)	Z4–8

WOOD SAGE Hybrid sage, of garden origin, the result of crossing *Salvia nemerosa* and *S. pratensis*. Clump forming with wrinkled, aromatic, green, lanceolate leaves, to 3 in. long. Spikes of showy flowers all season. Prefers moist, well-drained soil, but tolerates dry, poor ones. Available in the trade mostly as cultivars, which are many.

'Blue Hill' has true blue flowers. 18–24 in. **'Caradonna'**. Abundant spikes of violet flowers, on deep purple stems. 24 in. **'East Friesland'** ('Ostfriesland') has bluish green foliage; narrow spikes of violet flowers in late spring to early summer, repeats in early fall. Sterile. 16–20 in. **'Marcus'** ('Haeumanarc') is dwarf, long blooming with deep violet flowers. 8–10 in. **'New Dimension Rose'** is dwarf, with bright rose-pink flowers from early to midsummer. 8–10 in. Z5–7. **'Snow Hill'** produces white flowers in early summer; cut back for later rebloom. 18 in.

Salvia verticillata

(color)	lilac-blue
(bloom time)	early summer to late summer
(size)	18–30 in. × 18–24 in.
(light)	sun
(zones)	Z5–7

LILAC SAGE Europe, western Asia. Clumps of erect to arching stems, with hairy, coarse, and broadly ovate-triangular, medium green leaves, to 5 in. long. Terminal racemes of small, lilac-blue flowers all summer. Prefers average, moderately moist to dry, well-drained soils. Overly fertile soils encourage soft, lax growth. Drought tolerant. Shear plants after flowering to encourage neater growth and possible fall rebloom.

'Endless Love' has medium purple flowers; heavier blooming, improved form of the Piet Oudolf introduction, **'Purple Rain'**. 14–20 in. **'White Rain'** has a rounded, spreading habit; pure white flowers. 20 in. × 36 in.

SEA HOLLY

Eryngium APIACEAE

ALTHOUGH POPULAR AMONG European gardeners, the eryngiums remain largely unknown on this side of the Atlantic. Surely it is its spiny, unfriendly aspect that has prevented this striking genus from winning the place in our gardens that it deserves. Yet the same feature that makes these plants uncomfortable to handle, the spines that armor not only leaves but also the floral bracts and petals, also make them invaluable sources of texture and contrast; nothing else so emphasizes the softness or tactile qualities of other foliage than does a strategically placed sea holly.

Eryngiums flourish in dry, well-drained, and sunny spots, making them excellent specimens for xeriscapes, or where water supply is short. Steely blue foliage makes sea hollies natural companions for blue-flowered herbs such as Russian sages (*Perovskia*) and lavenders; they also harmonize well with taller yellows such as yellow foxgloves (*Digitalis grandiflora*) and hollyhocks (preferably some single-flowered cultivar such as 'Sunshine'). Sea hollies are sophisticated and stylish as cut flowers and dry well for winter arrangements. Deer and rabbit resistant.

The deep-reaching taproots of eryngiums do not respond well to transplanting or division. Do not disturb once a plant is well established. Propagation is by seed as soon as it ripens (start in containers) or by root cuttings taken in fall. Root cuttings may be taken from pencil-thick roots in winter.

Eryngium alpinum

color	blue
bloom time	early summer to late summer
size	1–2.5 ft. × 1–2.5 ft.
light	sun
zone	Z2–8

ERYNGO, ALPINE SEA HOLLY Alps and mountainous parts of southern Europe. Thrives in average to poor, dry to moderately moist soils as long as they are well-drained. Tolerates light shade, drought, and saline conditions—a good choice for seaside gardens. Thistle-like in appearance, with stiff stems clothed with gray-green to bluish, heart-shaped, spiny lower leaves, and palmately divided upper ones. Flowerheads are egg shaped, to 2 in. long, and framed by a collar of sharp, finely divided, blue-gray bracts. No serious insect pests or diseases, but won't tolerate wet soils in winter.

'Blue Star' has blue stems and foliage, and metallic blue flowerheads. **'Superbum'** has three tiers of bracts around the base of each flowerhead, lending the blossoms a lacy look.

Eryngium amethystinum

- blue
- mid- to late summer
- 18–30 in. × 24 in.
- sun
- Z2–8

AMETHYST SEA HOLLY Balkans, Italy, Sicily. Basal rosettes of grayish, deeply cut leaves are attractively speckled and veined with silver. Branching stems, gray-blue above, carry metallic-blue, thistle-like flowers surrounded by up-curving, long, silver bracts, armed with stiff spines. Prefers dry, poor to moderately fertile soil that drains freely.

The cold-hardiest species of the genus.

'Sapphire Blue' has steely blue flowers, foliage, and stems. Z5–9.

Eryngium bourgatii

- blue
- early summer to late summer
- 1–2 ft. high and wide
- sun
- Z5–8

ERYNGO Pyrenees. Has deeply lobed, silver-veined leaves, and vivid blue, branched stems. These bear conical, silver-blue or violet flowerheads set on collars of narrow, spiny bracts. Tolerates dry and poor soils; requires good drainage, especially in winter. No serious pests or diseases.

Eryngium maritimum

(flower color)	blue
(bloom time)	midsummer to late summer
(size)	8–24 in. × 12 in.
(exposure)	sun
(zone)	Z5–11

SEA HOLLY European native of coastal areas and sand dunes. Borne on tall stems, the evergreen foliage is showy: leathery, glaucous, and blue-gray in color, the ovate, three-lobed leaves have spiny teeth. Collars of spiny bracts frame the 1-in., thimble-shaped, light blue flowerheads.

Eryngium pandanifolium

(flower color)	green
(bloom time)	summer
(size)	4–6 ft. × 2–4 ft.
(exposure)	sun, part shade
(zone)	Z7–10

PANDANUS LEAF ERYNGIUM Argentina and Brazil. Forms clumps of blue-gray, strap-like, sawtooth-edged, screwpine-like leaves. Tall stalks emerge from the middle bearing branched clusters of gray-green thimble flowerheads.

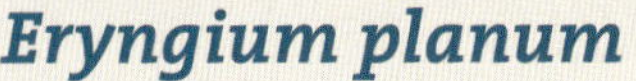

Eryngium planum

color	blue
bloom time	early summer to late summer
size	2–3 ft. × 1–2 ft.
light	sun
zones	Z5–9

SEA HOLLY, FLAT SEA HOLLY Central and southeastern Europe. Flourishes in dry, sandy soils; avoid overwatering and overly fertile soils that cause rank, lax growth. Basal rosettes of deeply toothed, oblong, blue-green leaves, to 4 in. long, from which sprout stiff, 3-ft. flower stems. These bear pale blue, round flowerheads collared with projecting spiny bracts. Generally pest-free, but subject to leaf spot.

'Blue Glitter' commonly blooms in its first year from seed. Large, intensely blue flowerheads on silver-blue stems. **'Blue Hobbit'** is dwarf, with flowerheads completely covering the foliage at the peak of its season. 8–12 in. **'Jade Frost'** has blue leaves edged with cream, and blue flowers. **'Silver Salentino'** has silvery-white cones sparsely ruffed with silver bracts. 2.5–3 ft. Z4.

Eryngium yuccifolium

color	greenish white
bloom time	early to late summer
size	4–5 ft. × 2–3 ft.
light	sun
zones	Z3–8

RATTLESNAKE MASTER Meadows and prairies, eastern half of the United States. Tussocks of lanceolate, 2.5 ft. × 2 in., grayish green leaves edged with spines—as the species name suggests, the foliage does resemble that of yucca. Flowerheads on stiff, upright stems that emerge from the center of the foliage rosettes; greenish white, globular heads to 1 in. across have sparse collars of long, sharp bracts at the apex of the central stem, and sometimes from the upper leaf axils. Prospers with dry to medium moisture on average soils; tolerant of clay, shallow, and rocky soils. Avoid very fertile soils that encourage soft, sprawling growth. No serious insect or disease problems. Staking may be necessary on windy sites. Equally at home in formal borders as in a meadow.

SEDUM | STONECROP

Sedum, Hylotelephium | CRASSULACEAE

THIS LARGE GENUS OF SUCCULENT PLANTS flourishes throughout the Northern Hemisphere; south of the equator species are confined to mountainous Peru. There are several hundred species; roughly a third are natives of the Americas. Most sedums store water in their fleshy leaves, which makes them outstandingly drought, sun, and heat tolerant. Sedums will not endure persistent wet, but many species flourish in moist climates, given excellent drainage. Sunny crevices in stone walls or sandy banks are good locations for sedums; they also sparkle in containers, and the lower growers do well as plantings for green roofs. The fine-textured and often richly colored foliage is evergreen in mild winters, semi-evergreen in colder ones, and is sedum's primary attraction; small, starry, usually five-petaled flowers cluster in showy heads or, in some cases, are just a bonus.

For convenience's sake, gardeners commonly divide the sedums into two groups: the "showy" or "border" sedums are upright, clump forming, and bear their colorful blossoms in expansive cymes; these are now mainly reclassified as *Hylotelephium*. The "creeping" sedums form low, spreading mats of foliage with tiny flowers borne more diffusely, and most remain in the *Sedum* genus (occasionally moved into *Phedimus*). The late-summer- and fall-blooming showy sedums are useful in borders, especially in dry summers; the creeping types are important as groundcovers, edgings, and as lawn alternatives. Both types are ideal for rock gardens.

Easy-care sedums flourish in average, dry to moderately moist, well-drained soils of poor to medium fertility. Drainage is critical, but poor soils do not faze them; most of the creeping kinds thrive even when their roots are confined to small interstices between stones, bricks, or stepping stones. Butterflies and pollinating insects are frequent visitors. Generally pest and disease free, though snails, slugs, and scale are a nuisance, as are deer and rabbits.

Several notable species not listed here are also cultivated widely. These include low, white-flowered *Sedum nevii*, *S. makinoi* 'Ogon', *S. aizoon*, and *S. ternatum* among others. *Sedum spathulifolium* is especially noted for green roofs.

Readily increased by tip cuttings or by division (creeping types); propagate cultivars vegetatively. Species are not difficult to grow from seed, although seeds are tiny, difficult to handle, and germination is often erratic. Many sedums self-seed in hospitable sites.

Sedum album 'Coral Carpet'

Sedum acre

Flower color	yellow
Bloom time	late spring to early summer
Size	3 in. × 10 in.
Light	sun
Zones	Z4–9

GOLDMOSS STONECROP Europe, naturalized locally in North America. Creeping, with small, light green, finely textured, plump leaves. Small, yellow flowers carried above the foliage. Fast growing; may develop into large patches.

'Aureum' has yellow-tipped foliage.

Sedum album

Flower color	white
Bloom time	early to midsummer
Size	3–6 in. × 12–18 in.
Light	sun
Zones	Z3–8

WHITE STONECROP Europe and northern Africa to Siberia, western Asia. Evergreen, mat-forming, creeping, with small, succulent, linear-oblong, cylindrical to flattened, green leaves to 0.75 in. long. Prostrate stems root at the nodes. Foliage turns reddish brown in fall. Starry, white flowers cluster above the foliage. Tolerates very light shade.

'Coral Carpet' has salmon-orange young growth that matures to bright green, becoming reddish bronze in winter. White to pale pink flowers. **'Orange Ice'** has red-tinted foliage that turns orange in cold weather. White to pink flowers.

Sedum cauticola

syn. *Hylotelephium cauticola*

flower color	pink
bloom time	late summer to early fall
size	4–6 in. × 18 in.
exposure	sun
zone	Z5–9

CLIFF-DWELLING STONECROP Japan. Forms mounds of rounded, blue-gray leaves. Pink to rosy-red flowers. Useful as a rock garden or front-of-border specimen.

'Lidakense' has pink-tinged leaves on pink stems.

Sedum kamtschaticum

syn. *Phedimus kamtschaticus*

flower color	yellow
bloom time	mid- to late summer
size	4–6 in. × 8 in.
exposure	sun
zone	Z3–9

ORANGE STONECROP Ural Mountains to Mongolia. Dense cushions of glossy deep green, scalloped and spoon-shaped, fleshy leaves that become pinkish red in winter. Blanketed with 0.5-in., golden flowers. Extremely drought resistant; excellent groundcover for challenging spots.

'Variegata' has smart, crisply yellow-rimmed leaves. Yellow-orange flowers.

Sedum rupestre

syn. *S. reflexum*

flower color	yellow
bloom time	early to midsummer
size	3–6 in. × 12–24 in.
exposure	sun
zone	Z5–8

SEDUM Central and western Europe. Creeping mats, to 2 ft. wide, of cylindrical, gray-green, 0.5- to 0.75-in. fleshy leaves flaunt vivid reddish color in fall. Yellow, 0.5-in., starry flowers. A tough, relatively fast-growing groundcover that often naturalizes.

'Angelina' has lime-green foliage; brilliant amber fall color in full sun. **'Blue Spruce'** has tightly packed, needle-like leaves, the color of a blue spruce.

Sedum sieboldii

syn. *Hylotelephium sieboldii*

flower color	pink
bloom time	late summer
size	6–12 in. × 12 in.
exposure	sun
zone	Z3–9

SIEBOLD'S STONECROP, OCTOBER DAPHNE Asia. Arching and trailing stems clothed with rounded, silvery blue, scalloped leaves, sometimes rose rimmed. Heads of dusky pink flowers. Great for containers, as well as tumbling over walls, for groundcover, and edgings.

'Mediovariegatum' ('Variegatum'). Deep pink flowerheads top mounds of blue-green leaves, centered with creamy yellow.

Other Notable Cultivars

Notable hybrids abound—most border sedums fall into this category, since they are often the result of *Sedum telephium* × *S. spectabile*. Sun loving and succulent unless stated otherwise.

'Autumn Joy' ('Herbstfreude') has light green, broadly obovate, toothed leaves. Large, green, broccoli-like flowerheads from late summer on; blooms open dusty pink and mature to rich bronzy red. Chop to 6 in. in early summer to control height and flopping. Divide every two to three years. 18–24 in. high and wide. Z4–10. **'Black Jack'** has purple-black leaves; clusters of bright pink flowers. Late summer to midfall. 18–23 in. high and wide. Z3–9. **'Cloud Nine'** has green foliage shaded with maroon; 6- to 8-in.-wide clusters of mauve flowers in late summer. 15–17 in. × 18–24 in. Z3–9. **'Matrona'** (syn. *Sedum telephium* 'Matrona') has thick, deep gray leaves that adorn upright purple stems. Pale pink flowerheads. Perhaps preferable to 'Autumn Joy'. Reportedly deer resistant. 24–36 in. Z3–9. **'Neon'** bears brilliant rosy heads. 18–20 in. **'Vera Jameson'** has smoky-blue leaves on arching stems, covered with 2- to 4-in., dusky-pink heads in late summer. 10–12 in. × 10 in. Z3–9.

Sedum spurium 'Dragon's Blood'

Sedum spectabile

syn. *Hylotelephium spectabile*

Flower color	pink
Bloom time	late summer
Size	12–24 in. × 12 in.
Light	sun
Zones	Z4–8

SHOWY STONECROP China, Korea. Often confused with *Sedum telephium*; these two very similar species have been hybridized extensively to produce a myriad of selections. Starry, pink flowers cluster into 2- to 4-in.-wide heads atop succulent stems clothed with alternate, fleshy blue-green or pale green, paddle-shaped leaves. The species is seldom grown, in favor of the available hybrids.

Sedum spurium

syn. *Phedimus spurius*

Flower color	red, pink
Bloom time	early summer
Size	4–6 in. × 12–18 in.
Light	sun, part shade
Zones	Z3–8

TWO-ROW STONECROP Caucasus Mountains. Dense mats of thick and succulent, obovate, 0.5- to 1-in., green to reddish leaves, toothed near the ends. Slow to medium growth rate. Red, pink, or pinkish white flowers bloom 2 in. above the foliage for two to four weeks. Deer resistant. Outstanding cultivars include:

'Dragon's Blood' has deep purple leaves, pinkish purple flowers. Z4–9. **'John Creech'** has mauve-pink flowers. Z5–9. **'Tricolor'** has green-and-white variegated leaves, tinged with pink. Pink, 0.5- to 0.75-in. flowers cluster in cymes, from late spring to midsummer. Vigorous. 3–6 in. × 12–18 in.

SHASTA DAISY

Leucanthemum | ASTERACEAE

OF ALL THE LEUCANTHEMUMS WORLDWIDE, only one species and a race of hybrids derived from it have made it into American gardens. Oxeye daisy (*L. vulgare*) is a Eurasian native; it is almost unkillable and has escaped from cultivation to establish itself in the wild throughout North America. It is listed as a Class C noxious weed in Washington, where it is on the quarantine list—meaning it is prohibited to transport, buy, sell, offer for sale, or distribute plants or plant parts into or within the state, and to offer for sale, or distribute seed packets of seed, flower seed blends, or wildflower mixes containing oxeye daisy seeds within the state.

Its offspring, however, is the much-loved, and better behaved, Shasta daisy (*L.* ×*superbum*) created by prolific plant hybridizer Luther Burbank. His breeding program included *L. vulgare*, the English field or dog daisy, the Pyrenees daisy (*L. maximum*), Portuguese field daisy (*L. lacustre*), and the Japanese field or Montauk daisy (*Nipponanthemum nipponicum*, or *Chrysanthemum nipponicum*). Burbank named his new plants Shasta daisies. Many fine and diverse cultivars have since been created.

Although closely related to chrysanthemums, and many were formerly classified in that genus, the 70 or so species in the genus *Leucanthemum* differ from their better-known relatives, lacking the pungent odor common in chrysanthemums and the grayish white hairs that clothe the leaves of "mums." Additionally, they lack the broad palette of colors found in chrysanthemums—oxeye daisy flowers are almost universally white. However, as a reliable and prolific source of this invaluable hue (white is technically an absence of color), leucanthemums are unequalled among perennials. Their showy, gleaming blossoms help to cool summer gardens filled with hotter reds, oranges, and golds; they serve to separate or to transition between floral shades that would clash if placed side by side. White flowers show up particularly well in weaker evening light, and practically glow in nocturnal gardens.

In general, leucanthemums are vigorous herbaceous perennials with daisy-like composite flowerheads, alternate leaves, and creeping rootstocks. All are fine cut flowers. Reliable, robust, and typically trouble free, Shasta daisies are somewhat susceptible to verticillium wilt, leaf spots, and stem rots; they are occasionally targeted by aphids, mites, and leaf miners. Deer seldom browse them.

Propagate by seed or division.

Leucanthemum ×superbum

color	white
bloom time	early to midsummer
size	8–48 in. × 12–24 in.
light	sun, part shade
zones	Z5–8

SHASTA DAISY Of hybrid origin. Alternate, glossy dark green leaves are oblanceolate to lanceolate, edged with coarse teeth. Typically flowerheads reach 2–5 in. across, with white rays surrounding a yellow disk. Bloom time lasts for about four weeks with intermittent bloom afterward; deadhead for further flowers. Best results are achieved in moist, rich, well-drained soil and full sun; provide partial shade on dry soils. Very prone to crown rot on wet or poorly drained soils. Mulch in winter with a loose blanket of evergreen boughs; avoid water-retentive mulch. Some cultivars may be hardier than zone 5, especially if drainage is perfect.

SHOOTING STAR

Dodecatheon

PRIMULACEAE

THIS GROUP OF SIMPLY BEAUTIFUL, ephemeral native plants blooms in spring, but when hot weather begins they go dormant and escape the heat underground. The best-known species is common shooting star, *Dodecatheon meadia*, a midwestern and eastern US native. Several other species are western US natives, with many from the Pacific Northwest. Tricky to grow and rarely available, these are cherished by specialist gardeners, particularly alpine plant enthusiasts. Be sure to purchase plants from reputable dealers who propagate their stock, rather than digging it from the wild, as wild populations are endangered in some states.

Typically, shooting stars produce a basal rosette of smooth, spatulate leaves, from which rises a naked stem (scape) topped with an umbel of charming pendent flowers like upside-down cyclamen. The number of flowers per stem varies, but may reach seven to ten or more. Each "shuttlecock" flower points downward with protruding, prominently pointed stamens and anthers like a beak. A spot shaded from noon and afternoon sun is best, where the soil remains moist but is not wet or waterlogged. Plant shooting stars along shaded pathways, in rock gardens, or in native and light woodland gardens. They also do well in troughs and other containers.

Propagate by division in spring, after flowering but before summer dormancy, or by seed sown as soon as it is ripe and allow it to overwinter outdoors. Seedlings require up to six years to reach blooming size.

Dodecatheon meadia

syn. ***Primula meadia***

	pink, white
	spring
	12–24 in. × 6–12 in.
	sun, part shade
	Z4–8

SHOOTING STAR, OHIO SHOOTING STAR, AMERICAN COWSLIP Native to glades, woodlands, and rocky bluffs from Wisconsin, east to Pennsylvania, Virginia, and further south, where they are shaded from intense sun and soil remains moist during the growing season. Tolerates alkaline soils. Thick, fleshy, and smooth basal leaves yellow and die as bloom time ends and plants enter summer dormancy. The lightly fragrant flowers range in color from white through pinks to a deep purplish pink, and are 1 in. long with strongly reflexed or swept-back petals, a yellow ring at the mouth, and exserted brown stamens. Attractive to foraging bees for their pollen. Plant in drifts or groups, but plan ahead for the foliage to disappear in summer. Christmas and other ferns, fringed bleeding hearts, partridgeberry, and maple-leaved alumroot are excellent companions. Reportedly resistant to deer and rodents.

'Alba' has pure white flowers. **'Aphrodite'** is a "good doer," vigorous with purplish pink flowers on 18- to 24-in. stems. Possibly a hybrid. **'Queen Victoria'** is showy with larger, light purplish pink flowers on red stems. Sterile.

SOLOMON'S SEAL

Polygonatum | ASPARAGACEAE

COMBINING TOUGHNESS WITH AN OFFBEAT ELEGANCE, the polygonatums are an asset to any shady planting. Their charming bell-shaped flowers dangle in rows like miniature carillons from the arching stems. But it is the foliage effects—the alternate, lanceolate leaves that climb the stems like rungs on a ladder—that give the plant its greatest visual impact. It contributes a precise architectural note often lacking in wild and woodland plantings, and that is always welcome in perennial borders.

Although Solomon's seals prefer rich, moist but well-drained soil in partial shade, they tolerate wet or fairly dry conditions, and make do in full shade. Though not aggressive, over time their rhizomatous roots spread to form dense but compact colonies. They mix well with other woodlanders including arisaemas, ferns, and May apples. Susceptible to deer browsing.

Sow seed in containers in autumn; overwinter outdoors. Germination is slow; up to a year. Otherwise divide established plants.

Polygonatum biflorum

Flower color	greenish white
Bloom time	midspring
Size	1–3 ft. × 1–1.5 ft.
Exposure	part shade, shade
Zone	Z3–8

SMALL SOLOMON'S SEAL Eastern United States, south-central Canada. Rhizomatous; mounds of arching, unbranched stems with parallel-veined leaves to 4 in. long, that turn attractive yellow in fall. Flowers, usually borne in pairs dangling from leaf axils, are small and greenish white; blue-black berries follow. Native peoples ate the starchy rhizomes.

Var. *commutatum*, giant Solomon's seal, regarded as a separate species by some authorities, has also been listed as *Polygonatum commutatum*, *P. canaliculatum*, and *P. giganteum*. Considerably more robust (though less heat tolerant) than *P. biflorum*, with stout, arching stems, 6- to 7-in. leaves; flowers cluster two to ten per leaf axil, followed by blue-black berries. Useful for erosion control, as well as in woodland and cottage gardens, and naturalized areas. Needs room to show to best advantage. 3–7 ft. × 3–4 ft. Z3–7.

Polygonatum humile

flower color	white
bloom time	late spring
size	6–12 in. x1–3 ft.
exposure	part shade, shade
zone	Z5–8

DWARF JAPANESE SOLOMON'S SEAL Native to mountains in Hokkaido, Japan. A petite counterpart to American Solomon's seals. Rhizomatous, develops slowly expanding clumps of arching stems with ovate leaves. Pendent, tubular flowers dangle from leaf axils, followed by round, blue-black fruits in fall. Prefers fertile, humus-rich, moist but well-drained soil. Drought tolerant once established. Shady borders, rock gardens, or woodlands. Occasional attacks by slugs and sawfly larvae.

Polygonatum odoratum

(flower color)	white
(bloom time)	spring to early summer
(size)	18–36 in. × 6–18 in.
(light)	part shade, shade
(zone)	Z3–8

FRAGRANT SOLOMON'S SEAL Europe, Asia. Clusters of arching stems bear elliptic leaves with one or two fragrant, tubular, green-tipped, creamy-white flowers hanging from each axil. Spherical black fruits follow contrasting with yellow autumn foliage. Occasional problems with slugs and sawfly larvae.

'Fireworks', to 2 ft., egg-shaped, green leaves, flecked with creamy white and developing creamy-white borders as they mature. **'Variegatum'** has soft green leaves tipped and rimmed with white; good fall color. Named the 2013 Perennial Plant Association Plant of the Year.

SPURGE

Euphorbia

EUPHORBIACEAE

THE BEST-KNOWN MEMBER of this genus is the decorative holiday poinsettia, *Euphorbia pulcherrima,* but this has a number of garden-worthy, perennial relatives. Upright or trailing stems well-clothed with oval, pointed leaves arranged in whorls or spirals are typical. The flowers are cup shaped with petal-like bracts ranging in color from red to yellowish green or lime. Flowers are borne in variously shaped heads or inflorescences, which are often quite large.

Best in sunny spots but appreciative of midday shade in areas with intense sunlight. Partial or light shade is acceptable, but avoid deeper shade. A moist, fertile soil, well drained and not overly rich, is ideal. The milky sap of the plants causes painful skin rashes in sensitive individuals, and in some species is actually poisonous, so avoid planting them near children's play areas. On the plus side, deer, rabbits, and most insects avoid these plants.

The larger spurges are perfect for flowerbeds and borders and for planting among shrubs, as well as for punctuating gates and entryways. Use drought-tolerant species in dry spots; site low-growers where they can tumble over walls and creep among pavers.

Beware of cypress spurge (*E. cyparissias*), an invasive European species. Many spurges make excellent and unusual cut flowers; flame the base or dip the base of the stems into boiling water to stop the flow of sap that will otherwise pollute the vase water.

Propagation is mainly from seed or by division of mature clumps. Leaf or stem cuttings may be taken in spring or summer to increase some species.

Euphorbia characias

(color)	yellow
(bloom time)	early spring to late spring
(size)	3–5 ft. × 3 ft.
(light)	sun
(zones)	Z6–8, HS

MEDITERRANEAN SPURGE Western Mediterranean. Strong, stout upright stems, woody at the base, crowded with spirals of pointed, blue-green leaves to 5 in. long; lower leaves may drop under stress. Large heads of greenish yellow flowers unfurl at the top. Great for winter and spring gardens. Often short-lived, especially in heat and humidity, but because it seeds freely, replacements abound. Cut back flowering stems after bloom.

Subsp. *wulfenii* (syn. *Euphorbia wulfenii*) differs from the above in having larger leaves and enormous cylindrical heads of yellow-green flowers, to 6–9 in. Drought tolerant. 3–4 ft. Z7–8.

'Lambrook Gold' is bushy with narrow, gray-green foliage and chrome-yellow flowerheads from early spring to midsummer. 3.5 ft. Z7–8. **'Tasmanian Tiger'** ('Variegata', 'Tassie Tiger') is a flashy variegated form of this species with slender, blue-green leaves edged with white. Heat and drought tolerant, but resents high humidity. Excellent in containers. 3 ft. high and wide. Z6–9.

Euphorbia griffithii

	orange
	summer
	24–36 in. × 24 in.
	sun, part shade
	Z5–7, HS

GRIFFITH'S SPURGE Himalayas. Makes robust mounds of sturdy stems clothed with green, lanceolate leaves, pink along the midrib. Flowers have dazzling brick-red bracts. Remains attractive well after bloom time. Best in part shade where sunlight is intense; elsewhere it tolerates full sun.

'Fireglow' has flame-orange floral bracts on bright red stems; green leaves take on wonderful autumn tints. 3 ft. Z6–8.

Euphorbia myrsinites

syn. *E. marschalliana* subsp. *marschalliana*

	chartreuse
	mid- to late spring
	15–18 in. × 2 ft.
	sun
	Z5–9

MYRTLE EUPHORBIA Eurasia. Beautiful trailer whose long prostrate stems are furnished with whorls of ice-blue leaves; looks good throughout the year. In spring, acid-yellow bracts decorate the flowerheads. Cut back hard after bloom time to avoid unwanted seedlings and promote handsome new growth, which appears at once and is particularly welcome in autumn and winter. Drought tolerant. Good between pavers, in rock gardens, and in hanging baskets. Unforgettable tumbling over a wall with *Origanum* 'Kent Beauty' in summer.

Euphorbia polychroma

syn. *E. epithymoides*

	yellow
	spring to late spring
	18–24 in. × 18 in.
	sun, part shade
	Z4–7

CUSHION SPURGE Europe. Clumping with strong stems clothed with 2-in.-long, oblong leaves. In spring the tops of the stems are covered with ruffs of brilliant chartreuse-yellow bracts. Best in full sun in cooler, less sunny areas, but midday shade is necessary in areas with intense sun and heat. Perennial cornflowers are attractive companions.

'Bonfire'. Slender, curvy-edged leaves are bluish green, purple at the tips when young. Brilliant sunny-yellow "flowers" in early spring. 12 in. Z5–7.

Other Notable Cultivars

Much breeding has taken place in recent years as euphorbias have gained in popularity. This is a sampling of what is available.

'Ascot Rainbow' has bluish green foliage broadly and irregularly variegated with creamy gold; pink flushed when temperatures drop. 20 in. Z6–8. **Blackbird** ('Nothowlee') has bushy, very dark purple foliage that persists through the year. Chartreuse flowers. 16–18 in. Z7– 9. **'Efanthia'** (syn. *Euphorbia amygdaloides* × *E.* ×*martinii*) is bushy and compact with evergreen, dark leaves, bright bronze when young and in cool weather. Chartreuse-yellow flowers. Drought tolerant. 12–36 in. Z4–11. **'Improved Efanthia'** ('Imprefant') is more compact at 10–14 in., but is otherwise similar. **'Glacier Blue'** (sport of 'Tasmanian Tiger') is strikingly beautiful with silvery-blue leaves rimmed with white. Evergreen. Cream flower bracts striped with gray-blue. Bluer than its parent. 12–18 in. Z7–11. **'Helena's Blush'** ('Inneuphhel', variegated form of 'Efanthia'). Rounded habit, with reddish young growth that matures to gray-green with cream variegations, with pink. Selected by Garry Grueber of Cultivaris. Resists powdery mildew. 12 in. Z4–11. **'Jade Dragon'** (syn. *Euphorbia characias* subsp. *wulfenii* × *E. amygdaloides*) has huge, chartreuse flowerheads in summer. Purple when young, the blue-green foliage is later flushed with reddish pink. 1–3 ft. Z7–9. ***×martini*** (syn. *Euphorbia amygdaloides* × *E. characias*). Martin's spurge, red spurge. This natural French hybrid is variable and selections may favor one parent or the other. Upright spikes of lime-green bracts with a red eye adorn stiff stems clothed with dark grayish green leaves. Short-lived. Cut back to the ground after bloom time. 2–3 ft. × 2 ft. Z6–8. **'Shorty'** is very compact with blue-green foliage that becomes bright red or purple tipped in cool weather. Chartreuse flowers in spring. Tolerates drought and heat. An introduction from ItSaul Plants in North Carolina. 15–18 in. Z7–11.

SUNFLOWER

Helianthus ASTERACEAE

THE SUNFLOWER TRIBE INCLUDES many fine perennials as well as the familiar annuals. All are native to North America, indigenous to a range of habitats including prairies, meadows, roadsides, seaside dunes, and even swamps. Economically the genus is important for the production of sunflower seed oil, birdseed, and Jerusalem artichokes or "sunchokes," consumed as a starchy vegetable.

Perennial sunflowers are generally imposing and durable plants. They include some of the tallest garden perennials as well as some of the showiest blossoms. As such, they make good backdrops for sunny borders and combine well with taller ornamental grasses, especially *Panicum virgatum* 'Heavy Metal' and purple muhly grass, whose blue or purple-toned foliage complement the yellow flowerheads. For a native plant display, pair sunflowers with big bluestem grass. Purple ironweed, Russian sage, and bluebeard also make good companions. Sunflowers mix easily with other "hot"-colored summer flowers—those with red, orange, or gold flowers. Their lofty, sunset-colored blooms show particularly well when planted on the western side of a garden so that the evening sun backlights the display. The flowers attract butterflies, and the seeds are a welcome food source for songbirds. Mostly resistant to deer browsing; pests and diseases are infrequent.

Propagate by seed or division.

Helianthus angustifolius

color	yellow
bloom time	late summer to fall
size	8–10 ft. × 2–4 ft.
light	sun
zones	Z6–9

SWAMP SUNFLOWER Native from Texas and Oklahoma, northeastward to New York, and south through Florida. This robust perennial has deep green, lance-shaped leaves, and bears a profusion of 2.5-in.-wide, bright yellow, daisy-like flowerheads with purple-brown centers, from early fall to frost. Prefers a moist soil. This species tends to spread aggressively and is best reserved for meadow or wild gardens. Salt tolerant, and a good choice for sheltered places in seaside gardens.

'First Light' forms a 4-ft.-tall, compact clump with bright yellow-orange, 2-in. flowerheads. Less aggressive than the species; a better choice for ornamental borders. **'Gold Lace'** has deep green, leathery leaves and produces a fountain of golden flowerheads. 5–6 ft. **'Matanzas Creek'** produces heads of light yellow flowers. 8 ft.

Helianthus debilis

color	yellow
bloom time	early to late summer
size	18–48 in. × 36–48 in.
light	sun
zones	Z8–11

BEACH SUNFLOWER, CUCUMBER-LEAVED SUNFLOWER Native to coastal regions from Texas, east through Florida and northward through North Carolina. Heart-shaped, coarse, rough-textured leaves 2–4 in. long and almost twice as wide. Slightly nodding, 2.5- to 3-in.-wide flowerheads are bright yellow with a red-purple central eye. Blooms repeatedly.

Subsp. *debilis* is prostrate; makes a pretty, drought-tolerant groundcover for seaside gardens and dry spots elsewhere. **Subsp. *cucumerifolius*** 'Italian White' has sparse, 4-in.-wide, black-centered flowerheads with only ten pale yellow or creamy-white, petal-like rays. 4–5 ft.

Helianthus giganteus

color	yellow
bloom time	midsummer to midfall
size	7–12 ft. × 2–3 ft.
light	sun
zones	Z5–9

TALL SUNFLOWER Native to the eastern half of North America, north of Florida. Less aggressive than swamp sunflower; requires staking and a site protected from strong winds. Purplish, often hairy stems branch toward the top. Slender, lance-shaped leaves are medium green, toothed along the margins; rather sparse flowerheads have 10 to 20 petal-like rays surrounding a yellow, 1.75- to 3.25-in. central disk. Prefers moist to wet, sandy soils.

'Sheila's Sunshine' produces loose clusters of light, primrose-yellow flowerheads.

Helianthus maximiliani

color	yellow
bloom time	midfall
size	4–10 ft. × 3–4 ft.
light	sun
zones	Z4–10

PRAIRIE SUNFLOWER, MAXIMILIAN SUNFLOWER Native to grasslands and meadows throughout the continental United States. Slender, erect stems bear alternate, slender, pointed, lance-shaped leaves folded down the mid-vein, and up to 12 in. long. Flowerheads, arranged in spikes rather than panicles, are 2–4 in. wide, yellow with brown-and-yellow centers, surrounded at their bases by pointed, green bracts which may stick straight out and curl at the tips. Tolerates a wide range of soils; an aggressive spreader best reserved for wildflower and prairie plantings.

Helianthus ×multiflorus

color	yellow
bloom time	summer to late summer
size	4–6 ft. × 2 ft.
exposure	sun, part shade
zones	Z3–8

THIN-LEAVED SUNFLOWER Ovate leaves, 8–10 in. long. Bright yellow flowerheads may be single, semi-double, or double, from 3.5–5 in. across. Many hybrids are lumped into this classification. It is wise to buy plants by cultivar name.

'Flore Pleno' has double, bright yellow heads of flowers. **'Capenoch Star'** has large, single, bright yellow heads. 5–6 ft. **'Loddon Gold'** is double flowered with gold flowerheads. **'Sunshine Daydream'** has rounded, golden, double blooms, almost 2.5 in. across. 5–6 ft. tall.

Helianthus salicifolius

syn. *H. orgyalis*

color	yellow-orange
bloom time	late summer to late fall
size	4–6 ft. × 15–24 in.
exposure	sun, part shade
zones	Z4–9

WILLOWLEAF SUNFLOWER Wisconsin, south and west to Texas, with populations in Ohio, New York, and Maryland. The pale green leaves are drooping and willow like, borne on rigid, whitish green stems. The flowerheads, carried in branched panicles, measure 2–2.5 in. across with bright yellow rays and dark brown central disks. Well adapted to any average, medium, well-drained soil in full sun, but also tolerates clays. Spreads by creeping rhizomes to form dense colonies; divide every three to four years to control expansion and maintain vigor. One of the brightest fall bloomers; a good source of cut flowers.

'Low Down' is a dwarf cultivar. 12–15 in. × 16–20 in.

Helianthus simulans

Flower color	yellow
Bloom time	early to midfall
Size	8–10 ft. × 3–4 ft.
Light	sun
Hardiness	Z6–9

TALL NARROW-LEAVED SUNFLOWER, MUCK SUNFLOWER

Native to the southern coastal plains from Florida to Louisiana and north into Tennessee and Arkansas. This species is similar to and was formerly considered a form of *Helianthus angustifolius*; it is, however, much more robust. Alternate leaves are hairy, slender, and willow like, with a conspicuous central vein. In fall, branched stems are spangled with a spectacular display of purplish red-centered, bright yellow, 3-in. flowers after most others are spent, even after light frost. Provides nectar for migrating butterflies. Prefers moist soil.

Other Notable Cultivars

'Lemon Queen' is one of the best. Pale yellow flowers, 2.5 in. across, are carried on 5- to 7-ft. stems. Can become aggressive, but ideal for wild gardens, meadows, or perhaps along a fence, as well as more formal spots.

TANSY | PAINTED DAISY

Tanacetum ASTERACEAE

MANY GENERA FORMERLY CLASSIFIED with *Chrysanthemum* have been integrated into *Tanacetum*; nursery catalogs may list these plants under the old names or new; both are included with their descriptions here.

Tansy foliage is aromatic, sometimes strongly so. For this reason, deer usually avoid it, but rabbits unfortunately are undeterred. The alternate, finely dissected leaves give the plants a fern-like look. Blooms are grouped into flat-topped clusters; flowerheads may be daisy-like with decorative ray flowers surrounding a central yellow disk, or lack rays and appear like yellow buttons.

Grow tansies in full sun, in light, well-drained soil. They thrive in coastal gardens, but inland should be sheltered from strong drying winds. Wet feet in winter are lethal. Low-growing species are suitable for rock gardens and as edgings for beds and borders. Showier, taller species can grace beds and borders or cutting and cottage gardens. They may need staking. Divide in spring every three to four years to maintain vigor. Pests and diseases are seldom troublesome, but be alert for red spider mites in hot, droughty periods. Gloves are recommended when working around tansies; leaf contact may irritate the skin.

Sow seed in fall for spring planting, or divide established clumps. Semi-ripe cuttings taken in summer root readily.

Tanacetum argenteum

syn. *Achillea argentea*

flower color	white
bloom time	summer
size	6–8 in. × 12 in.
light	sun
zone	Z5–7

SILVER TANSY Mediterranean. This beautiful, low, evergreen perennial develops mats of finely cut, silver foliage on much-branched, white-woolly stems. The leaves, like silver filigree, grow to 3 in. long with five to nine pairs of dissected leaflets. The white daisy flowerheads are relatively insignificant. Old plants become woody at the base. Pairs well with creeping thyme, 'Kent Beauty' oregano, and *Euphorbia myrsinites* planted between patio pavers and flagstones. They also mix well with colorful annuals, including trailing verbenas and calibrachoas.

Tanacetum coccineum

syn. *Chrysanthemum coccineum*, *Pyrethrum coccineum*, *P. roseum*

	pink, red, white
	early summer
	18–30 in. × 15–18 in.
	sun
	Z3–7

PAINTED DAISY, PYRETHRUM, PERSIAN INSECT FLOWER Iran, Caucasus. This cool-season, short-lived perennial produces tufted clumps of finely dissected, bright green leaves to 3–10 in. long, smaller above. Daisy-like, 2- to 3-in. blooms, each with a large, central yellow disk, rise on slender, wiry, usually unbranched stems. Flower forms include singles, doubles, and anemone centered, in a range of pinks, reds, and white. They are usually offered as seed mixes in mixed colors; to grow specific colors, look for plants in bloom in local nurseries. Remove spent flowers and cut stems to the ground to encourage rebloom. Best in cooler-summer climates; protect from intense sun in zone 7. Companion plants such as Shasta daisies and bearded iris can provide support for the painted daisies' rather weak stems. Excellent as cut flowers. Attracts hummingbirds and butterflies. This plant is the source of the natural insecticide "pyrethrin."

'Crimson Giant' has single, vivid cerise blooms. 3 ft. Z3–7. **Double Market** is a mixed (pink, rose, red, and white) strain of large, double-flowered blooms. 18–24 in. Z3–9. **'Duro'** has very large, purplish red blooms. 32 in. Z3–7. **'James Kelway'** has bright, almost crimson-red flowerheads. 18–20 in. Z3–7. **Robinson's Mix** includes red, deep and pale pinks, and white-flowered daisies. 24–30 in. Z3–9.

Tanacetum parthenium

syn. *Chrysanthemum parthenium, Matricaria parthenium, Pyrethrum parthenium*

Flower color	white
Bloom time	early to midsummer
Size	15–18 in. × 12 in.
Light	sun
Zone	Z4–9

FEVERFEW Caucasus, Europe. Tidy, well-branched mounds of strongly aromatic, ferny foliage. Smooth above and hairy beneath, the finely cut leaves are bright green, about 3 in. long. Small flowerheads have bright yellow disks and short, blunt, white ray flowers; these are grouped into flat-topped clusters. Self-seeds freely. Appropriate for herb gardens; the leaves are valued for homeopathic remedies. Good fillers in flower arrangements. Short lived; often treated as annuals.

'Aureum' (golden feverfew, golden feather) makes low bushes of divided, chartreuse foliage. Single, white daisy flowerheads. 12–18 in. Z3–9. **'Golden Ball'** produces low mounds of fragrant, deep green leaves; double yellow button flowers. 12–18 in. Z3–9. **'White Stars'** grows compact mounds of deep green leaves topped with small, double, white-and-yellow flowerheads. 8–12 in. Z3–9.

Tanacetum vulgare

syn. *Chrysanthemum vulgare*

Flower color	yellow
Bloom time	summer
Size	3–6 ft. × 3 ft.
Light	sun
Zone	Z4–8

COMMON TANSY, GOLDEN BUTTONS Europe. Vigorous and clump forming with fibrous, upright stems clothed with bright green, ferny foliage. Finely dissected and pinnately lobed, the leaves are 7–8 in. long below, smaller above. Flat, terminal heads are crowded with rayless, bright yellow, 0.3- to 0.5-in. button flowers. Mainly for herb gardens, but foliage is interesting contrasted with daylilies, peonies, and Oriental poppies in ornamental borders.

'Crispum' (curly tansy) is the most decorative with tightly crisped, bright green foliage; yellow button flowerheads. 3 ft. **'Isla Gold'** is grown for its aromatic, bright golden, dissected leaves. Makes companion plants appear to glow. 2–3 ft.

TROUT LILY | DOGTOOTH VIOLET

Erythronium | LILIACEAE

TROUT LILIES ARE NATIVE to forests and damp meadows across temperate regions of the world, and many can be found growing wild in parts of North America. They are one of the special joys of the spring garden, with gracefully nodding flowers commonly featuring swept-back petals and prominent stamens. Typically bloom time is two to three weeks long; the flowers present a pretty contrast to the tongue-shaped spotted or plain green leaves. The mottling of the leaves suggests the speckled side of a trout (hence the common name). The other traditional name for this genus, dogtooth violet, refers to the pointed, bulb-like, tuberous roots, which were imagined to resemble the shape of a dog's tooth—it's important to note that this genus is not related to violets (*Viola*).

Plant trout lilies in fall about 4 in. deep in a humus-rich soil that does not dry out. They prefer partly shaded places, and will not endure intense sun.

Seldom browsed by deer and generally pest and disease resistant. Allow to colonize in damp woodlands with ferns, summer snowflake, and other plants that enjoy shaded, damp places.

To propagate, mark the position of plants in spring, and dig in late summer to remove and replant offsets. Sow seed as soon as it ripens in late spring or early summer; seedlings are very slow growing and often require five to six years to reach flowering size.

Erythronium albidum

color	white
bloom time	mid- to late spring
size	4–8 in. × 9 in.
light	part shade, shade
zones	Z4–8

WHITE TROUT LILY, WHITE FAWN LILY, YELLOW SNOWDROP Moist, light woodlands of the eastern United States and Canada. Springing from a corm-like bulb, each plant has a pair of oval, 3- to 9-in.-long leaves that are irregularly mottled with silver. The solitary, 1.5-in., white flowers, flushed with yellow at the base, are borne on 6- to 12-in., leafless stems (scapes) and have reflexed petals reminiscent of cyclamen. When temperatures rise in early summer, the plants retreat underground. Spreads readily by offsets from the roots; these may take two years to bloom.

Erythronium americanum

color	yellow
bloom time	early spring
size	3–8 in. × 8 in.
light	part shade, shade
zones	Z3–8

ADDER'S TONGUE, YELLOW TROUT LILY, YELLOW DOGTOOTH VIOLET Rich, damp woods and wet meadows of the eastern seaboard of the United States. A pair of smooth, pointed, brown-and-purple-mottled leaves, 3–8 in. long, rise from a scaly bulb; immature bulbs produce only one solitary leaf. A single, 3- to 7-in. scape terminates in a nodding, yellow to brownish flower with recurved petals, brown on the underside. In the wild these plants colonize readily, and some stands are reputed to be 300 years old. Summer dormant. Seeds about freely; if growing in a lawn, delay mowing until the seeds have been disseminated.

Erythronium dens-canis

color	pink, white, purple
bloom	midspring to late spring
size	8–12 in. × 6 in.
light	sun, part shade
zone	Z3–8

DOGTOOTH VIOLET Mountain meadows of southern Europe. Flowers of this charmer are solitary, mostly rosy-purple with purple anthers and ringed with red-purple at the throat, about 2 in. long. Strongly purple-mottled, 4- to 6-in. basal leaves, in pairs, are reputedly tasty in salads. Several cultivars are available:

'Lilac Wonder' has light purple flowers accented with a chocolate ring at the base. Early. 6–8 in. **'Pink Perfection'** has clear bright pink flowers on 3- to 4-in. stems. Early. **'Purple King'** is bright pinkish purple, sometimes rimmed with white. Vigorous, and suitable for underplanting shrubs, in rock gardens, and for lining woodland paths. 6 in. **'Rose Queen'** has rosy pink flowers, with a deep brown blotch at the base. 4–8 in. tall. **'Snowflake'** is clean white with a taupe base. 6 in. **'White Splendor'** has white flowers, blotched with brown at the base. Early. 6–8 in.

Erythronium grandiflorum

color	yellow
bloom	late spring
size	12–20 in. × 15 in.
light	part shade
zone	Z4–8

YELLOW GLACIER LILY, YELLOW AVALANCHE LILY, LAMB'S TONGUE, TROUT LILY Clearings and open woods, often under Ponderosa pines and Gambel oaks, in the western United States, California to Alberta, Montana, and Colorado. Pairs of upright, elliptic, plain green leaves, undulating along the edges, to 8 in. in length, appear shortly after snow melt. Large, showy drifts of 2-in., bright yellow, starry flowers, several per scape, bloom for about a month.

Erythronium revolutum

Color	rose-pink
Bloom time	early to midspring
Size	12–14 in. × 10 in.
Light	part shade
Zone	Z5–8

MAHOGANY TROUT LILY, COAST FAWN LILY, PINK FAWN LILY Coastal areas from northern California to British Columbia, especially along streams and in damp forest clearings. One to several nodding, bright rose flowers top pinkish scapes above basal pairs of white-marbled, broadly lance-shaped leaves to 8 in. long. Seeds about freely to form colonies.

'Pink Beauty' has reflexed, clear pink petals. Self-sows readily and is charming in drifts in light woods. 12 in.

Other Notable Cultivars

'Pagoda' is a vigorous hybrid of western US species (*Erythronium tuolumnense* × *E. revolutum*) that produces several 1.5-in-wide, bright yellow flowers with a reddish brown eye on each naked stem. Blooms for up to a month in mid- to late spring. Each bulb may produce several stems, in contrast to other species that bear a solitary stem per bulb. The silvery green, sometimes mottled, basal leaves emerge somewhat later than those of *E. americanum* and disappear in hot weather. An attractive companion for naturalized narcissus and Spanish squills. Often listed as a cultivar of either parent. Later-blooming **'Kondo'** is similar and has the same parentage. The species *E. tuolumnense*, from the foothills of the Sierra Nevada, is seldom grown.

TURTLEHEAD

Chelone

PLANTAGINACEAE

NEVER DID A FLOWER'S COMMON NAME do it such a disservice. In fact, chelones bear only the most notional resemblance to a reptile's head; instead, they rank among the most desirable, if underutilized, native North American wildflowers.

Chelones' unusual blooms have an intriguing form, and their foliage is bold and handsome. They are undemanding and require only humus-rich, consistently moist, or even wet soil. Pinch back stem tips at 6–9 in. during spring to encourage bushy, compact growth and eliminate the need for staking. Mildew may be a problem where air circulation is poor.

Use versatile turtleheads to serve as focal points in shade or woodland gardens, moist meadows, bog gardens, and the edge of ponds or slow-moving streams. Their tolerance for wet feet equips them to be stars in rain gardens, although they are sufficiently refined to also hold their own in formal settings. Attractive to butterflies. Partner them with other damp-loving plants: ligularias, rose mallows, and cardinal flower, for example.

Propagate by seed or division in spring or fall.

Chelone glabra

Color	white, pink
Bloom time	midsummer to early fall
Size	2–3 ft. × 1.5–2.5 ft.
Exposure	sun, part shade, shade
Zones	Z3–8

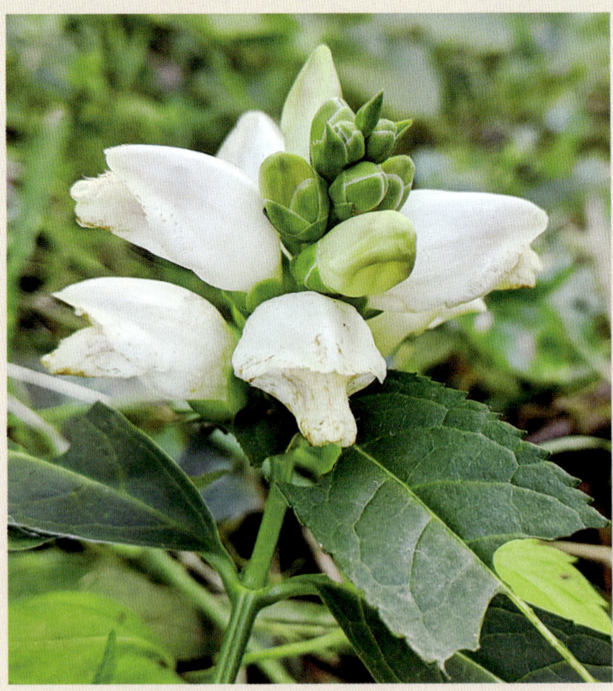

TURTLEHEAD, SNAKESHEAD United States east of the Mississippi, except for Florida and Louisiana. Clump forming, with stiff, erect stems well clothed with dark green, coarsely toothed, lance-shaped leaves, 3–6 in. long. The 1.5-in.-long, white, sometimes pink-tinged flowers are hooded, two-lipped, and snapdragon-like, borne in tight, spike-like, terminal racemes.

Deer often browse these plants.

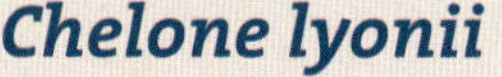

Chelone lyonii

Flower color	pink, purple
Bloom time	midsummer to early fall
Size	2–4 ft. × 1.5–2.5 ft.
Light	sun, part shade
Zones	Z4–8

SHELLFLOWER Southeastern United States. Similar to *Chelone glabra*, except with ovate, 6- to 7-in. leaves and rose-pink flowers; in general it is somewhat bolder and taller. Shellflower spreads by rhizomes and may self-seed to form a colony. Keep soil moist with a shredded leaf mulch in sunny sites. Reputedly, deer avoid this species.

'Hot Lips' has blooms of a richer pink than the species, red stems and purple-green foliage.

Chelone obliqua

Flower color	purple, pink, white
Bloom time	midsummer to early fall
Size	2–3 ft. × 1–2 ft.
Light	sun, part shade
Zones	Z4–9

RED TURTLEHEAD Throughout the United States east of the Mississippi. Dark green leaves are coarsely toothed and lance shaped. Flower color is variable, though most commonly a rich rose to rosy purple. Seldom browsed by deer.

TWINSPUR

Diascia | SCROPHULARIACEAE

DESPITE THE FAST-GROWING popularity of these long-blooming flowers, most gardeners mistakenly believe that all diascias are annuals. In fact, though many of the 75 members of this genus are indeed annuals, others perform as perennials. At least one species is reliably perennial as far north as Spokane, WA.

Natives of southern Africa, where rain falls in summer, twinspurs provide fine-textured mounds or mats of glossy green foliage and a succession of vivid flowers that continues for weeks or even months on end. The 1-in. leaves are ovate and toothed; the five-lobed flowers resemble those of snapdragons, except that each twinspur blossom sports (as the common name indicates) not one but two spurs. The flowers cluster at the stem tips.

Their sprawling habit of growth makes diascias ideal for spilling out over the edges of a border, over the lip of a container, or tucked in among stones in a rock garden. Some selections are more upright. Though sensitive to cold, diascias are heat hardy, tolerating intense sun as long as they are provided with sufficient water. Soil should be fertile, humus-rich, and well drained.

Twinspurs provide abundant color in the garden especially during spring and fall when night temperatures are still cool. They mix well in containers and in the landscape, notably with late spring bulbs and early alpine perennials, including rock cress and perennial candytuft. Other good companions include heucheras and heucherellas for their foliage throughout the season, miniature hostas, bacopas, and small ferns. In window boxes they are charming with calibrachoas, verbenas, and trailing ornamental oreganos.

Cut back in late winter or early spring to promote new growth. Deadhead regularly and pinch off branch tips periodically to encourage continued flowering and bushier growth. Diascias are rarely troubled by insects or diseases, but are vulnerable to snails and slugs; deer and rabbits leave them alone.

Propagate by soft cuttings of young growth or sow seed directly into the garden one to two weeks before the local last-frost date; alternatively start indoors six to eight weeks earlier.

Diascia barberae

Color	pink
Bloom time	midspring to fall
Size	9–12 in. × 12–18 in.
Light	sun
Zones	Z8–11

TWINSPUR Mountains of southern Africa. Perennial where winter temperatures seldom drop below 10°F. Flowers, to 0.75 in., are pink with yellow throats. When bloom flags in summer heat, shear plants to promote another flush in fall.

'Genta Giant Pink' is compact with large, pink, snapdragon-like flowers. Excellent for containers and as a groundcover. The Genta Series from Israel has stronger stems and is more upright than some strains.

Diascia integerrima

Color	pink
Bloom time	spring to fall
Size	18 in. × 30 in.
Light	sun, part shade
Zones	Z6–10

HARDY TWINSPUR A native of southern African mountains and thus an unusually cold-hardy species. It forms an upright clump of wiry, branching stems; the narrow leaves are mostly basal, with a few smaller ones up the stems. The pink flowers, up to 0.75 in. across, are borne in terminal racemes. They open in sequence over a long season, from the bottom progressing upward with new buds continually forming at the stem tips. Protect from full sun in hot climates.

'Coral Canyon' bears coral flowers with darker pink centers. Very long blooming. Tolerates dry soil. 15 in. × 18 in. **'Pink Adobe'** bears pale salmon-pink flowers, maroon at the throats. Appropriate for xeriscapes. 15 in. × 18 in.

Diascia rigescens

Color	pink
Bloom time	summer to fall
Size	10–12 in. × 15–20 in.
Exposure	sun, part shade
Zone	Z7–9

TWINSPUR Southern Africa. Trailing with semi-upright, branching stems clothed with heart-shaped leaves, toothed along the edges. Flowers are in various shades of pink, arranged along the stems in close erect spikes.

Other Notable Cultivars

There are numerous cultivars, with many more appearing on the market annually. Many of these have resulted from new technology applied to plant breeding, including tissue culture.

'Blue Bonnet' has pink flowers flushed with blue. 8 in. × 2 ft. Z8. **Flirtation Series**, currently only with pink or orange flowers, promises self-cleaning plants that do not require deadheading. However, when bloom decreases in response to hot nights, a shearing keeps the plants neat and encourages a further flush of bloom when nights cool. 8–12 in. Z7–10. **Flying Colors Hybrid Series** offers flowers in a range of pinks, apricot, and red on compact, heat-tolerant plants. Plants tolerate light fall frosts. Z8–9. A Proven Winners introduction. **Picadilly Series** was introduced from Holland and includes blues and lilac. **'Ruby Field'** has masses of strong salmon-pink flowers from summer to fall. 10 in. × 24 in. Z8–9. **Sun Chimes Series** offers large, coral, rose, blush-pink, peach, and coppery-purple flowers on mounded plants. The rose- and red-flowered selections are trailing types; excellent for hanging baskets. Z8–9. **Wink Series** blooms abundantly all season in containers and in the landscape. Flowers are sterile and self-cleaning. Cold tolerant. 10–12 in. Z5–8.

WALLFLOWER

Erysimum | BRASSICACEAE

DESPITE THE NAME, wallflowers are guaranteed to attract admiration wherever you may plant them. Traditionally they have been used mostly as cool-season bedding plants and treated as annuals; *Erysimum cheiri* (formerly *Cheiranthus cheiri*) has been the standard choice for this purpose. A number of species, however, perform as perennials in hospitable sites, and others, while normally biennial, self-seed readily so that they function as perennials.

Most species originated in hot, sunny climates subject to seasonal drought, and so make good subjects for rock or gravel gardens, and thrive (as the common name suggests) when tucked into the crevices of wall, where they often self-sow. Wallflowers prefer alkaline soil, but tolerate most soils as long as they are well drained. Slugs and snails are often a problem; seldom troubled by deer. Mingles well with perennial herbs such as rosemary, thymes, and lavenders, whose foliage complement the flowers. They are also a traditional element of cottage gardens. Several species, such as *E. cheiri* and *E. ×marshallii*, are toxic if ingested, and should not be accessible to children and pets.

Propagate by seed or by semi-hardwood cuttings of non-blooming stems taken in spring or summer.

Erysimum capitatum

syn. *Cheiranthus capitatus*

Color	orange, yellow
Bloom time	midspring to early summer
Size	1–2 ft. × 0.5–1 ft.
Light	sun, part shade
Zones	Z3–7

WESTERN WALLFLOWER, SAND-DUNE WALLFLOWER Western United States, as well as the upper South and Midwest. Produces evergreen basal rosettes of 3-in., linear to narrowly oblong leaves. In the second spring, upright stems, 1–2 ft. tall, emerge, each topped with a dense, rounded cluster of cruciform, four-petaled flowers, 0.75 in. across. Blooms are commonly some shade of yellow or orange, but may be maroon or near white. Flourishes in average soils with moderate to low moisture; tolerates shallow, rocky soils, and drought. Naturalizes where conditions are hospitable.

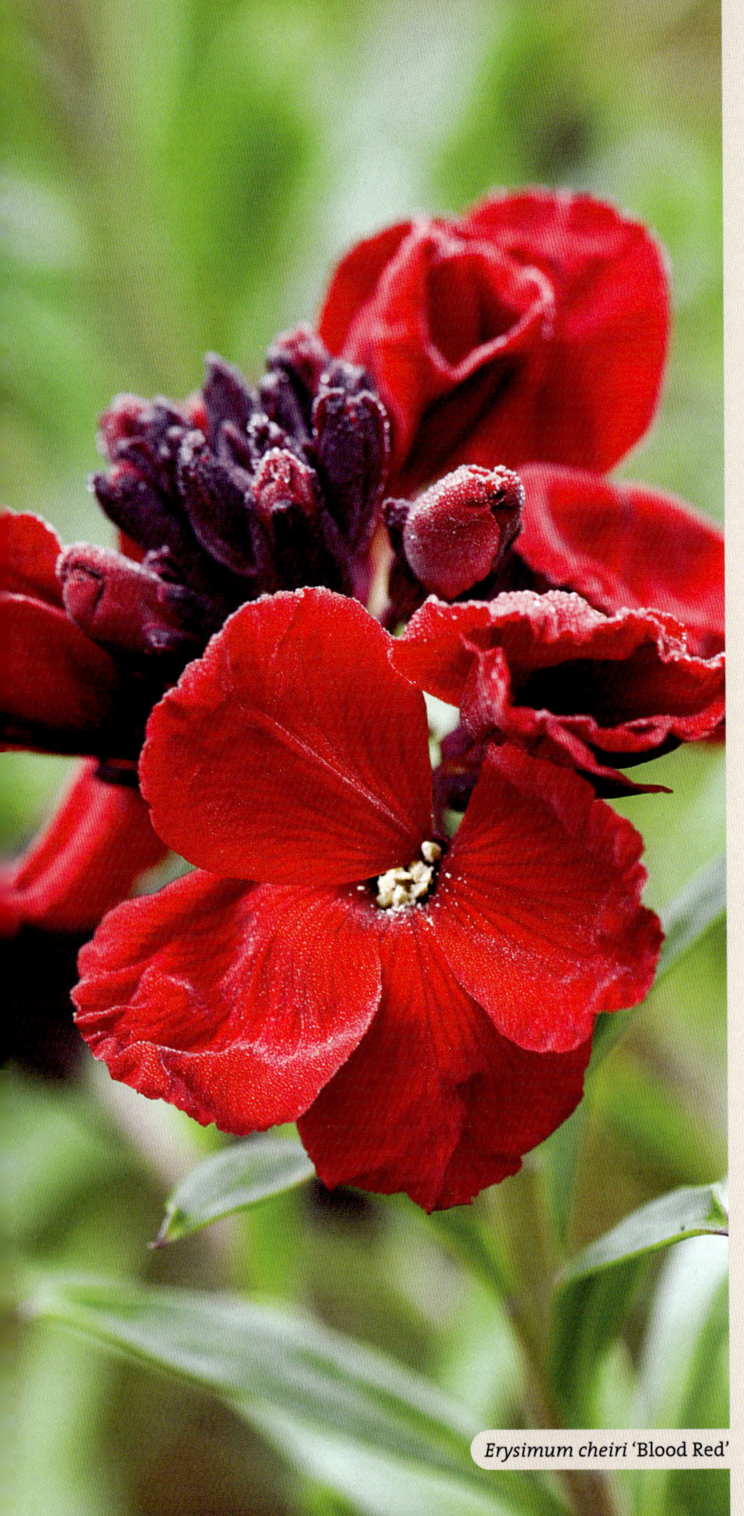

Erysimum cheiri 'Blood Red'

Erysimum cheiri syn. *Cheiranthus cheiri*

Color	red, orange, yellow
Bloom time	midspring to early summer
Size	18–24 in. × 15–18 in.
Light	sun, part shade
Zone	Z5–9, HS

AEGEAN WALLFLOWER, SIBERIAN WALLFLOWER, COMMON WALLFLOWER Southern Europe. This species is perennial in the Pacific Northwest. Prefers a moderately moist but well-drained soil with mildly alkaline pH—it often colonizes the cracks in the mortar of aging masonry walls. Forms rosettes of narrow, pointed leaves to 8 in. long in the first year's growth. The second and succeeding years bring mace-like inflorescences of cruciform, four-petaled flowers borne in dense racemes on upright stems. Flowers fragrant, in shades of yellow, orange, red, mahogany, and purple. Start from seed.

Bedder Series are compact to 12 in. Individual colors of gold, primrose, orange and scarlet. **'Blood Red'** has deep red flowers. **Charity Mix** is compact, about 8 in., and blooms in its first year of growth, with 0.5-in., rose-red, scarlet, yellow, or creamy-yellow blossoms. Fragrant. **'Harpur Crewe'** (syn. *E.* ×*kewensis* 'Harpur Crewe') is a double heirloom, with very fragrant, yellow flowers. 12 in. **Sunset Mix** is an F1 hybrid strain in a wide range of colors. Very fragrant. 10–12 in. **Tom Thumb Mix** is compact, ideal for furnishing window boxes and planters. Subtly scented blooms range from pale yellows to strong reds. 9 in. tall. **'Wenlock Beauty'** has long racemes of bronze-flushed, yellow flowers. Evergreen. 18 in.

Erysimum linifolium 'Bowles Mauve'

Erysimum linifolium

Flower color	pink, purple
Bloom time	early spring to late summer
Size	2–2.5 ft. × 1.5–2 ft.
Light	sun, part shade
Zones	Z6–9

ALPINE WALLFLOWER Native to Spain and Portugal. Vigorous, shrubby, evergreen perennial with narrowly lanceolate, gray-green leaves. Cruciform, four-petaled flowers bloom in terminal racemes over a long season.

'Bowles' Mauve' is probably a hybrid but is often assigned to *Erysimum linifolium*. It bears clusters of fragrant, mauve flowers more or less continuously, sometimes right through the winter in mild coastal areas. 2–2.5 ft. **'Variegatum'** has tufts of cream-and-green variegated leaves with profuse clusters of mauve and brown flowers. Attractive foliage for winter gardens. 20 in.

Erysimum ×*marshallii*

syn. ***Cheiranthus allionii***

Flower color	yellow, orange
Bloom time	midspring to early summer
Size	18–24 in. × 9–12 in.
Light	sun, part shade
Zones	Z3–8

SIBERIAN WALLFLOWER A hybrid of garden origin. Has gray to deep green, slightly downy, lanceolate, semi-evergreen, toothed leaves. The four-petaled flowers are yellow to bright orange, and strongly perfumed. If deadheaded it continues to bloom all summer.

'Apricot Delight' bears apricot-orange flowers on compact bushy plants.

Other Notable Cultivars

There are many other cultivars, but most are bred for bedding displays and not perennial.

Rysi Strain is more reliably perennial, to 16–18 in. high and wide, with cultivars bearing golden flowers flushed with bronze ('Rysi Bronze'), coppery orange ('Rysi Copper'), chrome yellow ('Rysi Gold'), cream fading to milky white ('Rysi Moon') and primrose yellow ('Rysi Star').

WILD GINGER

Asarum | syn. *Hexastylis, Heterotropa* ARISTOLOCHIACEAE

RHIZOMES OF THE WILD GINGERS have a spicy fragrance that recalls the culinary spice, but the two groups of plants are not related. Despite the advice offered by some wild food enthusiasts, do not use wild ginger to flavor your cuisine, as some species in this genus contain aristolochic acid, which according to the US Food and Drug Administration can cause serious and permanent kidney damage. Instead, enjoy these woodland perennials in the garden, where their large, kidney-shaped leaves furnish an elegant and shade-tolerant groundcover. Most species are evergreen or nearly so (some botanists have split the genus, moving the evergreen species into *Hexastylis*). The foliage is more of a presence in the garden than the calabash pipe- or cup-shaped flowers, which, though intriguing, are modest in size and commonly hidden beneath the leaves.

Most wild gingers prefer moist but well-drained, humus-rich soils with a neutral to acid pH. Typically they flourish on woodland sites, and though they appreciate regular irrigation during hot, dry weather, most are reasonably drought resistant once well established. They spread by creeping, fleshy roots or rhizomes, slowly forming expanding clumps or patches. Because even the deciduous wild gingers keep their foliage throughout the growing season, they make good companions for spring ephemerals such as spring beauties and trout lilies. The evergreen species are excellent as container plantings year-round.

Deer resistant; the only serious pests are slugs or snails.

Beyond the species featured here, the Asian *Asarum splendens* and its large-leaved cultivar 'Quicksilver', *A. maximum* and its selections 'Green Panda' and variegated 'Ling Ling', and our western US native *A. hartwegii* are also interesting and worth seeking.

To propagate, collect seeds in summer as soon as they ripen and sow in pots to overwinter in a cold frame or sheltered spot; or divide mature clumps into well-rooted pieces 6–8 in. across in early spring or fall. Alternatively, wash the soil from rhizomes and use a sharp knife to slice them into pieces, each including two leaves or a node; plant rhizome cuttings shallowly, with leaf-bearing end exposed; mulch to keep moist.

Asarum arifolium

flower color	brown
bloom time	late spring
size	6–8 in. × 12 in.
light	part shade, shade
zone	Z4–8

ARROW-LEAF GINGER Southeastern United States. Evergreen with smooth, variably mottled, triangular or arrow-shaped leaves to 8 in. long. Beige-brown flower buds are visible among last year's leaves in early spring; they open to little brown jugs, usually with spreading lobes. Handles heat and humidity with aplomb.

'Beaver Creek' may have more vigor. A Mt. Cuba Center, Delaware, introduction.

Asarum asaroides

flower color	purple-brown
bloom time	spring
size	4 in. × 15 in.
light	part shade
zone	Z5–9

ASARUM LEAF, PERENNIAL WILD GINGER Reliable and vigorous Japanese native that quickly forms 15-in.-wide clumps of evergreen, heart-shaped leaves marked with silver, to 6 in. long. At the base of the plant, 2-in., dark purple-brown flowers emerge in spring. Very easy to grow.

Asarum canadense

Flower color	purple-brown
Bloom time	midspring
Size	6–12 in. × 1–1.5 ft.
Light	part shade, shade
Zone	Z3–8

CANADIAN WILD GINGER Eastern half of North America, from Manitoba to North Carolina. An undemanding, deciduous species with downy, heart- to kidney-shaped, matte dark green leaves to 6 in. across; cup-shaped, purplish brown flowers are 1 in. wide.

'Eco Choice' has somewhat denser foliage.

Asarum caudatum

Flower color	maroon, white
Bloom time	late spring to early summer
Size	2–8 in. × 3 ft.
Light	part shade, shade
Zone	Z5–10, HS

WESTERN WILD GINGER, LONG-TAILED WILD GINGER Moist forests from British Columbia through southern California and eastward into Montana. Shiny, evergreen, heart-shaped leaves, 2–5 in. across; drought tolerant once established. Cup-shaped, three-lobed flowers end in long, graceful tails. The form *album* has creamy-white flowers.

Asarum europaeum

	purple-brown
	midspring
	6 in. × 8–12 in.
	part shade, shade
	Z5–9

EUROPEAN WILD GINGER Finland to Macedonia, France, and Italy. Slow to spread but perhaps the most elegant of the wild gingers with its dense cover of glossy dark green leaves. Excellent for woodland gardens but also for edging shady borders. Self-sows sparingly in hospitable locations. Protect from slugs. Avoid planting too deeply.

Asarum shuttleworthii

	purple-brown
	midspring
	6–9 in. × 6–12 in.
	part shade, shade
	Z6–9

SHUTTLEWORTH GINGER Moist woodlands in the Appalachian mountains. This species may offer the most beautiful foliage of all: silver mottling on the leaves creates a pattern almost like fish scales. Slow to spread, but lovely as an edging plant in a shady border, a groundcover, or container specimen.

'Callaway' is tighter than the species, with good-looking mottled leaves. Very slow to bulk up. Introduced by Fred Galle at Callaway Gardens, Georgia. **'Velvet Queen'** has the same distinguished leaves as 'Callaway' but is larger and bulks up more quickly.

WINDFLOWER | JAPANESE ANEMONE

Anemone | RANUNCULACEAE

WHEN THE BREEZE SETS their long-stemmed clusters of silken-petaled flowers dancing, anemones truly earn their common name of windflower. On a more practical level, the many species of this hardy and vigorous genus offer such a variety of blooming seasons that one could furnish a garden with flowers throughout the growing year with anemones alone. Wood anemones, for example, supply some of the first flowers of spring, while the fall-blooming Japanese anemone (*A. ×hybrida*) with its graceful, informal blossoms, provides the perfect counterpoint and companion to autumn's bombastic chrysanthemums.

Anemone blooms consist of single, or occasionally double, circles of petal-like tepals surrounding a central knot or boss of thread-like, usually golden stamens. The overall effect ranges from daisy-like in some species to looser, almost poppy-like flowers in others. Typically, anemone leaves emerge from the base of the plant on long stems. They may be divided palmately like fingers, lobed and toothed, or sometimes palmately compound; the lush but neat mounds of leaves furnish a handsome complement to other, showier foliage plants such as hostas, grasses, and ferns.

Though best adapted to partial shade, anemones tolerate full sun in cool climates, and flourish on most well-drained soils other than heavy clays. The spring- and summer-blooming species are tuberous rooted or rhizomatous, and these roots should be planted in fall like spring bulbs. The fall bloomers are more commonly fibrous rooted, best planted in spring or fall along with other perennials.

Include anemones in beds and borders, though they are also appropriate in woodland gardens. Spring-blooming species partner well with lungworts, woodland phlox, and foamflowers; the fall bloomers do well with Japanese toad lilies, *Allium thunbergii* 'Ozawa', and asters. The tuberous-rooted species (including *Anemone blanda*) can be forced in containers like spring bulbs. Seldom browsed by deer but need protection from slugs; anemones provide long-lasting cut flowers.

Propagate and reinvigorate named cultivars by division every two to three years, ideally in early spring; species may be started from seed sown as soon as it ripens.

Anemone coronaria De Caen Hybrid

Anemone blanda

syn. *Anemonoides blanda*

Color	blue, pink, red, white
Bloom time	early spring
Size	6–9 in. × 4–6 in.
Light	sun, part shade
Zones	Z5–8

GRECIAN WINDFLOWER Southeastern Europe and Middle East. This tuberous-rooted species naturalizes readily in well-drained soils. It spreads by seed or by root to form expansive mats of foliage and, in season, brightly colored, daisy-like flowers. Especially attractive under spring-flowering trees. Soak tubers overnight before planting. Prone to a variety of fungal diseases, though rarely seriously affected. Slugs and snails may be a problem. Deer damage is rare.

'Blue Shades' produces blooms in a range of blues. **'Charmer'** is deep lilac accented with a white ring around the stamens. **'Radar'** has magenta-pink flowers with contrasting white eyes. **'Violet Star'** has white-eyed, amethyst flowers and yellow stamens. **'White Splendour'** has pure white, daisy-like flowers accented with yellow stamens.

Anemone coronaria

Color	blue, red, white
Bloom time	midspring to early summer
Size	9–18 in. × 6–9 in.
Light	sun, part shade
Zones	Z7–10

POPPY ANEMONE Native throughout the Mediterranean basin and considered by some to be the Biblical "lilies of the field." Tuberous roots bear solitary, showy, poppy-like, single flowers to a diameter of 2.5 in. with six to eight colorful tepals and black centers, borne on 10- to 12-in. stems. May be grown in containers; popular and long-lasting cut flower.

De Caen Hybrids is an heirloom strain that has poppy-like, single flowers of scarlet, violet-blue, white, or mauve. **'Mr. Fokker'** bears single, violet-blue flowers. **St. Brigid Hybrids** is another heirloom strain with semi-double or double, dahlia-like flowers of scarlet, violet-blue, white, and mauve.

Anemone ×hybrida 'Konigin Charlotte'

Anemone hupehensis

syn. *Eriocapitella hupehensis*

flower color	pink
bloom time	mid- to late summer
size	18–24 in. × 12–18 in.
light	sun, part shade
zones	Z4–8

JAPANESE ANEMONE, JAPANESE THIMBLEWEED Actually native to central China, this misnamed perennial bears 2- to 3-in.-wide, slightly cupped flowers; typically these have five rose-pink tepals surrounding a prominent central ring of yellow stamens. Prefers a moderately fertile soil; ideal for partially shaded woodland gardens or borders. Seeds about and may become aggressive in ideal conditions. No serious pests.

'Praecox' is an exceptionally robust cultivar, blooming early in midsummer. To 50 in. tall. **Var. *japonica* 'Bressingham Glow'** (syn. *Anemone* 'Bressingham Glow') bears deep pink, semi-double or double flowers with a silvery sheen. **'Pretty Lady Diana'** belongs to a line of dwarf cultivars. Masses of single, 2-in.-wide, pink flowers. **'Pretty Lady Emily'** has semi-double, silver-pink flowers. Ideal in containers. 16 in. × 24 in. Z5–9.

Anemone ×hybrida

flower color	white, pink
bloom time	late summer to fall
size	24–48 in. × 12–18 in.
light	sun, part shade
zones	Z4–8

JAPANESE ANEMONE A collection of garden hybrids similar to *Anemone hupehensis*; some authorities treat these as a subdivision of that species.

'Andrea Atkinson' has white, single or semi-double flowers, to 3–5 ft. **'Whirlwind'** is similar. 2–4 ft. **'Honorine Jobert'** flowers are pure white and single. The benchmark for white-flowered introductions. This cultivar was named 2016 Perennial Plant Association Plant of the Year. **'Konigin Charlotte'** ('Queen Charlotte') is vigorous; 4-in.-wide, semi-double, pink flowers with purple backs. **'Pamina'** is double with deep rosy tepals. **'Prinz Heinrich'** ('Prince Henry') has semi-double rose-pink tepals. **'September Charm'** is silvery pale purple, single.

Anemone nemorosa

syn. ***Anemonoides nemerosa***

color	pink, purple, white
bloom time	late winter to midspring
size	6–12 in. × 6–9 in.
exposure	sun, part shade
zones	Z5–8

WOOD ANEMONE Northern Europe to western Asia. Naturalizes well in moist woodlands, expanding by rhizomes into large colonies; can become a pest if allowed to spread unchecked. Flowers about 1 in. across with six to eight tepals. Foliage is similar to that of *Anemone blanda*; it dies back right after bloom.

'Allenii' has large, lavender-blue flowers. **'Bowles' Purple'** has purple flowers. **'Bracteata Pleniflora'** is semi-double with green-tipped, double, white flowers. **'Vestal'** is double, with pompon-like white flowers. ***A. ×lipsiensis* 'Pallida'** (*A. nemorosa* × *A. ranunculoides*) has pale yellow flowers.

Anemone patens syn. *Pulsatilla patens*

color	blue-violet
bloom time	early spring
size	3–12 in. × 3–6 in.
exposure	sun
zones	Z3–7

EASTERN PASQUE FLOWER Northern Europe, Russia, North America (Alaska south to Washington, New Mexico, Texas, and Illinois). State flower of North Dakota. One of the first spring wildflowers of the northern Great Plains, with flowers opening while foliage is still emerging, often amid patches of snow. Basal foliage deeply divided, fern-like, and covered with silvery hairs. Flowers, usually blue-violet but occasionally white or yellow, are bell shaped and open, borne on 4- to 5-in.-tall stems that stretch to 8–12 in. as blossoms mature. Followed by plume-like, ornamental seedheads. Best in gritty, well-drained, dry to moderately moist soils in cool climates; tolerates light shade. Somewhat difficult from seed. No serious pests or diseases, welcome harbinger of spring in rock gardens, prairie plantings, and border fronts.

Anemone sylvestris

syn. *Anemonoides sylvestris*

color	white
bloom time	spring
size	12–18 in. × 9–12 in.
light	part shade, shade
zone	Z4–8

SNOWDROP ANEMONE Central and eastern Europe. A reliable and undemanding plant that prefers sandy, organic-rich soils. Naturalizes in hospitable sites and can be aggressive on loose soils; spreads less in clay. Nodding, fragrant, cupped, five-tepaled, white flowers with yellow anthers. The 1.5- to 2-in.-wide flowers are borne on 18-in. stems above medium green, deeply lobed foliage. White, woolly seedheads follow the flowers. Excellent for woodland gardens or meadows.

Anemone tomentosa

syn. *A. vitifolia, Eriocapitella tomentosa*

Color	pale pink
Bloom time	late summer to fall
Size	2–3 ft. × 15–18 in.
Exposure	sun, part shade
Zones	Z4–8

GRAPE-LEAF ANEMONE This native of northern China prefers a moist site, but rots on persistently wet soils. A source of spectacular late-season color, *Anemone tomentosa* is robust—indeed, it is most often available as the cultivar 'Robustissima'. It forms dense mounds of deep green, attractively cut foliage, above which rise branching stems topped with clusters of cupped, pinkish mauve flowers. Naturalizes readily, but it can be aggressive, overwhelming neighbors in the border. Impressive among shrubs.

Anemone vulgaris

syn. *Pulsatilla vulgaris*

Color	purple, white
Bloom time	early spring
Size	9–12 in. high and wide
Exposure	sun, part shade
Zones	Z4–8

PASQUE FLOWER Northern Europe. Flowers are five sepaled, goblet like, and solitary, 2–4 in. across. They range in color from blue to reddish purple, with a central knot of golden stamens; blooms appear before leaves, borne on stout stems. Pasque flower forms low clumps of silky, fern-like, deeply cut basal leaves, 3–6 in. long and gray-green. Flowers give way to showy, feathery seedheads. Prefers rich, humusy soil but tolerates most average, well-drained, moderately moist ones. No serious pests or diseases. Provides early color and texture for rock gardens and border fronts.

'Rote Glocke' ('Red Bells') has bright crimson flowers.

YARROW

Achillea

ASTERACEAE

SUMMER-BLOOMING YARROWS are major players in sunny ornamental gardens. Their ease of culture and sturdy constitution reward beginners and experienced gardeners alike. A few low-growing species, such as *Achillea ageratifolia*, are best suited to rock gardens, but the majority of yarrows are upright and suitable for mixed and perennial borders, and butterfly, wildlife, and cutting gardens.

Foliage is green or silvery gray-green, finely divided, and has an aromatic odor that deters browsing by deer and rabbits. Fibrous flower stems are crowned with flattened simple or compound heads of colorful, little daisy flowers, the outer all female and the inner bisexual and mostly yellow. Excellent as fresh or dried cut flowers; harvest in the cool of the day, taking flowers on which pollen is visible for longest vase life.

Yarrows thrive in most well-drained soils and tolerate drought when established. Also tolerant of salty winds, and excellent in coastal gardens. For best results, grow in full sun with lean soil; poor drainage and rich soil encourages soft, disease-prone growth that may need staking. After blooms are spent, deadhead to the ground. To maintain vigor, divide plants every two to three years.

Complement yellow-flowered achilleas with blue delphiniums, red hot pokers, monkshood, and bellflowers, or create a monochromatic design with yellow coreopsis, goldenrods, and yellow-toned daylilies. Pink and red yarrows are handsome planted with daylilies of similar hues; the habits and flower shapes contrast well.

Propagate named cultivars and hybrids by division or soft cuttings in spring; sow seed of species in spring.

Achillea filipendulina

syn. *A. eupatorium*

color	yellow
bloom time	early summer to early fall
size	3–4 ft. × 2–3 ft.
light	sun
zones	Z3–9

FERN-LEAF YARROW Caucasus. Rosettes of aromatic, deeply cut, greenish foliage give rise to strong stems topped with 4- to 5-in.-wide, golden flowerheads. Requires lean, very well-drained soil.

'Cloth of Gold' has brilliant yellow flowerheads. Tolerates very light shade. Comes true from seed. 4–5 ft. tall. **'Gold Plate'** is one of the tallest yarrows, with 6-in.-wide heads of bright golden flowers. Tolerates heat and humidity well. Z3–8. **'Parker's Variety'** is another fine selection with large, golden flowerheads. 4–5 ft. Z3–8.

Achillea grandifolia

color	white
bloom time	summer to late summer
size	3–4 ft. × 2 ft.
light	sun
zones	Z5–8

WHITE YARROW Turkey and the Balkans. An uncommon species worth seeking out. Large, fern-like, cut, gray-green leaves; strong stems bear 3-in.-wide heads of clean white flowers. Great companion for vibrant echinaceas, daylilies, and checker mallows.

Achillea millefolium 'Apricot Delight'

Achillea millefolium

(color)	white
(bloom time)	summer to early fall
(size)	2–2.5 ft. × 4 ft.
(exposure)	sun
(zones)	Z3–9

COMMON YARROW, SNEEZEWEED, SOLDIER'S FRIEND

Temperate regions. Weedy, a poor garden plant but parent of many fine selections and hybrids. Divide every two to three years to maintain vigor.

'Apfelblute' ('Apple Blossom') has soft lilac to rose flowerheads, and green foliage. Excellent for massing. **'Apricot Delight'**, sometimes called 'Tutti Frutti', has salmon, deep and light pink heads of flowers above grayish foliage. Compact, suitable for containers. 15 in. tall. **'Oertels Rose'** sports strong, non-fading pink flowers. 12–24 in tall. **'Paprika'** has dusty red flowers in 2- to 3-in. heads. Mid-green foliage. Pinch to control height, especially in hot, humid climates. Deadhead for rebloom. 18–36 in tall. **Seduction Series** is a strain bred for their stellar performance in hot, humid climates. Sturdy, upright, and compact. 18–24 in. Z4–8.

Achillea ptarmica

(color)	white
(bloom time)	early summer to fall
(size)	18–24 in. × 24 in.
(exposure)	sun, part shade
(zone)	Z3–9

SNEEZEWEED, SNEEZEWORT, BRIDEWORT Europe. With 2- to 3-in.-long, lanceolate, green leaves and branched stems, sneezeweed is not the average yarrow. Loose clusters of button-like, single or double, white flowers top slender stems like a bouquet. The foliage has been chewed to quiet a toothache or dried for use as snuff. May spread in average soil; best where the soil is poor and dry. The double forms are most popular.

'Ballerina', a dwarf version of 2-ft.-tall **'Angel's Breath'**, is a baby's breath lookalike. Long blooming. Deadhead to prevent self-seeding. 12 in. tall. **'Perry's White'**. Pure white, double flowers make this superior to rather dingy **'The Pearl'**. Upright and vigorous but may become floppy; provide support. 30 in. tall. **'Stephanie Cohen'** may be listed under *Achillea sibirica*. Pale pink flowers are carried in clusters 2–4 in. across. Named for American horticulturist Stephanie Cohen. 15–24 in. tall.

Other Notable Cultivars

'Anthea' ('Anblo') is a heat-tolerant, clump-forming British hybrid with summer to early fall bloom. Pale yellow flowerheads, 3 in. wide; soft silvery foliage. Deadhead or cut plants by half after the first flush. 18–28 in. × 36 in. Z3–9. **'Coronation Gold'** (*Achillea clypeolata* × *A. filipendulina*) is perhaps the most popular yarrow for long-lasting cut flowers. Plate-like, 3- to 4-in. inflorescences in late spring to late summer. Aromatic, gray-green, ferny foliage. Tolerates heat, humidity, and dry spells with aplomb. Divide every three to four years. Partner with mauve and purple asters. 2–3 ft. × 2 ft. Z3–9. **Galaxy Hybrids** (*A. millefolium* × *A.* 'Taygetea'), a fine strain with heads of pink, red, or yellow flowers from late spring to midsummer. Select superior colors; colors may fade in intense sun. Propagate by division. 2–3 ft. × 2 ft. Z3–9. **'Moonshine'**, an Alan Bloom hybrid, has wide, long-lasting, bright yellow flowerheads from early summer to fall; finely dissected, fragrant, silvery foliage. Cut back after first floral flush for rebloom. Sensitive to heat and humidity. Partner with daylilies and bellflowers. 18–24 in. × 18 in. Z4–8, HS. **Summer Pastels Strain** has green foliage and flowerheads in pinks, purples, yellows, and white. Less aggressive than many yarrows. Blooms first year from seed. 24–30 in. tall. **'Terra Cotta'** has silvery foliage and heads of flowers that range in color from peach and salmon to burnt orange. 3 ft. tall. **'Taygetea'**. Rich gray, dissected leaves provide a fine foil for soft lemon flowerheads; summer to fall. Easy to grow, undemanding, perfect for smaller spaces. Not to be confused with weedy, white Greek yarrow, *A. taygetea*. 12–18 in. × 18 in. Z3–10.

YELLOW WAXBELLS

Kirengeshoma | HYDRANGEACEAE

THIS GENUS IS NOTABLY COMPACT, including just two, closely similar species; some botanists regard them as one. However you define them, yellow waxbells offer woodland plantings with a difference: unlike so many forest dwellers, these plants wait until late summer to bloom. The yellow flowers are borne in cymes at the stem tips and upper leaf axils; individual blooms are bell shaped and waxy looking, 1–2 in. long. Out of bloom, the bold and maple-like foliage, borne on arching purplish stems, catches the eye, particularly when the leaves adopt their golden fall color. Seeds are carried in interesting, three-horned, brownish green capsules.

Kirengeshomas form slowly increasing clumps. They mingle well with shrubs and provide a fine textural contrast to astilbes, ferns, and other woodlanders. In addition, yellow waxbells provide ongoing summer and fall interest in areas planted with spring ephemerals.

Best suited to moist, acid, humus-rich, well-drained soils. No serious pests or diseases, except for deer that devour them.

Divide in spring, or sow fresh seed in a protected spot outdoors.

Kirengeshoma koreana

yellow

late summer to early autumn

3 ft. high and wide

part shade, shade

Z5–8

JAPANESE YELLOW WAXBELLS Native to Korea. Often treated as a variant of the following species, *Kirengeshoma palmata*. Flowers of *K. koreana* flare outward at the mouth of the bell.

Kirengeshoma palmata

yellow

late summer to early autumn

3–4 ft. × 2–3 ft.

part shade, shade

Z5–8

YELLOW WAXBELLS Native to Japan, Korea, and perhaps northeast China. Leaves are coarsely toothed, deeply lobed, and maple-like, to 8 in. across. Typically the drooping, waxy, slender, yellow bellflowers measure 1.5 in. long, and are usually borne three per cluster (or cyme).

YUCCA | ADAM'S NEEDLE

Yucca

ASPARAGACEAE

BOLD, BRASH, AND SPINY, yuccas are no shrinking violets, and can be used to dramatic effect. Most species are native primarily to arid high deserts, sand dunes, and hot plains of North, South, and Central America; they tolerate extreme dry conditions with aplomb, and are thus eminently suited to xeriscapes. However, yuccas are very adaptable, with a few species growing wild even in the hot humidity of the southeastern seaboard.

These striking evergreen succulents form loose or tidy rosettes of stiff, lanceolate to linear leaves that terminate in a wicked spike. Stunning panicles of creamy-white, bell-shaped flowers rise high above the foliage. Their evening fragrance attracts pollinators, mostly night-flying yucca moths that lay eggs of their caterpillars in the blossoms.

Several other species are well worth growing, especially where water is in short supply: the narrow-leaved *Yucca glauca* (*Y. angustifolia*), or soapweed (1–3 ft., Z4–8), which in addition to its ornamental value served Native Americans as a source of soap and fiber; weeping yucca, *Y. recurvifolia,* with its strongly arching, blue-green leaves, as well as its variegated selections 'Monca' (also known as 'Banana Split') and 'Gold Ribbons'; and the very slow-growing but ultimately huge Big Bend yucca, *Y. rostrata*, whose blue-gray leaves are borne in rosettes, reminiscent of giant porcupines, particularly in the selection 'Sapphire Skies'.

Few animals browse yuccas; susceptible to scale insects and cane borers; fungal leaf spots mar the leaves.

Increase by transplanting "pups" (rooted suckers) in spring, or take winter root cuttings. Sow seed of species in spring.

Yucca filamentosa 'Bright Edge'

Yucca filamentosa

flower color	white
bloom time	mid- to late summer
size	30–36 in. × 60 in.
exposure	sun
zones	Z4–11

ADAM'S NEEDLE, FILAMENT YUCCA, CENTURY PLANT Native to dry and sandy dunes of the coastal Southeast and west to Texas. Rosettes of long strap-shaped leaves, each tipped with a sharp spine and edged with curly fibrous threads. Robust flower stems may rise as much as 12 ft. or so above the leaves, carrying loose clusters of bell-shaped, white flowers, each with six tepals.

'Bright Edge' forms robust clumps of spiny-tipped, stiff, curly, thread-edged leaves, widely banded with cream. Long, 8- to 10-in. spires of white flowers. Z4–11. **'Color Guard'** leaves have a broad central stripe of creamy white flanked with green; sometimes coral flushed in cold weather. Vigorous, to 30 in. Similar **'Gold Heart'** grows to 20 in. Suitable as architectural accents for smaller-space gardens and containers. Z5. **'Hairy'** has blue-green leaves edged with white, twisted hairs. 18 in. × 36 in. Z4.

Yucca gloriosa

flower color	white
bloom time	late summer to fall
size	6–8 ft. × 6 ft.
exposure	sun
zones	Z7–11

SPANISH DAGGER Native from North Carolina to Florida. Dense evergreen clumps of stiff, gently arching, pointed leaves to 2 ft. in length. Large, white bell flowers sometimes flushed with purple, are arranged in stout panicles.

'Bright Star' has stiff, non-fading green leaves, edged broadly with gold. As temperatures drop in fall, leaf edges become dark pink. Pink flower buds open to white bells in summer. **'Variegata'**. Variegated mound lily. Leaves, narrowly edged with cream, blush pink in winter.

APPENDIX

PLANTING IDEAS

SHADE LOVERS

ASTILBE, PLUME FLOWER *(Astilbe)*
Beautiful fluffy plumes of pink, red, purple, or white flowers and attractive, fern-like leaves. Easy care, best in moist soil.
2-4 ft. × 2 ft., Z3-8

BISHOP'S HAT, BARRENWORT *(Epimedium)*
Hardy and shade tolerant, a groundcover and woodland favorite. Succeeds in dry shade, even under shallow-rooted trees.
6–18 in. × 9–18 in., Z4–8

BLEEDING HEART *(Dicentra and Lamprocapnos)*
Cottage-garden classics, many native to North America; many cultivars. Best in light or partial shade, always with damp but not waterlogged soil.
6–24 in. × 9–18 in., Z3–9

CORAL BELLS *(Heuchera)*
Form rounded mounds of leaves with woody basal rootstocks; roots are shallow and prone to winter heaving. Prefer partial shade; good drainage is a must.
6–24 in. × 6–24 in., Z3–9

DEAD NETTLE *(Lamium)*
In large part, grown for its foliage; among the most popular plants for groundcovers. Space closely to fill in quickly and smother leaves. Adapts to sun, part shade, or even shaded sites.
8-12 in. × 18 in., Z4–8

GOAT'S BEARD *(Aruncus)*
Vigorous, clump forming, with airy, plume-like blooms that inject a note of lightness. Best in partly shaded spots where the soil does not dry out readily.
10 in.–6 ft. × 1–4 ft., Z3-7

HELLEBORE *(Helleborus)*
Early bloomers with beautiful, long-lasting flowers and striking evergreen foliage. Notably tough, but prefer well-watered, well-drained rich, humus soil.
1–4 ft. × 1–3 ft., Z3–9

HOSTA *(Hosta)*
Valued for their attractive, sometimes textured foliage. An exposure with morning sun and afternoon shade is best; provide nutrient-rich, well-drained soil.
1–3 ft. × 1–4 ft., Z3–9

PERENNIAL FORGET-ME-NOT *(Brunnera)*
Foliage remains attractive throughout the growing season. Provide moisture-retaining fertile soil for best results; the leaf edges tend to crisp if allowed to dry out.
1–2 ft. × 18 in., Z3–9

SOLOMON'S SEAL *(Polygonatum)*
Combining toughness with an offbeat elegance, these are an asset to any shady planting. Adaptable, though they prefer rich, moist but well-drained soil in partial shade.
6 in.–3 ft. × 1–3 ft., Z3–8

WILD GINGER *(Asarum)*
Large, durable, kidney-shaped leaves furnish an elegant and shade-tolerant groundcover. Most prefer moist but well-drained, humus-rich soils. Slowly form clumps or patches.
4–8 in. × 8–18 in., Z4–8

WINDFLOWER, JAPANESE ANEMONE *(Anemone)*
Best adapted to partial shade. Flourish on most well-drained soils other than heavy clays. Include in beds and borders; also appropriate in woodland gardens.
Varies from 6 in.–4 ft. × 4–18 in.; Z4–8

DROUGHT RESISTANT

BEARDTONGUE *(Penstemon)*
A treasure trove for gardeners who favor North American natives; this large group offers great variety. Funnel-shaped or tubular flowers are borne typically in spikes.
1–5 ft. × 1–2 ft., Z4–10

CATMINT *(Nepeta)*
Tolerant of dry soils, heat, and full sun; ordinary garden conditions suffice. Outstanding for attracting butterflies and bees, deer resistant, and rarely troubled by insects and diseases.
9 in.–3 ft. × 9–18 in., Z3–9

COREOPSIS, TICKSEED *(Coreopsis)*
Colorful, showy daisy blossoms through a prolonged season of bloom. Tolerates dry soils and hot, sun-drenched sites, though in droughty conditions irrigation helps.
1–3 ft. × 1–3 ft., Z3–9

FALSE INDIGO *(Baptisia)*
Perform best on sunny sites, though they tolerate partial shade. Taprooted, difficult to transplant. The stems cluster in dense, shrub-like groups; pea-like flowers.
2–4 ft. × 2–4 ft., Z3–9

GIANT HYSSOP *(Agastache)*
Blooms from midsummer to early fall, attracting a steady stream of hummingbirds, butterflies, and other pollinators. Aromatic foliage. Vigorous and tough, but not invasive.
1–4 ft. × 1–3 ft., Z4–8

LAVENDER COTTON *(Santolina)*
Dwarf, aromatic evergreen subshrubs, invaluable for edging beds and paths. Prefers full sun and average to dry, well-drained soil; tolerant of alkaline and poor soils. Drought tolerant once established.
1–2 ft. × 2–3 ft., Z6–9

LEWISIA, CLIFF MAIDS *(Lewisia)*
Beautiful flowers on succulent plants. They demand free-draining soil and a dry situation during the winter. Grow lewisias in rock gardens, between rock crevices, or in containers.
6–12 in. × 6–8 in., Z4–9

RUSSIAN SAGE *(Perovskia atriplicifolia, Salvia yangii)*
This plant is remarkably tough and carefree. It thrives on well-drained, poor soils. Once established it shrugs off all except the most prolonged summer droughts.
3–5 ft. × 2–4 ft., Z5–9

SAGE *(Salvia)*
A critical source of color for containers and water-wise landscapes. Leaves may be coated with hairs that protect them from water loss and increase drought tolerance.
1–4 ft. × 4–8 ft., Z4–8

SEA HOLLY *(Eryngium)*
Flourishes in dry, well-drained, and sunny spots. Steely blue foliage makes them natural companions for blue-flowered herbs and other perennials; they also harmonize well with yellow.
1–3 ft. × 1–2 ft., Z3–9

SEDUM, STONECROP *(Sedum, Hylotelephium)*
Most store water in their fleshy leaves, which makes them outstandingly drought, sun, and heat tolerant. Excellent drainage is key.
Varies from 3–6 in. to 1–2 ft. × 12–18 in., Z3–8

YARROW *(Achillea)*
Summer-blooming, major players in sunny ornamental gardens. Their ease of culture and sturdy constitution reward beginners and experienced gardeners alike. Tolerate drought.
1–4 ft. × 2–4 ft., Z3–9

DEER RESISTANT

BELLFLOWER *(Campanula)*
Usually easy to grow, this large and diverse genus enables them to fill niches in plantings ranging from perennial borders to rock gardens. A range of blues, as well as whites and pinks.
4–36 in. × 6 in.–3 ft., Z3–8

BERGENIA *(Bergenia)*
Large leaves like ping-pong paddles, often heart-shaped at the base. Some are evergreen, and many turn red, purple or bronze in cold weather. Flower clusters atop thick stems.
6–24 in. × 12–30 in., Z3–8

BISHOP'S HAT, BARRENWORT *(Epimedium)*
Hardy and shade tolerant, a groundcover and woodland favorite. Succeeds in dry shade, even under shallow-rooted trees.
6–18 in. × 9–18 in., Z4–8

FUMEWORT *(Corydalis)*
Exquisite spurred flowers, usually held in dainty loose clusters at the tips of succulent stems. Finely divided leaves. Consistently cool, moist soil high in organic matter is ideal.
6–16 in. × 6–12 in., Z4–8

HELLEBORE *(Helleborus)*
Early bloomers with beautiful, long-lasting flowers and striking evergreen foliage. Notably tough, but prefer well-watered, well-drained rich, humus soil.
1–4 ft. × 1–3 ft., Z3–9

JERUSALEM SAGE *(Phlomis)*
Sage-like plants with attractive large, corrugated leaves covered with white or grayish woolly hairs. Eye-catching flowers of lavender-pink, yellow, or white. Sun, fertile, well-drained soil.
2–4 ft. × 2–3 ft., Z5–8

LEOPARD PLANT *(Ligularia)*
Statuesque, dramatic plants for damp, partly shaded sites. Large clumps of rounded, heart-shaped, or arrowhead-shaped leaves often held on dark stems. Some have attractive flowers.
3–6 ft. × 3–5 ft., Z4–8

LUPINE *(Lupinus)*
Handsome palmately divided leaves, spires of colorful, pea-type flowers. Species like loose, very well-drained, lean soils; showy garden hybrids prefer humus-rich, moderately fertile ground.
1–5 ft. × 1–3 ft., Z4–8

SAGE *(Salvia)*
A critical source of color for containers and water-wise landscapes. Leaves may be coated with hairs that protect them from water loss and increase drought tolerance.
1–4 ft. × 4–8 ft., Z4–8

SEDUM, STONECROP *(Sedum, Hylotelephium)*
Most store water in their fleshy leaves, which makes them outstandingly drought, sun, and heat tolerant. Excellent drainage is key.
Varies from 3–6 in. to 1–2 ft. × 12–18 in., Z3–8

SPURGE *(Euphorbia)*
Upright or trailing stems well clothed with oval, pointed leaves arranged in whorls or spirals. Cup-shaped flowers ranging in color from red to yellowish green or lime.
1–5 ft. × 1–3 ft., Z5–8

YELLOW WAXBELLS *(Kirengeshoma)*
Unlike other forest dwellers, these bloom in late summer. Yellow flowers in cymes at stem tips and upper leaf axils, bell-shaped and waxy looking. Bold maple-like leaves, arching purplish stems.
3–4 ft. × 2–3 ft., Z5–8

CONTINUAL BLOOMERS

BLACK-EYED SUSAN *(Rudbeckia)*
With their bright flowers, tolerance for drought, and prolonged bloom, these North American natives are a mainstay of midsummer and fall gardens.
2–3 ft. × 1–3 ft., Z3–9

CONEFLOWER *(Echinacea)*
Versatile and vigorous garden plants, in all sorts of colors and forms. Thrive in most well-drained soils, even endure periods of drought once established.
2–4 ft. × 1–2 ft., Z3–9

COREOPSIS, TICKSEED *(Coreopsis)*
Colorful, showy daisy blossoms through a prolonged season of bloom. Tolerates dry soils and hot, sun-drenched sites, though in droughty conditions irrigation helps.
1–3 ft. × 1–3 ft., Z3–9

DAYLILY *(Hemerocallis)*
Leafless stems (scapes) carry the colorful flowers. Hybridizers have added a range of new flower forms, including many doubles. Remove spent blooms daily to maintain a neat appearance.
2–4 ft. × 1–2 ft., Z3-9

CRANESBILL, HARDY GERANIUM *(Geranium)*
Undemanding and long-lived, requiring little maintenance in return for a vibrant floral display. They generally prefer sunny positions. Clusters or pairs of five-petaled flowers.
6 in.–2 ft. × 1–2 ft., Z3–9

JUPITER'S BEARD, VALERIAN *(Centranthus)*
Undemanding, flourishing even in poor, infertile, droughty soil. Dense cymes of fragrant, small, star-shaped flowers in shades of pink or red, also white. Bluish-green foliage.
1.5–3 ft. × 2–3 ft., Z5–8

ORNAMENTAL ONION *(Allium)*
The sulfur-based chemicals that give alliums their pungent aroma act as repellents to many animals and insects. Plant among bushy companion plants to help support their flower stalks.
1–4 ft. × 4–8 in., Z3–9

PERENNIAL FORGET-ME-NOT *(Brunnera)*
Foliage remains attractive throughout the growing season. Provide moisture-retaining fertile soil for best results; the leaf edges tend to crisp if allowed to dry out.
1–2 ft. × 18 in., Z3–9

RUSSIAN SAGE *(Perovskia atriplicifolia, Salvia yangii)*
This plant is remarkably tough and carefree. It thrives on well-drained, poor soils. Once established it shrugs off all except the most prolonged summer droughts.
3–5 ft. × 2–4 ft., Z5–9

SAGE *(Salvia)*
A critical source of color for containers and water-wise landscapes. Leaves may be coated with hairs that protect them from water loss and increase drought tolerance.
1–4 ft. × 4–8 ft., Z4–8

SHASTA DAISY *(Leucanthemum)*
As a reliable and prolific source of white flowers, these vigorous growers are unequalled among perennials. Their showy, gleaming blossoms stand out.
1–4 ft. × 1–2 ft., Z3–8

YARROW *(Achillea)*
Summer-blooming, major players in sunny ornamental gardens. Their ease of culture and sturdy constitution reward beginners and experienced gardeners alike. Tolerates drought.
1–4 ft. × 2–4 ft., Z3–9

NATIVE PLANTS

BANEBERRY, BUGBANE *(Actaea)*
Flourish in moist, well-drained, humus-rich soils in situations of partial shade, dappled sunlight, or even full shade. Attractive foliage, small but elegant flowerheads, and ornamental fruits.
1.5–3 ft. × 2–3 ft., Z4–9

BEARDTONGUE *(Penstemon)*
These tolerate and even favor nutrient-poor, very well-drained, even gritty soils. Attracts a variety of pollinators; seldom browsed by deer or rabbits.
1–5 ft. × 1–2 ft., Z3–9

BLANKETFLOWER *(Gaillardia)*
Bold, bright, and earthy. Plant in sunny spots with an average, well-drained soil; the latter is essential and critically important, especially for the hybrids.
1–3 ft. × 9–18 in., Z3–9

BLEEDING HEART *(Dicentra, Lamprocapnos)*
Cottage-garden classics, many native to North America; many cultivars. Best in light or partial shade, always with damp but not waterlogged soil.
6–24 in. × 9–18 in., Z3–9

COLUMBINE *(Aquilegia)*
Easy to grow, provided soil is well-drained. Full sun is fine. Well-suited to cottage gardens, excellent in containers, make good cut flowers.
1–3 ft. × 1–2 ft., Z3–8

CORAL BELLS *(Heuchera)*
Form rounded mounds of leaves with woody basal rootstocks; roots are shallow and prone to winter-heaving. Prefer partial shade; good drainage is a must.
6–24 in. × 6–24 in., Z3–9

FLEABANE, SEASIDE DAISY *(Erigeron)*
Though aster lookalikes, mostly bloom in spring and summer. Flowerheads may be single or semi-double. Well-drained soil is a must, and once established, plants tolerate dry soils well.
6–30 in. × 1–2 ft., Z4-9

GOAT'S BEARD *(Aruncus)*
Vigorous, clump forming, with airy, plume-like blooms that inject a note of lightness. Best in partly shaded spots where the soil does not dry out readily.
10 in.–6 ft. × 1–4 ft., Z3-7

LEWISIA, CLIFF MAIDS *(Lewisia)*
Beautiful flowers on succulent plants. They demand free-draining soil and a dry situation during the winter. Grow lewisias in rock gardens, between rock crevices, or in containers.
6–12 in. × 6–8 in., Z4–9

MILKWEED, BUTTERFLY WEED *(Asclepias)*
In many species, the milky sap is toxic, making them resistant to many pests and yet drawing and supporting monarch butterflies. Clump-forming plants, bright flower clusters.
2–5 ft. × 1–3 ft., Z3–9

SHOOTING STAR *(Dodecatheon)*
Typically produce a basal rosette of smooth, spatulate leaves from which arises a naked stem topped with an umbel of charming pendent flowers. Best in moist soil and part shade.
1–2 ft. × 6–12 in., Z4–8

WILD GINGER *(Asarum)*
Large, durable, kidney-shaped leaves furnish an elegant and shade-tolerant groundcover. Most prefer moist but well-drained, humus-rich soils. Slowly form clumps or patches.
4–8 in. × 8–18 in., Z4–8

POLLINATOR PARADISE

BEARDTONGUE *(Penstemon)*
A treasure trove for gardeners who favor North American natives; this large group offers great variety. Funnel-shaped or tubular flowers are borne typically in spikes.
1–5 ft. × 1–2 ft., Z4–10

BEEBALM *(Monarda)*
Hardy mint relatives with aromatic foliage and long-lasting blooms. Prefer a moderately moist, well-drained site. Nectar-rich flowers attract pollinators.
2–4 ft. × 2–3 ft., Z3–9

CALAMINT *(Calamintha)*
An aromatic, attractive member of the mint family, but they lack mint's aggressive nature. Typically in bloom for six weeks or more, attracting hosts of birds, butterflies, hummingbirds.
1–2 ft. × 1 ft., Z3–9

CATMINT *(Nepeta)*
Tolerant of dry soils, heat, and full sun; ordinary garden conditions suffice. Outstanding for attracting butterflies and bees, deer resistant, and rarely troubled by insects and diseases.
9 in.–3 ft. × 9–18 in., Z3–9

FOAMFLOWER, SUGAR SCOOP *(Tiarella)*
Outstanding handsome foliage, ethereal bloom and two patterns of growth—spreading and clump forming—to satisfy a diversity of needs. Some hybrids bloom for months.
9–20 in. × 8–24 in., Z4–8

JOE-PYE WEED *(Eupatorium, Eupatoriadelphus)*
Large, exuberant plants that contribute foliage mass and texture as well as flowers—borne in substantial to huge, parasol-like heads. Appreciate rich, organic soil.
3–8 ft. × 3–4 ft., Z3–9

LAVENDER *(Lavandula)*
Grow in lean, sweet soil—with excellent drainage. Bright sunlight in an airy location is best. An obvious choice for herb gardens, but suitable in many settings; dramatic when massed.
2–3 ft. × 2–4 ft., Z5–8

MILKWEED, BUTTERFLY WEED *(Asclepias)*
In many species, the milky sap is toxic, making them resistant to many pests and yet drawing and supporting monarch butterflies. Clump-forming plants, bright flower clusters.
2–5 ft. × 1–3 ft., Z3–9

RUSSIAN SAGE *(Perovskia atriplicifolia, Salvia yangii)*
This plant is remarkably tough and carefree. It thrives on well-drained, poor soils. Once established it shrugs off all except the most prolonged summer droughts.
3–5 ft. × 2–4 ft., Z5–9

SEDUM, STONECROP *(Sedum, Hylotelephium)*
Most store water in their fleshy leaves, which makes them outstandingly drought, sun, and heat tolerant. Excellent drainage is key.
Varies from 3–6 in. to 1–2 ft. × 12–18 in., Z3–8

SUNFLOWER *(Helianthus)*
Generally imposing and durable plants. They make good backdrops for sunny borders and other taller plants. Attract butterflies and are a welcome food source for songbirds.
4–12 ft. × 2–4 ft., Z4–9

YARROW *(Achillea)*
Summer-blooming, major players in sunny ornamental gardens. Their ease of culture and sturdy constitution reward beginners and experienced gardeners alike. Tolerates drought.
1–4 ft. × 2–4 ft., Z3–9

RABBIT RESISTANT

BEEBALM *(Monarda)*
Hardy mint relatives with aromatic foliage and long-lasting blooms. Prefer a moderately moist, well-drained site. Nectar-rich flowers attract pollinators.
2–4 ft. × 2–3 ft., Z3–9

CALAMINT *(Calamintha)*
An aromatic, attractive member of the mint family, but they lack mint's aggressive nature. Typically in bloom for six weeks or more, attracting hosts of birds, butterflies, hummingbirds.
1–2 ft. × 1 ft., Z3–9

CATMINT *(Nepeta)*
Tolerant of dry soils, heat, and full sun; ordinary garden conditions suffice. Outstanding for attracting butterflies and bees, deer resistant, and rarely troubled by insects and diseases.
9 in.–3 ft. × 9–18 in., Z3–9

GOLDENROD *(Solidago)*
Long-lasting and remarkably hardy late summer and fall color, as well as invaluable late-season nectar sources for butterflies and bees. Thrive in lean to moderately fertile soils in full sun.
1–3 ft. × 1–3 ft., Z3–8

HARDY GERANIUM, CRANESBILL *(Geranium)*
Undemanding and long-lived, requiring little maintenance in return for a vibrant floral display. They generally prefer sunny positions. Clusters or pairs of five-petaled flowers.
6 in.–2 ft. × 1–2 ft., Z3–9

HOSTA *(Hosta)*
Valued for their attractive, sometimes textured foliage. An exposure with morning sun and afternoon shade is best; provide nutrient-rich, well-drained soil.
1–3 ft. × 1–4 ft., Z3–9

ORNAMENTAL ONION *(Allium)*
The sulfur-based chemicals that give alliums their pungent aroma act as repellents to many animals and insects. Plant among bushy companion plants to help support their flower stalks.
1–4 ft. × 4–8 in., Z3–9

PINK *(Dianthus)*
Exquisitely beautiful and often sweet-scented flowers. They require a well-drained soil, ideally with a neutral to alkaline pH; mulch with limestone chips if soil is acid. Best in full sun.
6–18 in. × 12–15 in., Z3–9

RUSSIAN SAGE *(Perovskia atriplicifolia, Salvia yangii)*
This plant is remarkably tough and carefree. It thrives on well-drained, poor soils. Once established it shrugs off all except the most prolonged summer droughts.
3–5 ft. × 2–4 ft., Z5–9

SAGE *(Salvia)*
A critical source of color for containers and water-wise landscapes. Leaves may be coated with hairs that protect them from water loss and increase drought tolerance.
1–4 ft. × 4–8 ft., Z4–8

WILD GINGER *(Asarum)*
Large, durable, kidney-shaped leaves furnish an elegant and shade-tolerant groundcover. Most prefer moist but well-drained, humus-rich soils. Slowly form clumps or patches.
4–8 in. × 8–18 in., Z4–8

YARROW *(Achillea)*
Summer-blooming, major players in sunny ornamental gardens. Their ease of culture and sturdy constitution reward beginners and experienced gardeners alike. Tolerates drought.
1–4 ft. × 2–4 ft., Z3–9

BEST FOR SLOPES

BASKET-OF-GOLD *(Aurinia)*
Masses of brilliant school-bus yellow flowers that bloom over several weeks from spring into early summer. Woody base, evergreen, grayish leaves. Best in full sun, not fussy.
8–12 in. × 12–18 in., Z3–8

CANDYTUFT *(Iberis)*
Endow even the most modern garden with a touch of nostalgic charm. Numerous flower clusters mass above tufts of dark-green leaves. Shear plants after bloom to prevent legginess.
3–12 in. × 6–18 in., Z3–8

GOAT'S BEARD *(Aruncus)*
Vigorous, clump forming, with airy, plume-like blooms that inject a note of lightness. Best in partly shaded spots where the soil does not dry out readily.
10 in.–6 ft. × 1–4 ft., Z3-7

HOSTA *(Hosta)*
Valued for their attractive, sometimes textured foliage. An exposure with morning sun and afternoon shade is best; provide nutrient-rich, well-drained soil.
1–3 ft. × 1–4 ft., Z3–9

ICE PLANT *(Delosperma)*
Provide vivid splashes of color—bloom is most abundant in full sun. Mats of jellybean-like succulent foliage. They prefer rocky, average to poor soil, as long as it drains well.
2–5 in. × 1.5–3 ft., Z5–9

LILYTURF *(Liriope)*
Low, grass-like plants combine glossy foliage with grape hyacinth-like spikes of late summer flowers in purples, blues, or white. Refresh by mowing on a high setting in early spring.
12–18 in. × 9–24 in., Z6–10

PHLOX *(Phlox)*
Individual flowers, though modest in size, are abundant, grouped in panicles or solitary in blankets that almost hide the foliage. Extend bloom times with assiduous deadheading.
1–4 ft. × 9 in.–3 ft, Z3–8

SEDUM, STONECROP *(Sedum, Hylotelephium)*
Most store water in their fleshy leaves, which makes them outstandingly drought, sun, and heat tolerant. Excellent drainage is key.
Varies from 3–6 in. to 1–2 ft. × 12–18 in., Z3–8

SPURGE *(Euphorbia)*
Upright or trailing stems well clothed with oval, pointed leaves arranged in whorls or spirals. Cup-shaped flowers ranging in color from red to yellowish green or lime.
1–5 ft. × 1–3 ft., Z5–8

WILD GINGER *(Asarum)*
Large, durable, kidney-shaped leaves furnish an elegant and shade-tolerant groundcover. Most prefer moist but well-drained, humus-rich soils. Slowly form clumps or patches.
4–8 in. × 8–18 in., Z4–8

YARROW *(Achillea)*
Summer-blooming, major players in sunny ornamental gardens. Their ease of culture and sturdy constitution reward beginners and experienced gardeners alike. Tolerates drought.
1–4 ft. × 2–4 ft., Z3–9

YUCCA *(Yucca)*
Very adaptable, they tolerate dry conditions with aplomb. Bold, brash, and spiny—can be used to dramatic effect.
30–36 in. × 60 in., Z4–11

BEST FOR WET AREAS

ASTILBE, PLUME FLOWER *(Astilbe)*
Beautiful fluffy plumes of pink, red, purple, or white flowers and attractive, fern-like leaves. Easy care, best in moist soil.
2-4 ft. × 2 ft., Z3-8

BANEBERRY, BUGBANE *(Actaea)*
Flourish in moist, well-drained, humus-rich soils in situations of partial shade, dappled sunlight, or even full shade. Attractive foliage, small but elegant flowerheads, and ornamental fruits.
1.5–3 ft. × 2–3 ft., Z4–9

BEEBALM *(Monarda)*
Hardy mint relatives with aromatic foliage and long-lasting blooms. Prefer a moderately moist, well-drained site. Nectar-rich flowers attract pollinators.
2–4 ft. × 2–3 ft., Z3–9

IRIS *(Iris)*
Not all irises are suited to damp sites, but a few are, including Japanese and Louisiana. Most require a sunny position to thrive. Colorful blooms, mostly sword-shaped foliage.
1–3 ft. × 1–2 ft., Z3–8

GOAT'S BEARD *(Aruncus)*
Vigorous, clump forming, with airy, plume-like blooms that inject a note of lightness. Best in partly shaded spots where the soil does not dry out readily.
10 in.–6 ft. × 1–4 ft., Z3-7

HOSTA *(Hosta)*
Valued for their attractive, sometimes textured foliage. An exposure with morning sun and afternoon shade is best; provide nutrient-rich, well-drained soil.
1–3 ft. × 1–4 ft., Z3–9

JOE-PYE WEED *(Eupatorium, Eupatoriadelphus)*
Large, exuberant plants that contribute foliage mass and texture as well as flowers—borne in substantial to huge, parasol-like heads. Appreciate rich, organic soil.
3–8 ft. × 3–4 ft., Z3–9

LEOPARD PLANT *(Farfugium)*
Bold and intriguing, grown mainly for their handsome evergreen, long-stalked leaves that are held well above the crown. Average soil that is moist but not waterlogged is best.
18–24 in. × 24 in., Z6–11

MARSH MARIGOLD *(Caltha)*
Use to brighten up the margins of a pond or boggy area with sunny yellow flowers. Mounds of glossy, heart- or kidney-shaped leaves. May spread by seed on consistently damp soil.
10–12 in. × 12–18 in., Z3–7

SOLOMON'S SEAL *(Polygonatum)*
Combining toughness with an offbeat elegance, these are an asset to any shady planting. Adaptable, though they prefer rich, moist but well-drained soil in partial shade.
6 in.–3 ft. × 1–3 ft., Z3–8

TURTLEHEAD *(Chelone)*
Unusual blooms have an intriguing form, and their foliage is bold and handsome. Undemanding, requiring only humus-rich, consistently moist or even wet soil.
2–4 ft. × 1–2.5 ft., Z4–8

PHOTO CREDITS

Front cover, clockwise from top left: Clare Gainey/Alamy, Nahhana/Shutterstock, manuel m. v./Flickr, Juniors Bildarchiv GmbH/Alamy, Vahan Abrahamyan/Shutterstock, Tony Baggett/Shutterstock, imageBROKER.com/Alamy, Joshua Mayer/Flickr
Back cover: Andrey Zharkikh/Flickr

U.S. Geological Survey, Department of the Interior/USGS, U.S. Geological Survey/photo by Larry Allain, 156 (left)

Shutterstock
1Ljubisa78, 145
Adam Yee, 302 (left)
Aleksandr Naumenko, 103 (left), 104 (right), 225
Alex Manders, 87 (right), 111 (right), 127 (right), 166, 175 (right)
Algirdas Gelazius, 237 (left)
Alienor Llona Bonnard, 251
Amalia Lukash, 137 (right)
Annıbel, 326 (left)
Anna Gratys, 93, 374, 373 (left)
Anna50, 183 (right)
Antares_NS, 276 (right)
APugach, 6, 163
Arina Valiakhmetova, 87 (left)
branchesaroundme, 345 (right)
Brian Woolman, 199 (right), 267 (right)
Brookgardener, 254
ButtermilkgirlVirginia, 139 (bottom left)
C Belt, 235 (left)
C J Wheeler, 70
Carol Vandenbelt, 207
Catherine M Hollander, 52 (right)
Celine Kwang, 357 (left)
ChWeiss, 119 (right)
Dajra, 112 (right), 348
Dan Gabriel Atanasie, 208
Dan Hanscom, 324 (left)
Daria Kho, 274 (right)
Destartes, 370
dheotegar, 235 (right)
Diane N. Ennis, 194 (left)
Edita Medeina, 101, 296
Elena Tratsevskaya, 127 (left)
Eleonora Samenova, 110 (left)
Flower_Garden, 210 (right), 275 (right), 307 (right)
fotografiko eugen, 178
Gabriela Beres, 364 (left)
gailhampshire, 260 (right)
Galina Bolshakova 69, 174 (right)
Gardens by Design, 57 (right)
Gerry Bishop, 44 (right), 151 (right)
green scent, 153 (right)
Greens and Blues, 64 (right), 94, 175 (left)
GTW, 161
guentermanaus, 159 (left), 172 (right), 253 (left), 311 (right)
Gumirov, 172 (left)
High Mountain, 206 (right)
hoanglong, 212 (left)
Hope Easterly, 346
IanRedding, 97 (left)
Iva Vagnerova, 76 (right), 290 (right)
James Nature Pics, 369 (left)
Jana Loesch, 190 (left)
Jason Grant, 218 (left)
Joe Kuis, 218 (right), 322 (right)
JohnatAPW, 130 (right), 202
Josie Elias, 271 (right)
Julie MUTIN, 133 (right)
justkgoomm, 303
Kabar, 62 (right), 120 (right), 123 (right), 319 (right)
Katerina Maksymenko, 302 (right)
Kazakov Maksim, 275 (left)
Khairil Azhar Junos, 150 (left)
klemen cerkovnik, 301 (left)
krolya25, 142
lcrms, 203
Le Do, 232 (left)
lembi, 92 (left)
Lenstravel, 327 (left)
Lflorot, 68
LianeM, 277 (right)
Lidia Kovacs, 13, 124 (right), 271 (left)
m8setiawan, 379 (right)
MacBen, 340
Mai_Studios, 268 (right)
malamiute, 249 (left)
Manfred Ruckszio, 63 (left), 183 (left)
MAR007, 168
Marek M, 131 (left)
Mariola Anna S, 156 (right)
Marta Jonina, 242
Martin Hibberd, 141 (left)
Matt Hopkins, 236 (left)
Maximillian cabinet, 281 (left)
meunierd, 48
mizy, 60 (right)
Nahhana, 39 (left), 80 (left), 151 (left), 192 (right), 295 (left), 361 (right)

Nancy J. Ondra, 31 (right), 38, 129 (right), 233 (right)
Natalia Baran, 186
Nick Pecker, 53
Nikolay Kurzenko, 157, 324 (right)
nilovsergey, 341
Nokzd, 299 (right)
Norm Lane, 74 (right)
Ole Schoener, 239
Olga Glagazina, 214 (left)
Olga Kashubin, 246 (right)
Paul and Studio, 50 (left), 99 (right)
PAUL ATKINSON, 293 (left)
PaulSat, 43 (left)
Per Jacobsen, 41
Peter Turner Photography, 130 (left), 278 (right)
Petr Szymonik, 131 (right)
Rajko Simunovic, 368 (right)
Ramaprasad, 66
Robert Buchel, 141 (right)
RukiMedia, 60 (left)
Rumxde, 112 (left)
samray, 206
Sandra Alkado, 180 (right)
Sarycheva Olesia, 103 (right)
Sergey V Kalyakin, 99 (left), 100 (left), 100 (right)
shepherdsatellite, 69 (right)
Skrypnykov Dmytro, 349 (right)
speakingtomato, 120 (left)
SUJITRA CHAOWDEE, 209
Sunbunny Studio, 169 (right)
Sundry Photography, 150 (right)
Svetlana Mahovskaya, 108 (left), 369 (right)
tamu1500, 154 (right)
Tempus Aura Eugenie R, 139 (bottom right)
ThangNguyenPhoto, 316 (left)
theapflueger, 171 (left)
Thyary, 260 (left)
Timothy H Brown Jr, 32
Tony Baggett, 46, 52 (left), 295 (right)
Tracy Immordino, 307 (left)
Traveller70, 51 (right)
Ursula Perreten, 241 (left)
Usa.P, 258 (right)
vagabond54, 51 (left)
Vahan Abrahamyan, 5, 57 (left)
Walter Erhardt, 318 (left), 336
weha, 144, 185 (left)
Yala, 107
Yazovskikh Olga, 216 (left)
Zuzha, 185 (right)

Alamy

Alan Gregg, 323 (left)
Alex Polo, 44 (left)
Alexandra Glen, 39 (right)
Andrew Greaves, 230 (right)
AngieC, 290 (left)
Arctos Images, 92 (right)
Art Phaneuf, 328 (left)
Avalon.red, 357 (right)
AY Images, 30 (left)
B.O'Kane, 200
Bob Gibbons, 165 (right)
Botanic World, 217 (left), 267 (left)
Botany vision, 116 (left), 121, 147, 190 (right), 195, 249 (right)
Brian & Sophia Fuller, 95 (left)
Brian Hird (Wildflowers), 375
carla65, 311 (left)
Carpe Diem – Flora, 128 (right)
Clare Gaine, 26, 162 (right), 355 (right)
Clint Farlinger, 79 (right)
Craig Jack Photographic, 246 (left)
David Bagnall, 232 (right)
Derek Harris, 55, 223 (right)
Elly Miller, 301 (right)
Eugenie Robitaille, 343 (right)
Florapix, 229 (right)
Florapix, 45, 253 (right)
flowerphotos, 317 (left)
Frank Tozier, 363 (right)
Garey Lennox, 105
Gerry Bishop, 343 (left)
GKSFlorapics, 67
Heinz Hauser / botanikfoto, 165 (left)
HHelene, 40
Ian Redding, 368 (left)
imageBROKER.com, 221, 329 (left)
Jason Smalley Photography, 373 (right)
Jennifer Booher, 282 (right)
John Richmond, 84 (left), 86 (right), 108 (right), 129 (left)
Julia Färber, 367 (right)
Juniors Bildarchiv GmbH, 15, 160
Kathy deWitt, 216 (right)
Klaus Steinkamp, 107 (left), 119 (left)
Leon Werdinger, 281 (right)
Linda Freshwaters Arndt, 2, 344 (left)
Magica, 63 (right)
Martin Fowler, 272
Martin Hughes-Jones, 136 (left), 189 (left)
Michael Neelon, 293 (right)
Mike Truchon, 351 (left)
Nadya So, 371 (left)
Nigel Cattlin, 227
P Tomlins, 73 (right), 181 (left), 229 (left), 270 (left)
Panoramic Images, 287 (right)
Panther Media GmbH, 215 (right)
Paolo Reda - REDA &CO, 50 (right), 132 (right), 134, 288, 361 (left)
Perry Mastrovito, 328 (right)
Peter Mooij, 77
piemags/nature, 76 (left), 78, 236 (right), 323 (right), 365 (right)
Plantography, 358
Premium Stock Photography GmbH, 223 (left)
Ray Bulson, 359
RM Floral, 315 (right)
Robert Büchel, 347
Ros Drinkwater, 64 (left)

rumxde, 377 (left)
Sabena Jane Blackbird, 54
Sergey Kalyakin, 241 (right)
shapencolour, 237 (left)
SOURCENEXT, 182
Steffen Hauser / botanikfoto, 132 (left), 215 (left), 245 (left), 247, 256 (right), 309 (right), 327 (right)
Steffen Hauser, 198 (left)
Steve Taylor ARPS, 79 (left)
Stocktaker, 226
Svetlana Zhukova, 316 (right)
Tim Gainey, 210 (left)
Tim Wright, 171 (right)
Todd Bannor, 268 (left)
xulescu_g, 95 (right)
Zoonar GmbH, 306 (left)

Flickr (CC BY-SA 2.0)

Alvin Kho, 299 (left), 349 (left)
Amanda Slater, 244
Andreas Rockstein, 169 (left), 263 (left), 377 (left)
Andrey Zharkikh, 86 (left), 159 (left), 220 (left)
Andy Morffew, 204 (right)
Armin S Kowalski, 265
Bjorn S..., 176, 371 (right)
brewbooks, 256 (left)
Bruce Kirchoff, 335
candiru, 137 (left)
Carl Lewis, 80 (right), 331
Cecelia Alexander, 276 (left)
Daniel Jolivet, 97 (right)
Dinesh Valke, 211
Dwight Sipler, 72 (right)
F.D. Richards, 43 (right), 72 (left), 88, 104 (left), 139 (top left), 139 (top right), 199 (left), 245 (right), 270 (right), 298 (left)
Forest and Kim Starr, 124 (left)
Gail Frederick, 329 (right)
Guilhem Vellut, 340 (right)
Holger Wirth, 158
Ian Lee, 125
Ivan Radic, 309 (left)
Jakub T. Jankiewicz, 116 (right)
Jason Hollinger, 154 (left)
je_wyer, 136 (right)
Jean Jones, 274 (left)
Jeanne Grunert, 228 (left)
Jim, the Photographer, 355 (left)
jimduggan24, 198 (right)
John Brighenti, 291 (right)
John Richmond, 353
John Rusk, 287 (left)
Joshua Mayer, 111 (left), 180 (left), 187, 189 (right), 333 (left)
Judy Gallagher, 58, 82, 351 (right)
khmarais, 337
Koichi Oda, 278 (left)
Leonora (Ellie) Enking, 29, 365 (left)
m. m. v., 192 (left)
manuel m. v., 285
Matt Lavin, 194 (right), 344 (right)
Megan Hansen, 196, 377 (right)
Michele Dorsey Walfred, 73 (left)
MostlyDross, 110 (right)
Natasha de Vere & Col Ford, 181 (right)
Neil Turner, 338
nicolas_gent, 282 (left)
Patrick Standish, 263 (right), 297
peganum, 320
Peter D. Tillman, 162 (left)
Peter Stenzel, 204 (left)
Quinn Dombrowski, 292
Rüdiger Stehn, 222
Sara@Shotley, 345 (left)
Staudengärtnerei Forssman, 291 (left), 326 (right)
Udo Schmidt, 61 (left), 312
Under the same moon..., 354
Valleybrook Gardens, 139 (middle left), 319 (left)
xulescu_g, 352 (left)
yguaba, 220 (right)
阿橋 HQ, 153 (left), 233 (left), 283, 315 (left)

iStock

49pauly, 84 (right)
apugach, 31 (left)
Chris Leaver, 30 (right)
davelogan, 353 (right)
dawnhanna, 364 (right)
Kelli Kallenborn, 148
Kristine Radkovska, 298 (right)
Sundry Photography, 304
tc397, 113
Valerie Loiseleux, 115

GAP Photos

Adrian James, 74 (left)
Jonathan Buckley, 360
Nova Photo Graphik, 128 (left)
Robert Mabic, 69 (left)

Wikimedia

Alex Lomas, 322 (left)
Pipi, 174 (left)
Wouter Hagens, 62 (left)

CC BY-SA 2.0

Alvin Kho, 34
Andrey Zharkikh, 35
cultivar413, 149

CC BY-SA 3.0

Andy Mabbett, 313
Choess, 363 (left)
James Steakley, 230 (left)
Joshua Mayer, 260 (right)
Kor!An (Андрей Корзун), 133 (left)

CC BY-SA 4.0

Agnieszka Kwiecień, Nova, 37, 212 (right), 277 (left)

BeckyLaboy, 83

Krzysztof Ziarnek, 90, Kenraiz, 33

Photo by David J. Stang, source: David Stang. First published at ZipcodeZoo.com, 123 (left), 214 (right), 217 (right), 258 (left), 318 (right)

PumpkinSky, 379 (left)

Salicyna, 139 (middle right), 317 (right)

Uoaei1, 61 (left)

INDEX

A

Adam's needle *Yucca filamentosa*, 379
Adam's needle *Yucca* spp., 378–379
adder's tongue *Erythronium americanum*, 351
Aegean wallflower *Erysimum cheiri/Cheiranthus cheiri*, 359, 360
aizoon stonecrop *Sedum aizoon*, 125
allwood pink *Dianthus ´allwoodii*, 295
alpine campion *Lychnis alpina/Silene suecica*, 90
alpine catchfly *Lychnis alpina/Silene suecica*, 92
alpine columbine *Aquilegia alpina/Aquilegia montana*, 110
alpine poppy *Papaver alpinum/Oreomecon alpina*, 301
alpine rock rose *Helianthemum alpestre/Helianthemum oelandicum subsp. alpestris*, 311
alpine sea holly *Eryngium alpinum*, 321
alpine wallflower *Erysimum linifolium*, 361
alumroot *Heuchera* spp., 118–121
American cowslip *Dodecatheon meadia/Primula meadia*, 333
amethyst sea holly *Eryngium amethystinum*, 322
amur pine *Dianthus amurensis*, 295
anomalous peony *Paeonia anomala*, 281
Arkansas bluestar *Amsonia hubrichtii*, 86
Arkwright's catchfly *Lychnis ´arkwrightii*, 92
aromatic aster *Symphyotrichum oblongifolium/Aster oblongifolius*, 25
arrow-leaf ginger *Asarum arifolium*, 363
artic daisy *Chrysanthemum arcticum/Arctanthemum arcticum*, 103
artic poppy *Papaver nudicaule/Oreomecon nudicaulis*, 302
asarum leaf *Asarum asaroides*, 363
ashy cranesbill *Geranium cinereum*, 127
Asian forget-me-not *Myosotis asiatica/Myosotis alpestris* subsp. *asiatica*, 168
Asiatic poppy *Meconopsis grandis*, 210
aspen fleabane *Erigeron speciosus*, 165
aster *Aster* spp., 28–35, 205, 234, 308, 366
astilbe *Astilbe* spp., 36–39, 84, 86, 376, 381, 389
Atlantic poppy *Papaver atlanticum*, 301
Atlas poppy *Papaver atlanticum*, 301
August lily *Hosta plantaginea*, 216
autumn-flowering monkshood *Aconitum carmichaelii*, 270
autumn goldenrod *Solidago sphacelata/Brachychaeta sphacelata*, 200
autumn sage *Salvia greggii*, 316
avens *Geum coccineum*, 185
avens *Geum* spp., 46–49, 184–187
azure monkshood *Aconitum carmichaelii*, 270

B

baby's breath *Gypsophila cerastioides*, 40
baby's breath *Gypsophila* spp., 40
badger's bane *Aconitum vulparia/Aconitum lycoctonum*, 272
Balkan bear's breech *Acanthus hungaricus/Acanthus balcanicus/Acanthus longifolius*, 54
balloon flower *Platycodon grandiflorus*, 84
baneberry *Actaea* spp., 42–47, 385, 389
barrenwort *Epimedium pinnatum*, 70
barrenwort *Epimedium* spp., 68–70, 381, 383
basket-of-gold *Aurinia saxatilis/Alyssum saxatile*, 48
basket-of-gold *Aurinia* spp., 47–48, 388
beach aster *Erigeron glaucus*, 162
beach fleabane *Erigeron glaucus*, 162
beach sunflower *Helianthus debilis*, 343
bearded hybrid iris *Iris ´germanica*, 228
beardtongue *Penstemon barbatus*, 50
beardtongue *Penstemon digitalis*, 51
beardtongue *Penstemon* spp., 49–52, 382, 385, 386
bear's breech *Acanthus mollis*, 54
bear's breech *Acanthus* spinosus/*Acanthus spinossissimus*, 55
bear's breech *Acanthus* spp., 53–55

bear's foot hellebore *Helleborus foetidus*, 203
beebalm *Monarda didyma*, 57
beebalm *Monarda* spp., 15, 56–58, 386, 387, 389
belladonna delphinium *Delphinium ´belladonna*, 147
bellflower *Campanula* spp., 59–64, 372, 383
bergamot *Monarda* spp., 15, 56–58
bergenia *Bergenia* spp., 65–67, 383
bicolor monkshood *Aconitum cammarum/Aconitum napellus* var. *bicolor/Aconitum ´bicolor*, 270
Big Bend yucca *Yucca rostrata*, 378
bigflower tickseed *Coreopsis grandiflora*, 123
big leaf ligularia *Ligularia denata/Senecio clivorum*, 253
bigleaf lupine *Lupinus polyphyllus*, 261
bigroot geranium *Geranium macrorrhizum*, 129
biodiversity, 9
bishop's hat *Epimedium alpinum*, 68
bishop's hat *Epimedium* spp., 68–70, 381, 383
Bitterroot *Lewisia rediviva*, 255
bitterwort *Gentiana lutea*, 181
black bugbane *Actaea racemosa*, 44
black cohosh *Actaea racemosa*, 44
black-eyed Susan *Rudbeckia fulgida*, 72
black-eyed Susan *Rudbeckia hirta*, 72
black-eyed Susan *Rudbeckia* spp., 56, 71–74, 384
black iris *Iris tuberosa/Hermodactylus tuberosus*, 230
black snakeroot *Actaea racemosa*, 44
blanketflower *Gaillardia aristata*, 76
blanketflower *Gaillardia aristata ´grandiflora/Gaillardia aristata grandiflora*, 77
blanketflower *Gaillardia* spp., 75–77, 385
blazing star *Liatris scariosa*, 80
blazing star *Liatris* spp., 78–80
bleeding heart *Dicentra/Lamprocapnos* spp., 81–84, 381, 385
blood flower *Asclepias curassavica*, 267
bloodroot *Sanguinaria canadensis*, 81
bloody cranesbill *Geranium sanguineum*, 133
blue anise sage *Salvia guaranitica*, 317
blue corydalis *Corydalis elata*, 174
blue corydalis *Corydalis flexuosa*, 175
blue dogbane *Amsonia tabernaemontana/Tabernaemontana amsonia*, 88
blue false bleeding heart *Corydalis elata*, 174
blue false indigo *Baptisia australis*, 156
blue flax *Linum* spp., 160
blue globe onion *Allium caeruleum/Allium wallichii*, 275
blue leadwort *Ceratostigma plumbaginoides*, 86
blue-leaf red hot poker *Kniphofia caulescens*, 309
blue oak sage *Salvia chamaedryoides*, 315
blue poppy *Meconopsis betonicifolia*, 209
blue poppy *Meconopsis grandis*, 210
bluestar *Amsonia orientalis/Rhazya orientalis*, 87
bluestar *Amsonia* spp., 93–95
blue starflower *Amsonia tabernaemontana/Tabernaemontana amsonia*, 88
blue-stemmed goldenrod *Solidago caesia*, 198
boneset *Eupatorium/Eupatoriadelphus/Eutrochium* spp., 234–237
bonytip fleabane *Erigeron karvinskianus*, 162
border carnation *Dianthus ´allwoodii*, 295
border phlox *Phlox paniculata*, 292
bride's feathers *Aruncus/dioicus Aruncus sylvestris*, 196
bridewort *Achillea ptarmica*, 375
broadleaf chives *Allium senescens*, 277
brown-eyed Susan *Rudbeckia triloba*, 74
bugbane *Actaea matsumurae/Cimicifuga matsumurae/Cimicifuga simplex* var. *matsumurae*, 43
bugbane *Actaea simplex/Cimicifuga simplex/Cimicifuga racemosa*, 46
bugbane *Actaea* spp., 42–47, 385, 389
Bulgarian geranium *Geranium macrorrhizum*, 129
bush clematis *Clematis heracleifolia*, 107
bush lupine *Lupinus arboreus*, 260
Bush's purple coneflower *Echinacea paradoxa*, 116
butterfly gaura *Gaura lindheimeri*, 178
butterfly weed *Asclepias* spp., 266–268, 385, 386
butterfly weed *Asclepias tuberosa*, 268
button snakeroot *Liatris spicata*, 80

C

calamint *Calamintha* spp, 89–90, 386, 387
calibrachoa *Calibrachoa* spp., 356
calico aster *Symphyotrichum lateriflorum/Aster lateriflorus/Aster diffusus*, 32
Cambridge geranium *Geranium ´cantabrigiense*, 127

campanula *Campanula* spp., 59–64
campion *Lychnis* spp, 91–95
Canadian columbine *Aquilegia canadensis*, 111
Canadian wild ginger *Asarum canadense*, 364
candytuft *Iberis* spp., 96–97, 356, 388
Cantonese fairy bells *Disporum cantoniense*, 153
cardinal beardtongue *Penstemon cardinalis*, 50
cardinal flower *Lobelia cardinalis*, 205
Carolina phlox *Phlox carolina*, 290
Carpathian harebell *Campanula carpatica*, 60
catchfly *Lychnis* spp, 91–95
catmint *Nepeta racemosa*, 100
catmint *Nepeta* spp., 98–101, 382, 386, 387
Caucasus catmint *Nepeta grandiflora*, 99
century plant *Yucca filamentosa*, 379
checker bloom *Sidalcea malviflora*, 303
checker bloom *Sidalcea* spp., 303
cheddar pink *Dianthus gratianopolitanus/Dianthus caesius*, 298
Chilean avens *Geum quellyon/Geum chiloense*, 185
Chinese astilbe *Astilbe chinensis*, 38
Chinese chives *Allium tuberosum*, 278
Chinese delphinium *Delphinium gradiflorum*, 150
Chinese delphinium *Delphinium tatsienense*, 151
Chinese peony *Paeonia lactiflora*, 279
chocolate root *Geum rivale*, 186
Christmas fern *Polystichum acrostichoides*, 81
Christmas rose *Helleborus niger*, 204
Christmas rose *Helleborus* spp., 201–204
chrysanthemum *Chrysanthemum* spp., 102–105
citron daylily *Hemerocallis citrina*, 141
clematis *Clematis* spp., 117–119
cliff-dwelling stonecrop *Sedum cauticola/Hylotelephium cauticola*, 327
cliff maids *Lewisia cotyledon/Lewisia finchiae/Lewisia purdyi*, 256
cliff maids *Lewisia* spp., 255–256, 382, 385
climate change, 9
Clodius Parnassian butterfly *Parnassius clodius*, 84
closed-bottle gentian *Gentiana andrewsii*, 180
clustered bellflower *Campanula glomerata*, 61
coast fawn lily *Erythronium revolutum*, 353
Columbian lewisia *Lewisia columbiana*, 256
columbine *Aquilegia* spp., 65, 81, 83, 109–113, 385
common flax *Linum usitatissimum*, 158
common monkshood *Aconitum napellus*, 271
common sage *Salvia officinalis*, 317
common tansy *Tanacetum vulgare/Chrysanthemum vulgare*, 349
common torch lily *Kniphofia uvaria/Kniphofia. aloides/ Tritoma uvaria*, 309
common wallflower *Erysimum cheiri/Cheiranthus cheiri*, 359, 360
common yarrow *Achillea millefolium*, 374
coneflower *Echinacea* spp., 56, 114–117, 308, 384
Cooper's ice plant *Delosperma cooperi/Mesembryanthemum cooperi*, 220
coral bells *Heuchera americana*, 119
coral bells *Heuchera sanguinea*, 120
coral bells *Heuchera* spp., 118–121, 381, 385
coreopsis *Coreopsis* spp., 122–125, 372, 384
Corsican hellebore *Helleborus argutifolius/Helleborus corsicus,/Helleborus lividus subsp. corsicus*, 202
cottage pine *Dianthus plumarius*, 299
cottage pink *Dianthus ´allwoodii*, 295
cranesbill *Geranium ´riversleaianum*, 132
cranesbill *Geranium* spp., 126–134, 384, 387
crassula *Crassula* spp., 219
creeping baby's breath *Gypsophila repens*, 41
creeping bellflower *Campanula rapunculoides*, 59
creeping phlox *Phlox stolonifera*, 293
crested iris *Iris cristata*, 225
crevice alumroot *Heuchera micrantha*, 120
crisp-leaved hybrid astilbe *Astilbe ´crispa*, 39
cucumber-leaved sunflower *Helianthus debilis*, 343
culinary sage *Salvia officinalis*, 317
curled-leaf hosta *Hosta crispula/Hosta sieboldiana var. sieboldiana*, 214
cushion spurge *Euphorbia polychroma/Euphorbia epithymoides*, 341
cut-leaf coneflower *Rudbeckia lacinata*, 71
cyclamen *Cyclamen persicum*, 135
cyclamen *Cyclamen* spp., 135–137
cypress spurge *Euphorbia cyparissias*, 338

D

Dahurian gentian *Gentiana dahurica/Gentiana gracilipes*, 181
daisy fleabane *Erigeron speciosus*, 165
Dalmatian bellflower *Campanula portenschlagiana/Campanula muralis/Campanula poscharskyana*, 63
Dalmatian iris *Iris pallida*, 229
Davidson's penstemon *Penstemon davidsonii*, 51
daylily *Hemerocallis* spp., 138–142, 372, 384
dead nettle *Lamium* spp., 144–146, 381
delphinium *Delphinium* spp., 145–151, 184, 372
dense blazing star *Liatris spicata*, 80
desert candle *Eremus* spp., 170–172
desert hollyhock *Sphaeralcea ambigua*, 194
desert mallow *Sphaeralcea ambigua*, 194
dogfennel *Eupatorium capillifolium*, 235
dogtooth violet *Erythronium dens-canis*, 352
dogtooth violet *Erythronium* spp., 350–353
doll's eyes *Actaea pachypoda*, 44
dotted beebalm *Monarda punctata*, 58
downy amsonia *Amsonia ciliata/Amsonia angustifolia*, 86
Dumortier's daylily *Hemerocallis dumortieri*, 141
dusky cranesbill *Geranium phaeum*, 131
dusty miller *Lychnis coronaria/Agrostemma coronaria/Silene coronaria*, 94
Dutchman's breeches *Dicentra cucullaria*, 82
dwarf blazing star *Liatris microcephala*, 79
dwarf bluestar *Amsonia montana/Amsonia tabernaemontana* 'Montana'/*Amsonia tabernaemontana* var. *montana*, 87
dwarf cranesbill *Geranium renardii*, 132
dwarf crested iris *Iris cristata*, 225
dwarf goat's beard *Aruncus aethusifolius/Aruncus sylvester* var. *sylvester*, 195
dwarf iris *Iris* spp., 184
dwarf Japanese Solomon's seal *Polygonatum humile*, 336
dwarf larkspur *Delphinium tricorne*, 151
dwarf scarlet larkspur *Delphinium nudicaule*, 150

E

eastern bluestar *Amsonia tabernaemontana/Tabernaemontana amsonia*, 88
eastern cyclamen *Cyclamen coum*, 136
eastern Joe-pye weed *Eutrochium dubium/Eupatoriadelphus dubius/Eupatorium dubium*, 236
eastern pasque flower *Anemone patens/Pulsatilla patens*, 369
eastern purple coneflower *Echinacea purpurea/Rudbeckia purpurea*, 116
East Indies aster *Aster tongolensis*, 30
elecampane *Inula ensifolia*, 222
elecampane *Inula helenium*, 223
Endress's cranesbill *Geranium endressii*, 128
English lavender *Lavandula angustifolia*, 244
English monkshood *Aconitum napellus*, 271
eryngo *Eryngium alpinum*, 321
eryngo *Eryngium bourgatii*, 322
European colombine *Aquilegia vulgaris*, 113
European wild ginger *Asarum europaeum*, 365

F

fairy bells *Disporum flavens/Disporum uniflorum*, 153
fairy bells *Disporum* spp., 152–154
fairy's thimble *Campanula cochlearifolia*, 61
fairy wings *Epimedium epsteinii*, 68
false indigo *Baptisia* spp., 155–157, 170, 308, 382
false lamium *Lamium galeobdolon/Lamiastrum galeobdolon*, 144
false spirea *Filipendula rubra/Spiraea lobata/Spiraea palmata*, 307
fan columbine *Aquilegia flabellata/Aquilegia atkinesis*, 112
fernleaf corydalis *Corydalis cheilanthifolia*, 174
fern-leaf dropwort *Filipendula vulgaris/Filipendula hexapetala/Spiraea filipendulina*, 307
fernleaf peony *Paeonia tenuifolia*, 283
fern-leaf yarrow *Achillea filipendulina/Achillea eupatorium*, 373
feverfew *Tanacetum parthenium/Chrysanthemum parthenium/Matricaria parthenium/Pyrethrum parthenium*, 349
fig-leaf hollyhock *Alcea ficifolia*, 211
filament yucca *Yucca filamentosa*, 379
firewheel *Gaillardia aestivalis*, 76
flat sea holly *Eryngium planum*, 324
flax *Linum* spp., 158–160
fleabane *Erigeron* spp., 161–163, 385

foamflower *Tiarella cordifolia*, 366
foamflower *Tiarella* spp., 164–166, 386
foamflower *Tiarella wherryi*., 166
foetid iris *Iris foetidissima*, 227
foothill penstemon *Penstemon heterophyllus*, 52
forget-me-not *Myosotis* spp., 167–169
forget-me-not *Myosotis sylvatica*, 169
Fortune's hosta *Hosta fortunei*, 214
foxglove *Digitalis* spp., 65
fox's brush *Centranthus ruber/Valeriana rubra*, 239
foxtail lily *Eremurus ´isabellinus*, 171
foxtail lily *Eremurus stenophyllus/Eremurus bungei*, 172
foxtail lily *Eremus himalicus*, 171
foxtail lily *Eremus robustus*, 172
foxtail lily *Eremus* spp., 170–172
fragrant Solomon's seal *Polygonatum odoratum*, 337
French cranesbill *Geranium endressii*, 128
French hollyhock *Malva sylvestris/Malva sylvestris* var. *mauritiana*, 263
French lavender *Lavandula dentata*, 245
French lavender *Lavandula stoechas*, 246
Frickart's aster *Aster ´frikartii*, 29
frilly begonia *Bergenia ciliata/Bergenia ligulata*, 66
fringed bleeding heart *Dicentra eximia*, 83
fringed bluestar *Amsonia ciliata/Amsonia angustifolia*, 86
frostweed *Helianthemum mutabile/Helianthemum nummularium 'Mutabile'/Helianthemum nummularium subsp. nummularium*, 311
fumewort *Corydalis solida*, 175
fumewort *Corydalis* spp., 173–175, 383

G

gardening*See also* plant propagation; plants
  climate, 14
  diseases, 23
  fertilizer, 9
  mulch, 22
  pests, 23
  raised beds, 17
  shopping for perennials, 18–19
  soil preparation, 17
  staking/support, 22
garden maintenance
  deadheading, 21
  diseases/pests, 23
  irrigation, 20–21
  mulch, 22
  pinching, 21
  winter vs. summer hardiness, 20
garlic chives *Allium tuberosum*, 278
gas plant *Dictamnus albus/Dictamnus fraxinella*, 176
gas plant *Dictamnus* spp., 176
gayfether *Liatris* spp., 56, 78–80
gentian *Gentiana* spp., 179–183
gentian sage *Salvia patens*, 318
German catchfly *Lychnis viscaria/Viscaria vulgaris*, 95
germander sage *Salvia chamaedryoides*, 315
German garlic *Allium senescens*, 277
German iris *Iris ´germanica*, 228
geum *Geum* spp., 184–187
giant blue hyssop *Agastache foeniculum*, 189
giant desert candle *Eremus robustus*, 172
giant hyssop *Agastache* spp., 188–190
Gladwyn iris *Iris foetidissima*, 227
globe daisy *Globularia meridionalis/ Globularia bellidifolia/ Globularia subsp. bellidifolia/ Globularia cordifolia subsp. meridionalis*, 192
globe daisy *Globularia* ssp., 191–192
globe mallow *Sphaeralcea* spp., 193–194
gloriosa daisy *Rudbeckia hirta*, 72
goat's beard *Aruncus/dioicus Aruncus sylvestris*, 196
goat's beard *Aruncus* spp., 195–196, 381, 385, 388, 389
golden buttons *Tanacetum vulgare/Chrysanthemum vulgare*, 349
golden columbine *Aquilegia chrysantha*, 111
golden flax *Linum flavum*, 158
golden groundsel *Ligularia* spp., 252–254
golden Japanese stonecrop *Sedum makinoi*, 125
golden peony *Paeonia mlokosewitschii s/Paeonia daurica* subsp. *mlokosewitschii*, 282
goldenrod *Solidago* spp., 86, 102, 197–200, 234, 372, 387
goldentuft *Aurinia saxatilis/Alyssum saxatile*, 48
goldmoss stonecrop *Sedum acre*, 326
granny's bonnet *Aquilegia vulgaris*, 113

grape-leaf anemone *Anemone tomentosa/Anemone vitifolia/ Eriocapitella tomentosa*, 371
grass pink *Dianthus plumarius*, 299
grayleaf cranesbill *Geranium cinereum*, 127
greater musk-mallow *Malva alcea*, 263
great yellow gentian *Gentiana lutea*, 181
Grecian windflower *Anemone blanda/Anemonoides blanda*, 367
green lavender cotton *Santolina rosmarinifolia*, 249
Griffith's spurge *Euphorbia griffithii*, 340
ground clematis *Clematis recta*, 108
groundcover chrysanthemum *Chrysanthemum yezoense/ Dendranthema arcticum* subsp. *maekawanum*, 105
guara *Gaura* spp., 177–178

H

hairy alumroot *Heuchera villosa*, 121
hairy golden pink *Dianthus knappii*, 298
hardy ageratum *Eupatorium coelestinum/Conoclinium coelestinum*, 236
hardy begonia *Begonia* spp., 36
hardy cyclamen *Cyclamen cilicium*, 136
hardy geranium *Geranium* spp., 86, 126–134, 384, 387
hardy ginger *Asarum* spp., 68
hardy ice plant *Delosperma cooperi/Mesembryanthemum cooperi*, 220
hardy twinspur *Diascia integerrima*, 357
heartleaf foamflower *Tiarella cordifolia*, 165
heart-leaved brunnera *Brunnera macrophylla/Anchusa myosotidiflora*, 285
heart-leaved globe daisy *Globularia cordifolia*, 192
heath aster *Symphyotrichum ericoides/Aster ericoides*, 31
hellebore *Helleborus* spp., 36, 81, 201–204, 381, 383
Henry's monkshood *Aconitum henryi*, 271
hermes fingers *Iris tuberosa/Hermodactylus tuberosus*, 230
hibiscus *Hibiscus* spp., 205–208
Himalayan elecampane *Inula royleana*, 223
Himalayan foxtail lily *Eremus himalicus*, 171
Himalayan geranium *Geranium himalayense/Geranium grandiflorum/Geranium himalayense var. meeboldii/ Geranium meeboldii*, 128
Himalayan poppy *Meconopsis* spp., 209–210
hollyhock *Alcea/Althaea* spp., 62, 211–212
hollyhock *Alcea rosea/Althaea rosea*, 212
hollyhock mallow *Malva alcea*, 263
horny goatweed *Epimedium grandiflorum/Epimedium macranthum*, 69
horseheal *Inula ensifolia*, 222
horseheal *Inula helenium*, 223
hosta *Hosta* spp., 36, 81, 84, 213–218, 356, 381, 387, 388, 389
Hubricht's amsonia *Amsonia hubrichtii*, 86
hybrid astilbe *Astilbe ´arendsii*, 37
hybrid geranium *Geranium ´oxonianum*, 130
hydrangea *Hydrangea* spp., 308

I

Iceland poppy *Papaver nudicaule/Oreomecon nudicaulis*, 302
ice plant *Delosperma* spp., 219–221, 388
Indian blanket *Gaillardia* spp., 75–77
Indian poke *Veratrum viride*, 205
inula *Inula* spp., 222–223
iris *Iris* spp., 184, 224–230, 389
ivy-leaved cyclamen *Cyclamen hederifolium/Cyclamen hederifolium 'Rosenteppich'/Cyclamen neapolitanum/ Cyclamen immaculatum*, 137

J

Japanese anemone *Anemone ´hybrida*, 368
Japanese anemone *Anemone hupehensis/Eriocapitella hupehensis*, 368
Japanese anemone *Anemone* spp., 366–370, 381
Japanese bugbane *Actaea japonica/Cimicifuga japonica*, 43
Japanese catmint *Nepeta subsessilis*, 101
Japanese fairy bells *Disporum sessile*, 154
Japanese gentian *Gentiana scabra*, 183
Japanese iris *Iris ensata/Iris kaempferi*, 226
Japanese meadowsweet *Filipendula purpurea*, 306
Japanese onion *Allium thunbergii*, 278
Japanese thimbleweed *Anemone hupehensis/Eriocapitella hupehensis*, 368
Japanese toad lily *Tricyrtis hirta*, 366
Japanese water iris *Iris ensata/Iris kaempferi*, 226
Japanese yellow waxbells *Kirengeshoma koreana*, 377
Jerusalem cross *Lychnis chalcedonica/Silene chalcedonica*, 93

Jerusalem sage *Phlomis fruiticosa*, 232
Jerusalem sage *Phlomis russeliana*, 233
Jerusalem sage *Phlomis* spp., 231–233, 383
Joe-pye weed *Eupatorium/Eupatoriadelphus/Eutrochium* spp., 234–237, 386, 389
Jupiter's beard *Centranthus ruber/Valeriana rubra*, 239
Jupiter's beard *Centranthus* spp., 238–239

K

Kamchatka bugbane *Actaea simplex/Cimicifuga simplex/ Cimicifuga racemosa*, 46
Kashmir sage *Phlomis cashmeriana*, 232
keys-of-heaven *Centranthus ruber/Valeriana rubra*, 239
kingscup *Caltha palustris*, 264
king's spear *Eremus* spp., 170–172
Korean bellflower *Campanula takesimana*, 64
Korean hybrids *Chrysanthemum ´koreana*, 103
Korean hyssop *Agastache rugosa*, 190
Korean mum *Chrysanthemum ´rubellum*, 104

L

lady's leek *Allium cernuum*, 276
lady's mantle *Alchemilla mollis*, 242
lady's mantle *Alchemilla* spp., 240–242
lambs' tongue trout lily *Erythronium grandiflorum*, 352
lance-leaf blanket flower *Gaillardia aestivalis*, 76
lanceleaf coreopsis *Coreopsis lanceolata*, 124
large coneflower *Rudbeckia maxima*, 73
larkspur *Delphinium* spp., 145–151
lavandin *Lavandula ´intermediai*, 245
lavender cotton *Santolina chamaecyparissus*, 249
lavender cotton *Santolina* spp., 248–249, 382
lavender *Lavandula* spp., 243–247, 359, 386
lemon daylily *Hemerocallis lilioasphodelus/Hemerocallis flava*, 142
Lenten rose *Helleborus orientalis*, 204
leopard plant *Farfugium japonicum/ Farfugium tussilaginea/ Ligularia tussilaginea*, 251
leopard plant *Farfugium* spp., 250–251, 389
leopard plant *Ligularia denata/Senecio clivorum*, 253
leopard plant *Ligularia* spp., 252–254, 383
lesser calamint *Calamintha nepeta/Clinopodium nepeta/ Calamintha nepeta*, 90
lewisia *Lewisia* spp., 255–256, 382, 385
Lewis's blue flax *Linum lewisii/Linum perenne subsp. lewisii*, 159
lilac pink *Dianthus superbus*, 299
lilac sage *Salvia verticillata*, 319
liliy leek *Allium moly*, 276
lily-of-the-valley *Convallaria majalis*, 81
lilyturf *Liriope muscari*, 257
lilyturf *Liriope spicata*, 257, 388
lilyturf *Liriope* spp., 256–257
lobed tickseed *Coreopsis auriculata*, 123
long-petalled lewisia *Lewisia longipetala*, 255
longspur barrenwort *Epimedium grandiflorum/Epimedium macranthum*, 69
long-tailed wild ginger *Asarum caudatum*, 364
Louisiana iris *Iris* spp., 229
lungwort *Pulmonaria* spp., 36, 65, 68, 81, 83, 366
lupine *Lupinus* spp., 259–261
lupin *Lupinus* spp., 259–261, 383
lyreflower *Dicentra formosa*, 84

M

madwort *Aurinia saxatilis/Alyssum saxatile*, 48
Maga Colorada *Hibiscus grandiflorus/Thespesia grandiflora*, 207
mahogany trout lily *Erythronium revolutum*, 15, 353
maiden pink *Phlox deltoides*, 297
mallow *Malva* spp., 262–265
Maltese cross *Lychnis chalcedonica/Silene chalcedonica*, 91, 93
marchalan *Inula helenium*, 223
marsh marigold *Caltha* spp., 264–265, 389
Maximilian sunflower *Helianthus maximiliani*, 344
meadow clary *Salvia pratensis*, 318
meadow phlox *Phlox maculata*, 291
meadow sage *Salvia pratensis*, 318
meadowsweet *Filipendula* spp., 65, 305–307
mealycup sage *Salvia farinacea*, 316
Mediterranean spurge *Euphorbia characias*, 339
Mediterranean spurge *Euphorbia characias* subsp. *wulfenii/ Euphorbia wulfenii*, 339

Mexican butterfly weed *Asclepias curassavica*, 267
Mexican daisy *Erigeron karvinskianus*, 162
Michaelmas daisy *Symphyotrichum*, 28–35
milkweed *Asclepias* spp., 266–268, 385, 386
milkweed *Asclepias* spp,, 205
milky bellflower *Campanula lactiflora*, 62
Miyabe *Chrysanthemum weyrichii/Dendranthema zawadskii*, 104
Molly-the-witch *Paeonia mlokosewitschii* s/*Paeonia daurica* subsp. *mlokosewitschii*, 282
monkey grass *Liriope* spp., 256–257
monkshood *Aconitum* spp., 269–272, 372
moss phlox *Phlox subulata*, 293
mountain forget-me-not *Myosotis asiatica/Myosotis alpestris* subsp. *asiatica*, 168
mountain lady's mantle *Alchemilla alpina*, 241
mourning widow *Geranium phaeum*, 131
mouse-ear tickseed *Coreopsis auriculata*, 123
muck sunflower *Helianthus simulans*, 346
mullein pink *Lychnis coronaria/Agrostemma coronaria/Silene coronaria*, 94
mum *Chrysanthemum* spp., 102–105
Munro's globe mallow *Sphaeralcea munroana*, 194
musk mallow *Malva* spp., 262–265
myrtle euphorbia *Euphorbia myrsinites/Euphorbia marschalliana* subsp. *marschalliana*, 340

N

Nakai Korean meadowsweet *Filipendula glaberrima*, 306
narrow-leaved bluestar *Amsonia hubrichtii*, 86
narrow-leaved plantain lily *Hosta lancifolia*, 215
narrow-leaved yucca *Yucca glauca/Yucca angustifolia*, 378
narrow-spiked ligularia *Ligularia stenophylla/Ligularia stenocephala/Pojarkovia pojarkovae*, 254
Nevius' stonecrop *Sedum nevii*, 125
New England aster *Symphyotrichum novae-angliae/Aster novae-angliae*, 28, 33, 71
New York aster *Symphyotrichum novi-belgii/Aster novi-belgii*, 28, 34
ninebark *Physocarpus* spp., 86
nodding onion *Allium cernuum*, 276

O

October stonecrop *Sedum sieboldii/Hylotelephium sieboldii*, 328
Ohio shooting star *Dodecatheon meadia/Primula meadia*, 333
old-fashioned bleeding heart *Lamprocapnos spectabilis/ Dicentra spectabilis*, 84
opuntia *Opuntia* spp., 219
orange fleabane *Erigeron aurantiacus*, 161
orange stonecrop *Sedum kamtschaticum/Phedimus kamtschaticus*, 327
Oregon checker bloom *Sidalcea oregana*, 304
Oregon fleabane *Erigeron speciosus*, 165
oriental poppy *Papaver orientale*, 40, 302
ornamental onion *Allium atropurpureum*, 274
ornamental onion *Allium* spp., 273–278, 384, 387
ornamental oregano, 356
orris *Iris pallida*, 229
Oswego tea *Monarda didyma*, 57
Ozark coneflower *Echinacea paradoxa*, 116

P

Pacific bleeding heart *Dicentra formosa*, 83, 84
painted daisy *Tanacetum coccineum/ Chrysanthemum coccineum/ Pyrethrum coccineum/ Pyrethrum roseum*, 348
painted daisy *Tanacetum* spp., 347–349
pale purple coneflower *Echinacea pallida*, 115
pandanus leaf eryngium *Eryngium pandanifolium*, 323
parrot flower *Alstroemeria psittacina*, 288
pasque flower *Anemone vulgaris/Pulsatilla vulgaris*, 371
peach-leaved bellflower *Campanula persicifolia*, 62
penstemon *Penstemon* spp., 49–52, 382, 386
peony *Paeonia* spp., 279–283
perennial blue flax *Linum* spp., 160
perennial candytuft *Iberis sempervirens*, 97
perennial flax *Linum* spp., 158–160, 160
perennial forget-me-not *Brunnera macrophylla/Anchusa myosotidiflora*, 285
perennial forget-me-not *Brunnera* spp., 284–285, 381, 384
perennial wild ginger *Asarum asaroides*, 363
Persian epimedium *Epimedium pinnatum*, 70

Persian insect flower *Tanacetum coccineum/ Chrysanthemum coccineum/Pyrethrum coccineum/Pyrethrum roseum*, 348
Peruvian lily *Alstroemeria aurea/Alstroemeria aurantiaca*, 287
Peruvian lily *Alstroemeria huemulina*, 287
Peruvian lily *Alstroemeria* spp., 286–287
phlox *Phlox* spp., 274–278, 388
pigsqueak *Bergenia cordifolia/Bergenia crassifolia*, 67
pigsqueak *Bergenia* spp., 65–67
pineleaf beardtongue *Penstemon pinifolius*, 52
pine tickseed *Coreopsis rosea*, 124
pink *Dianthus* spp., 294–299, 387
pink fawn lily *Erythronium revolutum*, 353
plantain lily *Hosta* spp., 213–218
plant propagation
  cuttings, 24
  division, 23–24
  seeds, 24–25
plants
  attributes, 10–11
  best for slopes, 388
  best for wet areas, 389
  container-grown plants, 18–19
  continual bloomers, 384
  cultural tips, 12
  deer resistant, 383
  descriptions, 12
  drought-resistant, 382
  hardiness, 11, 20
  invasive plants, 9–10
  native plants, 385
  native range, 11–12
  plant names, 11, 15
  plant selection, 8, 10–12, 18–19
  pollinator plants, 386
  rabbit resistant, 387
  scientific names, 15
  shade plants, 381
pleurisy root *Asclepias tuberosa*, 268
plume flower *Astilbe* spp., 36–39, 381, 389
poker plant *Kniphofia uvaria/Kniphofia aloides/Tritoma uvaria*, 309
poppy anemone *Anemone coronaria*, 367
poppy *Papaver* spp., 300–302
Portuguese lavender *Lavandula latifolia/Lavandula spica*, 246
prairie blazing star *Liatris pycnostachya*, 79
prairie flax *Linum lewisii/Linum perenne subsp. lewisii*, 159
prairie mallow *Sidalcea malviflora*, 303
prairie mallow *Sidalcea* spp., 303
prairie smoke *Geum* spp., 184–187
prairie smoke *Geum triflorum/Erythrocoma triflora*, 187
prairie sunflower *Helianthus maximiliani*, 344
princess lily *Alstroemeria* spp., 286–287
Puerto Rican hibiscus *Hibiscus grandiflorus/Thespesia grandiflora*, 207
purple avens *Geum rivale*, 186
purple avens *Geum triflorum/Erythrocoma triflora*, 187
purple coneflower *Echinacea purpurea/Rudbeckia purpurea*, 116
purple coneflower *Echinacea* spp., 71, 114–117
purple corydalis *Corydalis solida*, 175
purple cyclamen *Cyclamen purpurascens/Cyclamen europaeum*, 137
purple geranium *Geranium ´magnificum*, 130
purple milkweed *Asclepias purpurascens*, 268
purple ornamental onion *Allium aflatunense*, 274
pyrethrum *Tanacetum coccineum/ Chrysanthemum coccineum/ Pyrethrum coccineum/ Pyrethrum roseum*, 348

Q

queen of the prairie *Filipendula rubra/Spiraea lobata/Spiraea palmata*, 307
queen of the prairie *Filipendula* spp., 305–307

R

ragged robin *Lychnis flos-cuculi*, 95
rattlesnake master *Eryngium yuccifolium*, 324
red baneberry *Actaea rubra*, 45
red hot poker aloe *Aloe aculeata*, 219
red hot poker *Kniphofia* spp., 308–309, 372
red hot poker *Kniphofia uvaria/Kniphofia aloides/Tritoma uvaria*, 309
Red Mountain ice plant *Delosperma dyeri*, 220
red-stemmed lady's mantle *Alchemilla erythropoda/ Alchemilla serbica*, 241

red swamp mallow *Hibiscus coccineus*, 206
red turtlehead *Chelone obliqua*, 355
rice button aster *Symphyotrichum dumosum/Aster dumosus*, 30
ring bellflower *Campanula armena/Symphyandra armena*, 60
rock anise hyssop *Agastache rupestris*, 190
rock candytuft *Iberis saxatilis*, 97
rock cress *Arabis* spp., 356
rock rose *Helianthemum nummularium*, 312
rock rose *Helianthemum* spp., 310–312
Rocky Mountain columbine *Aquilegia caerulea*, 110
rose campion *Lychnis coronaria/Agrostemma coronaria/Silene coronaria*, 91, 94
rose mallow *Hibiscus moscheutos*, 208
rose mallow *Hibiscus* spp., 205–208
rosemary *Salvia rosmarinus*, 359
rose *Rosa* spp., 98, 188
rough gayfether *Liatris aspera*, 78
rough goldenrod *Solidago rugosa*, 199
roundleaf heuchera Heuchera cylindrica, 119
roving bellflower *Campanula rapunculoides*, 59
royal blue gentian *Gentiana makinoi*, 182
Rubellium hybrids *Chrysanthemum ´rubellum*, 104
Russian hollyhock *Alcea ficifolia*, 211
Russian hollyhock *Alcea rugosa*, 212
Russian sage *Perovskia atriplicifolia/Salvia yangii*, 313
Russian sage *Perovskia/Salvia* spp., 382, 384, 386, 387
Russian sage *Perovskia* spp., 102, 313

S

sage *Salvia* spp., 184, 314–319, 382, 383, 384, 387
sand-dune wallflower *Erysimum capitatum/Cheiranthus capitatus*, 359
Santa Barbara daisy *Erigeron karvinskianus*, 162
scarlet larkspur *Delphinium cardinale*, 148
scarlet lightning *Lychnis chalcedonica/Silene chalcedonica*, 93
scarlet rose mallow *Hibiscus coccineus*, 206
Schubert onion *Allium schubertii*, 277
sea holly *Eryngium maritimum*, 323
sea holly *Eryngium planum*, 324
sea holly *Eryngium* spp., 320–324, 382
seaside daisy *Erigeron glaucus*, 162, 163–165
seaside daisy *Erigeron* spp., 161–163, 385
sedge *Carex* spp., 68
sedum *Sedum* spp., 86, 102, 219, 325–329, 382, 383, 386, 388
seersucker hosta *Hosta sieboldii/Hosta albomarginata/Hosta. lancifolia var. marginata*, 217
sempervivum *Sempervivum* spp., 219
Serbian bellflower *Campanula poscharskyana*, 63
Shasta daisy *Leucanthemum ´superbum*, 331
Shasta daisy *Leucanthemum* spp., 56, 330–331, 384
Shavalski's ligularia *Ligularia przewalskii/Senecio przewalskii*, 253
shellflower *Chelone lyonii*, 355
shining coneflower *Rudbeckia nitida*, 73
shooting star *Dodecatheon meadia/Primula meadia*, 333
shooting star *Dodecatheon* spp., 332–333, 385
showy calamint *Calamintha grandiflora/Clinopodium grandiflorum/Satureja grandiflora*, 89
showy fleabane *Erigeron speciosus*, 165
showy geranium *Geranium ´magnificum*, 130
showy goldenrod *Solidago speciosa*, 199
showy stonecrop *Sedum spectabile/Hylotelephium spectabile*, 329
shrubby clematis *Clematis heracleifolia*, 107
Shuttleworth ginger *Asarum shuttleworthii*, 365
Siberian bugloss *Brunnera macrophylla/Anchusa myosotidiflora*, 285
Siberian catmint *Nepeta sibirica/Dracocephalum sibiricum*, 100
Siberian delphinium *Delphinium gradiflorum*, 150
Siberian iris *Iris sibirica*, 65, 230
Siberian larkspur *Delphinium gradiflorum*, 150
Siberian wallflower *Erysimum ´marshallii/Cheiranthus allionii*, 359, 361
Siberian wallflower *Erysimum cheiri/Cheiranthus cheiri*, 359, 360
Sicilian honey lily *Allium bulgaricum/Allium siculum subsp. dioscoridis/Nectaroscordum siculum subsp. bulgaricum*, 275
Siebold's hosta *Hosta sieboldii*, 216
Siebold's stonecrop *Sedum sieboldii/Hylotelephium sieboldii*, 328
silver sage *Salvia argentea*, 315

silver tansy *Tanacetum argenteum/Achillea argentea*, 347
Siskiyou lewisia *Lewisia cotyledon/Lewisia finchiae/Lewisia purdyi*, 256
small-flowered alumroot *Heuchera micrantha*, 120
small rock hosta *Hosta gracillima*, 215
small Solomon's seal *Polygonatum biflorum*, 335
smooth aster *Symphyotrichum laeve/Aster laevis*, 31
smooth phlox *Phlox glaberrima*, 291
snakehead *Chelone glabra*, 354
snake's-head iris *Iris tuberosa/Hermodactylus tuberosus*, 230
sneezeweed *Achillea millefolium*, 374
sneezeweed *Achillea ptarmica*, 375
sneezewort *Achillea ptarmica*, 375
snowdrop anemone *Anemone sylvestris/Anemonoides sylvestris*, 370
soapweed yucca *Yucca glauca/Yucca angustifolia*, 378
soil
  drainage, 17
  mulch, 22
  preparation, 17, 20–21
  testing, 9, 15, 17
  types, 12
soldier's friend *Achillea millefolium*, 374
solitary clematis *Clematis integrifolia*, 107
Solomon's seal *Polygonatum* spp., 334–337, 381, 389
southern rose mallow *Hibiscus moscheutos*, 208
Spanish blue flax *Linum narbonense*, 159
Spanish lavender *Lavandula stoechas*, 246
Spanish needle *Yucca gloriosa*, 379
spike gayfeather *Liatris spicata*, 80
spike lavender *Lavandula latifolia/Lavandula spica*, 246
spotted bellflower *Campanula punctata*, 64
spotted dead nettle *Lamium maculatum*, 145
spotted geranium *Geranium maculatum*, 129
spotted henbit *Lamium maculatum*, 145
spotted horsemint *Monarda punctata*, 58
spotted Joe-pye weed *Eutrochium maculatum/Eupatoriadelphus maculatus/Eupatorium maculatum/Eutrochium purpureum subsp. maculatum*, 237
spurge *Euphorbia* spp., 338–341, 383, 388
spurless columbine *Aquilegia ecalcarata/Semiaquilegia ecalcarata*, 112
stagger weed *Dicentra cucullaria*, 82
star astilbe *Astilbe simplicifolia*, 39
sticky catchfly *Lychnis viscaria/Viscaria vulgaris*, 95
sticky Jerusalem sage *Phlomis russeliana*, 233
stinking Benjamin *Helleborus foetidus*, 203
stinking hellebore *Helleborus foetidus*, 203
stinking iris *Iris foetidissima*, 227
stonecrop *Sedum/Hylotelephium* spp, 325–329, 327, 382, 383, 386, 388
stonecrop *Sedum rupestre/Sedum reflexum*, 328
sugar scoop *Tiarella* spp., 164–166
sugar scoop *Tiarella trifoliata/Tiarella trifoliata subsp. unifoliata/Tiarella trifoliata var. unifoliata*, 165
summer gentian *Gentiana septemfida*, 183
summer gentian *Gentiana septemfida* var. *lagodechiana*, 183
summer phlox *Phlox carolina*, 290
summer phlox *Phlox paniculata*, 292
sundial lupine *Lupinus perennis.*, 260
sunflower *Helianthus* spp., 342–346, 386
sun rose *Helianthemum* spp., 310–312
swamp hibiscus *Hibiscus coccineus*, 206, 234
swamp milkweed *Asclepias incarnata*, 267
swamp rose mallow *Hibiscus moscheutos*, 208
swamp sunflower *Helianthus angustifolius*, 343
sweet coneflower *Rudbeckia subtomentosa*, 74
sweet goldenrod *Solidago odora*, 198
sweet iris *Iris pallida*, 229
sweet-scented Joe-pye weed *Eutrochium purpureum/Eupatorium purpureum*, 237
sweet william *Phlox barbatus*, 296
swordleaf inula *Inula ensifolia*, 222

T

tall boneset *Eupatorium altissimum/Ageratina altissima*, 234
tall hybrid delphinium *Delphinium ´elatum*, 149
tall mallow *Malva sylvestris/Malva sylvestris* var. *mauritiana*, 263
tall narrow-leaved sunflower *Helianthus simulans*, 346
tall sunflower *Helianthus giganteus*, 344
tansy *Tanacetum* spp., 347–349
Texas bluebonnet *Lupinus texensis*, 259
Texas hummingbird mint *Agastache cana*, 189

thickleaf phlox *Phlox carolina*, 290
thin-leaved sunflower *Helianthus* ´multiflorus, 344
threadleaf coreopsis *Coreopsis verticillata*, 125
thyme *Thymus* spp., 359
tickseed *Coreopsis* spp., 122–125, 384
toad lily *Tricyrtis* spp., 84
topped lavender *Lavandula stoechas*, 246
torch lily *Kniphofia* spp., 308–309
trailing ice plant *Delosperma cooperi/Mesembryanthemum cooperi*, 220
tree lupine *Lupinus* spp., 260
trout lily *Erythronium grandiflorum*, 352
trout lily *Erythronium* spp., 350–353
true forget-me-not *Myosotis scorpioides/Myosotis palustris*, 169
tube clematis *Clematis heracleifolia*, 107
tube clematis *Clematis tubulosa/Clematis tubulosa* var. *davidiana/Clematis heracleifolia* var. *davidiana*, 108
tuberous Jerusalem sage *Phlomis tuberosa/Phlomoides tuberosa*, 233
turkey corn *Dicentra eximia*, 83
turtlehead *Chelone glabra*, 354
turtlehead *Chelone* spp, 354–355, 389
twinspur *Diascia barberae*, 357
twinspur *Diascia rigescens*, 358
twinspur *Diascia* spp., 356–358
two-row stonecrop *Sedum spurium/Phedimus spurius*, 329

V

valerian *Centranthus* spp., 238–239, 384
velvet mallow *Hibiscus grandiflorus/Thespesia grandiflora*, 207
vervain *Verbena* spp., 356

W

Wallach's geranium *Geranium wallichianum*, 134
wallflower *Erysimum* spp., 359–361
water avens *Geum rivale*, 186
water forget-me-not *Myosotis scorpioides/Myosotis palustris*, 169
wavy-leaf plantain lily *Hosta undulata/Hosta lancifolia var undulata/Hosta media-picta/Hosta variegata*, 217
weeping yucca *Yucca recurvifolia*, 378
weigela *Weigela* spp., 86
Welsh poppy *Meconopsis cambrica/Parameconopsis cambrica*, 210
western bleeding heart *Dicentra formosa*, 84
western blue flax *Linum lewisii/Linum perenne subsp. lewisii*, 159
western peony *Paeonia brownii*, 281
western wallflower *Erysimum capitatum/Cheiranthus capitatus*, 359
western wild ginger *Asarum caudatum*, 364
white cohosh *Actaea pachypoda*, 44
white false indigo *Baptisia albescens/Baptisia alba*, 156
white fawn lily *Erythronium albidum*, 351
white goat's beard *Aruncus/dioicus Aruncus sylvestris*, 196
white stonecrop *Sedum album*, 326
white trout lily *Erythronium albidum*, 351
white wood aster *Eurybia divaricata*, 65
white yarrow *Achillea grandifolia*, 373
whorled tickseed *Coreopsis verticillata*, 125
wild bergamot *Monarda fistulosa*, 57
wild geranium *Geranium maculatum*, 129
wild ginger *Asarum* spp., 83, 362–365, 381, 385, 387, 388
wild hollyhock *Sphaeralcea ambigua*, 194
wild indigo *Baptisia* spp., 155–157
wild lupine *Lupinus perennis*., 260
wild sweet William *Phlox divaricata*, 290
wild sweet William *Phlox maculata*, 291
willow gentian *Gentiana asclepiadea*, 180
willowleaf sunflower *Helianthus salicifolius/Helianthus orgyalis*, 345
windflower *Anemone* spp., 366–370, 381
winter begonia *Bergenia ciliata/Bergenia ligulata*, 66
winter begonia *Bergenia cordifolia/Bergenia crassifolia*, 67
winter bergenia *Bergenia ciliata/Bergenia ligulata*, 66
wood anemone *Anemone nemorosa/Anemonoides nemerosa*, 369
wood cranesbill *Geranium sylvaticum*, 133
wood geranium *Geranium maculatum*, 129
woodland cranesbill *Geranium sylvaticum*, 133
woodland peony *Paeonia obovata*, 282
woodland phlox *Phlox divaricata*, 83, 290, 366
woodland stonecrop *Sedum ternatum*, 125

wood sage *Salvia ´sylvestris*, 319
wreath goldenrod *Solidago caesia*, 198

Y

yarrow *Achillea* spp., 372–375, 382, 384, 386, 387, 388
yellow archangel *Lamium galeobdolon/Lamiastrum galeobdolon*, 144
yellow avalanche lily *Erythronium grandiflorum*, 352
yellow catmint *Nepeta govaniana/Dracocephalum govanianum*, 99
yellow coneflower *Echinacea paradoxa*, 116
yellow dogtooth violet *Erythronium americanum*, 351
yellow fairy bells *Disporum lanuginosum/Prosartes lanuginosa*, 154
yellow flax *Linum flavum*, 158
yellow glacier lily *Erythronium grandiflorum*, 352
yellow ice plant *Delosperma nubigenum*, 221
yellow lavender *Lavandula viridis*, 247
yellow mandarin *Disporum lanuginosum/Prosartes lanuginosa*, 154
yellow marsh marigold *Caltha palustris*, 264
yellow snowdrop *Erythronium albidum*, 351
yellow trout lily *Erythronium americanum*, 15, 351
yellow waxbells *Kirengeshoma palmata*, 377
yellow waxbells *Kirengeshoma* spp., 376–377, 383
yellow wild indigo *Baptisia sphaerocarpa*, 157
yellow wolfsbane *Aconitum vulparia/Aconitum lycoctonum*, 272
yucca *Yucca* spp., 378–379, 388

Photo by Alan Detrick

Photo by William Burkhart

RUTH ROGERS CLAUSEN is the author of *50 Beautiful Deer-Resistant Plants*, and coauthor of *Essential Perennials* and *The Proven Winners Garden Book*. She received a Quill and Trowel award from the Garden Writers Association (now Garden Communicators International) and has written for the American Garden Guides series. She is the former horticulture editor for *Country Living Garden* magazine and a longtime contributor to *Country Gardens* magazine. Ruth lectures widely at horticultural conventions and symposia, flower shows, and to garden societies and clubs. In 2017, she was awarded the Garden Media Award by the Perennial Plant Association.

THOMAS CHRISTOPHER is the author of more than a dozen gardening books. He has written for *The New York Times*, *The Journal of the Royal Horticultural Society*, and *Horticulture Magazine*, as well as served as a columnist for *House & Garden* and a contributing editor at *Martha Stewart Living*.